Too Much

John Ruskin: The Argument of the Eye
  Thames & Hudson

Ruskin and Venice
  Thames & Hudson

New Approaches to Ruskin
  (editor) Routledge & Kegan Paul

Under Seige: Literary Life in London 1939–45
  Weidenfeld & Nicolson

In Anger: Culture in the Cold War 1945–60
  Weidenfeld & Nicolson

Irreverence, Scurrility, Profanity, Vilification and Licentious Abuse:
Monty Python – The Case Against
  Methuen

Footlights! : A Hundred Years of Cambridge Comedy
  Methuen

Robert Hewison

Too Much

Art and Society in the Sixties 1960–75

Methuen

First published in Great Britain in 1986
by Methuen London Ltd
11 New Fetter Lane, London EC4P 4EE
Copyright © 1986 Robert Hewison

Printed and bound in Great Britain by
Biddles Ltd, Guildford and King's Lynn

British Library Cataloguing in Publication Data

Hewison, Robert
  Too much : art and society in the
  Sixties 1960–75.
  1. Great Britain—Civilization—1945–
  I. Title
  941.085'6   DA589.4

ISBN 0-413-40790-X

for E.J.B.

Contents

List of illustrations

Acknowledgements

The sources of all quotations are acknowledged in the notes, but the author wishes to make a special acknowledgement for the use of copyright material to: the estate of Philip Larkin, for quotations from *High Windows*, reprinted by permission of Faber and Faber Ltd., and Farrar, Straus and Giroux Inc. (N.Y.); to Seamus Heaney, for a quotation from *North*, reprinted by permission of Faber and Faber Ltd., and Farrar, Straus and Giroux Inc. (N.Y.); to Ted Hughes, for a quotation from *Wodwo*, reprinted by permission of Faber and Faber Ltd., and Harper and Row Inc (N.Y.); for a quotation from 'Lady Lazarus' by Sylvia Plath, in *Collected Poems*, published by Faber and Faber Ltd., and Harper and Row Inc. (N.Y.), copyright Ted Hughes 1965 and 1981; to Adrian Henri for permission to quote from his poem 'Me'; and to James Fenton for a quotation from 'Letter to John Fuller' in *Children in Exile*, published by the Salamander Press Edinburgh, and Random House Inc. (N.Y.)

Sources of Illustrations

The author and publishers would like to thank the following for kind permission to reproduce the photographs and illustrations: Peter Blake, 1; *Private Eye*, 2; David Hockney 3; *Time* magazine, 4; Richard Hamilton, 5; Jeff Nuttall, 6; Topham Picture Library, 7 and 8; BBC Hulton Picture Library, 9; John and Barbara Latham, 10; the University of Wisconsin-Extension, 11; Knoedler Gallery, 12; Ray Sacks, 13.

Foreword

'For goodness, growing to a plurisy,
Dies in his own too-much.'

Hamlet Act IV Scene 7

The title of this, the third and final volume of my series, 'The
Arts in Britain since 1939' suggests the essential ambivalence of
people's feelings about 'the Sixties', then – and especially now.
'Too much' implies a fatal excess, but in the 1960s, as Partridge's
Dictionary of Slang reminds us, it meant 'excellent or wonderful'
or even, in those days of verbal as well as monetary inflation,
merely 'good at something or other'. The Sixties were good at a
number of things, especially at having a good time, and now,
when we are having a bad time, we are inclined to read the words
'too much' with a guilty awareness that the rich substance of the
Sixties has been dissipated in the Eighties – and that it was in the
Seventies that we began to pay the price.

Of course, it is much more complicated than that, and at this
distance from events there is still confusion about what took
place, as well as ambivalence about its significance. This is because
people in the Sixties were particularly prone to mixing myth and
reality, style and substance, image and fact. The Sixties have
themselves passed into myth more quickly than the period that
preceded them. Noting this as early as 1978, Peter York commented: 'When asked about the Sixties, there seems to be a
qualitative difference in people's responses – they seem confused
about what really happened (to them) and what the media had
said was happening. This kind of conceptualizing seems true

xi

across the social board. Most people under forty, in describing the Sixties, defer to the media Sixties.'

This book does not defer to the media Sixties. It is a continuation of *Under Siege* and *In Anger*, and it stays with the methodology and subject-matter of the earlier volumes. Its main topics are British art and literature and the institutional, economic and social conditions in which they were produced. In the Sixties this, what might be loosely defined as 'high', culture was considerably modified by the impact of the mass media and the so-called 'popular' culture that it reflected. I follow that modification, but my emphasis remains the same. Rock'n'roll is important, and its sounds are most evocative for those who first heard them when to be young was very heaven, but I have not concentrated on increasingly ephemeral aspects of the period (nor the mainly American and continental films) which are particularly attractive to makers of media versions of the Sixties.

Nor is this a personal Sixties (what happened to me). This is because my approach is consistent with the tone of the earlier volumes. I have not attempted the fine mixing of autobiographical and critical commentary that Morris Dickstein achieved in *Gates of Eden: American Culture in the Sixties* (1977). Though as he points out, contemporary cultural critics recognize that the historian's objectivity is a mask, and in my final pages I have tried to wrench mine off.

For the same reasons I have confined myself entirely to published sources (though some of these sources are obscure indeed). To have set out to interview witnesses to the period – besides meaning that it would take ten years to write the history of a decade – would have opened up large questions about selectivity, not least the selective memories of the witnesses, including myself. Interviews are valuable sources of information, and I have not hesitated to quote from those that have been published, but an account based on interviews would have been a very different book.

It would not necessarily have been an untruthful book. The Sixties have also taught us about the relativity of truth, and as I indicated earlier, the period has not settled down into any formal official version (though there is an increasingly comfortable myth). What I offer here is a hypothesis about the Sixties, about their shape, and the significance of that shape. In *Under Siege* I began a survey of the arts in Britain as a gathering of information from which discussion can begin, and though aspects of the Sixties have been examined in other books, and more thoroughly than cultural aspects of the Forties and Fifties, the material has not been assembled in the way it is here.

Part of my hypothesis is that the Sixties did not really begin until about 1963, and that they do not fade away until 1975. The Sixties that form the basis of popular myth lasted for a very short time, from 1964 to 1967, and even then two ideologies were developing in parallel: the affluent and hedonistic Sixties of 'Swinging London', and the oppositional culture of the underground. They have important cross-relationships; they both depended on a particular set of economic circumstances, they were both heralded by particular developments in the arts, and they both aimed at a kind of personal liberation. Yet the logic of the underground was ultimately opposed to the materialism which had created the opportunity for it to flourish. The materialist culture, for its part, could not sustain itself, and the climacteric of 1968 anticipates the social conflicts of the 1970s.

The search for a sense of autonomy and 'authenticity' – be it at the level of national identity or of individual happiness, both of which are carried by the idea of 'community' – was blocked by the change in the country's economic circumstances, which in the Seventies played into the hands of those who were alarmed by the forces that had been liberated. No new, authentic social identity with which the nation feels secure has emerged. This helps to account not only for the nihilism that has developed among young people in the face of increasing economic and political constraints, but also the fantasy heritage culture of country houses and museums that is now being promoted in Britain in the place of anything more substantial.

In my first chapter, which covers the preliminary period 1960 to 1963, a broad survey of the social and cultural anxiety which underlay the flush of affluence shows that there was already awareness that a sense of community had been lost. Cultural anxiety focused on the influence of that particular symbol of affluence, the television set. Another source of anxiety was the prospect of nuclear war, and I trace the development of a new radicalism through the rise – and then frustration – of the Campaign for Nuclear Disarmament. The case history of

Centre 42 illustrates the way in which the terms of the cultural debate were changing, as the mass media became more and more dominant.

The mass media were themselves changing, in particular the BBC. Sir Hugh Greene's regime as Director-General from 1960 to 1969 had such an influence in helping to ventilate social and cultural issues through current affairs, comedy and drama that in my first chapter I follow the BBC's history into the early 1970s, when it becomes a victim of the 'closure' that sets in after the adventurous mid-Sixties.

Part of that adventurousness was a new openness about sex, and customary British hypocrisy about these matters received particular attention in 1963, much to the discomfort of a Minister of the Crown. At first sight the Profumo affair has little to do with culture, but it undoubtedly had important social consequences, as both those who deplored the scandal, and those who enjoyed it, recognized at the time.

There were also political consequences, and these too contributed to the ambivalence in the public mood, which both welcomed change, and feared it. At this point two gurus of the Sixties begin to make their presence felt. Marshall McLuhan offered a theory that accounted for the anxiety about the state of affairs by analysing the means by which that anxiety was being communicated – the mass media, and in particular television. R.D. Laing went further, by suggesting that the 'real' world was a fantasy, willingly accepted and reinforced to suppress the deeper anxieties of a disordered identity. The British sense of identity was certainly disturbed (though not entirely disordered) in the early 1960s, and the mass media, as I show later, had a part to play in masking economic reality with pleasurable fantasy.

In the second chapter, I treat Pop Art as the herald of the celebratory side of the Sixties, the side that welcomed material affluence and the cultural and social changes that it brought. What is interesting is the way in which the advent of Pop Art not only precedes the general pleasures of Swinging London, but the critical *theories* of Pop precede the art with which they are associated. The theories of Pop Art set a style for the spectacle of the King's Road, but more importantly they suggested a new, democratic model of culture – the 'long front' – which broke down the old hierarchies of taste, admitted fresh cultural forms like rock music, and constructed a new, collage culture from the fragments of the old.

Pop Art, pop music, greater affluence and the sense of new possibilities brought by the convergence of 'high' and 'popular' culture led to a genuine sense of liberation, particularly among the young to whom this new culture was principally addressed, but the cultural revolution of the mid-Sixties was felt throughout the intelligentsia and the institutions through which they operated. The mood of expansionism was felt equally in the Arts Council and in architects' offices, and by 1966 a powerful new myth had emerged which *Time* magazine helped to define.

While Pop culture helped to release energies and break down former rigidities of taste and manners, the abandonment of constraints also liberated darker, irrational forces in the under-ground culture that developed in parallel to it. Pop culture, and the 'Bomb culture' of chapter III, shared an optimism about the material future, but the underground was more sceptical about materialism *per se*. The Theatre of the Absurd and the Theatre of Cruelty articulate some of the values of the emergent under-ground: a distrust of words, a desire to penetrate the mystery of human passions, and an insistence on authenticity of personal experience as the only valid measure of moral judgment. In the face of the material affluence which, ironically, made the underground possible, there is a turning towards inner space.

To act effectively as an oppositional culture, the underground needed its own means of communication, and, thanks to material advances in technology, it was able to develop the informal network that supported little magazines, poetry readings and pop concerts into an 'alternative press', with an alternative social calendar. Certain gatherings – increasingly tribal in character – reveal the burgeoning of this counter-culture, from the prophetic utterances of William Burroughs and Alexander Trocchi at the Edinburgh writers' conference in 1962, through the joyous poetry reading at the Albert Hall in 1965, to the sour 'Dialectics of Liberation' conference at the Round House in 1967.

This conference marks a turning point, as early as the summer of 1967, just as the release of the Beatles' *Sergeant Pepper* that same summer marks a climax of a different order. The opposition between the alternative culture and the official culture whose 'repressive tolerance' that conference analysed becomes much more marked. In spite of the series of liberal social reforms that the freer atmosphere of the middle Sixties helped to carry through, these were both too much for conservatives, and too little for radicals. In 1967 the use of drugs became a symbolic and actual *causus belli* between the authorities and the underground. The tension this created helped to generate the political explosions of 1968.

The underground began as a cultural movement, but its emphasis on a complete revolution in sensibility meant that it inevitably acquired a political dimension. As the 'Dialectics of Liberation' conference shows, the underground's analysis of contemporary conditions was simultaneously cultural and political. The response of the dominant culture was equally a combination of legal measures and cultural sanctions.

Sociologists in particular have analysed the inter-relation of political and cultural issues, and chapter V begins by discussing theoretical explanations for the student upheavals of 1968 and after, to try to establish a conceptual framework for the narrative of the events themselves. In particular, I try to show how the theatrical nature of events made sense to those who took part.

The upheavals had a correspondingly dramatic effect on spectators, who found it difficult to distinguish between the idealistic political arguments, and the purely gestural aspects of the scenes projected on the screen of the mass media. (In the 'charismatic' atmosphere of demonstrations and occupations, many participants had the same difficulty.) Those in authority interpreted all such arguments and gestures as a threat to their position, and took steps to block the drive towards autonomy and authenticity which had initiated first the cultural, and then the political, breaking of restraints. Meanwhile the economic summer of the Sixties turned to autumn, and external pressure and internal dissension caused what had been at best a temporary alliance between hippies and political hardheads to fall apart.

By 1970 the energies that had been focused in the explosion of 1968 had begun to dissipate. For some the journey through inner space led to the mental and physical self-destruction of drugs, for others it induced the self-surrender to the other-directed disciplines of religious cults. The feeling that a certain moment had passed increased with the passing of the decade.

Although there was a sense both of withdrawal, and of political bitterness following on disillusion as the Seventies began, chapter IV shows that the counter-culture had had its impact; firstly in the field of rock music (though rock's exploitation by the entertainment industry makes me less enthusiastic than some about the importance of its cultural messages), and secondly, in the spread of alternative or fringe theatre. Here the mixture of culture and politics which had seemed so confusing in the latter Sixties had genuinely creative issue, where cultural and political practice achieved an uncompromised harmony of interests. Although some practitioners argued that the fringe's gradual accommodation with official theatre *was* a compromise, it was inevitable that the talent and creativity involved should seek a larger audience than the fringe could provide.

The 'cultural politics' of feminism and gay rights were also the beneficiaries of the liberating drive of the Sixties, though here my choice of 1975 as an end-date means that only the beginnings of these movements are described. Feminist issues *outside* the groups that begin to evolve after 1968 did not fully make themselves felt until the mid-1970s.

Although relative to other expenditure the Arts Council's subsidy to fringe theatre was small, it was none the less vital, and with the changing economic climate of the early 1970s, subsidy and the Arts Council's relations with its clients becomes an increasingly important cultural and political issue. This is true of all the Arts Council's clients, great and small, but I found it logical to pursue this in the context of the theatre, before turning to the other arts. The levelling out, and then shrinkage, of Arts Council subsidies after 1975 is one of the firmest justifications for treating 1975 as the end of an era, one that had begun with the expansion of subsidy in 1964.

The new theatre, as I have argued, is the most visible and coherent product of 1968. In chapter VII, I survey the conditions of the visual arts, fiction and poetry in the late Sixties and early Seventies, and show how the certainties and status of all forms of official culture have been weakened.

In chapter VIII, I draw some conclusions, not only about the distance between theory and practice in radical social and cultural criticism after 1968, but about the relationship between British artists, writers and intellectuals and British society, as it has developed since 1939, the point at which I began this series. This relationship has been the central thread of all three volumes, and I have tried to show how three successive generations have responded to their material and political conditions, and in turn tried to influence the values of their culture.

As this study has progressed, and the events and topics discussed have approached the present day, I have become more and more conscious of my own involvement in this complex relationship. When I began the series a personal note was hardly appropriate, and I have maintained the convention of impersonality in historical prose. Now that this account of the past has almost caught up with the present, however, the impersonal tone seems less appropriate than when I began, and in my conclusion I offer a comment on the present that stems from my own reading of the past: I hope it also indicates something about work I have not yet undertaken.

My personal debts are many, and I should like to thank the Phoenix Trust for the grant they made towards the cost of research. The intellectual and literary debts to other writers are acknowledged in the source-notes at the end of the book, though there are many more than those from whom I have directly quoted. Three archives have been particularly helpful to me: the National Sound Archive, the little magazine collection in the library of University College, London; and the Poetry Library of the Arts Council. At University College Geoffrey Soar not only made their priceless collection of underground literature available to me, but supplied me with a great deal of additional material from his own sources. At the Arts Council Poetry Library Jonathan Barker has followed the accumulation of this survey all the way from 1939, and he has helped me at every step. I have also had useful advice from and enjoyable conversations with Barry Curtis, Chris Barlas and Paddy O'Sullivan. I should like to thank Blake Morrison and Malcolm Bradbury for their very helpful comments on the manuscript – and Christopher Hudson for contributing two words: the title.

I am proud that my sister Anthea has provided the index to all three volumes. John Curtis and Linda Osband helped to set this series in motion; Geoffrey Strachan and Anne Askwith have helped to draw it to a close. To both sets of editors, my sincere thanks.

College House Cottage
December 1985

CHAPTER 1

Understanding Media

'The situation could be described
by saying that we live in the
midst – or at any rate the
beginning – of a currency crisis.'

The Bishop of Woolwich *The Honest to God Debate* (1963)

'Damn you, England. You're rotting now, and quite soon you will disappear. My hate will outrun you, if only for a few seconds.' As successive international crises have brought us to the brink of nuclear destruction, the historical context of John Osborne's 'Letter to My Fellow Countrymen' of 8 August 1961 has almost been forgotten. For that matter, John Osborne's membership of the Committee of 100 and the significance of the letter's publication in a left-wing political paper, *Tribune*, have also been obscured by later events. In the summer of 1961 the crisis was over Berlin; the recently elected President Kennedy announced new military measures, in response to Khrushchev's declaration of his intention to sign a separate peace treaty between Russia and East Germany. Construction of the Berlin Wall began.

In the full flow of his conviction of the case for nuclear disarmament, Osborne attacked both the British Prime Minister, Harold Macmillan, and the leader of the Labour opposition, Hugh Gaitskell, for their support of the Americans. 'No, this is not the highly paid "anger" or the "rhetoric" you like to smile at (you've tried to mangle my language, too). You'll not pour pennies into my coffin for this; you are MY object. I am not yours. You are my vessel, you are MY hatred. That is my final identity.

1

True, it will no doubt die with me in a short time and by your unceasing effort.'

Osborne's denunciation is a suitably apocalyptic introduction to an increasingly apocalyptic period. The assassination of President Kennedy in November 1963 was only the first of a series of murders which dramatized the fusion of personal and political violence. In Britain, an underlying sense of dissatisfaction and disturbance was partially concealed by the rising tide of prosperity and the apparent security of Conservative Party rule. Social climates do not alter in accordance with the decades on the calendar, but 'change' was in the air, and on the lips of politicians, from Harold Macmillan's 'wind of change' blowing through the continent of Africa in February 1960 to Harold Wilson's 'white heat of technological change' of September 1963.

What this change was to produce was uncertain, and since in Macmillan's sense it meant the loss of Empire, it was also unwelcome, yet the talk of change helped to bring change about. Two other catch-phrases came into common currency in the early part of the decade: 'the affluent society' and 'the new morality'. Typically, neither was intended by its originator to have quite the meaning it acquired. J. K. Galbraith published his study of the American economy, *The Affluent Society*, in 1958. He argued that the growth of large independent corporations had diverted resources away from the control of the state, which was thus unable to carry out its social responsibilities; hence the condition he described as 'private affluence: public squalor'. This was not the case in Britain, where there was less affluence, and the Welfare State played a greater role, but after the austerities of 1945–56 'the affluent society' seemed to sum up something desirable and guiltily dangerous, bringing changes to British society.

'The new morality' came to be applied in senses even further from the intentions of its originator. In March 1963 Dr John Robinson, the Bishop of Woolwich, published a small paperback, *Honest to God*. 'The New Morality' was one of his chapter titles. It is emblematic of the changing cultural conditions that much of the controversy surrounding the publication was created, not by the book itself, but by a pre-publication article in the *Observer*. A sub-editor – not the bishop – supplied the headline 'Our Image of God Must Go'. Dr Robinson did have radical intentions, but not as radical as those summarized by the *Church Times*: 'It is not

2

every day that a bishop goes on record as apparently denying almost every Christian doctrine of the Church in which he holds office.'

Because Robinson challenged the traditional language of the Church, he was taken to challenge the traditional beliefs that this language expressed, but his 'new morality' turned out to be very like the old one, however much the idea of a personal God was redefined as a principle of harmony in the world. None the less, by questioning the ancient symbolism and language of the Church, Robinson was weakening its authority, and thus its power to exercise moral control. The Bishop believed that God is love; the 'love generation' of the mid-1960s was to make rather different sense of the personal chastity advocated by the Bishop of Wool-wich in his new morality.

The general anxiety about the current state of affairs shows in the number of books published which tried to assess the condition of Britain. They were in a sense expanded versions of the 'What's Wrong With Britain?' articles that were a popular feature of daily journalism (Penguin Books published a series of specials under the title.) The best known, not least because in its successive editions it has become something of an institution, was Anthony Sampson's *Anatomy of Britain*, published in 1962. Sampson commented in his introduction: 'A loss of dynamic and purpose, and a general bewilderment, are felt by many people, both at the top and the bottom in Britain today.'

Sampson's is an account of corporate and bureaucratic Britain, based on interviews with some two hundred 'top people' (*The Time*'s self-promotional phrase; see *In Anger* p. 167) in private and public management. He has no space for the discussion of arts or letters, but he describes the book in a telling image as 'an informal guide to a living museum'. Change is an important theme; economic expansion had been under way since 1957, but it had only begun to make its presence felt at the beginning of the Sixties.

Within two years, the credit squeeze ended, skyscrapers rushed up, supermarkets spread over cities, newspapers became fatter or died, commercial TV began making millions, shops, airlines, even coal and banks had to fight for their lives. After the big sleep many people

3

welcomed any novelty; any piece of Americanization seemed an enterprising change, and any thrusting tycoon, however irresponsible, was regarded as a phenomenon. Only now is Britain becoming *visually* aware of living in a state of perpetual and perilous change.

Although as an ambitious young journalist on the staff of the *Observer* Sampson was on the side of change, there are clear signs of cultural anxiety when he describes 'the new classless Americanized world of Wimpy bars, coffee-bars, television, mini-motors, pre-packaged food, ice-skating, Marks & Spencers, Vespas and airport lounges'. The mood of hectic novelty as Britain 'got with it' is captured by Timothy Birdsall's 1963 cartoon (Ill.2).

Sampson was not alone in detecting frustration with the current state of British society and relating it to the changes – and sometimes lack of changes – that had taken place since 1939. Anthony Hartley's *A State of England* (1963) puts forward the thesis that 'the diminution of Great Britain's position in the world and the relatively narrow economic margin on which we have lived since the war has caused a narrowing of horizons and a sense of frustration in English society, which has been frequently, though not always consciously, expressed by English intellectuals.' While Britain was morally right to divest herself of her Empire, the 'special relationship' with America behind which Britain hid her enfeeblement did not work, as America's exposure of Britain during the Suez crisis brutally made clear. At the same time, the arrival of the Welfare State had produced dissatisfaction, rather than a brave new society. Bureaucracy and inertia at home led to economic and cultural dullness.

Hartley's book had a specific political purpose other than to criticize the Welfare State: to urge on Britain an invigorating membership of the European Common Market. (Britain's application to join had been announced in July 1961, in the light of this search for a new world role, General de Gaulle's *non* of January 1963 was all the more humiliating.) But in its criticism of bureaucracy *A State of England* also contributes to the theme along which the political debate generally ran: was Britain becoming a corporate state? Brian Chapman argued in *British Government Observed* (1963): 'What in fact has been created in Britain is not the pluralist society, dreamt of in more innocent days, but a

4

special form of corporate state, in which public institutions become private property.' W. L. Guttsman's *The British Political Elite* suggested whose property these institutions had become. He echoed the arguments of left-wing American political theorist C. Wright Mills's *The Power Elite*, which did away with Marxist notions of a 'ruling class' and substituted the idea of a society modelled on the structure of 'mass' and 'élite'. In the late 1950s Britain's governing élite with its intricate network of relationships, had become popularly known as 'the Establishment' (see *In Anger* pp. 166–174).

Anthony Sampson's *Anatomy of Britain* is indeed an excellent anatomy of the Establishment, and he is critical of those Establishment values – the cult of the amateur, the cult of Oxbridge and the public school, the cult of conformism – which appeared to hold up progress and economic growth. But the new dynamism which Sampson wished to see would not necessarily lead to a better quality of life. So warned Raymond Williams in 'Britain in the 1960s,' the conclusion to *The Long Revolution* (1961), his sequel to *Culture and Society* (1958). This is another contribution to the 'state of Britain' debate. The chapter is pessimistic about the prospects for the arts, but Raymond Williams is also disquieted by the contradictions in the economic outlook. On the one hand Britain seems 'a country with a fairly obvious future: industrially advanced, securely democratic, and with a steadily rising general level of education and culture'. Yet 'the ordinary optimism about Britain's economic future can be reasonably seen as simple complacency. It is very far from certain that on present evidence and given likely developments the directions and rate of growth of the economy guarantee us, over say fifty years, a steadily rising standard of living in this economically exposed and crowded island.'

The irony of unintended meaning applies to one of the phrases which expressed the 'simple complacency' Williams criticized. At a rally in Bedford in July 1957 Harold Macmillan had said, 'Let's be frank about it. Most of our people have never had it so good.' This is the source of the catch-phrase which summed up the material benefits of Tory government, 'You've never had it so good', but Macmillan's intention had been quite opposite: he was warning against the very complacency of which he was later

5

accused. He said in the same speech, 'amidst all this prosperity there is one problem that has troubled us in one way or another since the war. It is the problem of rising prices'.

Yet it was self-evident that most people *had* never had it so good. Between October 1951 and October 1963 wages were estimated to have risen by 72 per cent, prices by 45 per cent. There was full employment, and the availability and consumption of pleasurable possessions such as cars, washing machines, record players and television sets testified to the expansion of the 'affluent society'. Now that the most glaring social inequalities were taken care of by the Welfare State, the debate 'What's Wrong With Britain?' shifted from the political and economic field to the cultural. In his introduction to a special number of *Encounter* in 1963, a 'state of Britain' enquiry ominously titled *Suicide of a Nation?*, Arthur Koestler argued that 'psychological factors and cultural attitudes are at the root of economic evils' and not the other way round. His mainly conservative-minded contributors – Henry Fairlie, Cyril Connolly, Malcolm Muggeridge, Aiden Crawley – agreed with him. The nation that *Encounter* describes has two rearguards: the Old Boy Network and the trades unions. In these conditions a fresh élite could emerge but slowly, and even then this new technocracy was also to be feared.

The cultural debate had been started by the Left during the upsurge of radical feeling that followed the Suez débâcle of 1956, but as affluence became general the uses of the leisure that the new prosperity afforded became a matter of concern. Anthony Sampson wrote:

In spite of the slow industrial growth, the adverse balance of payments, the economic crises, Britain continues for most people to be an increasingly pleasant place to live in. Behind the daunting facades of British institutions, the drab architecture, economists, imperialists and the Board of Trade, Britain is in a state of galloping consumption, in the age of Bingo, Babycham or Chemmy. At one extreme leisure is organized and commercialized with juke boxes or glossy magazines, at the other it revolves round philosophical paperbacks and correspondence courses. But either way there's more of it, and more money to spend on it. The average working week has dropped from about fifty hours in 1939 to forty-four hours in 1961, the teenagers alone spend £800 million a year on themselves.

6

The 1959 General Election was the first in which support for the arts became an electoral issue. The Labour Party published *Leisure for Living* and promised in their manifesto to establish a National Theatre and to give more money to the Arts Council. The Conservative Party kept culture out of their manifesto, but their pamphlet *The Challenge of Leisure* matched the Labour Party's promises.

In *A State of England* Anthony Hartley saw a gradual blending taking place between politics and culture. What might previously have been seen as moral choices were now matters of taste, and with the collapse of a general system of accepted moral values culture acquired greater importance as a guide to political choice. This is to the advantage of culture, but politics 'will tend to suffer from the association, the ultimate result of which is the state of mind that is to be found among many young supporters of CND, where banning the Bomb, Socialism, good modern architecture and the accoutrements of Bohemianism all take on something of an equivalent importance as gestures against everyday conformity.' Hartley is warning against the substitution for policy of style; a warning increasingly justified by the actions of politicians and advertising men as the decade went on.

The blending of culture and politics is evident in the merging of their respective models of society. The theory of government which posited, as opposed to the old pluralist pattern, the leadership of a more or less *lumpen* mass by an élite is also the model for a theory of culture which depends on the opposition between an élite 'high culture' and an inferior 'popular' one. There is no longer a pyramid of cultural aspirations, and no middle ground. The significance of the élite/mass model is that in both politics and culture the élite controls the mass, through the institutions of the corporate state, and the control of mass communications by corporations run by élites.

The distinction between true and false popular culture worried the Left. In 1962 Arnold Wesker's *Chips With Everything* was a critical and commercial success. The play, which depicts the experience of a squad of young men in their first weeks of National Service in the RAF, uses a Christmas party in the NAAFI canteen to show the difference between genuine and ersatz popular culture. The Wing Commander urges the band to sing Elvis Presley, but an aircraftsman counters with a recitation

7

from Robert Burns and then 'The Cutty Wren', 'an old peasant revolt song'. According to the stage directions, 'Boys join in gradually, menacing the officers'. The irony of this scene is that the opposition is led by an ex-public schoolboy, who is temporarily in revolt. He is also given lines expressing hostility to the working class as it really was: 'Chips with every damn thing. You breed babies and you eat chips with everything.'

The anatomists of British society were all alarmed by the cultural pattern that was emerging. Anthony Sampson: 'The *total* annual government grant to the arts in 1961 was £8 million – one two-hundredth of the defence budget, of this the main state patron, the Arts Council gets a meagre £1.7 million. . . . Private patronage, with its huge potential influence, is largely in the hands of commercial middlemen who sponsor the safest mediocrity – the cinema distributors, property developers, building societies, television tycoons.' Raymond Williams did not believe that even the Arts Council, a closed and inflexible institution, could be of much practical help against the increasing corporatization of publishing, the theatre, cinema and television.

The condition of cultural growth must be that varying elements are at least equally available and that new and unfamiliar things must be offered steadily over a long period, if they are to have a reasonable chance of acceptance. Policies of this degree of responsibility seem impossible in our present cultural organization. The encouragement of valuable elements is restricted to what is little more than a defensive holding operation, which of course is better than nothing but which is hardly likely to make any general change. The rest of the field is left to the market, and not even to the free play of the market, for the amount of capital involved in financing our major cultural institutions restricts entry to a comparatively few powerful groups, so that both production and distribution are effectively in few hands.

Martin Green's *A Mirror for Anglo-Saxons* (1961), written from the point of view of an intellectual deliberately expatriated to America, noted 'there has been no enthusiasm in England for a long time', and blamed this absence on 'that paralysed and paralysing hegemony of gentlemanliness'. His prescription for cultural renewal turns on acceptance of the new political and economic conditions which other writers have described. 'What is needed is a modern British type which has some vigour and glamour, and which is adapted to modern conditions, which has

8

no desire for elegance or panache, no nostalgia for world greatness, which can accept poverty and irony without losing zest for life, which will feel itself at home in an overpopulated, post-industrial, post-imperial, raining little island in the North Sea.' His examples of the new man are D. H. Lawrence, F. R. Leavis, George Orwell and Kingsley Amis, in retrospect an unlikely collective source of cultural regeneration, but one unified by their opposition to the Mandarin high culture of Bloomsbury.

At the beginning of the 1960s the focus of the debate shifted. The point at issue was no longer the high culture that had been attacked by the Angry Young Men of 1956. Instead, the question centred on the quality of the popular culture enjoyed by the majority of the population. In particular, concern was expressed about the quality of British television.

The history of British television goes back to 1936, though programmes stopped during the war. The coverage of the coronation of Queen Elizabeth II in 1953 established television's predominance over radio as a mass medium, but as long as it (and the cultural transmission it involved) remained exclusively the responsibility of the BBC, it was seen as merely an extension of radio broadcasting. Then in September 1955 the Independent Television network began operations. Because of the powerful example of the BBC its programmes were not radically different from those the BBC offered, but the fact that it was funded by advertising placed it in a completely different relationship to the public. Independent Television was *commercial*, its objective was to deliver audiences for advertising in as large quantities as possible; its programmes were therefore perceived by its critics as a further means of exploiting the lowest common denominators of desire and appetite aroused by the advertisements' lies and half-truths. Commercial television was seen as a stimulus to materialism – an attitude of mind deplored by the culturally concerned of both Left and Right. When the proposal to permit commercial television was put to Parliament in 1953 the Conservative Party was initially as hostile as Labour, and only a skilful lobby persuaded Parliament to change its mind.

Commercial television caught the rising tide of affluence, and with the rapid expansion of television ownership the commercial television companies became outrageously, even embarrassingly profitable. Gross expenditure by television advertisers rose from an estimated £13 million in 1956 to an estimated £76 million in 1960, and £93 million in 1961. By 1958 the companies were averaging profits of 130 per cent, but the terms of the Independent Television charter meant that nothing could be done to change the situation until the first set of operating licences expired in 1964. Even Norman Collins, a former Head of BBC TV who resigned in 1950 in order to become one of the chief advocates of commercial television, called the profitablity of ITV 'immoral'. His own investment of £2,250 had turned into £500,000.

The 'licence to print money' – as one television baron put it – that had unwittingly been issued to the independent television companies was one cause for concern. Another was that if advertisers had such faith in the medium's ability to sell products, the mass medium must be in a position to change other attitudes as well. Television was coming of age, as programme-makers gained confidence in their skills and journalists gradually freed themselves of the severe restrictions imposed by the politicians. The 1959 General Election was acknowledged to be the United Kingdom's first television election, with the BBC and ITV enjoying editorial freedom for the first time to provide a full news coverage of the event. In 1961 Joseph Trenaman and Denis McQuail of Leeds University television research unit published *Television and the Political Image*, a study of the 1959 election. Their cautious conclusion was that 'with three incidental and slight exceptions, no medium or source of propaganda . . . had an ascertainable effect on *attitude* changes.' Television enlarged political knowledge, but did not change pre-existent opinions. The significance of this conclusion is that while television became an acceptable part of the information process, the introduction of *new* ideas via the medium, as opposed to the reporting of those already in circulation, was more difficult, and, as we shall see, when an issue was actually raised by television, its reception was highly controversial.

The attitude of intellectuals to television was almost universally hostile. R. H. S. Crossman's Fabian tract *Labour in the Affluent Society* (1960) sums up the disappointment of those who had hoped that the Labour post-war reforms would do more than improve material conditions. 'The commercialized media of mass communications have been systematically used to dope the critical faculties which would normally have been stimulated by the improvement of popular education since 1945.'

A significant source of this hostility to television was the teaching of F. R. Leavis. *Scrutiny*, the critical magazine he had launched as 'an outlaws' enterprise' in Cambridge in 1932, had an enormous influence on a generation of academics and teachers, and continued long after the magazine ceased publication in 1953. Leavis believed himself embattled against the academic Establishment in Cambridge, and against the fashionable literary world of London. He believed in the moral worth of literature, and in the former existence of a popular culture shaped by it, but this popular culture had long been corrupted by the mass media, of which television was only the latest. Thus the history of culture was one of inevitable decline and fall, resisted only by 'a key community of the élite' – the 150 or more contributors to *Scrutiny*.

Leavis's influence can be seen in the contributions to the symposium, *Discrimination and Popular Culture* (1964), which grew out of a National Union of Teachers' conference on popular culture. The essay in *The Modern Age* (1961) contributed by a close colleague of Leavis, G. H. Bantock, on 'the Social and Intellectual Background' to contemporary literature sums up the horror with which television was viewed:

> . . . night after night a selection of programmes of inane triviality sterilize the emotions and standardize the outlook and attitudes of millions of people. And these, it is necessary to remind ourselves, are the 'educated' and literate descendants of people who produced the folk song and the folk tale, who built the parish churches and nourished Bunyan.

In the same volume Richard Hoggart's essay 'Mass Communications in Britain' emphasized the trivializing effect of television in particular. Mass communications 'do not ignore intellectual matters; they tend to castrate them, to allow them to sit at one side of the fireplace, sleek and useless, a family plaything.' In *Communications* (1962) Raymond Williams argued that the so-called popular culture purveyed by television was spurious.

> In the worst cultural products of our time, we find little that is genuinely popular, developed from the life of actual communities. We find instead a synthetic culture, or anti-culture, which is alien to almost everybody, persistently hostile to art and intellectual activity, which it

11

spends much of its time misrepresenting, and given over to exploiting indifference, lack of feeling, frustration, and hatred. It finds such common human interests as sex, and turns them into crude caricatures or glossy facsimiles.

There is an important element of anti-Americanism in Williams's attack. The popularity of American programmes on British television served as a focus for the intelligentsia's general hostility to America. As Williams put it, 'At certain levels, we are culturally an American colony.' He acknowledged that not all American cultural influences were bad, but in the field of popular culture America was having a disastrous effect. Martin Green, from his American viewpoint, drew a political moral from the sense of inferiority, the 'malice and misunderstanding and dislike' displayed by British intellectuals towards American culture. 'It is because . . . Englishmen think or suspect that their country is "in decline" that they resent America's growth.' There were some Englishmen beginning to take an interest in American culture, 'but most of this new interest is neither intelligent nor whole-hearted. It either remains academic or concentrates on the exotic, and is likely to create an Americanization as false and superficial as the Europeanization Orwell used to complain of in British intellectuals.'

In July 1960 the concern about the quality and influence of British television was officially recognized by the establishment of a Royal Commission on Broadcasting under the chairmanship of Sir Harry Pilkington, an industrialist who freely admitted that he knew almost nothing about television. The need for an enquiry was urgent because of the imminent expiry of the BBC's charter, and the growing demand for the opening of a third television channel. In the event, the BBC's charter was extended by two years to 1964, so that its renewal would coincide with the expiry of the first commercial television company licences. Richard Hoggart, about to become Professor of English at Birmingham University, served on the Pilkington Committee, and played an important part in drafting the final report. His conviction of the corruption of working-class culture by mass media, first expressed in *The Uses of Literacy* (1957), runs through the committee's criticism of the trivializing effect of television.

The Pilkington Committee examined all aspects of broadcasting except the BBC's External Services, and when the report appeared in 1962 it confirmed not just the anxiety about television, but the general sense of unease and change in British society.

From the representations which have been put to us, this is the underlying cause of disquiet about television: the belief, deeply felt, that the way television has portrayed human behaviour and treated moral issues has already done something and will in time do much to worsen the moral climate of the country. That this is at a time when many of the standards by which people have hitherto lived are often questioned is not in itself regrettable.

The committee tried earnestly to evolve a philosophy of broadcasting which (as in Trenaman and McQuail's *Television and the Political Image*) took into account the fact that the medium was believed to have a profound influence on values and moral attitudes, although nobody knew quite how this influence worked. It tried to decide what 'giving the public what it wants' actually means, for the public is as difficult to analyse as the medium's effect upon it. It concluded negatively that the idea of a mass audience was 'patronizing and arrogant', since there is more to the individual viewer than the average of common awareness. That, however, did not answer the question of what to do about the commercial companies who depended on mass audiences for their profitable existence.

The report did not evolve a satisfactory philosophy. It decided that what the public wanted to be given was freedom to choose. But it did serve its purpose as a disciplinary hearing for the commercial television companies, who had been alarmingly smug and complacent in their submissions. 'We conclude . . . that the disquiet about television is mainly attributable to independent television and largely to its entertainment programmes.' ITV was criticized for the level of violence in its programmes, for its quiz games, and its failure to reckon sufficiently 'with the effect of television on values and moral standards generally'. But the committee's main recommendation, that ITV should be restructured, and the functions of making programmes and selling advertising be completely separated, was ignored. It was not until Channel Four was launched in 1982 that such a system was put into operation. The BBC, meanwhile, was given a clean bill of health, and was rewarded with the allocation of a second channel, to open as BBC2 in 1964.

The difficulty for the critics of television and of the mass culture that television represented was that their ideals were clearly at variance with reality. As Anthony Hartley pointed out in *A State of England*, 'instead of holding discussion groups or organizing amateur theatricals the English working classes have been reading women's magazines and comics or watching television – and commercial television at that. What is worse, they have appeared positively to enjoy doing so.' To the social theorists mass communications were the cultural expression of mass society, from which the individual was alienated, capitalist individualism being as illusory as the working classes' degraded enjoyment of quiz shows. The antithesis of alienation was 'community', those working-class values sanctified by Richard Hoggart in *The Uses of Literacy* (1957), and concern for whose preservation underpinned the moral judgements of the Pilkington Report. But what precisely were these values, and how were they to be expressed? The debate about mass communications turned back to the general political debate that had been launched with the emergence of the New Left after 1956.

The problem for the early New Left thinkers like Hoggart, Raymond Williams and E. P. Thompson was that while they admired the values of solidarity and mutual support fostered by working-class institutions, the British working class showed no signs of being the force for change that it was supposed to be. It was in the main culturally backward, socially conservative, nationalistic and racially prejudiced. The distance between theory and reality was measurable by working-class attitudes to the one issue which might upset the formal dance of consensus politics, the Campaign for Nuclear Disarmament.

CND failed to attract sufficient working-class support. In 1960 the Labour Party conference adopted a unilateralist disarmament policy, but the price of this political success was that disarmament became an issue in a power struggle within the Labour Party. Several of the unions that had supported the disarmament motion did so because they disapproved of Hugh Gaitskell's attempt to alter the Party's commitment to nationalization under Clause Four of its constitution. When in 1961 Gaitskell threatened to split the Party over disarmament, trades unions reversed their position and the unilateralist commitment was withdrawn. After

Gaitskell's death in January 1963 the issue lost its symbolic importance in the Right/Left struggle within the Labour Party, and Labour's narrow majority after the General Election in 1964 once more made unity paramount. The successful resolution of the 1962 Cuban missile crisis – when there were very real fears that nuclear war was about to break out – and the test ban treaty of 1963 lessened the apparent urgency of the issue in the public's mind.

Yet if CND failed to attract mass, working-class support, it did offer a focus for the 'commitment' which had exercised radical intellectuals in the late 1950s, and proved a seedbed for later developments. In 1960 the Campaign for Nuclear Disarmament split within itself. The 1961 Easter march from Aldermaston was the biggest ever, but the initiative in the movement passed to the Committee of 100, formed in the previous year to press for civil disobedience and direct action. (A prime mover in the Committee was Ralph Schoenman, the first of a succession of American radicals in this period to act as catalysts in cultural and political life and who became Bertrand Russell's secretary.) Backed by Bertrand Russell, who split with Canon Collins on the issue of direct action and resigned his presidency of CND, the Committee of 100 attracted many of those who had gathered under the banner of the Royal Court Theatre on Aldermaston marches, among them John Osborne, Lindsay Anderson, Vanessa Redgrave, Arnold Wesker, Robert Bolt, John Arden and Shelagh Delaney. After a number of sit-down demonstrations in 1961, thirty-six members of the Committee were summonsed for planning civil disobedience. The majority of them refused to undertake not to break the law, including Bertrand Russell, Arnold Wesker, Robert Bolt and Christopher Logue, and went to prison for up to two months. There were further demonstrations and arrests – 1,314 in Trafalgar Square in September – and in December five of the main organizers were arrested under the Official Secrets Act and given sentences of a year to eighteen months. The arrests stifled the Committee of 100, and demoralized its supporters, and, after a last flare of activity during the Aldermaston march of 1963, the Committee was wound up in 1968.

In the later 1960s CND was virtually defunct as a political force, yet in mobilizing the support of a significant number of young people it had created a new constituency from which more radical movements sprang. As David Widgery describes in *The Left in Britain* (1976), the annual Aldermaston march 'was a student movement before its time, mobile sit-in or marching pop festival; in its midst could be found the first embers of the hashish underground and premature members of the Love Generation as well as cadres of forthcoming revolutionary parties.' When the 'counter-culture' did form it opposed itself to the old system of reformist politics of which CND was a part, but the temporary communitarian spirit created on marches and demonstrations gave many people a first taste of what an alternative society might be like. It was also a first political experience and, excluded from the mainstream of consensus politics, ex-marchers were recruited by the radical or anarchist Left. The very failure and decline of CND after 1963 was a stimulus to some of those active in the counter-culture, as we shall see in chapter III.

The failure of CND to live up to its radical promise was a bitter disappointment to the intellectuals of the New Left, and it had immediate repercussions for the *New Left Review*. Perry Anderson has written that the New Left

never became a tight, compact intellectual formation, any more than it became a mass political movement. It was a certain *milieu*, in which there was an open interflow of professions and preoccupations, ranging between the extremes of the theoretical and the pragmatic: it included students, journalists, teachers, doctors, architects, academics. Potentially, this was a very creative and hopeful phenomenon. Where it has occurred, the constitution of a separate pariah-élite of intellectuals, cut off from the rest of society, has had innumerable damaging consequences on the socialist movement in Europe. Avoidance of it appeared to be one of the greatest advantages of the New Left. Unfortunately, however, it was also the source of paralysing confusions.

Some of these confusions were over the purpose of the *New Left Review*.

As with CND, which included liberals and even conservatives in its ranks, there were those who wished to keep the review 'a broad church', and tackle cultural as much as political issues. In the first number in January 1960 the editor Stuart Hall explained:

The purpose of discussing the cinema or teenage culture in *NLR* is not to show that, in some modish way, we are keeping up with the times. These are directly relevant to the imaginative resistances of people who

16

have to live within capitalism – the growing points of social discontent, the projections of deeply felt needs.

Thus the magazine began by continuing on the lines of the *New Reasoner* and *Universities and Left Review* from whose merger it had been created.

In 1960 the magazine and the New Left Clubs that supported it flourished, but its fortunes fell with CND in 1961. By issue eleven in September 1961 'considerable reconstruction' was reported to be under way, both in the magazine and the movement. The next issue announced that the editor, Stuart Hall, was resigning to take up a post with the Centre for Contemporary Cultural Studies, then being established at Birmingham University by Richard Hoggart as a faculty for long-term research and cultural criticism. At Birmingham Stuart Hall was to have considerable influence on the development of cultural analysis, as we shall see.

At the beginning of 1962, under a shared editorship, the *New Left Review* was in poor financial shape. A palace revolution followed, and the 24-year-old former editor of *New University*, Perry Anderson, emerged as sole editor. The chairman, the former communist historian E. P. Thompson, who had founded the *New Reasoner*, was deposed, and the whole episode caused a deep split in the New Left movement. Thompson moved to the *Socialist Register*, from whence he engaged in regular polemics with Anderson. For his part, Anderson shifted the magazine's interest away from popular culture towards a much more rigorous enquiry into the theoretical principles of revolutionary politics, concentrating on European Marxism and the Third World, and publishing articles on Lukács, Gramsci, Sartre, and Marcuse in an effort to make up for the philosophical and intellectual deficiencies of English thought. He described the task as 'forging a revolutionary and internationalist political culture', but he considerably narrowed the appeal of the *New Left Review* in the process.

There was, however, one serious attempt to put into practice the cultural ideals that were an essential part of the political debates of the late 1950s and early 1960s: Arnold Wesker's Centre 42. In 1960, with the completion of his trilogy of plays, *Chicken Soup With Barley*, *Roots* and *I'm Talking About Jerusalem*, which place cultural issues at the centre of any hopes of political regeneration, Arnold Wesker was riding high on the success of the new wave of committed theatre launched at the Royal Court in 1956. He wanted to carry out the programme of cultural reform urged by Raymond Williams and others, and evolve an alternative means of promoting the arts to close the divide between high and popular culture that was reinforced both by commercial entertainment and the patronage of the Arts Council. In an article for the *New Statesman* in July 1960 he described his vision of the new Jerusalem.

> You start off with a picture: orchestras tucked away in valleys, people stopping Auden in the street to thank him for their favourite poem, teenagers around the jukebox arguing about my latest play, miners flocking to their own opera house; a picture of a nation thirsting for all the riches their artists can excite them with, hungry for the greatest, the best, unable to wait for Benjamin Britten's next opera, arguing about Joan Littlewood's latest.

Wesker wished to wrest control of the forms of art from both market forces and aristocratic patronage, and return it to the makers of art themselves. He proposed to do so by appealing to the trades unions. At the *Sunday Times* student drama festival in 1960 he made a speech attacking the labour movement for its neglect of the arts. The speech became a pamphlet, and with the help of a trades unionist and New Left supporter Bill Holdsworth a copy was sent to the general secretary of every union. A second pamphlet put forward proposals for nationwide sponsorship of the arts by trades unions. Out of the 187 unions 4 replied sympathetically, and at the annual Trades Union Congress in September 1960 the film and television technicians' union, the ACTT, presented a resolution, number forty-two, which called on the TUC to recognize its responsibilities towards the arts in an age of increased leisure. In spite of opposition from the TUC General Council, the resolution was carried unanimously.

While the TUC responded to the resolution by handing the problem over to their Education Officer for a report, Wesker found that his ideas had focused the enthusiasms of a number of people with similar concerns. He was invited to join in the discussions being held independently by a group of writers centreing on Doris Lessing, Clive Exton, John McGrath, Bernard Kops,

Shelagh Delaney, Ted Kotcheff, Ted Allen, Alun Owen and others, who were equally anxious to close the gap between artist and public. (They were also involved in CND and the Committee of 100.) From these discussions emerged the idea of a pool of artists and a network of people's festivals. It was decided to form a non-profit-making company with a Council of Management that included four trades unionists and one Labour MP, Jennie Lee. Centre 42 was officially launched at a party on 24 July 1961.

It is important to stress that Wesker was not trying to evolve new cultural forms, or promote proletarian art. He did not believe that there was such a thing as 'working-class' culture – except at the level of keeping whippets and pigeon-fancying or the ways in which people celebrate marriage. Nor did he believe that 'high' culture was exclusively class-based. He wanted to make the best – in an aesthetic and moral sense – available to everyone. This was clear from Centre 42's launching brochure.

Centre 42 will be a cultural hub which, by its approach and work, will destroy the mystique and snobbery associated with the arts. A place where artists are in control of their own means of expression and their own channels of distribution; where the highest standards of professional work will be maintained in an atmosphere of informality; where the artist is brought into closer contact with his audience enabling the public to see that artistic activity is a natural part of their daily lives.

Though he was clearly of the Left, and associates like Doris Lessing, John McGrath and Adrian Mitchell gave Centre 42 a Left slant, Wesker believed that art and politics were separate fields of action. (Lessing and McGrath soon resigned, and McGrath later attacked Wesker for promoting 'bourgeois' culture.) As we shall see, Wesker manifestly failed to get the Left to support him.

It was unfortunate timing that in the same month that Centre 42 was launched, Joan Littlewood, one of the people Wesker most admired, and who had gone some way towards achieving a popular theatre, should resign as director of Theatre Workshop, and go abroad. She resigned for paradoxical reasons of failure and success. Theatre Workshop, which she had co-founded in 1945 with Ewan MacColl, had been based in London at the Theatre Royal, Stratford East since 1953, and although they had gained a following in the working-class area that was their home, it was never large enough to support them entirely. Transfers of productions to the West End were a necessary part of their economy, and the company was becoming increasingly successful. At one point in 1961 three Theatre Workshop productions were running in commercial London theatres, *The Hostage*, *A Taste of Honey* and *Fings Ain't Wot They Used T'Be*. But that meant that there was no longer a genuine Theatre Workshop company for Joan Littlewood to work with, and she stayed away until March 1963, when she began work on the highly successful *Oh What a Lovely War*. She also put her energies into promoting her idea for 'fun palaces', popular recreation parks which were to offer 'juke-box information, adult toys, star-gazing, science gadgetry, news service, tele-communication, swank promenades, hide-aways, dance-floors, drinks rallies, battles of flowers, concerts, learning machines, observation decks, nurseries, music, theatre clownery' etc. (The project came to nothing, but it anticipated the mixed-media pleasures of the underground in a way that Centre 42 did not.)

Centre 42, meanwhile, was being rushed into action in order to maintain momentum, but before it was really ready. Having decided during his imprisonment for Committee of 100 activities to commit himself fully to the project, Arnold Wesker became artistic director, and as a result he was to have little time for writing. The plan was to raise funds and establish an actual centre, a building, from which Centre 42 could operate. But before funds or building were found, there was an invitation from Wellingborough Trades Council to help them organize a festival. Trades Councils are local committees representing all the trades unions in an area, and Wesker believed that these were the best organizations to work with. As it turned out, their quality and influence varied a great deal from place to place, and real power lay with individual unions and their shop stewards, who were rarely sympathetic to anything beyond the struggle to improve wages and conditions.

Five members of Centre 42 worked for eight days in Wellingborough, and the experiment was sufficiently successful for five more Trades councils, in Leicester, Nottingham, Birmingham, Bristol, Hayes and Southall to follow Wellingborough in organizing festivals in 1962. The result was a rolling festival, with one week in each town and a week off in between. As much encouragement was given to local efforts, amateur artists exhibited alongside professionals, and so forth. Centre 42 supplied a jazz band and organized folk concerts and folk documentaries – Charles Parker's series *The Maker and the Tool*, Wesker's *The Nottingham Captain*; there were dance competitions, poetry readings in pubs and factories. The reception varied. The local press were generally enthusiastic, but the national critics were either uncomprehending or patronizing, for they were suspicious of trades union influence and what they thought was supposed to be working-class art. Centre 42 lost money.

And that, so far as the material achievements of Centre 42 are concerned, is the end of the story. Yet the history of Centre 42 is a prologue for many of the themes encountered during the 1960s, and indeed Centre 42 is bound up with one of the symbols of the Sixties, the Round House. After the 1962 festivals it was decided to wait two years before accepting any more invitations, while money was found to pay off accumulated debts and a proper base was created. Wesker was tipped off by the critic Alan Brien that the old railway-engine turning-shed in Camden, then being used as a liquor store, had been bought by the millionaire property dealer and art patron, Louis Mintz. (Mintz, for instance, was a governor of Bernard Miles's Mermaid Theatre in the City of London.) The Round House, as it was known, had obvious potential as an arts centre in a working-class district of London, but it would cost a great deal to convert. Like many artistic projects in the 1960s, the fate of Centre 42 became inextricably entangled with the fate of a building.

After lengthy negotiations, in July 1964 Louis Mintz formally handed over the sixteen years remaining on the Round House's lease to Centre 42. Architects' plans were drawn up, and Centre 42 launched an appeal, backed by some of the most prestigious names in the cultural world: Lord Harewood, Peggy Ashcroft, Benjamin Britten, Albert Finney, Graham Greene, Yehudi Menuhin, Henry Moore, Sir Laurence Olivier, John Piper, J. B. Priestley, Terence Rattigan, Sir Herbert Read, Vanessa Redgrave, Sir Carol Reed, Sir John Rothenstein. There was also support from business patrons of the arts. The appeal was for £600,000. A month later they had raised £1,600. In the following years inflation and revisions to plans raised the target to £750,000. By 1971 about £150,000 had come in from all sources.

21

The need for funds drove Wesker unwillingly into the arms of the political and cultural Establishment. Harold Wilson had supported the scheme while in opposition, and introduced his friend George Hoskins to act as a financial adviser. When Labour won the election in October 1964 Jennie Lee became the first ever Minister for the Arts, but that did not mean that Centre 42's problems were solved. (Previously Centre 42 had survived on grants from the Gulbenkian Foundation, but had had only £200 from the Arts Council.) In December 1965 a Round House Trust was established, in order to raise funds and keep them separate from Centre 42's debts. George Hoskins became Administrator, and Robert Maxwell MP Treasurer. Wesker reluctantly agreed to a scaled-down scheme for a gradual conversion of the building, which would then operate a mixed economy of plays and commercial events like pop concerts. The pressing need, however, was for money. Wesker and Hoskins attended the 1966 Labour Party conference in order to lobby for support, and Harold Wilson suggested that his wife Mary would arrange a tea party at 10 Downing Street. After much delay and political wrangling, the party duly took place on 25 July 1967, attended by many of Labour's more wealthy supporters. £80,000 was raised, enough for the initial conversion.

Wesker's relations with the Labour establishment on which he depended gradually deteriorated. His first play for six years, *Their Very Own and Golden City* (1966), is a tacit admission of defeat. Centre 42 was in suspension, and he did not agree with the commercial exploitation of the Round House. He did not like the 'smug trustees', he had to work with, whom he thought of as 'rich thugs'. He also had a public quarrel with Jennie Lee when she sat in on a council meeting held at the House of Commons. Unable to raise money from the Arts Council, and exasperated by the trustees, Wesker had come to believe that someone was sabotaging their efforts, and said so. Challenged by Jennie Lee, he replied that she was responsible. Lee, for her part, accused him of being 'a bloody communist'. Political suspicion, and the supposed threat of Centre 42 to her own efforts as Arts Minister appear to have cost Wesker valuable support.

Centre 42 was finally wound up in 1970. Wesker's last throw was a production of a new play, *The Friends*, which he directed himself. (In 1964 he spent four months in Cuba, and returned there in 1967 to direct his play, *The Four Seasons*. He wished to continue to direct his own work, and therefore refused to allow *The Friends* to be produced by a commercial management.) *The Friends*, which he had directed in Sweden in January 1970, was a flop when it opened at the Round House on 19 May. It must have been particularly mortifying that Kenneth Tynan's sex-revue *Oh Calcutta!* which followed at the Round House in July was a commercial success. In November 1970 Wesker resigned as director, and Centre 42 was officially wound up on 18 December, leaving debts of £40,000. In 1971 the Round House received its first grant from the Arts Council (other than for building work) of £7,500.

As for Wesker's original hopes for support from the TUC, the 1961 Trades Union Congress received a report from its Education Officer which concluded that there was little the TUC could or should do, except at a regional level by putting pressure on local authorities to levy the rates they were entitled to spend on cultural activities. The report was accepted, and shelved, for no money was voted to help encourage local festivals. Wesker believed that the unions had a responsibility for the society they had helped to create, and that they would act as channels of communication. He was proved wrong, for the unions were bureaucratic machines with – except in one or two rare cases – very narrow horizons.

The inability of Centre 42 to attract the funds it needed shows that even in the years of apparent cultural boom in the 1960s it was difficult to promote the genuinely unorthodox as opposed to the merely avant-garde. Wesker's chief mistake (and his idealism should not be counted as an error, however much it made for practical difficulties) was to become trapped by the pursuit of a building in which to house the activities he proposed. (In theory, the Round House was to be only the first of several centres.) But if Centre 42 was itself a failure, it was a stimulus to cultural activity in the regions, and a challenge to local authorities to undertake proper arts funding. It was a stimulus to the provision of locally supported theatres, and to the creation of arts centres. It was even a stimulus to the creation of Ministry for the Arts with which it had such poor relations. Ironically, it secured the future of the Round House as a building for the arts.

* * *

The failure of Centre 42 suggests that there was an inevitability about the changes that were taking place in the cultural patterns of British life, as the economics of the arts separated out a small, but artistically rich, high culture, from a general low level of impoverished expectations and cheap satisfactions. Wesker's idealism could not sustain the Round House where George Hoskins's commercialism could. But the very terminology used to describe high and low culture implies a judgement fixing them in a relationship that condemns them both, and deepens the divide between them. As Raymond Williams points out in *Communications*, it is a matter for argument 'whether "the masses" and "the minority" are inevitable social facts, or whether they are communication models which in part create and reinforce the situation they apparently describe.'

What did appear to be happening was the disappearance of the middle ground between mass and minority. In 1960 the last of the 'middlebrow' magazines, *John Bull*, folded. *John Bull* had supplied a diet of popular feature articles and short stories neither sensational nor pretentious to a general reading public since as long ago as 1882, but its market had disappeared. A former *John Bull* writer Robert Holles commented in *Encounter*: 'We are left with a magazine and Sunday newspaper coverage which presupposes that the population is composed of 10 per cent articulate egghead and 60 per cent sniggering half-wit, with a balance of women who are obsessed with frustrated romance and the latest knitting patterns.'

The absorption of the *News Chronicle* by the *Daily Mail* in October 1960 (which occasioned a Royal Commission on the Press in parallel with the Pilkington enquiry) was another sign of the shrinkage of the middle ground. The *Chronicle* did not compete with *The Times*, the *Telegraph*, or the *Manchester Guardian* (about to move to London and become simply the *Guardian*), but its content was far more serious-minded than that of the tabloid press. The fact that such a paper could not survive with a readership of 1¼ million was evidence of the pressure on mass communications to gain as large an audience as possible, with all the invitations to sensationalism that implied. Yet if the middle ground was disappearing, the constituency appealed to by the 'quality' newspapers was growing. In February 1961 the *Sunday Telegraph* was launched, and with the *Sunday Times* and the *Observer* gained a steadily increasing readership. In February 1962 the *Sunday Times* published the first number of its colour magazine; the *Observer* followed suit in 1964.

For all that television hurt the reading of middlebrow magazines and light fiction (in 1961 the booksellers W. H. Smith wound up their commercial lending libraries and began to sell records instead; Boots libraries closed in 1966), there were signs that television encouraged the circulation of serious books. People stayed at home, and what they saw on television stimulated their interest in current affairs, history and popular science. The public libraries, which were obliged by the 1964 Public Libraries and Museums Act to provide a comprehensive service, steadily increased the number of annual loans to over 600 million by 1970. The rapid expansion of the paperback market meant that many more serious books were becoming available at an accessible price, as literary and academic publishers launched paperback imprints. The sales of recordings of classical music were similarly on the increase, so were attendances at art galleries and museums. The market for high culture was expanding; the only art form in difficulties was the cinema, as audiences shrank and cinemas closed in the face of competition from television.

It was just at this moment that an important change took place in the institution that had the greatest single cultural influence: the BBC. The BBC had always had a commitment to high culture that was protected from commercial pressures by its status as a public corporation. In the field of culture it was virtually the equivalent of the nationalized industries set up by the Labour Government after 1945; as employer and patron of artists it far outweighed the Arts Council; actors, musicians, composers and writers were able to subsidize their work elsewhere with fees earned from the BBC. The corporation itself employed 16,000 people, making it the largest single broadcasting organization in the world outside the Soviet Union. Managed by a small élite, and largely staffed by graduates of Oxford and Cambridge, the BBC was very much a corporate structure appropriate to a corporate state.

Yet the BBC had become ossified. It still thought in terms of the national responsibilities it had acquired during the war, and its executives still thought largely in terms of radio. In 1960 the BBC's television revenue was half that of Independent Television, and it is not surprising that ITV took as much as 70 per cent of the audience. The bureaucratic traditions of the BBC did not encourage competitive thinking. The playwright David Mercer described his reception by the BBC in 1960 when he delivered his first television play, *Where the Difference Begins*: 'I was slightly overawed by the kind of benign, paternalistic civil service temperament, not only of people, but the whole atmosphere. What I thought were very posh people, Cambridge and Oxford degrees, being kind of, you know, free and liberal and gentle and all that, rigorously sticking within the meaning of the charter.'

In January 1960, however, the mandarin atmosphere of the BBC was disrupted by the appointment of Hugh Carleton Greene as Director-General. Greene, brother of the novelist Graham Greene, had been a journalist before the war, and then joined the BBC, where he ran the wartime German Service. He then helped to restart broadcasting in West Germany; he rose to become the Head of the BBC's Overseas Service, and later Director of News and Current Affairs. Although 'an inside man', Greene had a clear idea of what he wanted to do as Director-General.

I wanted to open the windows and dissipate the ivory-tower stuffiness which still clung to some parts of the BBC. I wanted to encourage enterprise and the taking of risks. I wanted to make the BBC a place where talent of all sorts, however unconventional, was recognized and nurtured, where talented people could work and, if they wished, take their talents elsewhere, sometimes coming back again to enrich the organization from which they had started. I may have thought at the beginning that I should be dragging the BBC kicking and screaming into the Sixties. But I soon learnt that some urge, some encouragement, was all the immense reserve of youthful talent in the BBC had been waiting for, and from that moment I was part of a rapidly flowing stream. Otherwise the job could never have been done. Most of the best ideas must come from below, not from above.

In the face of increasing opposition from both politicians and outside pressure groups, Greene totally changed the creative atmosphere inside the BBC. Television acquired priority over radio. (The new Television Centre at Wood Lane began operations in 1960.) The opening of BBC2 in April 1964 enabled the corporation to continue the campaign for audiences that it had launched against ITV on BBC1, while producing programmes of

26

the highest quality for the minority audiences on BBC2. Independent Television's programmes stuck to safe formulas, but under Greene's influence the BBC began to take risks. This was true just as much in news reporting as drama, but the development which caused the most controversy was the decision to confuse the categories of light entertainment and current affairs, and produce something called satire.

'Satire' had such a brief vogue that several of those most involved have questioned whether it ever existed. Yet between 1961 and 1963 there was a powerful concentration of influences and attitudes that in turn opened the way for fresh ideas. The model was vague recollections of political cabaret in Berlin in the 1930s, though Britain in the early 1960s was hardly the equivalent of the Weimar Republic. Yet satire did offer a way round the difficulties of registering effective social protest. In 1956 the British landings at Suez had made people angry, but the crushing of the Hungarian rising by the Russian army finally discredited the old Marxist Left. Grand schemes for social regeneration were out of fashion, and the masses showed no inclination to stir. Outside the fairly narrow circles of the New Left there was a general cynicism about politics, and the seemingly static nature of the political debate stood in the way of a direct assault. Most of the means of expressing dissatisfaction with the *status quo* – the BBC, the newspapers, the weekly magazines and almost all the theatres – were in the hands of those most interested in preserving it.

English satire had a cosy relationship with the institutions it criticized, for it grew up within them, and so found it difficult to avoid being stifled by the indulgence of its targets. Jonathan Miller was quite right to point out in an article on the boom in satire for the *Observer* in October 1961 that the interest the *Observer* showed indicated a benevolence 'which could well disarm the toxic intentions of the project.' The movement began, if anywhere, in the ancient institutions of Oxford and Cambridge, and more especially in a privileged and well-established undergraduate revue club, the Cambridge Footlights, which had been putting on light entertainment since 1883. But Cambridge was influenced by the more radical atmosphere of the late 1950s, and in 1959 the annual Footlights revue took a new tack with *The Last Laugh*. Most of the usual jokes about undergraduate life were dropped in favour of critical comments on social attitudes, and in particular on the threat of nuclear war which provided the framework for the revue. Several of the performers associated with later developments – Eleanor Bron, Timothy Birdsall and the director John Bird – were with *The Last Laugh*, but the star was Peter Cook, who began to write for London revues while still an undergraduate.

In August 1960 Peter Cook and a Footlights performer of a slightly earlier generation, Jonathan Miller, joined forces with two Oxford graduates, Dudley Moore and Alan Bennett, to put on a revue as part of the official programme of the Edinburgh Festival – hence the title *Beyond the Fringe*. The revue was taken up by a commercial management, and opened in London in May 1961. It was a huge success, and marks the beginning of English satire's brief boom. It was in fact a gentler revue than *The Last Laugh*, for there was an element of surreal fantasy in the humour that was quite unaggressive, but there were sketches critical of nuclear defence, capital punishment and racism, and a parody of Harold Macmillan by Peter Cook which, for all of the affectionate guying of Macmillan's Edwardian aura, shocked by breaking the convention of respect for public figures. It was intelligent, literate comedy that made people think as well as laugh.

The other developments coincided in October 1961. Peter Cook opened a nightclub in Soho where it was possible to bare some of the teeth that were otherwise drawn by the theatrical censorship of the Lord Chamberlain. Cook neatly encapsulated all the earnest debate of the late 1950s by calling his club *The Establishment*. At the same time Richard Ingrams, Christopher Booker and William Rushton produced the first number of a satirical magazine, *Private Eye*. In April 1962 the two groups drew closer together when Peter Cook became principal shareholder in *Private Eye*.

What finally brought satire to the centre of public attention was Hugh Greene's decision to attempt political cabaret, such as he recalled from pre-war Berlin, on television. He made the key decision to give the project to the current affairs department, as opposed to light entertainment. Since 1957 the magazine programme *Tonight* had, in the senior producer Grace Wyndham Goldie's phrase, done much to erode the air of 'intellectual condescension' in television broadcasting. Its reporters, several of whom had come from *Picture Post*, were not rebellious, but they were sceptical of the pretensions of politicians and other Establishment figures. *Tonight*'s editor, Donald Baverstock was put in charge of the new project, and he chose one of the *Tonight* team, Ned Sherrin, as director. The first transmission of *That Was The Week That Was*, better known as *TW3*, was on 24 November 1962.

TW3 was a new genre, created by television, and this in itself helped to cause controversy. Sherrin naturally drew his team from the writers and performers launched on the new wave of satire. The *Beyond the Fringe* cast was in America, as were some of the stars of *The Establishment*, but another Footlights graduate, David Frost, became presenter alongside William Rushton, Timothy Birdsall and other more established cabaret performers like Lance Percival and Millicent Martin. But Sherrin also drew on the talents of critic and Parliamentary sketch-writer Bernard Levin, and writers like Christopher Booker, Peter Shaffer, Keith Waterhouse and Willis Hall, John Braine, Dennis Potter, John Mortimer and even on occasion Kenneth Tynan. All these were more literate contributors than the usual line of light entertainment gag-smiths. That did not mean that *TW3* was without a fair amount of abuse, aggression and bawdy, but, as variety comedian Frankie Howerd observed while appearing on *TW3*, 'These days you can't be filthy unless you've got a degree.'

The programmes, transmitted live, were a heady cocktail of instantaneous comment on the week's events in songs and sketches, combined with more investigative items, waspish interviews by Bernard Levin, and a number of personal attacks on public figures which, since the Conservative Party was in power, included a preponderance of Tory ministers. Little of this was threateningly subversive, but this one programme, transmitted once a week from November 1962 to April 1963, and from September to December later that year, did give the impression that a new attitude was being taken by the BBC, and, by inference, the rest of British society. This change was interpreted by the Moral Rearmament supporter Mrs Mary Whitehouse, who was about to launch her campaign to Clean Up TV, as spiritual decay: *TW3* 'was the epitome of what was wrong with the BBC – anti-authority, anti-religious, anti-patriotism, pro-dirt, and poorly produced, yet having the support of the corporation and apparently impervious to discipline from within or disapproval from without.'

The second run of *TW3* was not as successful as the first, and it was ended earlier than scheduled. The official reason was that 1964 was to be an election year, but another consideration was that 1964 was also the year when Parliament debated the renewal of the BBC's charter. Hugh Greene, who had evidently succeeded in opening some windows at the BBC, and had given a new impetus to young talent, commented, 'It was in my capacity as a subversive anarchist that I yielded to the enormous pressure from my fellow subversives and put *TW3* on the air; and it was as a pillar of the Establishment that I yielded to the Fascist hyena-like howls to take it off again.'

What Greene had done, by allowing the programme on the air, was to show that beneath a bland surface there *was* a lack of consensus in British society. By mixing comedy and current affairs *TW3* brought politics and show business closer together, and show business became an increasingly important part of politics. This was evident in the 1964 General Election, when Harold Wilson was comfortable with the medium of television and knew how to use it, while the outgoing Tory Prime Minister Sir Alec Douglas-Home evidently did not.

The new spirit of enterprise and expansion introduced by Greene was felt throughout the BBC. In 1963, in order to compete with the highly successful *Armchair Theatre* produced by ABC on the commercial network, the BBC persuaded its creator, Sidney Newman, to become the BBC's Head of Drama. Newman made an important decision to divide the department into three sections: series, serials and single plays. He had realized that television drama has a distinct relationship with its audience: a series, where the same characters appear in a number of different stories is a halfway house between the twice-weekly serial (such as Granada's *Coronation Street*, begun in 1960), and the single play, where the audience has to familiarize itself with both characters and plot. In all three cases the writer's role is also changed: in single plays he becomes a member of a team, rather than a single creator; in series and serials the writers themselves form a team. As Martin Esslin has observed 'if the single play is a product of craftmanship, the series is an *industrial product*, mass produced.'

Access to a mass medium, however, offers the writer certain possibilities, and it was a new *series*, launched in 1962 before

Newman arrived, that demonstrated a fresh approach at the BBC. Two writers, Troy Kennedy Martin and John McGrath, then working as a director, took the genre of the cops and robbers story and set out to use it to explore a community. For McGrath 'the series was going to be a kind of documentary about people's lives in these areas, and the cops were incidental – they were the means of finding out about people's lives.' The documentary element in *Z Cars* meant that the police were treated with more gritty realism than in the earlier *Dixon of Dock Green*, but as recurring characters they became the focus of interest. Later chiefly written by John Hopkins, *Z Cars* ran until 1965, and was succeeded by *Softly Softly* and *Softly Softly, Task Force*.

On his arrival at the BBC Sidney Newman decided to win for single plays the size of audience attracted to series and serials, by creating an identifiable image for them, as though they were part of a series. 'The Wednesday Play', launched in October 1964, has become an image of the radicalism of the BBC in the 1960s, though in fact this rests on a relatively small number of plays. The Newman reorganization had the effect of enhancing the role of the producer over the director and the writer, and institutionalized the use of a script-editor as an intermediary between the three. Certain combinations of personality could bring powerful results: in 1965 *For the West*, written by Michael Hastings with Toby Robertson as director; the two *Nigel Barton* plays by Dennis Potter, directed by Gareth Davies; and *Up the Junction*, by Nell Dunn, directed by Ken Loach, and all produced by James MacTaggart. After producing thirty-two plays in 1965 MacTaggart reverted to the role of director, and overall responsibility was divided between the contrasting personalities by Lionel Harris and MacTaggart's former script-editor, Tony Garnett. Garnett's first Wednesday Play as producer was *Cathy Come Home*, first transmitted in November 1966.

Cathy Come Home was based on the writer Jeremy Sandford's investigation into homelessness, and it exposed the destructive effects on family life of the official measures to cope with the problem. Again, it was the apparent documentary realism of the story of Cathy, played by Carol White, which gave the play its force. The effect was so powerful that it led to changes in local authority policy, and eventually to the foundation of the charity Shelter. Garnett and his director Ken Loach used as much film as possible, and, beginning with *Cathy Come Home*, concentrated their efforts (and considerable budgets) on plays that handled 'issues' on a cinematic scale (In 1969 Garnett and Loach did break into the cinema, with *Kes*.) *The Lump*, written by Jim Allen and directed by Jack Gold (1967), *In Two Minds*, by David Mercer and directed by Loach (1967), *Drums Along the Avon* (1967) by Charles Wood and directed by James MacTaggart, and *The Big Flame* with Jim Allen and Ken Loach (1969) continued the tradition that Tony Garnett's productions had established with *Cathy Come Home*.

The Wednesday Play helped to make writing for television respectable, so that even Samuel Beckett wrote *Eh Joe* for BBC2 in 1966, but the power that the medium had to command large audiences – the average for a Wednesday Play was 8 million, for *Cathy* it was 12 million – made the authorities anxious about its manipulation. By 1965 the ventilation introduced into the BBC by Hugh Greene had led to even a comedy show, *Till Death Us Do Part*, raising questions of politics and racism, albeit in a satirical context. In the same week as the transmission of *Up the Junction* in November 1965, the news broke that the BBC had decided to forbid the broadcast of a drama-documentary by Peter Watkins about the effects of a nuclear attack, *The War Game*.

As with the Wednesday Play, it was the creative use of documentary techniques which exercised senior officials in the BBC. In 1964 Watkins had made a programme about the Battle of Culloden as though film reporters were present in 1745; in *The War Game* he applied the same techniques to the build-up and aftermath of a nuclear war. Although it was claimed that the results were visually too horrifying to be shown, what concerned the BBC was that here was a documentary that gave no balancing argument in favour of nuclear weapons. *The War Game* and the Wednesday Play challenged previously secure categories of 'fact' and 'fiction' in such a way that the authority of the institution which sustained these categories was undermined. *The War Game* was eventually released for cinema showing through the British Film Institute, but it was not seen on television until 1985.

It is possible to exaggerate the directly political effects of the BBC's occasional controversial plays and documentaries. (By 1972 *Screen* magazine was denouncing *Cathy Come Home* as 'a classic of bourgeois individualism' and 'close to a Lassie movie'.)

To a certain extent the BBC was only reflecting the changes that were going on around it, but in the mid-1960s it did seem to be a little ahead of public opinion, rather than in its more usual position, a little behind. Certainly, by 1967 politicians and the pressure groups that worked upon them had decided that the BBC was too far ahead. In *The Least Worst Television in the World* (1973) Milton Shulman records that

At the beginning of 1967, although pursued and harassed by politicians and pressure groups, the BBC reached the apex of this controversial phase in its history. In its current affairs programmes, it defiantly resisted all the direct and indirect pressures being brought against it by the Labour Government. In the field of satire, although quality had deteriorated and brilliance was at a premium, there was still the *Late Show* mocking aspects of religion and authority. In drama, the Wednesday Play was still frankly and imaginatively dealing with social problems involving sex, poverty, lunacy. In the light entertainment field, the ignorant, foul-mouth, intolerant Alf Garnett of *Till Death Us Do Part* was delighting half the nation.

In 1967 however, the BBC found itself with a financial deficit for the first time in its history. BBC2, and the move into colour transmissions, had overstretched its resources; but the size of its revenue was determined by the licence fee, and that was controlled by the Government. Harold Wilson was no friend of the BBC, and in September 1967 he astonished the staff by appointing a former Conservative Minister, Lord Hill, as the BBC's Chairman. Hill had just ended a term as Chairman of the Independent Television Authority, where he had earned a reputation as an interventionist. Unlike Hugh Greene, whose position as Director-General was now threatened, he was willing to receive Mrs Mary Whitehouse at Broadcasting House. The balance of power had clearly altered within the BBC by 1969, when Hugh Greene resigned.

The effects of the new circumstances in which the BBC found itself slowly worked through the corporation, and there was a major controversy over reorganization plans in 1970 which reduced the BBC's commitment to 'high' culture. The anarchic comedy series *Monty Python's Flying Circus* was launched in 1969, a sign that good ideas could still come from below, but in that year Shaun Sutton became Head of Drama, a man who had made his reputation with series like *Softly Softly*, *Dr Who* and adaptations like *The Forsyte Saga*. (Newman had left in 1967.) In 1970 the Wednesday Play became Play for Today, when the transmission day was changed to Thursday, and this simple change seemed to end an era in provocative television drama, even though Jeremy Sandford's *Edna, the Inebriate Woman* (1971) and Tony Parker's plays produced by Irene Shubik maintained the Wednesday Play tradition. In the 1970s the single play had a struggle to survive, for it was the most expensive form of television to make, and the emphasis in both the BBC and commercial television was on audience-building series. It is noticeable that later examples of committed drama – Jim Allen's *Days of Hope* with Loach and Garnett in 1975, and Trevor Griffiths's *Bill Brand* for Thames Television in 1976 – were both series productions.

As Milton Shulman points out, the satire boom soon faded, although *Beyond the Fringe* ran, with changes of cast, until 1966. In 1963 *The Establishment* club foundered, and the circulation of *Private Eye* temporarily collapsed. *Private Eye* shows how the satire movement was a means of ventilating ideas rather than challenging society with some complete new blueprint. The magazine's attacks were very much in Establishment terms; the laws of libel and the nature of their sources meant that *Private Eye*'s gossip was conveyed in the private language of a public school (whence most of the contributors came). The nicknames, the humour, the prejudices meant that this language was only understood within the Establishment, to which *Private Eye* became a parasitic attachment. 'In the City' has become indispensable reading for stockbrokers, which seems a contradiction. None the less, the serious investigative journalism which developed in the back pages of the magazine did earn a reputation, and gave the first warnings of the notorious scandals of the later 1960s.

In June 1963 *TW3* was off the air for the summer, when a scandal broke that left the Establishment wide open to the abuse the satirists were hurling at it. Only *Private Eye* was in at the kill. But rumours concerning sex and security in high places had been buzzing for some time, and *TW3* did manage a hint of what was to be revealed in a new version for Millicent Martin of 'She Was Poor But She Was Honest'.

> See him in the House of Commons
> Making Laws to put the blame
> While the object of his passion
> Walks the street to hide her shame.

'He' was the Minister for War, John Profumo; she was Christine Keeler, a call girl who was believed also to have slept with a Russian naval attaché, Captain Ivanov. In March Profumo, who had been prominent in the lobby for commercial television ('We are not a nation of intellectuals', he told Anthony Sampson), denied that there was anything improper in his relationship with Keeler, but the rumours persisted, and a private investigation on behalf of the Prime Minister revealed the truth. Profumo confessed that he had lied to the House of Commons and resigned. An official enquiry by the judge, Lord Denning, later concluded that there had been no breach of security, but by then the Profumo affair had become a much wider political issue. In October 1963 Harold Macmillan, confined to hospital by a prostate operation, resigned.

To many of the old guard, such as the editor of *The Times* Sir William Haley, the Profumo affair was confirmation of the general upheaval and loss of direction that was afflicting Britain. It was a case of 'The New Morality', the title of a long editorial. This was only the most notorious of a series of cases where the Government, the security services or the police had acted incompetently: the Vassal spy case of 1962, the Enahoro affair, the brutalities of police officers in Sheffield and during demonstrations against the Greek Government, the revelations about the exploitation of the Rent Act by a slum landlord, Peter Rachman (also a Keeler connection) and the salacious coverage of the divorce of the Duchess of Argyll – all helped to paint a picture of corruption in high and low places.

In *Private Conscience: Public Morality* (1964) the journalist Brian Inglis took very seriously the proposition that society was experiencing 'the doubts and uncertainties of the new morality', and his is another of the books expressing anxiety about Britain. But his conclusion on the Profumo affair shows that while the politicians and churchmen were upset, the affair had also provided a considerable amount of enjoyment.

Although Profumo was indeed ruined politically, it certainly was not because of any fit of morality on the part of the English public. During

35

the rumour months, he and other ministers were resented because they seemed to be getting away with it; the feeling was that if they had involved themselves in any dubious practices, they should not be allowed to exercise political influence to have the whole business hushed up. But what they had done, or were supposed to have done, was not recounted with any noticeable disapproval: the rumours were passed on with gusto rather than disgust.

A similar conclusion was reached by the authors of *Scandal '63*, an instant account of the affair. They wondered whether Fleet Street's exposés were really read in a spirit of moral shock, 'or was it all regarded as just one long glorious summer of vicarious excitement, novelettish intrigue and sexual titillation, laced with the amusement of seeing the hypocrisy and pretensions of the Establishment exposed? As the dust began to settle, politicians were coming to believe that the last attitude was predominant.'

The politicians were right, but the summer of 1963 did contribute to the change that was under way, as society began to take a more permissive attitude to sexual morality. Politically, the scandal helped to end the feeling so pervasive in 1960 that Conservative rule was inevitable. And when the General Election finally came in October 1964 the parties were led by new men. Harold Wilson had taken over the Labour Party leadership after the death of Gaitskell in January 1963, and had made his mark in Parliament during the Profumo scandal; the Conservatives were led by an earl who had hurriedly renounced his peerage, Sir Alec Douglas-Home. Change was definitely in the air.

For those concerned with the quality of British culture, the 'perpetual and perilous change' noted by Anthony Sampson, and the 'galloping consumption' that accompanied it, were causes for alarm. Television was largely blamed for the spread of a commercial culture that undermined traditional values. But it was not clear how, if at all, this process was to be halted, or indeed precisely why television had such a subversive effect. Then in 1964 a Canadian academic trained at Cambridge published a book with the helpful title, *Understanding Media*.

The author, Marshall McLuhan, was just as concerned about the deleterious effect of television on culture as everyone else, but he did at least have an explanation to offer that accounted for its effects. His argument was that the medium used to transmit information modifies what is communicated. His famous dictum 'the medium is the message' meant that ideas were structured by the means used to convey them. The world of print which he had discussed in *The Gutenberg Galaxy* (1962) encouraged linear organization, the division of tasks, individualism and the growth of social hierarchies. Intellectuals inhabit the world of print. But the discovery of electricity had led to the telegraph, the telephone, radio and television, which transmitted information instantaneously, in a mode which threatened that linear world, just as the invention of movable type had threatened the culture of the Middle Ages.

All media exist to invest our lives with artificial perception and arbitrary values. All meaning alters with acceleration, because all patterns of social and political interdependence change with the acceleration of information. Some feel keenly that speed-up has impoverished the world they knew by changing its forms of interassociation. There is nothing new or strange in a parochial preference for pseudo-events [McLuhan's term for developments in communication technology, in this case printing] that happened to enter into the composition of society just before the electric revolution of this century.

But, McLuhan argued, conservatism was not the answer, for the print culture was totally incapable of resisting the change that electric communication was bringing about.

The new media facilitated mass communication at a scale and speed that far outstripped books or newspapers. More people were being enabled to see and hear the same thing, at the same time, and the result was an implosion. Distance was eliminated, everyone and everything was closer together, so that division and hierarchy were lost. Instead, there was a retribalization and a loss of individuality in a single homogenizing culture, the culture of what McLuhan called 'the global village'.

In particular, *Understanding Media* had something to say about television. McLuhan posited a division between 'hot' and 'cool' media. The hot media were high in definition, like print, and therefore required little participation by its audience. The cool media, especially television, were low definition, and therefore required more contributory participation by the audience. (Film, according to McLuhan, is a 'hot' medium.) All media carry the messages of other media, with their own effects (television carries speech, for example), but television, with its own absorbing influence, carries a particularly dense mixture. When television

encounters a literate culture, it necessarily thickens the sense-mix, transforming fragmented and specialist extensions into a seamless web of experience. Such transformation is, of course, a 'disaster' for a literate, specialist culture. It blurs many cherished attitudes and procedures. It dims the efficacy of the basic pedagogic techniques, and the relevance of the curriculum. If for no other reason, it would be well to understand the dynamic life of these forms as they intrude upon us and upon one another.

The young people who have experienced a decade of TV have naturally imbibed an urge toward involvement in depth that makes all the remote visualized goals of visual culture seem not only unreal but irrelevant, and not only irrelevant but anaemic. It is the total involvement in all-inclusive *nowness* that occurs in young lives via TV's mosaic image. This change of attitude has nothing to do with programming in any way, and would be the same if the programmes consisted entirely of the highest cultural content. The change in attitude by means of relating themselves to the mosaic TV image would occur in any event. It is, of course, our job not only to understand this change but to exploit it for its pedagogic richness.

McLuhan's arguments were neither fully accepted, nor understood. His aphoristic, repetitive and punning style made its own contribution to his argument that the linear organization of books was obsolete. But from his texture of ideas some important perceptions were taken up. One was that literary culture was on the wane. (Others had already come to the same conclusion. Richard Hoggart in 'Mass Communications in Britain' in *The Modern Age* (1961) forecast that 'literature will have relatively a much smaller place in the society which is now emerging'; and G. H. Bantock in the same book: 'really serious literature has become a peripheral occupation.') Verbal culture was being supplanted by a visual one, and ideas were now being discussed in terms of 'image'. McLuhan became a victim of this as *Understanding Media* became a cult book. Jonathan Aitken's *The Young Meteors* (1967) quotes this illuminating conversation with a young man of the Sixties: 'It's the visual age. Read your Marshall McLuhan. The media is the message.' [sic] The passing of print culture was a threat to those who lived by it, the intellectuals, and this helps to account for the negative attitudes displayed by most cultural critics. As Anthony Hartley put it: 'Culturally England is being divided into intellectuals and the rest. What we are seeing is the equalization of everything below a rather high cultural level, and this process does not reflect class difference in the usual sense, since, though intellectuals generally live like the professional middle classes, they cannot be identified with them.'

The question of image had already attracted the attention of another cult figure of the Sixties, though in a rather different sense. In 1960 the psychiatrist R. D. Laing published *The Divided Self*, a study of schizophrenia that sought to understand what 'madness' really means. He argued that the divided mind of the schizophrenic developed a false image of itself because it could not cope with its true relations with the world: 'the self, in order to develop and sustain its identity and autonomy, and in order to be safe from the persistent threat and danger from the world, has cut itself off from direct relatedness with others, and has endeavoured to become its own object, in fact, related directly only to itself.' The self imagines whatever it likes, but does nothing; its creativity produces only fantasy. (In 1963 John Le Carré published *The Spy Who Came in from the Cold*, introducing an extensive literature of false identities.)

It is possible to see Britain in the early 1960s as a divided self. It had lost its Empire, but still wished to play a world role and could not find the means to do so. It was enjoying increasing affluence, and yet there was a deeper anxiety about the direction society was taking. In the affluent, aggressive Sixties what seemed to be lacking most of all was a sense of community, a feeling of unity and common purpose such as had been felt during the war years, and which has since become such a powerful source of myth. The first volume in this series, *Under Siege*, tried to show some of the realities beneath that myth, but so long as a myth is believed it does not matter if it is based on fact or fantasy. A myth is a source of national identity, just as much as is a successful foreign policy and domestic well-being. Yet that identity was now in question, and while politically frustrated abroad, the country also seemed to be in an ideological stalemate at home, with both parties offering a mixed economy, full employment and a Welfare State, but no great national purpose.

It was at this point that the Labour Party's new leader stepped forward to present the country with a fresh self-image. In a series of campaign speeches, Harold Wilson offered Britain a confident new future of a planned and efficiently managed economy that would extricate the country from its underlying difficulties. He dispersed the nightmare fears of change by talking about 'restating our Socialism in terms of the scientific revolution' so as to forge the new Britain. He removed apprehensions about the technological developments that were taking place and radically altering the landscape – airports, motorways, high-rise buildings, television – by harnessing them to the idea of the new bright Britain that Wilson, his economists and technocrats would create 'in the white heat of this revolution'. At the Labour Party conference at Scarborough in October 1963, his first as party leader, he contrasted this shining new image with the fusty world of unearned privilege of the Conservatives. It was this contrast of image, between Wilson the trained economist, and Home, the former earl who did his sums with matchsticks, that decided the 1964 General Election. In the event, Labour gained only 41 per cent of the vote, and was faced with governing the country with a working majority of only four. But a change had been made.

CHAPTER 2

The Young Meteors

'*Sexual intercourse began*
In nineteen sixty-three
(Which was rather late for me) –
Between the end of the Chatterley *ban*
And the Beatles' first LP.'

Philip Larkin 'Annus Mirabilis' *High Windows* (1974)

Almost all the responses to change quoted in the last chapter were hostile. They were hostile for reasons of uncertainty about the future, cultural snobbery, anti-Americanism and, in some cases, because of moral and political fears about the nature of the society the new affluence was creating. But there were also those who welcomed the change in social expectations, not least the millions who were enjoying the possession of motor cars, television sets, washing machines, record players and the opportunity for foreign travel for the first time. As early as January 1957 a 35-year-old artist teaching at Newcastle University, Richard Hamilton, had noted that all the material requirements of the domestic environment, 'e.g. some kind of shelter, some kind of equipment, some kind of art', were being met by mass production. The aesthetic that governed all three of them was something he called Pop Art.

> Pop Art is:
> Popular (designed for a mass audience)
> Transient (short-term solution)
> Expendable (easily forgotten)
> Low cost

Mass produced
Young (aimed at youth)
Witty
Sexy
Gimmicky
Glamorous
Big business

Richard Hamilton's observations were the result of a series of
exploratory exhibitions on themes of design and technology to
which he had contributed, exercises which were themselves the
result of even more wide-ranging discussions held with like-
minded friends at the Institute of Contemporary Arts. The Independent Group, so-called to distinguish it from a Painters Group
which also met at the ICA, began meeting in 1952 at the
prompting of the design historian Reyner Banham, in order to
exchange enthusiasms about technology, design, the mass media,
art historical and general socio-cultural issues. The nearest thing
to a common denominator was an enjoyment of the popular
urban culture of magazines, feature films, music and motor cars
which seemed most developed in the United States. 'Art' was not
the issue. At its first meeting the sculptor Eduardo Paolozzi used
an epidiascope to project found images from the field of mass
communications in order to investigate their persuasive symbolism. By the time Richard Hamilton prepared his collage *Just
What is it that Makes Today's Homes so Different, so Appealing?*
for the exhibition *This is Tomorrow* in 1956 (see *In Anger* p. 191
and ill. 12) the term 'Pop Art' was being used within the group to
describe the ever-intensifying assault of visual information from
the mass media.

The significance of the Independent Group's enthusiasm was
that it ran entirely counter both to the snobbery of those who
clung to the mandarin values of a pastoral romanticism, and to
the folksy nostalgia of those who would revive a pre-industrial
culture. Quite simply, it was pro-American; American urban
culture seemed energetic and colourful, whereas British life in the
mid-1950s was deprived and dull. At this stage few of the
Independent Group had actually been to America (in 1955 the
artist John McHale electrified the Group with the collection of
magazines he brought back from his first trip), but thanks to the
Marshall Plan there was plenty of evidence of American affluence

in Europe. This material prosperity was a very real argument in
the propaganda struggles of the Cold War, though the attractive
popular culture of the United States, from jeans to rock'n'roll to
movies and musicals, hardly needed covert support in Britain. At
the same time, however, the Central Intelligence Agency, through
the New York Museum of Modern Art, was busy promoting
Abstract Expressionism as 'symbolic demonstrations of freedom
in a world in which freedom connotes a political attitude', as
MOMA's Director Alfred Barr put it in the catalogue to *The New
American Painting*, which visited London in 1958. A series of
American exhibitions from 1956 onwards asserted the supremacy
of the contemporary New York school over European painting,
much as Hollywood dominated European cinema programmes,
and American singers topped the hit parades.

Such salesmanship was bound to produce results. In the field of
fine art the most obvious response was the non-geometric abstraction of Rodrigo Moynihan, Patrick Heron, Bryan Winter, Alan
Davie and others, and the 'hard-edge' colour field abstractions of
contributors to the *Situation* shows at the RBA galleries in 1960
and 1961. But when Richard Hamilton made his list in 1957 there
was no painting that corresponded to the characteristics of Pop
Art that he described, even though his collage for *This is Tomorrow* did contain most of the movement's iconography. In their
practical work, both Hamilton and Paolozzi continued very much
in a fine art mode. Paolozzi's machine-based sculptures, bearing
the impressions of cogs, grilles, and even toys have an element of
collage, but they are unified (and elevated) by being cast in costly
aluminium or bronze. Hamilton's sparse paintings deploy the
visual vocabulary of chrome bumpers, home technology and
sexual gloss, but his chief interest is in rendering the techniques
of commercial art within the format of an easel painting. Can the
ad-man's dream world of urban living, he asks of *$he* (1958–61)
'be assimilated into the fine art consciousness?'

Two younger painters, Richard Smith and Peter Blake, who
were students at the Royal College of Art when both Hamilton
and Paolozzi held short-term posts there, brought the projected
Pop Art closer to reality. Blake graduated in 1956, Smith in 1957.
At one time they shared a studio, but their work is quite different,
representing as it does the opposite extremes of what was eventually recognized as Pop. Both set out to travel, but whereas Blake

went in search of 'popular culture' in Europe, Smith visited America. Smith says he set himself 'the task of mingling commercial atmosphere with abstract art'. Certainly the degree of abstraction in his work enabled him to exhibit comfortably with the *Situation* group, but his bold stripes, poster-bright colours and shaped canvasses (suggestive of painting-as-sculpture) were derived from commercial packaging. His concerns reflect the issues raised in the discussions of the Independent Group.

I paint about communications. The communications media are a large part of my landscape. My interest is not in the message so much as in the method. There is a multiplicity of messages (smoke these, vote this, ban that), fewer methods. Can how something is communicated be divorced from what is being communicated and can it be divorced from who it is being communicated to?

By contrast, Peter Blake was, and has remained, a figurative painter. His excursions into abstraction have been by way of jokes such as *The First Real Target* (1961), a play on contemporary American flag and stripe painting, where Blake simply displayed a real archery target manufactured by Slazengers. Jokes, however, are an essential ingredient of Pop. Blake's diploma piece *On the Balcony*, completed in 1957, is an eclectic homage to a wide range of influences, from a 'Royal College Realist' still life to paintings by contemporaries Smith, Robyn Denny and Leon Kossoff, to *Life* magazine and *Illustrated*. It is a disparate collection of objects littering a children's fantasy world. Blake's fascination with badges and other pop music ephemera reappears in *Self-portrait with Badges* (1961) (Ill. 1), where Blake has the same 'Midwich Cuckoo' stare of the children in *On the Balcony*. Blake is an inveterate collector, a passion he celebrated in *Toy Shop* (1962), a scaled-down shop window crammed with gaudy ephemera. But, as with many of his post-card and pin-up collages, there is an element of nostalgia and distancing that seems to echo Anthony Sampson's description of Britain as a 'living museum'.

Nostalgia can weaken into whimsy, as in the case of Blake's series of circus artistes and imaginary wrestlers, but childlike fantasy was another essential element in British Pop, most noticeably developed by David Hockney, where it is used for very sophisticated purposes (ill. 3). The canons of accepted taste are disrupted by jokes and childish behaviour. At the same time

Blake's nostalgic assemblies could be seen to refer back to an earlier 'popular' tradition of sign painting and illustration. Blake achieved a convergence between high-art practice and low-art taste. He was a painter *and* he liked Elvis Presley. Even his licked surfaces manage a synthesis: on the one hand they have the finish once admired in nineteenth-century academic painting, and on the other they reflect 'the glossies', the magazines that were often his source. Yet the self-consciously uncompleted plimsoll and deliberately painterly sky and trees behind him in *Self-portrait with Badges* remind us that this is a unique *object d'art*.

While Blake, Smith and Richard Hamilton were exploring the visual possibilities of different areas of popular culture, others in the Independent Group were evolving critical theories that could accommodate the new art, when and if it emerged. In 1954, after a year's lapse, the critic Lawrence Alloway helped to restart the Group's discussions, this time expressly focused on popular culture. (Others in the Group besides Reyner Banham and John McHale were the architects Alison and Peter Smithson, photographer Nigel Henderson and art historian Toni del Renzio.) There was a clear need in the late 1950s to find a way out of the cultural stalemate that matched the ideological and military stalemate of the Cold War. Both capitalism and communism seemed to have produced authoritarian, hierarchical, bureaucratic and intellectually alienating systems, with mass destruction the bleak concomitant of mass production. The old cultural models seemed worn out, and ways were sought to subvert the established categories that enforced conformity. Marshall McLuhan pointed out in *Understanding Media*:

The highbrow, from Joyce to Picasso, has long been devoted to American popular art because he finds in it an authentic imaginative reaction to official action. Genteel art, on the other hand, tends merely to evade and disapprove of the blatant modes of action in a powerful high definition, or 'square' society. Genteel art is a kind of repeat of the specialized acrobatic feats of an industrialized world. Popular art is the clown reminding us of all the life and faculty that we have omitted from our daily routines.

Pop Art – like pop music – turned out to be a form of aggression against the established order, and like pop music it used sex, humour and even banality as means of disruption. It was, as we have seen, pro-American, but the principle achievement of the Pop Art theorists like Alloway and John McHale was to offer an alternative cultural model. Traditionally, the arts had been imagined as a pyramidical structure, with fine art at the top, mass art at the bottom. Instead Alloway suggested that there was a 'Long Front of Culture', the title of an article published in *Cambridge Opinion* in 1959.

According to Alloway, mass production and general affluence had changed the terms in which culture could be understood. 'The aesthetics of plenty oppose a very strong tradition which dramatizes the arts as the possession of an élite.' Once an object can be produced in quantity – for instance a reproduction of *The Mona Lisa* – it can no longer be possessed only by a few. 'Mass production techniques, applied to accurately repeatable words, pictures and music, have resulted in an expendable multitude of signs and symbols. To approach this exploding field with Renaissance-based ideas of the uniqueness of art is crippling. Acceptance of the mass media entails a shift in our notion of what culture is.'

'Culture' becomes the exercise of multiple choices across a wide spectrum. The mass-produced image and the unique art object 'can be placed within a continuum rather than frozen in layers in a pyramid'. Along the long front of culture there can be no hierarchy of value, and no traditional hierarchy of subject-matter either. As attitudes become more flexible and mobile, a splendid pluralism of forms becomes possible. The confusion of categories is matched by the mixing of media. Collage has been part of the fine art tradition since the Cubists, but it is particularly appropriate to Pop. Imagery is no longer drawn from nature, but can be 'found', having been already processed by any one of a number of industrial techniques. The closed categories of both low and high art are equally undermined. McLuhan argued that mass communications had replaced the hierarchical culture of print with a global village; Alloway's cultural continuum suggests that at its centre there is a mass market-place.

The celebrators of Pop culture usefully stressed the falsity of the assumption that 'mass' meant 'uniform'. Mass production and the mass media made possible a far greater number of individual cultural choices than under a pre-industrial or craft economy.

Richard Hamilton made this point when he addressed the National Union of Teachers conference, whose deliberations emerged as *Discrimination and Popular Culture* (1964, see chapter I, p.11). He argued that the mass media had an important function as a stimulus to production, and disparaged the negative attitudes of cultural critics like Vance Packard and Richard Hoggart. 'The story is the same: the end of the world is upon us unless we purge ourselves of the evils of soft living and reject the drive for social and economic advantages. The effect of this criticism of our culture, coloured as it is by the hysterical overtones of its re-interpretation within the mass media, has been to create an atmosphere of unrest, which can itself be dangerous.' This was plainly unpopular with the conference organizers for, unlike the gloomy condemnations quoted in chapter I, Hamilton's speech was not reprinted in *Discrimination and Popular Culture*.

Hamilton realized that Pop Art was unusual among avant-garde art movements in that although provocative it was an art of affirmation. Most new movements begin as criticism of the contemporary cultural situation, as revolts of some kind, but Pop Art celebrated mass culture, and positively enjoyed it.

Affirmation propounded as an avant-garde aesthetic is rare. The history of art is that of a long series of attacks upon social and aesthetic values held to be dead and moribund, although the avant-garde position is frequently nostalgic and absolute. The Pop-Fine-Art standpoint, on the other hand – the expression of popular culture in fine art terms – is, like Futurism, fundamentally a statement of belief in the changing values of society. Pop-Fine-Art is a profession of approbation of mass culture, therefore also anti-artistic. It is positive Dada, creative where Dada was destructive.

Hamilton's reference to Dada is important, for it stresses the fine art tradition to which Pop belonged. Dada – and Hamilton was making a close study of Marcel Duchamp between 1957 and 1966 – anticipated many of the techniques of Pop Art in Britain and America: jokes, surprise, aggression, decontextualization, recontextualization. British and American Pop have different histories – American Pop developed from the 'happenings' of 1959, which in turn were the result of developments in Abstract Expressionism to which Pop has been presented over-simplistically as a reaction – but Dada is a common source. One of the ironies

47

of the Pop artists' position was that while they enjoyed mass culture, they felt the need, as fine artists, to repossess the territory that popular art seemed to have taken from them. Hamilton warned that 'if the artist is not to lose much of his ancient purpose he may have to plunder the popular arts to recover the imagery which is his rightful inheritance.'

While Pop Art decided to plunder the mass media and mass production, industry had cause to plunder Pop Art. McLuhan put it portentously:

> To prevent undue wreckage in society, the artist tends now to move from the ivory tower to the control tower of society. Just as higher education is no longer a frill or luxury but a stark need of production and operational design in the electric age, so the artist is indispensable in the shaping and analysis and understanding of the life of forms, and structures created by electric technology.

Pop indeed evolved in a close relationship with industry. Mass-media symbols and styles were taken up by the artists, and then recycled in advertising, design and other forms of production. The long front of culture was being established through an even more thorough process of industrialization which ended the traditional hierarchic transmission of taste. Yet in order to maintain production, the laws of built-in obsolescence demanded that fashion should constantly change.

This was made brutally clear by the experience of artists who were interested in the purely optical effects that certain patterns could have on the eye. Bridget Riley, dubbed as an 'Op' artist by *Life* magazine in December 1964, two months before her abstracts were shown at the *Responsive Eye* show at the Museum of Modern Art, was horrified to discover that her paintings, along with those of Richard Steele, had been copied by fabric designers and were already on display in shop windows on Fifth Avenue. The hard-edge designs of Op Art translated very easily into the crisp, black-and-white graphics of early-Sixties magazine layout, black-and-white television credits, and even the geometrical haircuts of Vidal Sassoon and the cut-out dresses of Mary Quant. Bridget Riley had worked as an illustrator for the advertising agency J. Walter Thompson, and designed a display in Piccadilly for British Wool, whose 'Woolmark' echoes a Riley painting. Edward Lucie-Smith has suggested that Op Art (which went out of fashion almost as quickly as it arrived, although Riley won the painting prize at the Venice Biennale in 1965) 'seems to represent the reassimilation of fine art by the applied arts. . . . It has all the qualities that popular art needs: it is easily recognized, easily characterized and easily reproduced.'

In 1961 the term 'Pop Art' made the transition from in-group reference to common cliché. The critical discussions and individual experiments of the previous years had set the scene for the emergence of a new generation of mainly Royal College of Art students who dominated that year's 'Young Contemporaries' show. (The 'Young Contemporaries' exhibitions were mounted to display the cream of art students' work; both 'young' and 'contemporary' were selling words.) Lawrence Alloway served on the selection committee, Peter Phillips (RCA 1955–62) was President, Allen Jones (expelled from the Royal College after one year in 1960) was exhibition secretary. They exhibited along-side Derek Boshier (RCA 1959–62), Patrick Caulfield (RCA 1960–63), David Hockney (RCA 1959–62), and R. B. Kitaj.

Kitaj's presence is a reminder of the increasing cross-fertiliz-ation between Britain and America. Born in Ohio, he studied first at the Ruskin School of Drawing in Oxford on a G.I. scholarship in 1958, and was then at the Royal College from 1959 to 1963. He was an influential personality, older than his Royal College contemporaries, and with a formed professional commit-ment. Though, like Peter Blake, his example turned minds towards figuration and problems of representation, he has emphasized the continuity between Pop and the Abstract Expressionists. 'Who wouldn't have been influenced by Abstract Expressionism? It is in all of us: Jim Dine, Rauschenberg, Johns; it is part of what we experienced and we cannot avoid it. There is no break from one to the other – it is clear continuation.'

Pop Art, as it emerged in 1961, contained a number of very individual styles, from David Hockney's smeared and scribbled childlike figurative paintings to Peter Phillip's hard-edged games-board designs to Patrick Caulfield's schematic explorations of the most banal decorative subject-matter, but there was now a sufficient body of work to match the theorizing that had prepared the way. In the more confident and iconoclastic mood of the early Sixties the theorists' original respect for the fine art tradition was forgotten. Looking back in 1969, the critic John Russell borrowed the rhetoric of the Angry Young Men to describe Pop Art's programme:

On the English side, and for many though not all of its participants, Pop was a resistance movement: a classless commando which was directed against the Establishment in general and the art-Establishment in particular. It was against the old-style museum-man, the old-style critic, the old-style dealer and the old-style collector. (Banham later described its success as 'the revenge of the elementary schoolboys'.) Much of the English art-world at that time was distinctly and unforgivably paternalistic. Pop was meant as a cultural break, signifying the firing squad, without mercy or reprieve, for the kind of people who believed in the Loeb classics, holidays in Tuscany, drawings by Augustus John, signed pieces of French furniture, leading articles in the *Daily Telegraph* and very good clothes that lasted for ever.

The natural alliance between Pop Art and the mass media ensured a rapid success for the newly recognized movement. Peter Blake featured in the first *Sunday Times* colour supplement; in the same year BBC TV's arts programme *Monitor* broadcast a Ken Russell documentary *Pop Goes the Easel*, with Blake, Derek Boshier, Peter Phillips and Pauline Boty. David Hockney was reported to have refused to take part, but his appearance in dyed blonde hair and gold lamé jacket to receive the Royal College of Art Gold Medal in 1962 launched him on a career that has always enjoyed good publicity. In April 1963 Hockney was seen leaving a private view of his work shouting 'I am not a pop painter', which seemed to confirm that he was.

The new movement rapidly gained official recognition. Blake, Kitaj and Hockney all won prizes at the 1961 John Moores exhibition in Liverpool; the Arts Council sent selections from the 1961 and 1962 'Young Contemporaries' exhibitions on tour and bought Hockney's *We Two Boys Together Clinging* in 1961 (ill. 3). In 1963 Blake, Boshier, Hockney, Jones and Phillips were chosen for the Paris Biennale, and Pop Art was accepted for the first time in the Royal Academy summer show. The success of Pop on both sides of the Atlantic encouraged the critic Mario Amaya to write a history of the movement before the paint had dried. He introduced *Pop as Art* (1965) with the justification that 'the new art has had instant fame and instant success, unlike any other movement in modern art. It is self-confessed to being an instant art form, for an instant society, and as such lends itself to instant art history.'

Instant success also provoked instant competition. In 1964 a group of Slade painters – John Bowstead, Bernard Jennings, Roger Jeffs and Terry Atkinson – launched themselves as 'Fine Artz Associates', announcing 'the intention of taking art back into society at large and give it a real public'. Their joint work, 'The Kandilac Kustomized Asteroid Action Seat' featured at the 1964 'Young Contemporaries'. The delight to be found in Californian car-styling, beat music and teenage cults seemed to herald a 'new Golden Age in which culture can fulfil its real function and enhance and stimulate the non-functional leisure time.' By contrast, the marginally senior Pop artists, 'the hipsters of the New York and London art scenes are really playing a very old-fashioned game.'

Although the hipsters lasted longer than Fine Artz Associates, defunct by 1968 (by which time Terry Atkinson had taken quite another direction, as we shall see), it is not surprising that Pop Art has itself conformed to the law of built-in obsolescence. When John Russell and Suzi Gablik came to arrange the major Pop retrospective at the Hayward Gallery in 1969 they felt it necessary to attempt to restore its reputation, and, as their title, *Pop Art Redefined*, implies, to reclaim the movement for the canon of fine art. Pop was to be viewed 'in terms of formal ideas and not in terms of the jokey, gregarious, eupeptic and loosely organized phenomenon which was seized upon with such relish by the mass media in the early 1960s.'

Of these formal ideas, the most significant came from the use of collage. However illusionistic a collage may appear to be (for instance Hamilton's seminal *Just What Is It. . . .*) the derivation of the material from a pre-existent source emphasizes that this is a man-made object without direct reference to the natural world. The material selected may be representational, but its surface is emphatically flat. The work is an object, and although the nostalgic, referential element in British Pop tends to contradict this, it asks to be taken as an object in itself, without deeper allusions. You are expected to take the object as it is, and enjoy it for itself, without associations. Collage destroys the hierarchy of subject-matter; its material has come from anywhere, and may return to anywhere, so that the plane of the picture can be broken up, or the shape of the canvas changed, or, as in the case of Joe Tilson's carpentry or Blake's *Toy Shop*, it is only loosely connected with easel painting at all.

Collage effects in formal terms the confusion of categories that Pop and the 'long front of culture' brought about. It admits any material, from anywhere; it liberates choice, and it celebrates chance. It also transforms the meaning of its material in potentially subversive ways. The anthropologist Claude Lévi-Strauss has noticed that one culture can take the symbols employed by another, and by placing them in a different context, change their meaning. Collage is the aesthetic equivalent of what Lévi-Strauss called *bricolage*; Pop, with its eclectic approach and bizarre combinations, could take a symbol of nationality and imperial pride like the Union Jack, and turn it into an ironic item of fancy dress: a union jacket. As an heir of Dada, Pop contributed to the breaking-down of formal categories that preoccupied the emergent counter-culture, even though Pop's enjoyment of the fruits of mass culture set it at odds with other counter-cultural values. Pop took a positive attitude to industrialization; its enjoyment of the mass media and mass consumption undoubtedly helped to create the optimistic and hedonistic atmosphere of the mid-1960s.

Hamilton's programme of 1957 was remarkably thoroughly carried out. Pop indeed proved popular, transient – and although the museum and gallery system has preserved some of its objects – many of its fashionable ideas have proved expendable. It was, at least to begin with, low cost. Now a collector's item, Peter Blake's *Babe Rainbow* (1967), a pin-up in his wrestlers series, was silk-screened onto tin in an edition of 10,000, and sold for £1; much Pop was mass produced, in that it was mass-*re*-produced, through photographs, record sleeves and graphic design. The painters themselves were young, and wit was part of the armoury. Sex was an essential part of their appeal – in the case of Allen Jones, almost to the exclusion of everything else – and the whole movement succeeded through the use of gimmicks and glamour.

All art, meanwhile, from Pop prints to old masters, was becoming big business. The relatively mild inflation of the mid-Sixties was an encouragement to invest in marketable objects; the steady rise in old-master prices pulled up those paid for modern works. The

London art-auction firms were clearing houses for an international
market stimulated by the investment activities of banks like the
Chase Manhattan, a Rockefeller institution with links to the New
York Museum of Modern Art. In 1964 Sothebys took over the
New York auction house Park Bernet; the following year
Sothebys' turnover was £13·25 million, about half of it from
American sources. In 1964, £29 million worth of art-works were
exported from Britain, and £21·2 million imported. The impo-
sition of a 30 per cent tax on art resales in 1966 shows that the
British Treasury had discovered a new area where money was to
be made.

Foreign buyers were chiefly responsible for driving up prices,
but British institutions – the Tate, the Arts Council, the British
Council and the Contemporary Art Society – were active, and
there were also wealthy British collectors interested in contemporary art: Sebastian de Ferranti, Robert Sainsbury, Christopher
Selmes, Alister McAlpine. In a lower price-range there was a
steady boom in the sale of artists' original prints, from 1961 until
the market collapsed in 1973. The Curwen press opened its
lithographic studio in 1959; Editions Alecto began operations in
1960, and broke through with Hockney's suite, *The Rake's Progress*, in 1963. Marlborough Fine Art started a print department
in 1964. The buoyancy in British art circles is reflected in the
scale of the Contemporary Art Society's 1963 show *British
Painting in the Sixties*, which was divided between the Tate
Gallery and the Whitechapel. The catalogue states that besides
the Society's usual budget for purchases of works of art for
presentation to museums, 'a substantial sum' has been set aside
to buy from this exhibition. 'It is a moment that, with the
international art situation for once in our favour, seems remarkably full of promise and potentiality for English art.' Hockney,
Jones, Kitaj, and Phillips were among those selected for the
show.

Big business directly promoted contemporary art. The Liver-
pool-based football pools and mail-order firm John Moores
launched their biennial awards in 1957. From 1964 to 1968 the
Peter Stuyvesant corporation sponsored an annual *New Generation* show at the Whitechapel Art Gallery. In the first *New
Generation* catalogue (Derek Boshier, Patrick Caulfield, Anthony
Donaldson, David Hockney, John Hoyland, Paul Huxley, Allen

Jones, Peter Phillips, Patrick Prockter, Bridget Riley, Michael Vaughan, Brett Whitely, cover photograph by Lord Snowdon) David Thompson writes of 'a boom period for modern art. British art in particular has suddenly woken from a long provincial doze, is seriously entering the international lists and winning prestige for itself. The atmosphere is one of self-confidence.'

Public as well as private patronage contributed to the increasing prosperity of painting and sculpture. Since its creation, the art department of the Arts Council had always set aside a certain amount each year for the purchase of contemporary British work. In 1961–2 it spent £6,275, in 1962–3 £18,269, in 1967–8 £21,625. The steady increase was in line with the 1964 Labour Government's *Policy for the Arts*, which as we shall see led to a large rise in general arts subsidy, but the key recommendation in that document as far as fine art was concerned was that direct subsidies to young artists should go up from £10,000 to £50,000 a year.

There was a marked increase in the number of private commercial galleries to service the expanded market that was being created. Fifteen new galleries are reported to have opened in London in 1961 alone. Of the key dealers Victor Waddington opened in Cork Street in 1958; his son Leslie opened a second gallery for younger artists in 1966. Mateus Grabowski, who gave first shows to Hockney, Jones, Boshier and Phillips, and mounted an important mixed show, 'Image in Progress', in 1962, opened in Sloane Avenue in 1959. Robert Fraser opened in 1962 after working in the United States, and represented Claes Oldenburg, Jim Dine, Paolozzi, Harold Cohen, Peter Blake, Richard Hamilton and Patrick Caulfield. In 1967 his turnover was reported to be £200,000 a year. In 1963 John Kasmin, backed by the Marquess of Dufferin and Ava, launched the Kasmin Gallery. In 1964 Paul Keeler and David Medalla launched the Signals Gallery and in 1966 John Dunbar and Barry Miles opened the short-lived Indica Gallery in Mason's Yard. Nearly a hundred commercial art galleries were in business in London in that year. In 1966 *Art and Artists* and the *Studio*, restyled as *Studio International*, were launched into this sea of activity.

The symbolic high-tide mark of British self-confidence was the title of an article in *Studio International* for December 1966: 'The Ascendancy of London in the Sixties'. The author was the painter Patrick Heron, who during the 1950s had pioneered non-geometric abstraction in both his criticism and his own paintings. Naturally he had welcomed the development of Abstract Expressionism in America, but he now rebelled against the relentless propaganda emanating from New York. Unlike the Pop artists who had shown such envious admiration for American culture, he resented the 'gutless obsequiousness to the Americans which prevails amongst so many British artists and art pundits generally'. Whereas the formats of American abstractionists had become exhausted, the perspicacity shown by British artists when they had so eagerly responded to the Americans in the 1950s had led them on to develop fresh and exciting forms in the 1960s. 'In Britain today there are not one but three generations of painters whose vitality, persistent energy, inventiveness and sheer sensibility is not equalled anywhere else in the world.' Unfortunately he names none of these ascendant painters besides himself, Peter Lanyon, Alan Davie, William Scott and Ben Nicholson, but the vigour of his assertion shows the extent to which British painters no longer felt themselves provincial members of a decayed School of Paris, and insisted on their independence from the School of New York. In 1974 Patrick Heron published a series of articles claiming that British artists had anticipated the procedures of the Americans.

Whether he was aware of it or not – and in the summer of 1966 it was difficult for anyone to be unaware of the phenomenon – Patrick Heron's declaration of the ascendancy of London as the city of painters is an echo of *Time* magazine's declaration of the ascendancy of London as the city of pleasure in its famous feature, 'London: the Swinging City'. London's artists and dealers feature prominently in *Time*'s *galère*, and although the feeling of confidence and creativity that article attempts to encapsulate was not the responsibility of a few successful painters alone, the internal history of Pop art and the critical theory that sustained it were important factors in creating the mood *Time* describes. What Pop and 'the Sixties', in its first phase, have in common, is a belief in cultural convergence and economic expansion.

In the prevailing atmosphere, it was not so surprising that when property developer Harry Hyams commissioned the skyscraper at the east end of Oxford Street known as Centre-Point, the building should be described as 'London's first Pop-Art office block'. There is no real connection between the formal properties of Pop and the architect Richard Siefert's design, but the fashionable phrase caught the expansive mood that had begun to inform the more visible aspects of British life. New buildings, like paintings, were attractive investments that profited from inflation. The building boom of 1958 to 1964 was the consequence both of the urgent need for urban renewal and the upturn in the economy. The prime profits were made in London, where the chief customer for new offices was the Government itself, but up and down the country local authorities cooperated with private developers. The authorities wanted new town centres with new traffic plans and enhanced rateable values; their powers of compulsory purchase provided the developers with their raw material. The boom in the retail trade encouraged the creation of vast shopping precincts; in 1963 no fewer than seventy comprehensive redevelopment schemes were on the drawing-board.

In 1964 the new Labour Government began to put a brake on the boom by banning fresh office building in London, but by then many projects were under way, only to reach completion years later. The Labour ban also played into the hands of the speculators by drying up the market just as a surplus had been created. This reinforced the strange principle that it was often more profitable to keep a building empty than to let it. The value of the building was an expression of the rent it would eventually fetch. It was cheaper to pay tax-deductible interest on the money borrowed for the project until such time as a client was found who was ready to pay the price demanded. The capital gain on the building when it was let handsomely covered the loss of rent while waiting. Centre-Point cost some £5 million to build; by 1967 it was valued at £16.7 million, and it was still empty. Harry Hyams was only one of 108 men and 2 women who became millionaires as a result of the boom.

It was not until the vast redevelopments like the Bull Ring in Birmingham came to fruition that enthusiasm began to wane. In the early 1960s the tall buildings that rose in city centres were treated as symbols of aspiration and renewal. 'High-rise' housing developments also seemed to be the answer to slum clearance, and acres of decayed but human-scale housing were swept away, replaced by tall blocks of flats built with the latest systems-technology. (This was the heyday of the futuristic schemes for mobile cities and disposable architecture of *Archigram* magazine, launched in 1964.) By 1965 there were some 27,000 flats in new buildings of over ten storeys, 6,500 in blocks of twenty storeys or more. The social and technological consequences of tower-blocks did not emerge until after they were built. By the time of the partial collapse of a London tower-block, Ronan Point, in 1968, technocratic optimism had begun to falter.

The arts were the incidental beneficiaries of the building boom. Comprehensive redevelopment schemes created what were known as 'planning gains', rewards to local authorities from developers in the shape of new civic amenities: town halls, libraries and art galleries. The Fairfields Halls complex at Croydon in South London, with its concert-hall, gallery and theatre is a good example of the trade-off between commercial developers and the local authorities. While old touring theatres were being closed and demolished, provincial cities acquired new civic theatres. Fifteen new theatres were built between 1958 and 1970. In London, the Barbican Arts Centre, the new Museum of London, a new British Library, the Hayward Gallery and the Queen Elizabeth Hall were all committed projects by 1964. Funds for the construction of the National Theatre (whose foundation-stone had been laid on the South Bank in 1951) were released in 1962; originally the theatre was to have been paired with an equally large new opera house, but in 1966 the opera-house plans were scrapped and the site of the National Theatre was shifted downstream to its present location. Ten years later the National opened its doors in an atmosphere very different from the one that had at last got the project under way.

In the light of the increased demands such schemes would make on its resources, it was as well that the Arts Council should also experience a boom. Expansion began in 1963, when the Conservative Government undertook a three-year programme to increase the Arts Council's grant-in-aid by 10 per cent annually. The new Labour Government of 1964 was not to be outbid. In February 1964 the White Paper *A Policy for the Arts: The First Steps* announced that responsibility for arts expenditure was to be transferred from the Treasury to the Department of Education

57

and Science; Jennie Lee, an Under Secretary of State in the Department, became the first ever Minister for the Arts, a title intended to show that the Government was committed to a long-term expansion in arts funding. In 1967 the Arts Council received a new charter which established separate Councils for Wales and Scotland; its new terms called upon it to 'develop and improve knowledge and practice of the arts' and increase their accessibility, and it was given the money to begin the job.

The Arts Council grant of £3,205,000 for 1964–5 was increased to £3,910,000 in 1965–6, to £5,700,000 in 1966–7, and £7,200,000 in 1967–8, reaching £9,300,000 in 1970–71. The White Paper allowed the Arts Council for the first time to concern itself with housing the arts. £150,000 was committed for building in 1965–6, £200,000 in 1966–7. The figure rose steadily until 1973, when the demands of the National Theatre pushed it up to £1,270,000. The Housing the Arts fund was very successful in stimulating other parties, chiefly local authorities, into finding the balance of the money for arts buildings to go ahead, but once built – as in the case of the National Theatre – the buildings had to be maintained, and the revenue consequences for the companies that occupied them were not foreseen.

The rhetoric of *A Policy for the Arts* (which echoes that of the Festival of Britain in 1951) spoke of a rising generation that 'will want gaiety and colour, informality and experimentation' and of financial help for artists 'particularly in the years before they have become established.' Literature in addition to poetry was to be supported for the first time. 'High points of excellence' were to be created throughout the country, and it was hoped that an arts centre would be established in every town. Ironically, Centre 42 is mentioned as a potential source of professional expertise. The drafters of the White Paper appear to have been converted to the language of the long front of culture:

It is partly a question of bridging the gap between what have come to be called the 'higher' forms of entertainment and the traditional sources – the brass band, the amateur concert party, the entertainer, the music hall and pop group – and to challenge the fact that a gap exists. In the world of jazz the process has already happened; highbrow and lowbrow have met.

Jazz was supported by the Arts Council for the first time in 1967.

Just as clients of the Arts Council were able to enjoy improved opportunities and conditions, the expansion in higher education improved the general lot of the intelligentsia. The population of the universities doubled in the 1960s, but this was only part of a wider increase in the total number of students – and their teachers. In 1960 4 per cent of school leavers went on to higher education; by 1975 the proportion was 16 per cent. The Robbins report of 1963 accepted the principle that higher education was the right of anyone whose ability merited it, and recommended the foundation of six new universities and the up-grading of ten Colleges of Advanced Technology to university status. Following the pattern established at the University of Sussex, founded in 1961, work began on the construction of the universities of East Anglia, York, Canterbury, Warwick, Lancaster and Essex. The 1966 *Plan for Polytechnics* outlined the continued expansion of non-university higher education and designated thirty merged institutions as 'New Polytechnics'. By 1966 the figure projected in the Robbins report of student demand in 1970–71 had already been exceeded.

In a period of enhanced opportunity, such as the one provided by the period 1960–68, underlying structural difficulties tend to be obscured. In the academic field Oxford and Cambridge maintained their dominance, but that seemed less of an issue when there were so many other openings for bright young graduates in the new universities. Oxford and Cambridge, like other universities, also expanded their post-graduate programmes and facilities. Opportunities increased throughout Britain's cultural institutions. The argument of the sociologist T. R. Fyvel's study *Intellectuals Today* (1968) was that economic expansion had led to a convergence between British society and the intelligentsia which now served it.

Fyvel rightly points out that before the Second World War those employed in the spread of academic, journalistic, creative and culturally-administrative jobs that have been the British intelligentsia's main occupations since the late nineteenth century had come almost exclusively from a narrow band of the upper-middle classes, that 'Intellectual Aristocracy' identified by Noel Annan in a 1955 essay (see *In Anger* p. 65). In the 1920s and 1930s intellectuals had tended to feel socially and politically alienated from the mainstream of British life, but according to Fyvel their wartime employment in administration, broadcasting and intelligence started a process of social integration. Although immediate post-war exhaustion and austerity produced some dissatisfaction and a sense of *ennui*, educational reform widened access to the ranks of the intelligentsia, and, with the return of affluence, from the mid-1950s social integration proceeded apace as the arts, journalism, broadcasting and higher education enjoyed the expansion of opportunities that has been described.

Fyvel believed that in the accomplishment of what amounted to a social revolution a new 'technical intelligentsia' had evolved in order to operate the new, mass, team-based innovative technology. Whereas in the old bourgeois society access to enjoyment and culture was restricted to the upper and middle classes, the new consumer society depended on mass participation to sustain its momentum. Bourgeois values of family and class structure were maintained, but the consumer society was administered by the products of a changed educational system, and kept informed by the mass media, whose homogenizing influence produced a general level of material and cultural aspiration. Though he does not use the term, Fyvel is describing the evolution of the long front of culture.

For artists and intellectuals this revolution had created a 'massive sense of class liberation'. Access to McLuhan's control tower of society was no longer restricted by age or social background. The effect of the arrival of 'young historians, sociologists and other academics, of the young theatre, film and television personalities and all the young geniuses from the provinces, has been to give voice to a large section of the British populace which had previously been determinedly kept out of the dominant literary culture.' The revolt begun by the Angry Young Men in the 1950s and pressed by the post-Suez generation appeared to have become a peaceful takeover.

Fyvel's celebration of the emergence of a new intelligentsia is a typical example of mid-Sixties optimism. Disaffection was already manifesting itself when his book appeared. His account of the expansion of opportunity for intellectuals and of their integration into the academic and cultural system is valid, but what is significant about his description is the submerged use of two value judgments that unconsciously coloured much contemporary writing about culture: the new intelligentsia was essentially young, and it was somehow 'classless'. Youth, classlessness and a third factor which might be loosely summarized as 'sex, drugs and rock'n'roll', formed the ideological underpinnings of what has become identified as the Sixties style. Since these words suggest images, values or states of being rather than concrete ideas, it is not surprising that we have to talk of style, rather than anything as coherent as a philosophy.

We have seen how youthfulness and the pleasure principle contributed to the 'classless' style of Pop Art, but this was only one expression of those submerged values which also influenced Fyvel. The idea that there was something that could be separately identified as 'youth' became current in the mid-1950s, when the Americanism 'teenager' began to be used to identify a distinct section of the population, often in order to isolate it as a problem. There had always been young people, but their emergence as a separate social category which none the less did not correspond to political notions of class supplied a useful metaphor for social change. The Teddy Boys were the first youth cult that attracted public attention as something both enviable and dangerous, and with a distinct cultural style. Young people joyously responded to being identified as a 'problem' by dancing in the aisles and breaking up the seats during showings of Bill Haley's *Rock Around the Clock* in 1956. But it was the simultaneous emergence of 16–25-year-olds as a distinct economic group that made them more than sub-cult curiosities. While their total spending power represented only 5 per cent of that of all consumers, it was remarkably concentrated in a number of highly visible areas, where the young were the dominant purchasers: records and record players, fashion and entertainment. Much of the material, in fact, which supplied the iconography of Pop Art. Because of their influence their taste had to be respected, if only so that their spending power might be better exploited. Emblematically, the title given to the singer Cliff Richard's 'autobiography', published in 1960, was *It's Great To Be Young*.

With a degree of economic power comes an identifiable voice, in this case the voice of what had come to be known by the late 1950s as the pop singer. How far this genuinely expressed the values of the constituency it claimed to speak for, and how far it was merely manipulated by the entertainment industry, has been regularly called into question. George Melly's *Revolt into Style*

61

(1970) argues that the sexual drive of young people, as expressed by the rhythm and lyrics of pop songs, was successfully exploited by commercial interests who turned this genuine potentiality for revolt into a more or less harmless style. (Melly's title comes from Thom Gunn's poem 'Elvis Presley': 'He turns revolt into a style'.) According to Melly, in order to maintain for the purposes of exploitation an illusion of the spontaneous sexual revolt of rock'n'roll, the male sexual principle was diverted into an object of adolescent female fantasy.

It is true that rock'n'roll has not led to revolution, but the fact that revolt *did* become a style, as we shall see in the next chapter, does not diminish the genuine effect that style had on the culture which contained it. Whereas the process of absorption and manipulation which George Melly describes did turn early British singers like Tommy Steele and Cliff Richard into harmless 'all-round entertainers', the growing economic power of young people and the change in the cultural pattern which they were helping to promote brought pop music, and the messages of pop, however modified, much closer to the centre of cultural life. We can see this in the convergence of pop and high culture in the first half of the 1960s.

In the 1950s a taste for jazz was an acceptable attribute of the intellectual, but within the spectrum of popular music jazz was a minority interest. It was relatively unexploited commercially, and the antiquarianism associated with traditional jazz gave this interest the added endorsement of being a scholarly pursuit. (The hidden messages of racial protest and black eroticism in the music seem to have been ignored.) Skiffle, which grew out of traditional jazz, had more commercial success, but its roots in American folk music again made it enjoyable on the grounds of its supposed authenticity, and not just the noise it made. In the 1950s rock'n'roll and its pallid British imitators remained almost exclusively a youth cult.

The convergence in tastes began, most appropriately, in the art schools. The 'traditional' jazz band The Temperance Seven, an ironic mixture of Edwardian clothes and 1920s and 1930s music, which had considerable success in the late 1950s and early 1960s, is an early example of 'art school' music, for most of its personnel were art students or teachers. The vocalist Roddy Maude-Roxby

1. Pop artist as pop fan: Peter Blake *Self Portrait with Badges* 1961

2. Public affluence and the new morality:
Timothy Birdsall *Britain Gets Wythe Itte* 1963

3. Sophisticated innocents:
David Hockney *We Two Boys Together Clinging* 1961

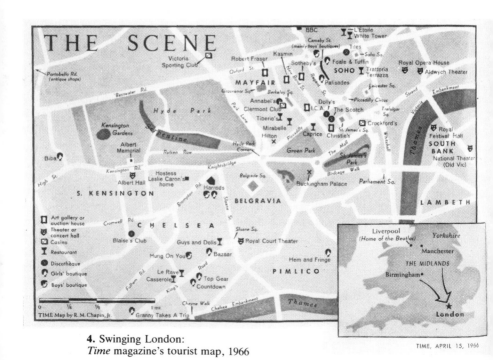

4. Swinging London:
Time magazine's tourist map, 1966

TIME, APRIL 15, 1966

once edited the Royal College of Art magazine *Ark*. Bruce Lacey, who had begun his career as a 'Royal College Realist' in the early 1950s, and then turned to kinetic sculpture, teamed up with the eccentric Grey brothers to form The Alberts, a wild jazz and performance group, best known for their *Evening of British Rubbish* with Spike Milligan at the Comedy Theatre in 1963. The nostalgia of the Temperance Seven and the surrealism of the Alberts were entirely consonant with British Pop art.

Art schools were a haven for imaginative people otherwise neglected by the educational system. (David Halliwell's play *Little Malcolm and His Struggle Against the Eunuchs* (1966) evokes the atmosphere.) Few would become commercially successful artists, but the relative freedom of the art schools encouraged experiments with style. For working-class students they were an escape route from the factory, for middle-class students they were the entry to bohemia. The shift in art school curricula away from craft techniques – led by the post-graduate Royal College of Art – encouraged students to make a more commercial assessment of their talents, to move from the ivory tower to the control tower of society. And pop music reverberated in the art-school canteens. Nick Cohn's *A WopBopaLooBopALopBamBoom: Pop from the Beginning* (1969) describes the potent mixture of Beat and beat.

In those very early Sixties, before the age of T-shirts and baseball boots, the heavy art school cults were Ray Charles and Chuck Berry and Bo Diddley, Muddy Waters, Charlie Mingus and Monk, Allen Ginsberg and Jack Kerouac, Robert Johnson. If you were pretentious about it, you might stretch to a paperback translation of Rimbaud or Dostoyevsky, strictly for display.

Rhythm and Blues, rather than Rimbaud, produced a convergence within the youth cults, as Jeff Nuttall (himself a jazz trumpeter and former art student) describes in *Bomb Culture* (1968).

Art students and popular music had, until this point, been separate, except for an odd overlapping in the world of trad and skiffle. But R & B was that bit less commercial than rock had been. It appealed to the authenticity cult *and* the rock'n'roll cult. The students and the Mods cross-fertilized, particularly in Liverpool. Purple hearts appeared in strange profusion. Bellbottoms blossomed with wild colours. Shoes were painted with Woolworths lacquer. Both sexes wore make-up and dyed their hair. The art students brought their acid colour combinations, their lilacs, tangerines and lime greens from abstract painting. The air in the streets and clubs was tingling with a new delirium. The handful of art-student pop groups appeared, with their louder, more violent music, their cultivated hysteria, their painful amplifiers, the Rolling Stones, the Pretty Things, the Kinks, the Beatles.

Nuttall, who wished to distance himself from aspects of the underground, 'particularly marijuana and rock'n'roll', emphasizes the increasing noise and violence of the proceedings. Aggression found an outlet in the group rivalries of the Mods and Rockers, who emerged as distinct sub-cults in the early 1960s. The Rockers, who cultivated the sado-masochistic style of motorcycle gear, were essentially the heirs of the Teddy Boys; the Mods on their motor-scooters were cooler, priding themselves on the Italian elegance of their dressing. The Mods' heavy expenditure and lifestyle matched the affirmative consumerism of Pop. Both Mods and Rockers were male-oriented groups, and a key expression of their identity was found in fighting, culminating in their seaside *fracas* in 1964.

Colin MacInnes's novel *Absolute Beginners* (1959) was the first literary exploration of the Mod milieu. The narrator is a young working-class freelance photographer living off his wits in a run-down immigrant section of Notting Hill Gate. He is essentially amoral, but a passion for black music has created a firm belief in racial tolerance, and when white youths (identifiable as Rockers) attack the local blacks, he defends them. MacInnes was fictionalizing the circumstances of the race riots in Notting Hill in 1958, and at the age of forty-five could not be said to be part of the youth culture himself, but his evocation of a marginal world of jazz-clubs and coffee-bars, where music and clothes stood as symbols of independence from the normal categories, gave *Absolute Beginners* a cult following among the very generation that had given MacInnes so much of his subject-matter.

Anthony Burgess's *A Clockwork Orange* (1962) also uses a first-person narrator from the generation he describes, but transposes the urban violence of MacInnes's London to some undated future. Underneath the richly invented slang there are the same intonations of MacInnes' hero – without any of his redeeming features. The aggression and amoral violence of youth comes into conflict with the equally amoral violence of the state, and whereas in 1962 Burgess concluded the novel with an epilogue showing his victimized narrator subsiding into conformity, later editions leave the ending more ambiguous, as though Burgess no longer believed that the revolt of youth could be contained by a style. To Burgess, the subsequent film version of the novel seemed to celebrate all the violence and corruption against which he was writing.

Burgess, like MacInnes, was an outsider, but in the same year that *A Clockwork Orange* appeared 23-year-old Ray Gosling published 'a sort of autobiography', *Sum Total*. Gosling was a provincial lower-middle-class grammar-school boy who dropped out of Leicester University and founded what would now be called an 'alternative' youth club, but under authoritarian pressure the project collapsed. His account, which again is about a marginal existence outside the normal social categories, reads like a cross between John Wain's *Hurry on Down* and Colin Wilson's *The Outsider*, with the novels of Jack Kerouac as a guiding model, but though the Beats and the Angry Young Men clearly influenced his writing, Gosling's revolt is more visceral. 'The aggression and the hate came in – to be able to say, look you British bastards this land isn't a land of red pillar-boxes and straight faces, it's a living land, a land of violence and passion and change.'

Sum Total devotes a long section to the emotional ideology of the pop star, 'the show in the flesh', which argues that this is not simply a question of commercial interests seizing on the sexual aggression of the young male and harnessing it to profitable and harmless ends. The exploitation is in fact mutual. He says of the singer, 'you love it, and you believe in it, and you worship it and if the man with the big cigar is there, it is because you wanted him to be there. If you have bin corrupted, then it was with your own consent and it wasn't corruption.'

Gosling implies that the relationship between the pop musicians and their manipulators was more dynamic than George Melly suggests. Both sides in the partnership were eager to make money, but the more intelligent performers also had some perception of what their own experience had told them about repression and revolt which sustained them against the emasculating effects of the record companies and the mass media. There is no better example of this than the career of the Beatles, who developed a genuine voice of their own by grafting working-class provincial accents onto black American rock'n'roll rhythms. They evolved their style in the rough bohemias of Liverpool and Hamburg; their manager, Brian Epstein, cleaned up their act (literally, by sending them to a venerologist) and prettified their appearance, but as we shall see, the Beatles ran ahead of the commercial forces that wished to control them. As Paul Willis comments in his study *Profane Culture* (1978), in the mid-Sixties 'for a strange brief period creative authenticity and the purities of consumer marketing coincided. Select groups were simply allowed to get on with it.' The Beatles took all that the man with the big cigar could offer, but they managed to remain spokesmen and exemplars for their generation.

In a sense, for the Beatles the convergence between pop and art was achieved as early as 1961. During their second trip to Hamburg John Lennon's fellow student from Liverpool College of Art, Stu Sutcliffe – a better painter than guitarist – met Eduardo Paolozzi, who had started teaching at Hamburg State Art College. Paolozzi recognized Sutcliffe's talent and arranged for him to study there. (Sutcliffe died in 1962, probably as a result of an earlier injury during a post-concert fight.)

The Beatles' arrival on the scene in the year of the Profumo scandal was fortunately timed, for they provided the popular newspapers with one of the few positive (and innocent) stories of 1963. Their second record, 'Please Please Me', a mixture of sexual invitation and adolescent pathos, reached number one in the sales charts in March; by September they had the top selling LP, Extended Play and single all in the same month. The pattern was repeated in America. 'I Want To Hold Your Hand' reached number one in America in February 1964, just before their first visit to New York. It was three months after the assassination of President Kennedy, and their arrival was a relief, even a release. The discovery that Britain could export pop singers to America only increased their popularity in the United Kingdom. Their influence was very real. Between 1960 and 1963 only ten records by British artists were bestsellers in the United States; between 1964 and 1967 there were 173, 25 of them by the Beatles.

As is well known, the Beatles opened the gates for a horde of groups, few of whom had great talent or staying power. The satirists of *That Was The Week That Was* showed that it was possible to be listened to, and young; the Beatles showed that it was possible to be listened to, and be young, provincial and working-class. The Beatles did not achieve this on their own, for they were served by the mass media that they served. In August 1963 Rediffusion launched *Ready, Steady, Go* on the commercial television network, which with the BBC's more sedate *Top of the Pops* provided a weekly means of communicating youth styles both to its own generation, and to a much wider area besides. (The BBC's monopoly over what was suitable for radio broadcasting was broken when Radio Caroline started transmissions on Easter Day 1964. For the next three years a band of pirate radio stations jostled the airwaves with the subversive messages of pop.)

Of the groups that followed in the Beatles' wake the Rolling Stones and the Who, launched in 1963 and 1964, added to the momentum rather than simply exploited it, chiefly by raising the level of aggression whenever pop music threatened to become too engaging. The Who deliberately employed the iconography of Pop Art, and added to it a violence of their own. Pete Townshend (an ex-art student) remarked of their act, 'You've got to be drastic and violent to reach the audience now. They've been getting too much *given* to them.'

The Beatles drew attention to Liverpool's poets as well as singers. It is unlikely that they would have had quite the success they did without the sudden fashionability of their city, but the Liverpool poets are an important example of the cultural convergence that was taking place. Far from Pop poetry developing as a result of pop music, it has a parallel history, and common roots in the oral tradition of Liverpool's working-class culture. Being an essentially spoken form, it was necessarily close to the sung lyric.

Since the mid-1950s provincial cities like Manchester and Newcastle had supported an underworld of coffee-bars and jazz clubs (the world of Ray Gosling's *Sum Total*) and Liverpool, with its distinctive character as a seaport, was no exception. Liverpool was the main port for the trans-Atlantic trade, and just as American music unobtainable elsewhere could be heard in Liverpool, the Beat poets of New York and San Francisco supplied Liverpool's bohemia with a model. The reputation of the city's jazz-and-poetry sessions was already strong enough in 1960 to attract the attention of London-based poets Pete Brown and

Spike Hawkins. In 1961 Adrian Henri and Johnny Byrne started to hold regular readings at Streate's Coffee-Bar, and Roger McGough and Brian Patten (who was running a pioneer poetry magazine, *Underdog*) became regular performers.

Henri, who had studied art at Newcastle and Durham, was a painter as well as poet, and after reading an article by Allan Kaprow about the New York happenings he staged the first English mixed-media events for the Merseyside Arts Festival in 1962. Henri describes them as a mixture of 'poetry, rock'n'roll and assemblage', in other words a cross-category collage. The events stayed close to their rock'n'roll roots. 'Bomb' (1964) and 'The Black and White Show' (1965), written with Brian Patten, were staged at the Cavern Club, made famous by the Beatles. In 1963 Roger McGough, John Gorman and Mike McGear (brother of Paul McCartney) formed The Scaffold, which became well known for its records, but which did its best work as a poetry-and-black-comedy group. Adrian Henri's group, Liverpool Scene (1967–70), was a later attempt to synthesize rock'n'roll and poetry.

Since performance was essential to Liverpool poetry, the verse was direct and rhythmic, like the songs to which it was so close. It aimed at an immediate effect, without complexities of literary allusion. Brian Patten's 'Prosepoem Towards a Definition of Itself' asserts this oral poetry's independence of metropolitan literary criticism.

When in public poetry should take off its clothes and wave to the nearest person in sight; it should be seen in the company of thieves and lovers rather than that of journalists and publishers.

In its immediate address, and lack of reverential profundity, Liverpool poetry was entirely in tune with the intentions of Pop Art – and shared its limitations. It was meant to be accessible, and humour gave easy access, but, as with some forms of Pop Art, there is a tendency to fall into nostalgia and sentimentality, particularly in the love lyrics. It was impossible for the verse to be entirely without allusions, but often they were imported, as it were, ready-made. Adrian Henri's poem 'Me' ('if you weren't you, who would you be?') is a collage of twelve stanzas constructed entirely of proper names.

Paul McCartney Gustav Mahler
Alfred Jarry John Coltrane
Charlie Mingus Claude Debussy
Wordsworth Monet Bach and Blake

Charlie Parker Pierre Bonnard
Leonardo Bessie Smith
Fidel Castro Jackson Pollock
Gaudi Milton Munch and Berg

Henri presents an image of himself as a scrap-book of borrowed ideas, without a hierarchy of cultural value – 'McCartney . . . Mahler', any ordering of forms – 'Leonardo Bessie Smith', or subject-matter – 'Castro . . . Pollock'. It is the poetic equivalent of Blake's *Self-portrait with Badges*, where the fan identifies himself with his models by wearing their brand names.

Although disparaged by orthodox critics, the Liverpool poets' success outside conventional literary circles ensured, in a fashion-conscious age, that they would receive at least some acknowledgment within them, and in 1967 Henri, McGough and Patten were published in the Penguin Modern Poets series. Their volume, No. 10, was given the additional title *The Mersey Sound* and was an enormous success. The accessibility of the verse gave it a popularity far beyond the narrow confines of the traditional poetry readership. Liverpool poets and their imitators may be dismissed for the lack of density or complication in their work, but, just as the Beatles' music encouraged the use of a simple rhythmic drive and direct presentation, so their verse (together with the songs of Bob Dylan) encouraged Lennon and McCartney to complicate the verbal texture and allusions of their songs. Numbers like 'Strawberry Fields' and 'Penny Lane', released in 1967, are Liverpool poems in music.

For the Beatles, commercial success enabled them to extend their range; critical success spread their influence over more than just a large section of the youth culture. The publication of John Lennon's surrealistic jottings *In His Own Write* in 1964 was another sign of cultural convergence, but their first film, *A Hard Day's Night*, released in the same year, was a more solid achievement. Until then films by pop singers had been feeble vehicles, but the script by Liverpool playwright Alun Owen and the direction by Dick Lester had a freshness that caught the attack in the performers' music. The film fuses pop with Pop Art procedures, for Dick Lester's experience mixed the surrealism of the Goons – he had directed Spike Milligan's *The Running, Jumping and Standing Still Film* in 1960 – with the ability to produce instantaneously persuasive and seductive images learned from directing television commercials. The grainy black and white of *A Hard Day's Night*, and the bleached textures of Lester's film version of Anne Jellicoe's play *The Knack* (1965) epitomize the smart visual style of the mid-1960s.

Such was the fame of the Beatles that it is difficult to know who was patronizing whom when high and low cultures met. *The Times* classical music critic William Mann wrote in all seriousness of the 'chains of pandiatonic clusters' and the 'submediant switches from C major to A flat major' in 'I Want To Hold Your Hand'; Paul McCartney became a regular attender of first nights and private views with his girlfriend, the actress Jane Asher. The Arts Council report for 1965–6 noted smugly: 'Luciano Berio crowded out the large double lecture-room at the Italian Institute one night for an electronically illustrated lecture on his own work: the noticeably youthful audience included a Beatle (unannounced).' An interest in art – especially Pop Art – became fashionable among the new rich of the record world. Gallery-owner Robert Fraser claimed that the Beatles and the Rolling Stones were his best customers, although the property developer Peter Palumbo, who was already laying plans for a Mies Van der Rohe building in the City of London, proved to be a more serious client.

Such mutual exploitation was entirely beneficial to the development of the long front of culture. The symbolically closest point of convergence was political, when in June 1965 the Beatles were awarded the MBE. Even while in opposition Harold Wilson, who represented a Liverpool constituency, had exploited the publicity value of an association with the Beatles; the award of the MBE was a political gimmick. (The event was satirized in Anthony Burgess's *Enderby Outside* (1968).)

The Beatles were welcomed to the centre of a free-wheeling, hedonistic social world where art was fashionable, and fashion art. Jonathan Miller described this potent mix in a review of the *New Generation* show at the Whitechapel in May 1964:

Mod, of course, is the word one is groping for, since it gets, better than the over-used 'pop', the emotionally indifferent swish of these paintings, so many of which are decorative in a camp sort of way. There is now a curious cultural community, breathlessly *à la Mod*, where Lord Snowdon and the other desperadoes of grainy blow-ups and bled-off lay-out jostle with commercial art-school Mersey stars, window-dressers and Carnaby pants-peddlers. Style is the thing here – Taste 64 – a cool line and the witty insolence of youth. Tradition has little bearing on any of these individual talents and age can go stuff itself.

This 'curious cultural community' was a mingling of the old aristo-bohemian Chelsea Set evoked in Andrew Sinclair's *The Breaking of Bumbo* (1959)) and the new money created by fashion, advertising and the world of pop. When Mary Quant opened her first Bazaar shop in the King's Road in 1955 she symbolically initiated a shift in London's bohemia from the decayed streets of Fitzrovia to the eighteenth-century village atmosphere of Chelsea (although artists since Turner had favoured the nearby reach of the Thames). Quant's boutique, closely associated with her husband Alexander Plunket Greene's restaurant, Alexander's, in the basement below, launched a fashion for small-shop retailing that the menswear designer John Stephen turned into a revolution when he made a dingy lane in northern Soho, Carnaby Street, into a Mecca for the Mods. By 1967 there were some two thousand shops describing themselves as boutiques in the Greater London area. While Quant, who began mass producing clothes in 1963, and Stephen dressed the newly affluent young, Terence Conran set the style for furnishing their homes. After working as a restaurateur, textile designer and interior decorator (he designed the Knightsbridge branch of Bazaar) Conran opened his first Habitat shop in the Fulham Road in 1964.

These personalities, and the other professionals they mixed with were the heroes of the glossies, the expensive monthly magazines whose visual style Miller links to the *New Generation* paintings. *Vogue* had long served as a beacon of style for the truly affluent and aristocratic who could possess the objects and places imaged in its pages, and for those who envied or sought to emulate them. But in the late 1950s two minor magazines that had served a traditional, quasi-aristocratic market were taken over by young entrepreneurs and relaunched on the new wave. In 1957 25-year-old Jocelyn Stevens bought the society magazine

Queen and appointed as art editor a young Cambridge graduate, Mark Boxer, who created a new and aggressive lay-out. *Man About Town*, a tailoring magazine, was bought by Michael Heseltine and Clive Labovitch in 1960, and was similarly restyled by Tom Wolsey.

Queen and *Man About Town* (which gradually abbreviated its title to *Town*) shared an aggressive journalistic as well as visual style. They enjoyed the new affluence and celebrated those who were creating it. They offered a whole style of life, not just in terms of what to wear, but where to go, what to see and what to read. As in *That Was The Week That Was*, the style had room for an element of serious journalism that used a new form to challenge established views. In January 1961 *Man About Town* was urging its readers in typically imperative tones to 'Raze the boom towns. Read Lawrence Durrell. Drink champagne. Get wise to Europe. Live it rich. Cheat the cold.' Which sums up its values and preoccupations. In 1962 Mark Boxer became the first editor of the *Sunday Times* colour magazine, and though its design and approach was less radical than *Queen* or *Town*, it and subsequent newspaper colour supplements stimulated photo-journalism, while projecting the images of affluence that its advertisers wished to exploit.

As Jonathan Miller hinted, the photographer played a vital role as mediator between the constituent elements of the glossy community. The fashionable photographers supplied the images for advertising and editorial matter with profitable impartiality. Just as their craft was a mixture of visual sensibility and technical flair, their work allowed them to move freely between art and commerce. Michelangelo Antonioni's attempt to capture this milieu in the film *Blow-Up* (1966) has as its protagonist a photographer who in the same day photographs down-and-outs and high fashion. (The arch mystery of the film creates a deliberately disturbing feeling of alienation intended as moral criticism.)

Photographers were the intermediaries along the long front of culture; they fed it images of itself, and in the process of making heroes, they became heroes themselves. Antony Armstrong-Jones was a Cambridge contemporary of Jocelyn Stevens, and made his reputation on *Queen* before joining Mark Boxer on the *Sunday Times*. In 1960 he achieved the ultimate in hypergamy by marrying Princess Margaret, and became the Earl of Snowdon in 1961.

Snowdon was at least from Eton and Cambridge, but other photographers appeared on the scene with cultivated East End backgrounds: David Bailey, Terry Donovan, Terry Duffy.

These photographers, with their fast, high-contrast film and grainy prints created the black-and-white 'hard-edge' style of the early 1960s. They were young, and, like the pop singers, enjoyed a rapid success that depended as much on a personal style and aggressiveness as on content. Economic expansion in the media led to an acceleration of people's careers in journalism, some businesses, theatre and art. Mary Quant, David Hockney, the photographers, all became famous for being well below the age of 40. Peter Hall took over the direction of the Royal Shakespeare Company at 30; Harry Hyams, 39 in 1967, was the wealthiest man to have made his fortune since the war. These are *The Young Meteors* that the 25-year-old journalist (and great-nephew of Lord Beaverbrook) Jonathan Aitken chose to celebrate in his book published in 1967.

Because social barriers would impede the meteoric rise of such young, ambitious people, they chose to present themselves as 'classless', and indeed some, like the Beatles, had risen to fame and fortune from lowly origins. Others, like Snowdon and Quant, had not. 'Classlessness' manifested itself in social gestures, from the 'classless' accents of Cliff Richard, David Frost or Cathy McGowan (all evolved in order to broadcast on a mass medium), to Peter Hall's decision to stop printing the RSC's posters and programmes with special billings for the stars. Instead, the cast appeared in alphabetical order. Hall said in 1963: 'We don't want to be an institution supported by middle-class expense accounts. We want to be socially as well as artistically open.'

By attempting to escape the categories of class, they were trying to escape the conventions of category, but the young meteors (the phrase suggests both their rapid trajectory and inherent evanescence) really emerged as a new class, or at least a class-fraction. 'Classlessness' was not a resolution of the problems of class, but an expression of the stress the previously rigid class structure was undergoing. Even Jonathan Aitken had to admit, 'Britain is still a very class-obsessed country, and because some young Londoners have recently become highly successful in their class mobility, this has added to rather than detracted from the class obsession.' The members of the classless society were in fact a new 'talent class'. 'We now have something that looks like meritocracy, and for this three hearty cheers.'

The aristocrats of this meritocracy received their apotheosis in 1965 in *David Bailey's Box of Pin-ups*, a photographic extension of Blake's *Self-portrait with Badges* and Adrian Henri's 'Me'. It is exactly what it describes itself as: thirty-six black-and-white portraits of leading members of Miller's 'curious cultural community'. They are studio portraits, key-lit for contrast against plain white backgrounds. The unifying element is the direct address of the sitters, the '*Midwich Cuckoo* stare which marks the Beatles style' that Jonathan Miller had noticed some of the 1964 *New Generation* paintings, and which goes back to Blake's children in *On the Balcony*. The collection was laid out by Mark Boxer, and supplied with a brief text by the old-Etonian film-critic Francis Wyndham.

Wyndham emphasized the *Box*'s conformity to Hamilton's Pop principle of expendability. 'David Bailey is fascinated by tinsel – a bright, brittle quality, the more appealing because it tarnishes so soon.' According to Wyndham the photographs

make a statement not only about the man who took them, but also about London life in 1965. Many of the people here have gone all out for the immediate rewards of success: quick money, quick fame, quick sex – a brave thing to do. Glamour dates fast, and it is its ephemeral nature which both attracts Bailey and challenges him. He has tried to capture it on the wing, and his pin-ups have a heroic look: isolated, invulnerable, lost.

The professions of the pin-ups reveal the constitution of this brave new world: photographers (Cecil Beaton, Terry Donovan, Michael Cooper, Bailey photographed by Mick Jagger); singers (Lennon and McCartney, The Rolling Stones, P. J. Proby, Gordon Waller); managers (Brian Epstein, Andrew Oldham); actors (Michael Caine); dancers (Rudolf Nureyev); models (Jean Shrimpton, Susan Murray); dress designers (Gerald McCann); boutique owners (James Wedge); interior decorators (David Hicks); hairdressers (Vidal Sassoon); artists (David Hockney); crooks (the Kray brothers); and Brian Morris, the manager of the night-club of the moment, the Ad Lib.

The self-defining gesture of David Bailey's collection is that it is based on the erotic fantasy of the pin-up: the photographs appear hard and glossy, but they are insubstantial and impenetrable. Richard Hamilton's definition of the categories of Pop

Art could hardly be more precisely fulfilled. But the sexual element in the package has become more blatant, so that Wyndham equates sex with fame and money as a symbol of success. Pop music provided the erotic pulse of the pleasure principle, films and advertising harnessed it to commercial ends, but the admission of the existence of sexual enjoyment extended itself well beyond the group of entertainers and film stars who had always served to objectify the fantasies of the mass, and who were now the peers of the 'permissive society'. Philip Larkin's poem 'Annus Mirabilis', quoted at the head of this chapter, though set in the context of a general relaxation in sexual repression, celebrates his personal liberation. It continues:

> Up till then there'd only been
> A sort of bargaining,
> A wrangle for a ring,
> A shame that started at sixteen
> And spread to everything.
>
> Then all at once the quarrel sank:
> Everyone felt the same,
> And every life became
> A brilliant breaking of the bank,
> A quite unlosable game.

As we shall see in greater detail in the next chapter, sex and its Sixties concomitant, drugs, had a symbolic meaning beyond the material problems of sexuality, a meaning which is concerned with the politics of ecstasy, and questions of cultural control through censorship. In 1967 Jonathan Aitken could write 'At the moment there is no real sign of a secular equivalent of the Jesuits, fighting to inaugurate a moral counter-reformation. It seems that the triumph of London's sexual revolutionaries has been complete and absolute, and that their opponents have fled.'

But Aitken, like T. R. Fyvel in a different context, was optimistically self-deluded. Mrs Mary Whitehouse had launched her campaign to Clean Up TV in 1964. A more telling response, because it imaginatively expresses and hostilely identifies so many of the elements of the sexual and material revolution, comes in John Osborne's *Inadmissible Evidence*, first performed in September 1964. The corrupt, adulterous and despairing solicitor Bill Maitland addresses his seventeen-year-old daughter in a quasi-fantastical monologue. This is the voice of Jimmy Porter at forty:

I cause you little else but distaste or distress, or, at least, your own vintage, swinging indifference. But nothing, certainly not your swinging distaste can match what I feel for you. *(Small pause as he changes tack.)* Or any of those who are more and more like you. Oh, I read about you, I see you in the streets. I hear what you say, the sounds you make, the few jokes you make, the wounds you inflict without ever longing to hurt; there is no lather or fear in you, all cool, dreamy, young, cool and not a proper blemish, forthright, unimpressed, contemptuous of ambition but good and pushy all the same. You've no shame of what you are, and very little, well, not much doubt as to what you'll become. And quite right, at least so I used to think. They're young, I said, and for the first time they're being allowed to roll about in it and have clothes and money and music and sex, and you can take or leave any of it. No one before has been able to do such things with such charm, such ease, such frozen innocence as all of you seem to have, to me.

By 1966 a cultural revolution inconceivable in 1960 appeared to have been achieved. A Conservative political establishment had been disgraced; in March 1966 a general election gave Harold Wilson a decisive majority, and the Labour administration presented the image, if not the actuality, of a new approach to economic management. Superficially, Harold Macmillan's good times were even better; unemployment was at its lowest ever and exports were booming. There was a welcome feeling of confidence in the air that encouraged investment in new buildings and new technologies on a grand scale, from new universities to the development of the Concorde aircraft. The success of the arts, especially in painting and the theatre, helped to create the mood of expansion, and their contribution to the general confidence was rewarded with increased public and private patronage. That dominant cultural institution, the BBC, was in an expansive and controversial phase.

Each decade appears to have its own moment of myth: in the 1940s it was the pride and communality of suffering during the Blitz; in the 1950s it was the aggressive ambition of the Angry Young Man; in the 1960s it was Swinging London. In all three cases the myths reflect an imaginative rather than literal truth, but that does not destroy their validity. They would not have become the sustaining images they became without a basis in fact, but, more importantly, they were observably believed to be true at the time of their origination.

Such myths met the needs for some general explanation of the circumstances in which people found themselves. However much the evident truth that 'London [and by implication the rest of the country] Can Take It' was inflated during the war by the Ministry of Information, Government propaganda could only reinforce what was already there. The image of the Angry Young Man answered a different need, as a means of expressing resentment at the austerities of post-war Britain and the national humiliation of Suez. It was nurtured by popular journalists and critics like Kenneth Tynan who found in the Angry Young Man a personification of their own dissatisfaction, but no group of individual (and individualistic) writers could have imposed an image of discontent if that dissatisfaction had not also been more general. Once such myths are discovered in the national consciousness, their validity is proved by the rapidity with which they become self-reinforcing.

The myth of Swinging London was, like the Angry Young Man, a journalists' creation, and more than any it was the creation of the team of American journalists who worked on the article 'You Can Walk Across It on the Grass' for the 15 April 1966 issue of *Time* magazine. The phrase 'London: The Swinging City' was emblazoned across *Time*'s cover, a collage that parodied the mutually sustaining iconographies of pop music and Pop Art. It is ironical that it took an American magazine to reveal a British phenomenon to itself, but the *Time* editorial method has always been one of compilation, and the article gathers in many of the separate developments surveyed in this chapter. In particular, it is a distillation of the images of the way of life that *Queen*, *Town* and the colour supplements had been both reporting and promoting. It synthesizes the worlds of *Pop As Art*, Bailey's *Box of Pin-ups* and the *New Musical Express*. The opening sentence, 'In this century, every decade has had its city', sets out to confirm the myth.

Today, it is London, a city steeped in tradition, seized by change, liberated by affluence, graced by daffodils and anemones, so green with parks and squares that, as the saying goes, you can walk across it on the

77

grass. In a decade dominated by youth, London has burst into bloom. It swings; it is the scene.

The analytical reporting in the article is slight. The one statistic produced is that London had a far younger population than the rest of the country, with 30 per cent in the 15 to 34-year-old bracket. What tell are the images. 'In a once sedate world of faded splendour, everything new, uninhibited and kinky is blooming at the top of London life.' The capital has been invigorated by the influx of young and often working-class talent from the provinces, who have helped to create 'a new and surprising leadership community; economists, professors, actors, photographers, singers, admen, TV executives and writers – a swinging meritocracy.' Spokesmen for this meritocracy celebrate the new cultural mix.

. . . says Peter Hall 'we've got rid of that stuffy middle-aged lot that go to the theater as a sop for their prejudices. We're getting a young audience who are looking for experiences and will take them from the latest pop record or *Hamlet*.' The In Hamlet this year is David Warner, 24, who plays the Dane with Beatle haircut and a Carnaby Street slouch.

Most of the article is devoted to visiting the places identified on the helpful map (Ill. 4) and describing those encountered there, but the conclusion attempts a deeper seriousness.

The London that has emerged is swinging, but in a far more profound sense than the colorful and ebullient pop culture by itself would suggest. London has shed much of its smugness, much of the arrogance that often went with the stamp of privilege, much of the false pride – the kind that long kept it shabby and shopworn in physical fact and spirit. It is a refreshing change, and making the scene is the Londoner's way of celebrating it.

The truth is that London, and the rest of the country, had chosen an image of itself which obscured the far deeper divisions and uncertainties of its true identity. Swinging London, for all but a very few, was a fantasy. Yet the appeal of the self-image that *Time* offered was so great that British journalists, especially feature-writers, picked up the myth and fed it back to those who were its subject. The myth was so powerful that in the summer of 1966 it appeared to come true. But Britain's economic reality could not sustain the fantasy for very long.

Since 1960, the underlying decay in Britain's economic position had been signalled by a series of crises in the external balance of payments. The Conservative Chancellor Reginald Maudling's 'dash for growth' before the 1964 Election left the incoming Labour Government with a record balance of payments deficit of £750 million. The deficit was partly the result of domestic wage inflation, partly the expense of maintaining a British military presence abroad – the foreign role that Britain continued to play, though she had lost the Empire that gave it substance. To some extent Britain was the victim of circumstances beyond her control – namely the foreign policy of America. In *The British Experience* (1978) Peter Calvocoressi argues that 'it was the behaviour of the international economy under American direction, or non-direction, which from the Sixties onwards most severely boosted inflation in Britain.'

In 1964 the immediate answer to the problem of the balance of payments might have been devaluation, but Wilson was in a weak position politically, having a majority of only five. It is also probable that Wilson recalled the previous Labour devaluation of 1949, and its devastating effect on Socialist morale. (As President of the Board of Trade in the Attlee government Wilson had presided over the virtual collapse of the British film industry; see *In Anger* pp.14–16.) Rather than devalue, Wilson built up a large external debt, while the economic devices of the technological revolution – higher taxes, credit squeezes, wage freezes, expenditure cuts and prices and incomes policies – failed to have their deflationary effects and provoked domestic resistance in the form of the seamen's strike of 1966 and the dock strike of 1967. (The introduction of Selective Employment Tax in 1966, which struck at the commercial theatre as a service industry while exempting film and television, stimulated the municipalization of theatres.)

Inflation began to rise perceptibly from 1965, but was not seen as a particular threat. In his contribution to *The Decade of Disillusion: British Politics in the 1960s* (1972) Peter Sinclair asserts, 'Why did inflation suddenly accelerate in the mid-Sixties? The simplest and most cogent explanation is simply that people came to expect it.' Evidence of this attitude can be found in the Arts Council's report for 1965–6, *Key Year*.

It is our experience that the effects of inflation lead to increased costs in the world of entertainment and the arts faster and further than elsewhere. It was therefore no surprise to us to find that the estimates of expenditure for 1965–6, which we had to present to the Government at the end of 1964, were far in excess of the amount that would have been available to us on a strict application of the triennial agreement.

As we have seen, this complacency was justified, for the new Labour Government responded with a large increase in arts subsidy, so that, the report continues, with these increased funds 'We could even begin to contemplate the most revolutionary change of all, namely a transition from the poor-law technique of limiting our assistance to a bare subsistence level, with stringent means tests, towards a system of planned subsidies for improvement and growth.' Although in macroeconomic terms the increased subsidy of the arts was insignificant, psychologically the mood of expansion in the arts helped to create an atmosphere of optimism and self-indulgence. As Peter Calvocoressi suggests, 'wage-push inflation was promoted as much by economic exuberance as by economic gloom.'

It must be acknowledged that this is written some time after the party was over, but even at its height there was some awareness of an underlying unease. A property boom has a visible effect on the townscape, but it does not create real wealth – and by 1967 the property boom was over. Jonathan Aitken's Tory, capitalist celebration of youthful enterprise, *The Young Meteors*, began as a series of articles for the *Evening Standard* following in the optimistic wake of *Time*'s 'Swinging London' report. But in his conclusion Aitken admits that during the preparation of the book his mood has shifted from optimism to pessimism. The boutique revolution is only 'gifted amateurism', and the economic reality of post-Imperial Britain is grimmer and more absurd. He concludes, 'The generation which I belong to and have been trying to write about is schizophrenic and insecure.'

CHAPTER 3

Bomb Culture

'And what's the point of a revolution without general copulation?'

De Sade in Peter Weiss's *The Persecution and Assassination of Marat as Performed by the Inmates of Charenton under the direction of the Marquis de Sade* (1964)

One reason for the insecurity that Jonathan Aitken detected in his generation was the success with which its meteoric rise to fame and fortune appeared to have disrupted traditional social and cultural categories. The long front of culture abolished hierarchies of taste, but it did not establish firm critical standards in their place: as Richard Hamilton had perceived, the primary value of Pop Art was that it was ephemeral. An ever-accelerating demand for what is new places increasing strain on the innovators, who have less and less time to distinguish between the genuinely inventive, and the merely meretricious. Schizophrenia, as R. D. Laing had pointed out, induces escape into fantasy, and Swinging London was one such mythical projection. But as the distance between Britain's true economic position and the gaudy affluence of the King's Road widened in 1966 and 1967 it became clear that another section of the same generation had chosen a different path. Their project was not simply to achieve a long front of culture that removed the old hierarchies; they wished to bring together a set of values that would constitute a radical alternative to it: not a long front, but a counter-culture.

In 1960 in *The Divided Self* Laing wrote of the schizophrenic as an outsider estranged from himself and from a society which he cannot accept as real. The patient in turn presents a false self to society, but the split between his true and false selves cannot be sustained, so that his whole personality is in increasing danger of disintegration. By 1970 Laing and others had come to apply this interpretation to the whole of what they saw as a sick society. Thus in *The Making of a Counter-Culture* (New York 1969, London 1970) Theodore Roszak explains its emergence as the result of a 'radical cultural disjuncture' in Anglo-American society, where technological advance has produced an affluent totalitarianism in which mankind is completely estranged from its true nature. The 'normality' defined by the scientific world view is in fact an absurd fiction, and mankind must develop a false self in order to be able to cope with its demands. The counter-culture aims to recover the 'visionary splendour' of life by dissolving that false self.

What is important here is not the validity or otherwise of the argument, but the terms in which it is expressed: the counter-culture proved as much a fantasy as Harold Wilson's technological revolution. What is significant is that they are united by their mutual opposition to each other. Each depends on the other for its definition; for the counter-culture to be presented as a radical alternative to bourgeois civilization, and not just a marginal adjustment to it, it had to appear in terms at the furthest opposite to the disputed 'normal'. The rhetoric of division and disintegration imposed a language of revolution and anti-structure, to the point of apparent incomprehensibility. As Roszak put it, it became 'a culture so radically disaffiliated from the mainstream assumptions of our society that it scarcely looks like a culture at all, but takes on the alarming appearance of a barbaric intrusion.'

The 'underground' (a military metaphor transferred to cultural as opposed to political resistance and sabotage) surfaced in Britain between 1965 and 1967. In that time it ceased to be simply a literary and artistic movement and became a lifestyle that at its extremes had a purely political rationale. In its origins it had much in common with the affluent culture to which it was opposed. As with Pop, its most important aesthetics were derived from Dada and collage. Also like Pop, it could only sustain itself in a period of economic surplus. As Peter Fryer remarked in his survey for *Encounter*, 'A Map of the Underground', in October 1967: 'From one point of view, the whole phenomenon can be seen as a complex of business enterprises.'

The point at issue between the underground and the culture it opposed was no more and no less than the definition of reality. Was reality the ordinary, contingent day-to-day experience of Western society with its strictly limited pleasures and pains, or was this merely a mask that obscured some profounder and greater reality whose 'visionary splendour' involved a far more harmonious relationship between ourselves, and with our environment? Was the material wealth, to whose production we are devoted, a means of release from want, or the price of a far greater personal freedom? Such a challenge to the social definition of reality involved a challenge to the means with which that reality was expressed. Was not language itself a mask of true experience, and did not the logic and grammar of language help to impose a false ordering of society? Those who were alarmed by these challenges to the authority of language called it a 'retreat from the word'.

One such was the critic George Steiner, who gave two radio talks on the topic in 1960, later reprinted as an essay in his collection *Language and Silence* (1967). Steiner acknowledged the Eastern view that 'it is only by breaking through the walls of language that visionary observance can enter the world of total and immediate understanding', but the Western cultural tradition asserts the primacy of the word. Yet that tradition is under pressure both from science and contemporary art. Since the seventeenth century, mathematics had evolved a world of numbers that gradually encroached on economics, history, sociology and, worst of all, philosophy, to the point where such disciplines have become near 'illiterate, or more precisely, anti-literate.' At the same time

the retreat from the authority and range of verbal language plays a tremendous role in the history and character of modern art. In painting and sculpture, realism in the broadest sense – the representation of that which we apprehend as an imitation of existent reality – corresponds to that period in which language is at the centre of intellectual and emotive life . . . [when] . . . we can give a linguistic account of the subject of the work of art. The canvas and the statue have a title that relates to the verbal concept.

But modern art has rebelled 'precisely against such verbal equivalence or concordance'. The world of words has shrunk, squeezed by mathematics and the 'sub-languages or anti-languages of non-objective art and *musique concrète*.' Music, indeed, which in its most modern form had abandoned its classical language of statement, variation and recapitulation of theme in preference for mathematical formulae, is taking the place of literature in Western culture. 'The new middle class in the affluent society reads little, but listens to music with knowing delight. Where the library shelves once stood, there are proud, esoteric rows of record albums and high-fidelity components.'

Steiner's essay is a protest and a warning, but there was a sense in which those who deplored the retreat from the word also contributed to it. On the one hand the sheer volume of words made available through the mass media of cheap printing, television and radio (note that Steiner's protest was first broadcast, then printed) had led to their devaluation; on the other the academic approach to literature so prevalent in the 1950s had narrowed its appeal. Steiner remarks in his preface to *Language and Silence* that 'literary criticism, particularly in its present cohabitation with the academic, is no longer a very interesting or responsible exercise.' But beyond that, there was a sense in which the literate culture which Steiner was trying to defend had failed. 'My own consciousness is possessed by the eruption of barbarism in modern Europe; by the mass murder of the Jews and by the destruction under Nazism and Stalinism of what I try to define in some of these essays as the particular genius of "Central European humanism".' Against such barbarism an art of humanism had proved no defence. 'The blackness . . . rose from within, and from the core of European civilization. The cry of the murdered sounded in earshot of the universities; the sadism went on a street away from the theatres and museums.' As the novelist William Golding later wrote of Belsen and Hiroshima: 'We have discovered a limit to literature.'

Since the word seemed incapable of coming to terms with the horrors of the twentieth century – and in the hands of propagandists and the self-interested it served to perpetuate them – there was an argument to be made for a retreat into silence, the mystical silence of a higher understanding such as was sought by the students of Zen. There was a case for the dethronement of language and logic, which could not convey a greater truth that was at once too complex, and too unified, for the analytical procedures of grammar and conceptual thought. Dadaists like Tristan Tzara had anticipated such things in 1917; as we shall see, at the beginning of the 1960s the word was to suffer some of its fiercest physical assaults with the cut-ups of William Burroughs and John Latham's book burnings.

It was in keeping with the dialectical logic of opposites that the truth that could not be expressed in language could not be discovered in the material world that language structured and described. The retreat from the word into silence also implies a retreat from contingency and technology into the inner spaces of the imagination. Laing's *The Politics of Experience and the Bird of Paradise* (1967) provides a typical example.

We are far more out of touch with even the nearest approaches of the infinite reaches of inner space than we now are with the reaches of outer space. We respect the voyager, the explorer, the climber, the space man. It makes far more sense to me as a valid project – indeed, as a desperately urgently required project for our time, to explore the inner space and time of consciousness.

Laing is not being original; he draws on a long tradition both of Eastern and Western mysticism, but the materialism of the 1960s gave the mystical element in counter-cultural ideology a particular urgency. And his reference to actual outer space is not accidental. The international politics of the decade were dominated by the race to the Moon between Russia and America. In his survey of British science fiction in the 1960s, *The Entropy Exhibition* (1983), Colin Greenland observes that the avant-garde writers associated with Michael Moorcock's editorship of *New Worlds* magazine turned away from outer space just as the actual space race was getting under way. 'Angst in space, detestation of the stars, were not simply affectations of the new writers, but disenchanted expressions of their feeling that SF and mankind were both travelling in wrong directions.'

The conquering of inner space became a common theme in the alternative ideology of the underground. In their preface to *BAMN (By Any Means Necessary): Outlaw Manifestos and Ephemera 1965–1970* (1971) Peter Stansill and David Mairowitz explain that they chose to begin their anthology in 1965 because 'suddenly, the debate is no longer between right-wing/left-wing, but rather between the oppressions of the external world and the desire for internal liberation, between activist commitment to the continuing social struggle and dropping out of a cultural milieu that won't allow it.' Part of the reason for dropping out of politics (which is a political gesture) was indeed, as we saw in chapter I, that the political route had become blocked. The Campaign for Nuclear Disarmament, where many of the founders of the counter-culture had had their first experience of an 'alternative' life-style had proved a failure as far as its own ends were concerned, and was trapped in the net of party politics.

As a system (or rather anti-system) of aesthetics, the counter-culture wished to destroy artistic categories altogether. It wished to destroy the distinction between art and life by turning art into a life-style, and vice versa, for it recognized that cultural categories are also social definitions. Thus its arguments would necessarily be at the same time political and aesthetic. The convention was to ignore all boundaries and conventions, and as far as possible to escape the imposed definitions of material reality by exploring inner space. Noble as this project was in many ways, its consequences for the explorer could be heavy. The destruction of the categories of art could lead to the self-destruction of the artist, and the inner world turn out to be purgatory rather than paradise. The risk of abandoning logic and language was that this could lead to a nonsensical, catatonic silence.

As Steiner's protest shows, the authority of language was under attack before the formation of the counter-culture: the assaults on the word in the 1960s were a continuation of what the Dadaists and Surrealists had begun. In the theatre, the theories of the French surrealist Antonin Artaud (1896–1948) were a direct influence, and it was in the theatre that the case for a revaluation of the function of language was first made. Artaud's writings, and the plays of Samuel Beckett and Eugene Ionesco began a process of creative disintegration and reduction that the 'happenings' of the 1960s sought to complete.

Beckett's *Waiting for Godot* (1952) and Ionesco's *The Lesson* (1951) were both first produced in English in 1955, when Peter Hall ran the Arts Theatre Club for a year before beginning his association with the Shakespeare Memorial Theatre (relaunched under his direction as the Royal Shakespeare Company in 1960). A production of Ionesco's *The Bald Prima Donna* (1950) followed in 1956, and of *The Chairs* in 1957. These plays – where a teacher murders his pupil, where a married couple communicate the obvious to each other in the fragmented clichés of a phrase-book, where two ancients solemnly fill a room with chairs as though these are people – created an atmosphere of disturbing unreality and menace which suggested that the world had lost any rational meaning; that it was absurd. It was meaningless because belief in God was no longer possible, and no other ruling explanation for our existence had been found. As Martin Esslin sums up in *The Theatre of the Absurd* (1961), the theatre of Beckett, Ionesco, Arthur Adamov, Jean Genet and those influenced by them

bravely faces up to the fact that for those to whom the world had lost its central explanation and meaning, it is no longer possible to accept art forms still based on the continuation of standards and concepts that have lost their validity; that is, the possibility of knowing the laws of conduct and ultimate values, as deducible from a firm foundation of revealed certainty about the purpose of man in the universe.

The Theatre of the Absurd had a vogue in London between the transfer of *Waiting for Godot* to the West End in 1955 and Orson Welles's production of Ionesco's *Rhinoceros* with Sir Laurence Olivier in 1960. The term provided a useful umbrella for the early work of Harold Pinter, who acknowledged the influence of Beckett and Kafka, but did not know the work of Ionesco until after his first plays, *The Room* (1957) and *The Dumb Waiter* (written 1957, first performed 1960) had already been written. In *The Dumb Waiter* two killers are waiting Beckett-like in a basement room for something to happen, while a service-lift (the inexplicable machinery of the universe) sends down incomprehensible demands to the pair, one of whom becomes the victim of unanswerable questions. Pinter's first full-length play *The Birthday Party* (1958) similarly deploys a pair of gangsters who invade a seedy seaside boarding-house and take away the pathetic lodger Stanley, having reduced him to near imbecility.

Although Pinter's plays, especially the early ones, depicted extreme and potentially violent situations, he conveyed the absurd through a closely observed use of ordinary speech which revealed how extraordinary it really is. Language masks our true meaning

– if in fact we mean anything at all. This reflection of the everyday world distinguishes him from other absurdist writers; *The Caretaker* (1960), which established Pinter's reputation, is an entirely plausible situation. The mutual helplessness and fear of the tramp, the brain-damaged man who has taken him in and his fantasizing brother are actual as well as symbolic.

The absurd can be menacing, but it is also comic, and audiences found Pinter's dialogue often very funny, partly because the repetitions, pauses and *non sequiturs* were so recognizable. At a completely different level of apprehension the surrealistic characters of the radio comedy *The Goon Show* (1949–60) peopled an absurd parallel world to reality. Its chief creator, Spike Milligan, went on to write the post-nuclear farce *The Bed Sitting-room* (1963) with John Antrobus, and has kept the comic absurd alive in poems, stories and television series. N. F. Simpson introduced some of this distinctly British absurd into the theatre with *A Resounding Tinkle* (1957) and *One Way Pendulum* (1959). In the latter a suburban household contains a son who is teaching a collection of speak-your-weight machines the 'Hallelujah Chorus', while his father is building a replica of the court-room at the Old Bailey in the living-room. With absurdist logic the court-room fills with judge and lawyers, and the son goes on trial for murder.

The London productions of Ionesco, Beckett, Genet, Pinter and Simpson ran in counterpoint to the social realism associated with Arnold Wesker and ideas of the drama as a historical narrative derived from Brecht. There was no major Brecht production in English until 1962 when the Royal Shakespeare Company mounted *The Caucasian Chalk Circle*, but Robert Bolt's *A Man for all Seasons* (1960) and John Osborne's *Luther* (1961) had already familiarized British audiences with a 'Brechtian' style that was, as the editors of *The Encore Reader* (1965) put it, 'politically concerned, theatrically bold and artistically disciplined.' By contrast the Theatre of the Absurd seemed irresponsibly nihilistic. In 1958 Ionesco became engaged in public controversy with one of the leading propagandists of committed theatre, the *Observer*'s drama critic Kenneth Tynan.

Tynan claimed that Ionesco's anti-theatre heralded a 'bleak new world from which the humanist heresies of faith in logic and belief in man will forever be banished'. Ionesco replied that it was not the playwright's duty to convey a political message, and indeed political and social adjustments were no solution to the essentially metaphysical anguish of mankind. 'No society has been able to abolish human sadness, no political system can deliver us from the pain of living, from our fear of death, our thirst for the absolute; it is the human condition that directs the social condition, not vice versa.' To explore these problems, the playwright must turn to his inner self, for 'I am certain then to find the problems and fears of literally everyone. That is the true road into my own darkness, our darkness, which I try to bring to the light of day.' That exploration involved breaking down the language used by society to conceal the truth from itself. The language of political ideologies must be 'relentlessly split apart in order to find the living sap beneath.'

For Ionesco the theatre, where the imagination is free, where anything can happen, where logic is suspended and inner states of being can be rendered as effectively as outward events, is the ideal location for the dethronement of language. It is but one element in the ensemble of action, gesture, sound and sight, and it can make its impact felt as easily through nonsense as sense. He wrote in an essay of 1958 'to give the theatre its true measure, which lies in going to excess, the words themselves must be stretched to the utmost limits, the language must be made almost to explode, or to destroy itself in its inability to contain its meaning.'

In the early 1960s the fashion for the absurd faltered, partly because new ways were being developed of going to excess: the Theatre of the Absurd gave way to the Theatre of Cruelty. The term is Antonin Artaud's; his pre-war performances and the theoretical writings collected as *The Theatre and its Double* (first published 1938, translated 1958) were an inspiration to the post-war European avant-garde, while his life as drug addict and mental patient gave him a special place in the mythology of the counter-culture. His 1932 manifesto 'The Theatre of Cruelty' argued that the theatre has its own independent physical language which reaches a deeper level of understanding by appealing beyond reason, directly to the senses. 'It makes no difference whether these other levels are really conquered by the mind, that is to say by our intellect, for this curtails them, a pointless and meaningless act. What matters is that our sensibility is put into a deeper, subtler state of perception by absurd means, the very

89

object of magic and ritual, of which theatre is only a reflection.' Magic and ritual will make the theatre into a truly holy place, where mankind can explore the inner mysteries of being, and, by discovering in a truthful way the hidden urges that are part of our nature, the theatre can purge them.

Theatre will never be itself again, that is to say will never be able to form truly illusive means, unless it provides the audience with truthful distillations of dreams where its taste for crime, its erotic obsessions, its savageness, its fantasies, its Utopian sense of life and objects, even its cannibalism, do not gush out on an illusory make-believe, but on an inner level.

Such a theatre is one of extremes, but for Artaud 'this cruelty is not sadistic or bloody; or at least not exclusively so.' He later explains, 'I use the word cruelty in the sense of hungering after life, cosmic strictness, relentless necessity . . . the inescapably necessary pain without which life could not continue.'

Artaud thought it essential 'to shatter language in order to contact life' and that meant 'creating or recreating theatre'. (In a completely different medium, the paintings of Francis Bacon depict violence and emotion in such a way as to disrupt his deliberately traditional formats.) The argument had appeal for directors who wished to take the theatrical revolution of the 1950s a stage further. *Look Back In Anger* had broken into the make-believe world of boulevard theatre, but its social realism was still only an imitation of life. New forms of theatre had to be discovered where life itself occupied the stage. In *The Confessions of a Counterfeit Critic* (1971) Charles Marowitz gives an account of his own conversion from the realism of the Method school of acting which he had originally helped to import from Lee Strasberg's Actors' Studio in New York. Marowitz came to London in 1957, and combined writing for the drama magazine *Encore* with running an experimental theatre group 'In-Stage' and his Method Workshop. He began to read Artaud and found

a lure in the work of Genet and Beckett, Obaldia and Arrabal which had nothing in common with the naturalistic minutiae and sociological homilies in the work of writers such as Osborne, Wesker and (Heaven forfend) even Harold Pinter. Before long – one can never date these things but it was around the early Sixties – I realized I had been blinded by Strasberg in precisely the same way he had been conned by

Stanislavsky, and that in some kind of prophetic way, my attempt to apply the Method to classics was really an indication of a entirely different temperament, one which found its realization in the ideas of Artaud.

In 1963 Marowitz was invited by Peter Brook to collaborate with him on a project that would explore Artaud's ideas. In 1962 Brook had joined the Royal Shakespeare Company as a permanent director, specially charged with experimental work, and from this point on his career took a radical turn. Peter Hall's policy had prepared the ground at the RSC for what was to follow with the rituals and tortures of John Whiting's *The Devils* in 1961, and the 1962 RSC season at the Arts Theatre presenting seven plays on the theme of lust and horror, from Middleton and Gorky to David Rudkin's *Afore Night Come*. The same year Peter Brook directed a powerful Beckettian *King Lear*, with Marowitz as his assistant.

Brook has said he used Artaud's 'striking title to cover our own experiments'; Marowitz has called the resulting Theatre of Cruelty season 'a kind of surrealist vaudeville-show'. Brook's aim was to discover whether it was possible to evolve a new theatrical language of such directness that 'the play, the event itself, stands in place of a text.' Twelve actors (including Glenda Jackson) were chosen for a series of intensive workshops, and the results were shown at the London Academy of Music and Dramatic Art early in 1964. The month of performances were very much 'work-in-progress', for Brook was working towards a production of Genet's arduous play about the Algerian war *The Screens*. Improvizations were changed every night, and suggestions from the audience were invited. Artaud's sketch 'A Spurt of Blood' was played first with the dialogue replaced by screams, and then as written. A short story by Alain Robbe-Grillet was dramatized in movement only. Peter Brook contributed two collage texts, 'The Guillotine' and 'The Public Bath', an exploration of ritual in which Glenda Jackson was 'stripped, bathed and dressed in a prison uniform to the words of a report of the recent Christine Keeler case; the same words were then used to transform her into Mrs Kennedy at the President's funeral.' The use of collage continued in Marowitz's twenty-minute version of *Hamlet*, which he described as an 'exercise in Burroughs-like cut-ups.'

The presentation of these experiments was followed by private performances of the first twelve scenes of *The Screens*, but censorship and the sheer difficulty of the piece caused Brook to abandon the production. (The customary censorship imposed by the Lord Chamberlain had been avoided by treating LAMDA as a private 'club' theatre for the Theatre of Cruelty season.) Instead, the work bore fruit in Brook's production in August 1964 of Peter Weiss's *The Persecution and Assassination of Marat as Performed by the Inmates of Charenton under the Direction of the Marquis de Sade*. Weiss was an acknowledged disciple of Artaud: what could be more Artaudian than to choose the Marquis de Sade as a chief character, and the madhouse of Charenton as his setting? But Weiss was Marxist as well as Artaudian, and he used the play-within-the-play devices of Brecht. Brook exploited Brechtian alienation techniques to the full. At the end of the play the lunatics advance menacingly on the audience (who themselves have been inveigled into playing the part of spectators at a Charenton performance) when a stage-manager appears and blows a whistle to stop the play-outside-the-play. The conflict between Brechtian political theatre and Artaudian psychodrama is mirrored within the text by the revolutionary violence of Marat, and the self-explorations of de Sade.

There is no doubt about the impact of Brook's production, yet the sheer terror and eroticism of the piece (the wild antics of the insane, Glenda Jackson as Charlotte Corday beating de Sade with her hair) overwhelmed the audience. Charles Marowitz, who was no longer working with Brook, was in a good position to judge Brook's application of Artaud's ideas. Returning to the role of drama critic, he wrote 'the ordering mentality of an audience tries to collate the shocks and the sense, only to find that they don't really go together; that, in fact, the intellectual dialogues are themselves a kind of theatrical effect.' In his search for 'a theatre, more violent, less rational, more extreme, less verbal, more dangerous' Peter Brook learned the counter-productivity of shock.

This lesson was reinforced in 1966, when Brook turned to the directly political subject of the war in Vietnam. Britain was not militarily involved, but Harold Wilson's Government supported President Johnson's policy, which had led to escalating American involvement in a war of increasing violence and cruelty. Under the punning title *US*, Brook did not so much explore America's role in the war, as Britain's attitude towards it. The production was prepared over four months in an atmosphere of great intensity. The cast lived communally and rehearsed in secret. By choice there was no author; Adrian Mitchell, who had versified the English translation of the *Marat/Sade*, was credited with the lyrics. Mitchell's 'To Whom It May Concern', with the refrain 'Tell me lies about Vietnam', already familiar from readings and demonstrations, was heard once again. The playwright Denis Cannan helped to script the non-documentary parts of the text. Brook conducted workshops with the Polish director Jerzy Grotowski, whose theatre he has described as 'as close as anyone has got to Artaud's ideal' and sought the advice of Joe Chaikin, the American actor-director who has similarly explored Artaudian techniques with the Living Theater and his own Open Theater.

The results were theatrically impressive, but politically inconclusive. A lengthy history of the Vietnamese conflict depicted in a series of violent tableaux was framed by the dilemma of a British journalist sent to cover the war. The dilemma remains unresolved in the second act in a succession of encounters with symbolic figures: the liberal, the artist, the addict, none of whom has any positive answer. The final scene is the most negative; a long speech by Glenda Jackson which accuses the emotionally and politically impotent (by implication, the British audience, us) of wishing the war in Vietnam to go on. The only answer is to increase the violence and destruction, by calling for the war to come to Britain, so that napalm will rain on English lawns. Images of fire predominate, from the opening mimed self-immolation of a Buddhist monk to the burning of a butterfly at the conclusion (a piece of theatrical illusion that fooled the RSPCA.) This time, instead of advancing on the stalls, Brook's cast stayed silently on stage, as though daring the audience to leave.

Brook's attempt to transfer the sincerely felt liberal guilt of his cast to the audience was generally derided, no doubt because almost without exception the audience was already fully aware of its responsibility and impotence towards Vietnam. In early performances the first act ended with the cast as moaning, blinded war victims (expressed by wearing paper bags over their heads) who descended into the auditorium beseeching people to help them find the way out. This scene (later cut) was too much for the critic Irving Wardle, writing in *New Society*. 'Like other things in the show it conveys a sense of moral superiority which no one, actors included, has any right to assume.'

Morally superior or not, *US* marks a particular moment. Brook's conclusion appears to have been that the theatre was an inadequate vehicle for direct political statement. His next production was Seneca's *Oedipus*, in a new text by the poet Ted Hughes, for the National Theatre. In 1968 he went to Paris to do experimental work with an international group of actors, but was interrupted by the political upheavals in May, and it was not until 1971 – by which time he had directed a striking *Midsummer Night's Dream* for the RSC – that his International Centre for Theatre Research finally came into being. Their first project, for the Shiraz Festival in Iran, involved the creation by Ted Hughes of an entirely new language that would escape the tyranny of conventional meaning and be appropriate to universal theatrical communication.

What is important here is the extent to which the experiments of the Theatre of Cruelty had opened up new means of expression, but at the expense of rational discourse. The tension between political statement and theatrical effect in *Marat/Sade* and *US* was to be revealed once more in extravagant gestures of the counter-culture. At the same time the theme of violence, the violence of governments – as in Vietnam, and the violence of the artist towards the forms he had inherited, was coming to the fore. Such a situation breeds its own conflict and confusion, and however much he was criticized for it, Brook's failure to provide any answer to the dilemma of Vietnam accurately reflected the dilemma of his audience. As he said in 1968, 'every element in it [*US*] had come into being just for the particular cross-section of London that sat in the Aldwych Theatre in 1966.'

The first issue of *International Times* was published on Friday 14 October 1966, the day after *US* opened. It led with a front-page review by Charles Marowitz which attacked the play for its 'romantic liberalism'. A new radicalism was in the air; the launching of Britain's first underground newspaper marks the point at which the counter-culture acquired a recognizable voice.

Though the first of a new kind of publication in England, *International Times* came from a long tradition of small-scale publishing that goes back at least as far as the development of the steam press. *IT* (for the owners of *The Times* objected to the use of the full title) drew partly on the experience of newspapers like *Peace News* and the anarchist weekly *Freedom*, and partly on the tradition of the little magazine. It differed from its literary antecedents in that it was able to take advantage of the new cheapness of offset photolithography, while the burgeoning economy of the counter-culture gave it a ready market. The first issue had a print run of 5,000, in 1968 it reached 50,000 copies per issue.

IT's forerunners were a crop of magazines that sprouted all over Britain in the late 1950s. As we shall see, these were unlike the handful of literary magazines that had managed to keep going through the narrow Fifties and enjoyed semi-official status as part of the established literary culture. Few were published in London or took much notice of it; they were often hand-produced on duplicating machines; their life was ephemeral and their readership sometimes little larger than the circle of contributors and their friends. But their very cheapness and simplicity gave their creators freedom to experiment and express their enthusiasms. Anyone who felt they had something to say in print could launch a magazine, and many people did. In 1959 Michael Horovitz launched *New Departures* from Oxford; Gael Turnbull and Michael Shayer launched *Migrant* from Worcester; and Barry Miles, a future editor of *IT* published his first magazine, *Tree*, while an art student in Cheltenham. These, and magazines like *Poetmeat* (Blackburn), *Underdog* (Liverpool), *Outburst* (London), *Sidewalk* (Edinburgh) catered to the coffee-bar bohemias such as nurtured the Liverpool poets and pop groups. These are only the pioneers: John Noyce's *Directory of British Alternative Periodicals 1965–74* has 1,256 entries, from *Aardvark* to *Zoar*.

The more persevering developed from cyclostyled, hand-stapled bundles into printed and bound magazines, and their editors founded small presses: the Migrant press had actually preceded *Migrant* in 1957; *Poetmeat* spawned Screeches Publications; Tom Raworth of *Outburst* founded the Goliard Press, eventually taken over by Jonathan Cape Ltd. After Raworth's departure from Goliard he was published by Asa Benveniste's Trigram Press, founded in 1965. In that year Deirdre and Stuart Montgomery decided to launch a magazine, but found themselves immediately

becoming book publishers instead. Their first title, *Loquitur*
(1966) was the first British publication for the 65-year-old Basil
Bunting, who had become the focus of a small cult at the Mordern
Tower Poetry Centre in Newcastle, opened by Tom Pickard in
1964. The Association of Little Presses, formed in 1966 with
fifteen members, grew to over a hundred.

The new magazines looked not to London, but to San Francisco,
where Lawrence Ferlinghetti's City Lights Press (1956) formed a
focus for the American Beat movement. The Beats had established their own version of McLuhan's global village in New
York, on the West Coast, in Paris, Tangiers and London. The
poetry of Allen Ginsberg, Gregory Corso, Michael McLure, Gary
Snyder, Robert Creeley and Charles Olson rejected the bland
materialism of official culture and substituted a sometimes joyful,
sometimes self-destructive hedonism that broke free of social
constraints, just as their verse broke free of conventional metre
and rhyme. Jazz stimulated a new lyricism, open forms, a poetry
of chant and breath, and the young British poets who were
rediscovering the modernism of Ezra Pound and Bunting after
the conservatism of the Movement, followed their American
models by writing specifically for performance. As Michael Horovitz put it, 'Jazz: sacred river, deeply embedded in the American
idiom, was a seminal influence for many of us: underground
movement, living mythology and international language of our
upbringing: which addressed its primal message to the whole
world – and through which all could speak.'

The new poetry was rough, dynamic and inter-active; it broke
down the categories dividing poetry and music, and the separation
between poet and audience.

Jazz-and-poetry readings became a regular feature of an underground network; these anarchic but essentially celebratory affairs
were important forerunners of the conferences, teach-ins and
demonstrations of the later Sixties, and as the Liverpool poets
showed most effectively, they escaped the conventional patterns
of literary life. In 1960, after meeting the poet and jazz player
Pete Brown at the Beaulieu Jazz Festival, Michael Horovitz
launched 'Live New Departures' in order to present regular jazz
and poetry concerts, funding the intermittent publication of *New
Departures* from the proceeds. Looking back in 1965 on some 500

performances, Horovitz observed: 'Liverpool and Newcastle and other towns with a thriving club scene, a multi-racial late-night population and widespread unemployment tend to provide the most intelligent, fresh and responsive audiences; college and literary society platforms the most tired, jaded and inhibited.'

The distance between this developing, though still amorphous, world of readings in pubs, clubs and art schools and the world of the recognized literary magazines can be measured in a survey by Peter Levi published in *Encounter* in February 1963. *Encounter* was of course part of that established world, but Peter Levi was well aware of the need for a thriving sub-culture of magazines to keep literature alive. His comments must be seen in the context of a general decline in reviewing and literary discussion in the 1950s and 1960s. Weeklies like the *New Statesman* and the *Spectator* were paying less attention to literary topics, and book reviews were getting less space in the newspapers. Looking back in 1971 in *The Social Context of Modern English Literature*, Malcolm Bradbury commented that what he called the literary dialogue 'has on the one hand, consolidated into a few ventures and, on the other, diminished in range'.

This was certainly Peter Levi's view in 1963. He concludes his article for *Encounter* with a protest against

the sophisticated, sensitive, talented poetry which is occupying too much of the space that ought to go to more naked and experimental writers. . . . It reflects not only the drowsy and timid tastes of literary editors, but the steam-roller effects of the British examination system: this is the poetry not exactly of an upper class, though a social category could also be found for it, but of the class educated in grammar or public schools or universities, and it mirrors their dull self-involvement, their pretentious language, and their sheep-like segregation from popular life.

This narrowness is reflected by the predominantly academic and critical – as opposed to experimental – bias of the dozen magazines he names: the 'unashamedly academic' *Review of English Literature*, the 'chaste, classic, decently learned and mildly brisk' *Critical Quarterly*, and even the critical standards 'so high as to be frightening' of Ian Hamilton's recently founded magazine *The Review*. In all this the influence of the academic tone set by the Movement poets of the 1950s can be seen at work. Indeed, the Movement writers published by *Listen* seemed to constitute the only coherent group with control of its own magazine, but 'we are all too familiar with the wry, urbane poet's *persona* of a dying culture coughing up its syntax like a haemorrhage.'

Outside university poet circles the *London Magazine* had 'attained the odd position of having a sort of official status.' In 1961 its founder John Lehmann sold the magazine to Alan Ross, who introduced a new format and added features on theatre, painting, cinema and music. Levi comments 'criticism of this magazine is criticism of conventional literary life.' Although Levi mentions the Cambridge-based *Delta* and the Poundian *Agenda*, he could only find evidence of other strands of writing in *X* (which had just died after seven issues in three years) and the bilingual *Two Cities*, launched in 1959 in Paris and London, and featuring Lawrence Durrell, Henry Miller, Anäis Nin, Gregory Corso, and William Burroughs. 'If anything of real experimental interest were to appear in an English little magazine, this would probably be where.'

Peter Levi makes no mention at all of any of the post-1959 magazines where the new writing of the Beats and their British followers was already on display. For all of his criticism of the academic bias of the established journals and his gentle mocking of the *London Magazine*, his own tastes were traditional and metropolitan. *Stand*, relaunched by Jon Silkin from Newcastle in 1960, is dismissed as 'provincial'. He seems unaware of the international scale of the concrete poetry movement and of Ian Hamilton Finlay's magazine *Poor. Old. Tired. Horse.*, launched from Edinburgh in 1962.

It would be wrong, however, to present the little magazines Peter Levi acknowledged and those he ignored as entirely opposed. Outside the immediate circle of the Movement poets there was a growing revolt against modesty and control towards a greater expressiveness, of which the Beats were the most extreme examples. In the *London Magazine* in 1962 Julian Mitchell asked 'Why *is* British poetry so nicely, charmingly, diffidently dull?' The answer was that not all of it was, as *A Group Anthology* (1963) and A. Alvarez's *The New Poetry* tried to show. As was said in *In Anger* (p.185) the 1962 edition of Alvarez's anthology was more prescriptive than descriptive, but his polemical introduction 'Beyond the Gentility Principle' claimed to detect a new urgency in the work of the Americans John Berryman and Robert

Lowell, and of British poets like Ted Hughes, Thom Gunn and Peter Redgrove, even if the anthology also includes Movement poets such as Philip Larkin and Kingsley Amis.

Alvarez makes points that would be familiar to Steiner and Laing:

What, I suggest, has happened in the last half century is that we are gradually being made to realize that all our lives, even those of the most genteel and enislanded, are influenced profoundly by forces which have nothing to do with gentility, decency, or politeness. Theologians would call these forces evil, psychologists, perhaps, libido. Either way, they are the forces of disintegration which destroy the old standards of civilization. Their public faces are those of two world wars, of the concentration camps, of genocide, and the threat of nuclear war.

Wars have always been with us, but the twentieth century has produced mass society, mass cruelty, and the imminence of mass destruction, while psychoanalysis has made us recognize 'the ways in which the same forces are at work within us.' Lowell and Berryman wrote poetry which coped openly with the quick of their experience, experience sometimes on the edge of disintegration and breakdown.

Alvarez's case looked much stronger in the revised edition of *The New Poetry* in 1966, when he was able to add poems by Peter Porter, Jon Silkin, George Macbeth, Ian Hamilton and the Americans Sylvia Plath and Anne Sexton. Sylvia Plath had married Ted Hughes in 1956, but they separated in 1962 and she committed suicide in 1963. Alvarez later wrote that Plath, more than anybody, vindicated his argument that the emotional pressure exerted on the individual artist by the violent forces at work in the world had to be truthfully borne, even at the risk of self-destruction. He included in the revised edition Plath's 'Lady Lazarus':

> Dying
> Is an art, like everything else.
> I do it exceptionally well.

In August 1962 the publisher John Calder was the *eminence grise* behind a writers' conference at the Edinburgh International Festival. Calder, by birth a Scot, had started publishing seriously in 1957, and quickly established a reputation as the British publisher of the European and American avant-garde. Besides Henry Miller and Robert Creeley, he published the French *nouveau roman* authors: Nathalie Sarraute, Alain Robbe-Grillet, Margarite Duras, and the works of Artaud, Ionesco, Arthur Adamov, Fernando Arrabal, Peter Weiss and, most important of all, Samuel Beckett. In 1960 the new Obscene Publications Act had been successfully tested when Penguin Books were acquitted of all charges for publishing *Lady Chatterley's Lover*, and this had made it easier to publish 'difficult' books, but there were few signs of a British contribution forthcoming to the international modernist movement. The Edinburgh conference was part of his plan to launch a new British school of writing that would be reflected by the Calder list.

Assisted by Sonia Orwell and a young American, Jim Haynes, who had recently started the first ever British paperback bookshop in Edinburgh, Calder assembled a group of distinguished writers in Edinburgh University's McEwan Hall to discuss the present and future of the novel, Scottish writing, censorship, and the hardy perennial, 'The Writer and Commitment'. The discussions were held over five afternoons in front of an audience of 2,000. British writers included Angus Wilson, Lawrence Durrell, Colin MacInnes, Rebecca West, Stephen Spender, Rosamond Lehmann, L. P. Hartley, Simon Raven and David Caute; there were contributions from India, Ceylon, Greece, Holland, Austria and Yugoslavia, though the expected Russian delegation did not attend. It was the Americans – Mary McCarthy, Norman Mailer and Henry Miller – who attracted most attention.

Miller in fact had little to say in public, beyond pronouncing that the novel had been 'dead for at least a hundred-and-fifty years.' But Mary McCarthy startled the audience on the first day by referring to another American delegate as, along with Vladimir Nabokov, the one hope for the future of the novel. His name was William Burroughs, and it is extremely unlikely that either he, or the book she referred to, *The Naked Lunch*, had ever been heard of by most of those listening to her.

Burroughs was an ex-heroin addict who had published one novel, *Junkie*, in 1953 before moving to Tangiers, where he started work on the manuscript that became *The Naked Lunch*. In 1957, the year Burroughs obtained a cure for his addiction in

London, Allen Ginsberg drew the attention of the Parisian pornographer-publisher Maurice Girodias to Burroughs's work, but it was not until 1959 that *The Naked Lunch* was published by his Olympia Press. The text is more a compilation of violent, homo-erotic fantasies, drug-dreams and paranoid projections than a novel in the accepted sense of a narrative, but it constructs an absurd world where the will to life has become, in the hands of the rulers, a perverted will to power. Drugs and sex are both metaphors for the commodity-fetishism which governs all human transactions in a monstrous universe.

Sections of *The Naked Lunch* had begun to appear in magazines from 1958, notably in the first issue of *New Departures*, and the Chicago magazine *Big Table*, which attracted the first of the obscenity cases which dogged the novel throughout the 1960s. Appropriately, Burroughs's dust-dry voice was first heard in Edinburgh during the discussion on censorship. His contribution outlined a theme that was to become increasingly emphasized as the debates of the decade developed. Anticipating Herbert Marcuse's *One-Dimensional Man* (1964), Burroughs discussed censorship in terms of the threat of sexual licence to mass production. While 'the bourgeois capitalist world' hated sex, advertising and popular fiction were 'channelling the sexual instinct into production and purchase of consumer goods'. Censorship is a matter of sexual politics. The psychologist Wilhelm Reich (whose work was then virtually unknown outside specialist circles) had been prevented from conducting serious research into sex; Reich had been exiled from several countries and had died in a Federal prison for his pains.

Censorship, said Burroughs, was thought-control, thus introducing the major theme of *The Naked Lunch* and his later writings. The existence of a world conspiracy to dominate and exploit is a science-fiction fantasy that grew out of his legitimate paranoia as a drug addict and homosexual, but words themselves are treated as part of the system of manipulation and control. Thus, although words were his medium, they had to be attacked in some way. He wrote in *The Soft Machine* (1961), 'Cut word lines – Cut music lines – Smash the control images – Smash the control machine – Burn the books – Kill the priests – Kill!!!'

Burroughs had taken his own advice and begun to produce texts by cutting them up. (Although it is a literary collage, he did not use the method for *The Naked Lunch*.) While staying in the Parisian hotel favoured by the Beats at 9 Rue Git le Coeur in 1959 he watched the American painter Brion Gysin cut up newspaper articles to make texts for *Minutes to Go*, a collaboration between Gysin, himself, Sinclair Beiles and Gregory Corso. Burroughs immediately recognized the possibilities of the technique. He, Brion Gysin and the British film-maker Anthony Balch also experimented with film, notably the performance film *Bill and Tony*, in which images were projected onto faces, and the collage of Burroughs themes in *Towers Open Fire*. Burroughs alluded to these experiments at Edinburgh when in the final day's discussion on 'The Future of the Novel' he explained the cut-up and fold-in method to a bemused audience. 'If writing is to have a future, it must at least catch up with the past and learn to use techniques that have been used from some time past in painting, music and film.'

The cut-up method, which Burroughs used for *The Soft Machine* and *The Ticket that Exploded* (1962), took a series of texts, his own or other people's, cut them, usually into four, and then pasted them together in a different order and read off the results. The fold-in similarly folded a page in half and set it against another, extending to writers the flash-back and flash-forward used in films. Thus 'the *déja vu* phenomenon can be produced to order', while cut-ups even allowed collaboration between the living and the dead. Burroughs stressed that although these techniques allowed for chance and multiple choice, 'I edit, delete and rearrange as in any other method of composition.' He evidently exercised more control than might be supposed, but he insisted that the texts so created were clearer than the originals he used. Like all techniques, cut-up and fold-in would be useful to some writers and not to others; none the less 'a new mythology is possible in the space age. The future of writing is in space and not in time.' .

The allusion to space is important, for the space of Burroughs's science fiction is inner, not outer. He had begun his speech by describing himself as 'a map maker, an explorer of psychic areas. To use the excellent phrase of Mr Trocchi, "as a cosmonaut of inner space".' Burroughs was acknowledging that he was not alone in his explorations; Alexander Trocchi had also startled the audience with his claim that 'modern art begins with the destruction of the object. All vital creation is at the other side of nihilism. It begins *after* Nietsche and *after* Dada.'

Trocchi, like Burroughs, used heroin, but unlike Burroughs he continued the habit until his death in 1984. Born in Glasgow of Italian parents, after wartime service as a seaman, he studied philosophy at Glasgow University but fled what he called – in the course of a spectacular argument with the poet Hugh McDiarmid during the discussion on Scottish writing – all 'the turgid, petty, puritan, stale-porridge, Bible-class nonsense' and went to Paris in search of Henry Miller. There he became editor of the avant-garde magazine *Merlin* (1952–5), which published work by Beckett, Robert Creeley and Christopher Logue, among others. Like Christopher Logue, he supplemented his income by writing pornography for Maurice Girodias's Olympia Press, including a parodic fifth volume to Frank Harris's *My Life and Loves*, which in subsequent paperback editions has become absorbed into the original. Girodias's 'Collection Merlin' published Beckett's *Watt* and translations of Genet's *Our Lady of the Flowers* and *The Thief's Journal*. In 1955 Girodias published Trocchi's semi-autobiographical novel *Young Adam*. During his time in Paris Trocchi encountered the ideas of the International Situationists, for whose anarchist philosophy he became a conduit in the 1960s.

From Paris, Trocchi moved to New York, and in 1960 published *Cain's Book*, an autobiographical novel that revolves around his addiction. It opens with a quotation from de Sade, and the description of a fix. By his own account, in 1962 Trocchi crossed the border into Canada using false papers, and made his way back to Scotland, bringing with him a wife and child. Calder was about to publish *Cain's Book* in Britain, and the Edinburgh conference served to launch him and Burroughs on the British public. (Burroughs's *Dead Fingers Talk*, a bowdlerized amalgam of his first three novels, was published by Calder in 1963, *The Naked Lunch* in 1964.) At a press conference in Edinburgh Trocchi caused a scandal by admitting his addiction, and it was here that he coined the phrase 'cosmonaut of inner space', the phrase that subsequently has been taken as Burroughs's own.

Although his novels do not go as far as those by Burroughs, Trocchi was similarly trying to break out of the straight-jacket of conventional form. At Edinburgh he declared that 'the categories

103

of painting and the novel are no longer significant.' Thanks to the wave of experimentation at the beginning of the twentieth century, 'the destruction of the object came about: in painting, non-objective abstraction, in writing the anti-novel. The vital poetic substance that once flowed naturally into these forms finally burst out and couldn't be contained.' The appropriate attitude for the artist was now 'tentative, intuitive and creative passivity. A spontaneity leading to what André Breton called the found object. A found object is at the other end of the scale from the conventional object. To free themselves from the conventional object and thus to pass freely beyond non-categories, the twentieth-century artist finally destroyed the object entirely.'

Little of this can have made much sense to Trocchi's audience or to many of the delegates; the chief theme of the conference became the conflicting roles of the writer as realist and humanist, and the writer as suffering individual who bore witness to a general anguish through the struggles of his own soul. Trocchi, who at one stage announced provocatively, 'I am only interested in lesbianism and sodomy. . . . It is the question of a man alone', plainly belonged to the latter group. But he and Burroughs had begun to urge, not just the retreat from the word that Steiner feared, but its annihilation.

The theme of 'the death of the word' continued in John Calder's second Edinburgh conference in 1963, this time given over to drama. Again it was a distinguished occasion, under the chairmanship of Kenneth Tynan, with contributions from J. B. Priestley, John Mortimer, Arthur Adamov, Joan Littlewood, John Arden, Alain Robbe-Grillet, Max Frisch, and the Polish critic Jan Kott, whose essays *Shakespeare Our Contemporary* (published in English in 1964) had a profound influence on Peter Brook and other British directors. But it was again the Americans who stole the show in a spectacular manner. 'Happenings' were a verbal and visual collage, where the ideas of Artaud, the demonstrations of the Dadaists and the experiments of American abstract expressionists were brought together in New York in the late 1950s as a distinct art form, more the province of painters than dramatists. Two leading exponents, Allan Kaprow and Kenneth Dewey were guests at the conference, and with the help of Charles Marowitz they devised a happening for the last day.

It was brief: there was a wail of bagpipes, the sound of recorded voices from earlier in the conference, and a naked girl art student was trundled in a wheelbarrow along the gallery above the conference hall. Its effect was out of all proportion to its substance (there was even an unsuccessful prosecution). Kenneth Tynan denounced happenings as 'totalitarian' and 'apocalyptic'. Martin Esslin commented in *Encounter*: 'Six days of intensive argument, hundreds of speeches, six Third Programme broadcasts, dozens of thoughtful press reports on the conference – all utterly obliterated by a forty-second appearance of a nude in a public place. . . . Is there significance here for our *kultur*-critics?' In one sense the event succeeded in destroying the object, for John Calder's projected 1964 poets' conference was cancelled by the authorities as a result.

After the Edinburgh writers' conference of 1962 Trocchi moved to London; the young American bookshop-owner Jim Haynes stayed to start the Traverse Theatre Club. It was in Edinburgh that 'fringe theatre' – the term applied to the independent productions students and others presented 'on the fringe' of the official Edinburgh Festival – first found a permanent home. Little theatres and clubs had long existed in London, but most had decayed, while the Arts Theatre Club served as an annexe to the West End. The Traverse was an original venture, not simply for its policy of presenting new plays all the year round, but because it was an attempt to create a complete cultural environment. In a narrow building on the Royal Mile Haynes created a tiny seventy-seat theatre, an art gallery run by the Italian-born Scot Richard Demarco, a restaurant and a bar. Haynes 'saw it from the beginning as a social centre open morning, noon and night, where people could have a drink or lunch, see an exhibition, go to the theatre, meet each other. The social aspect of it was just as important as what was going on in the theatre.'

The only comparable institution in London was the Institute of Contemporary Arts, which had a small suite of rooms in Dover Street. There was a bar and gallery and the ICA also put on readings, discussions and small concerts. ('Live New Departures' appeared there regularly from 1964 to 1966). But the atmosphere at the ICA was more inward-looking, cosy and staid. The size of London caused the literary and artistic network to be informal and dispersed, though there were always natural organizers trying to draw the strands together. In the northern suburb of Hendon the concrete and 'soundtext' poet Bob Cobbing had founded the Hendon Experimental Art Club as early as 1951; in 1954 it became the Hendon Group of Painters and Sculptors and in 1957 simply Group H. Bob Cobbing also ran the Writers' Forum of Arts Together, a section of the Finchley Society of Arts, and with John Rowan ran the intermittent poetry magazine *And*, whose first issue is dated 1954, and fifth 1969. The project developed into the Writers' Forum Press, which published a hundred titles in the ten years after 1963. (In 1966 Cobbing helped to form the London Film Makers' Cooperative.)

The first Writers' Forum publication was *Limbless Virtuoso* (1963), by Keith Musgrave and Jeff Nuttall. Nuttall also exhibited with Group H, alongside John Latham and Bruce Lacey. In November 1963, inspired by the example of William Burroughs, Nuttall began producing *My Own Mag: A Super-Absorbent Periodical*, a typed and cyclostyled magazine that followed the cut-up and fold-in procedures of Burroughs and added some burn-through effects of his own. But as Nuttall describes in his account of the development of the underground up to 1968 in *Bomb Culture*, the magazine was not an end in itself. Disenchanted by the failure of CND, Nuttall had become involved in a project to found a 'committed' art group that would confront the problems of living in the shadow of imminent destruction. The plan was to set up an environmental exhibition, but there were difficulties in finding a location, so *My Own Mag* began as 'an example of the sort of thing we might do. My intention was to make a paper exhibition in words, spaces, holes, edges and images which drew people in and forced a violent involvement with the unalterable facts.' As an artist Nuttall was interested in the visual effects of cut-ups, but he saw what such collages could lead to. 'The first step . . . was the dislocation of the word, the main line of power control. A writer, Burroughs was well situated to sabotage language.'

In January 1964 Nuttall met Burroughs in London, when Burroughs was allowed entry to the United Kingdom for fourteen days for the hearing of a libel case against *Time* magazine for its review of *The Naked Lunch*. (He won, but was awarded only five guineas damages.) In May 1964 Burroughs began contributing cut-ups to *My Own Mag* under the title 'Moving Times', which

Nuttall described as 'a programmed assault on reality'. Though produced in very small numbers, *My Own Mag* also attracted attention in other quarters. In the summer of 1964 Nuttall began to receive the typewritten sheets of Alexander Trocchi's *Sigma Portfolio*. Trocchi too was looking for a way to synthesize the avant-garde in art and politics.

For Trocchi, the 'sigma project' meant 'a possible international association of men who are concerned individually and in concert to articulate an effective strategy and tactics for . . . cultural revolution.' He set about its creation by circulating friends and contacts with a series of typewritten pamphlets and manifestos, which were to be assembled as the *Sigma Portfolio*.

The project began in July 1964, and although Trocchi was still proselytizing for the scheme in *IT* in 1966, the written materials peter out in December of that year. The last item in the *Sigma Portfolio*, number 28, is the pamphlet produced by Timothy Leary to promote the activities of the LSD-taking community he started in up-state New York, named the Castalia Foundation after Herman Hesse's mythic society in *The Glass Bead-Game* (1943). (Leary's periodical, *The Psychedelic Review* promoted the use of the term – meaning mind-expanding – if not the drug, world-wide.) Item 17 is a 'list of people interested', with the caveat 'the persons named are in no sense a group; they wear no badge and possess no card of membership; they are INDIVIDUALS who have, at one time or another, expressed serious interest in the possibilities implied in the sigma experiment.' Lord Goodman is listed as legal adviser, so the caveat is justified, but the fifty names provide a first sketch of the counter-cultural network.

It is transatlantic: Lawrence Ferlinghetti, Allen Ginsberg, Norman Mailer, Timothy Leary, William Burroughs; at its centre is a group of radical poets and artists: Tom McGrath, Michael McClure, John Latham, Jeremy Moon; there are links with an older generation: Felix Topolski, Colin Wilson; there are contacts with other cultural entrepreneurs: Jim Haynes and Joan Little-wood, then promoting her fun palaces; there are also contacts with radical psychiatrists: R. D. Laing, and his colleagues David Cooper and Aaron Esterson. Laing's paper 'The Present Situation', given at the 6th International Congress for Psychotherapy in August 1964, is item 6 in the *Portfolio*. Trocchi also lists

Michael Hollingshead, the English artist who first introduced Leary to LSD, and who returned to London in September 1965 to set up the World Psychedelic Centre in Pont Street. (The Centre closed following Hollingshead's conviction for drug offences in March 1966.)

It is difficult to judge how far Trocchi's ideas penetrated beyond this circle, or even within it, but his two most important statements, 'The Invisible Insurrection of a Million Minds' and 'Sigma, a Tactical Blueprint' did reach a wider audience through being reprinted in the *Journal of the Architectural Association* and the *City Lights Annual*. Appropriately, 'The Invisible Insurrection' opens with a quotation from Artaud: 'And if there is still one hellish, truly accursed thing in our time, it is our artistic dallying with forms, instead of being like victims burnt at the stake, signalling through the flames.'

Trocchi proposed a non-political revolution in consciousness: 'the cultural revolt must seize the grids of expression and the power-houses of the mind.' A revitalized art – which did not yet exist – would help to generate and be generated by this revolt. At present 'art anaesthetizes the living; we witness a situation in which life is continually devitalized by art' which, with the exception of jazz, has degenerated into passive spectacle. Even Dada was killed off by being narrowed down to an art movement. To create the new art, artists (and he alludes to Centre 42) must have control over their own means of expression.

The chief source of Trocchi's ideas is the French Situationists' 1960 *Manifeste Situationniste*, a translation of which is item 18 in the *Portfolio*. The Situationist International was founded in 1958, a non-organization claiming to be without leaders which, while anti-communist, synthesized Marxist and anarchist revolutionary ideals. Their chief target was the consumer society, to which they opposed a philosophy of 'joy'. (The Situationists had links with student groups in Germany, Italy and Berkeley in California, but their chief success was in Strasbourg, where their activities helped to foment the Paris events of May 1968.) The Situationists had a touching belief that the problems of production had been solved, and that what was needed was a revolution in distribution. In Trocchi's version of their manifesto in the *Sigma Portfolio*:

Automation, and a general 'socialization' of vital goods will gradually and ineluctably dispense with most of the necessity of 'work': eventually, as near as dammit, the complete liberty of the individual in relation to production will be attained. Thus freed from all economic responsibility, man will have at his disposal a new *plus-value*, incalculable in monetary terms, a *plus-value* not computable according to the accountancy of salaried work . . . PLAY-VALUE. What is becoming is *homo ludens* in a life liberally constructed. There is no solution within the conventional economic framework.

The phrase anticipates by a decade the title of Richard Neville's primer for the counter-culture, *Play Power* (1970). Trocchi echoes the Situationists in 'The Invisible Insurrection' when he accepts that the problem is no longer one of production, but of leisure. The alienating distinction between work and life must be dissolved, so that the whole of existence is a form of art. In 'Sigma: A Tactical Blueprint' this becomes 'a new conscious sense of community-as-art-of-living; the experiment situation (laboratory) with its "personnel" is itself to be regarded as an artefact, a continuous making, a creative process, a community enacting itself in its individual members.'

Three myths can be seen at work: first the traditional alienation of the artist from society that can be resolved only by reintegration as a separate community of artists, either as a bohemia or a secret cell. Secondly, that the achievement of this community will not just make art possible, but a new form of art that breaks down the old formal categories, and so the distinction between art and life. Finally, there is the myth of the affluent Sixties, which touches even a self-exiled artist like Trocchi: the economic problem to be faced was not work, but leisure, not production, but distribution. In this respect, although totally opposed to the commercial, celebratory and affirmative 'curious cultural community' of the King's Road, in 1964 Trocchi shared their optimism, as he shared their desire to remove social restraints on drugs, sex, and personal expression.

Trocchi could not describe the art that would result from his cultural revolution, since the conditions for its production did not yet exist. The first step would be for a group of like-minded souls to withdraw from the city to an appropriate spot where 'we shall foment a kind of cultural jam session: out of this will evolve the prototype of our *spontaneous university*.' The idea of a retreat is as old as *The Decameron*; the immediate model for the community was the defunct Black Mountain College in North Carolina that had seen the collaboration of artists like Merce Cunningham, John Cage and Robert Rauschenberg in the 1950s.

The original building will stand deep within its own grounds, preferably on a river bank. It should be large enough for a pilot-group (astronauts of inner space) to situate itself, orgasm and genius, and their tools and dream-machines and amazing apparatus and appurtenances; with outhouses for 'workshops' large as could accommodate light industry; the entire site to allow for spontaneous architecture and eventual town planning.

There is an element of fantasy in this description, brutally destroyed by the events of a weekend in the summer of 1964 when Trocchi and like-minded friends did indeed withdraw to Braziers Park, a Quaker community in Oxfordshire, to discuss the sigma project. The party included R. D. Laing, David Cooper, Aaron Esterson, Tom McGrath, Bob Cobbing, John Latham, Clancy Sigal, and Beba Lavrin, a former assistant at Centre 42. The weekend is described by a disillusioned Jeff Nuttall in *Bomb Culture*. Instead of holding serious discussions the group bickered, drank heavily, and terrorized their hosts. On Saturday night Nuttall was woken by a strange smell.

I opened the lounge door. John Latham met me with a steady staring eye. There's something about Latham at such moments that is mad beyond madness. A staring immovable shocked and shocking inner violence. Latham had taken a book (an irreplaceable book belonging to a pleasant little Chinese friend of Alex's) stuck it to the wall with Polyfilla, and shot black Aerosol all over the book and wall in a big explosion of night. . . . Until breakfast-time John reassured me that [their hosts] had given him permission to do a mural. Later it caused serious mental distress to aged community members. That Sunday morning it stood, overlooking the talk, a stark, beautiful, violent emblem to pure action, the most graphic condemnation possible of our evasive ineffectual waffle.

The psychiatrists, who had their own plans for an alternative community, withdrew from the project. In June 1965 the Philadelphia Foundation, a charity set up by Laing, Cooper and Esterson in the previous year, took a lease on Kingsley Hall, a former community centre in Bow, and turned it into a psychiatric commune. Cooper had already experimented with an 'anti-psychiatry unit' at Shenley Mental Hospital, but it was easier to operate outside the formal structures of health care. The principle purpose of Kingsley Hall was to allow patients to work through their crises in an atmosphere where there was no rigid line between patient and counsellor, or between 'sane' and 'insane', and where madness was seen as an inner voyage towards rebirth. The experiment attracted visits from artists, writers and film-makers, and Kingsley Hall became another link in the chain of counter-cultural centres until it closed in 1970.

The artists persevered with a scheme to give sigma some visual form. The bookseller, later publisher, Tony Godwin had opened a paperback bookshop, Better Books, in the Charing Cross Road and employed first the poet Bill Butler and then Bob Cobbing as manager. While the shop became one of the few reliable places to find avant-garde books and magazines, the basement was made available as a meeting-place. 'Better Books Writers' Nights' were inaugurated with a panel discussion between Peter Brook, John Arden and Adrian Mitchell on 'The Theatre and its Future', but events rapidly became more anarchic. Ken Dewey and Charles Marowitz performed happenings there, and early in 1965 the sigma group began work on the long-discussed environmental exhibition.

The overall plan for 'The sTigma' came from Group H member Criton Tomazos, but individual sections were built by Bruce Lacey, John Latham, Nick Watkins, Keith and Heather Musgrave, Dave Trace and Jeff Nuttall. In spite of tensions and conflicts similar to those at Braziers Park, the exhibition opened in February 1965. Nuttall describes the result as 'propagandist rather than art'. (Ill. 6.)

The entrance to the sTigma was through three valve-doorways lined with old copies of *The Economist*. The last you could just squeeze through, but not back, no return. The corridor this led to was lined with hideous bloody heads, photos of war atrocities, Victorian pornographic cards, tangles of stained underwear, sanitary towels, french letters, anatomical diagrams; the passage narrowed into complete darkness – tin, glass, wet bread, plastic, sponge rubber, then a zig-zag corridor of polythene through which you could glimpse your goal, a group of figures. They were gathered around a dentist's chair which had itself been turned into a figure, with sponge-rubber breasts and a shaven head. On the seat

111

of the chair was a cunt made of a bed pan lined with hair and cod's roe. Detergent bubbles spluttered from between the slabs of roe, which remained spluttering and stinking for four weeks . . .

In March, they tore it all down again, with relief, for the horror of the exhibition had as violent an effect on its creators as the spectators who vandalized it, or added graffiti which revealed a sadistic enjoyment of the images of disgust with the modern world that had been created. The Better Books basement, however, continued in use, and in October 1965 Criton Tomazos exhibited his scheme, 'The Cage', and in 1966 Nuttall created his environment 'The Marriage'. Nuttall was responsible for introducing the recently formed People Show to the basement where, as we shall see, they created the prototype for alternative theatre, but when Hatchards took over Better Books in August 1967 the basement activities were swiftly shut down.

Stimulated rather than deterred by events like the sTigma, the underground continued to expand. In April 1965 Jim Haynes, following disagreements at the Traverse in Edinburgh, moved to London and was encouraged by the Arts Minister Jennie Lee and Lord Goodman to open a London Traverse at the Jeanetta Cochrane Theatre, a small and unsuitable building next door to the Central School of Art in Holborn. Haynes was given a grant by the Arts Council, and secured the backing of an impresario, Frank Coven, who was looking for material to transfer to the West End. Haynes, Michael Geliot and the designer Ralph Koltai were artistic directors, Charles Marowitz an associate. Their big success was Marowitz's 1966 production of Joe Orton's black farce *Loot*, which transferred to the Criterion, and briefly to Broadway, but in spite of a mixed programme of new plays, jazz, underground films and happenings, it was difficult to create the free and easy social atmosphere of the Edinburgh Traverse in a building designed exclusively as a theatre, and Haynes moved on at the end of 1966.

The first truly public demonstration of the new spirit of celebratory improvisation came on 11 June 1965, when, at a week's notice, members of the sigma group joined with *New Departures* to form a 'Poet's Cooperative' and hired the Albert Hall for the first

International Festival of Poetry. The star of the evening was Allen Ginsberg, who had arrived in England in May on a world tour, but the chief organizers, New Zealander John Esam and the Americans Daniel and Jill Richter also put on Lawrence Ferlinghetti, Gregory Corso, Paolo Leonni and Harry Fainlight. The English poets included Pete Brown, Anselm Hollo, Michael Horovitz, Spike Hawkins, Tom McGrath, Christopher Logue, George Macbeth and Adrian Mitchell. Simon Vinkenoog, the founder of *sigma nederland*, came from Holland and Ernst Jandl from Austria. Three communist poets were due to appear, the Chilean Pablo Neruda, the Cuban Pablo Fernandez and the Russian Andrei Voznesensky. But Ginsberg had recently been expelled from Cuba and made a rumbustious visit to Poland, and in the event only Voznesensky turned up, and he did not read. Thanks to advance publicity from television, seven thousand people came to the reading, which lasted four hours. For Alexander Trocchi, who acted as compère, this was an hour of triumph. (Ills. 7, 8, 9.)

Even the *Times Literary Supplement* had to concede that the reading 'made literary history by a combination of flair, courage, and seized opportunities.' It was recognized as important, not so much for the poems themselves, which were often interrupted, and sometimes inaudible, but the atmosphere created in the echoing vastness of the Albert Hall. *Wholly Communion*, the title of Peter Whitehead's film of the event, suggests its essence. At a press conference on the steps of the Albert Memorial to announce the reading the assembled poets produced a spontaneous collaged invocation to the spirit of William Blake, who had been adopted as their patron saint.

> World declaration hot peace shower! Earth's grass is free!
> Cosmic poetry Visitation accidentally happening carnally!
> Spontaneous planet-chant Carnival! Mental Cosmonaut poet-
> epiphany, immaculate supranational Poesy insemination!
> Skullbody love-congress Annunciation,
> duende concordium, effendi tovarish illumination,
> Now! Sigmatic New Departures Residu of Better Books and
> Moving Times in obscenely New Directions! Soul
> revolution City Lights Olympian lamb-blast!
> Castalia centrum new consciousness hungry generation
> Movement roundhouse 42 beat apocalypse energy-triumph!
> You are not alone!

Here was an international declaration of the formation of a new cultural network. As Michael Horovitz later wrote, 'What did happen – for whoever suspended disbelief – is that poem after poem resonated mind-expanding ripples of empathy – uncut and precious stones in a translucent pool. The buds of a spreading poetry internationale, the esperanto of the subconscious sown by Dada and the surrealists and the beats bore fruit.'

For Jeff Nuttall, who with John Latham had dressed in blue body-paint and a structure of books to perform another of Latham's attacks on the word, 'all our separate audiences had come to one place at the same time, to witness an atmosphere of pot, impromptu solo acid dances, of incredible barbaric colour, of face and body painting, of flowers and flowers and flowers, of a common dreaminess in which all was permissive and benign.' Flowers, public nudity, dope and – for a few – LSD, along with the sound of Allen Ginsberg's finger cymbals, were becoming the regular props of such quasi-mystical celebrations of community.

Not everyone, however, to use Horovitz's phrase, suspended disbelief. The poet and critic Edward Lucie-Smith likened the evening to 'a bad bull fight'. Adrian Mitchell won the loudest applause for his Vietnam poem 'To Whom It May Concern': 'Yet there was awareness that this was applause without catharsis, that the spectators were applauding the echo of their own sentiments, and willing themselves to be moved without truly being so – the stock response at work.' In his introduction to the anthology *Wholly Communion* Alexis Lykiard reveals another aspect of the evening when he describes the audience successively turning 'football crowd, Boy Scout rally, and wolf pack' during the reading by Ernst Jandl.

As his sound poems rose to a crescendo, a rhythmic furore aided and abetted by the claps and cries of the crowd, so, suddenly, the destruction of words and their conversion to a shouted, half-hysterical series of sounds became sinister – took on a Hitlerian aspect: the Hall became almost a Babel. It was perhaps the most extraordinary event of the evening: parody and warning, cacophony with its own logic, rational collapse of reason, and despair of communication communicating itself. Artaud, who understood the sanity of madness, would have relished it.

The underground was now out in the open. Within eighteen months its styles would be translated onto the High Street and its music pervade the airwaves in the summer of flower power. In June 1966 the Albert Hall was once again invaded by poets waving flowers when Michael Horovitz held his Festival of the New Moon: Robert Graves and Stevie Smith shared the platform with the Liverpool poets and Spike Milligan. But within the heady atmosphere of benevolence and celebration there were also gusts of violence and destruction. In painting, as in poetry, there were those who had evolved an aesthetic of violence which smashed the formal categories of art – and released sinister forces in the process.

This development involved a whole range of activities in the visual arts which crossed the formal divisions between painting, sculpture, theatre and music. There is a common root in Dada and collage. Collage led to three-dimensional assemblage and the creation of complete environments; Dada demonstrations suggested the inclusion of live performers to inhabit the environment. This implies that the 'happening' turned into theatre, but narrative was excluded from such 'event-art'. The first happening is credited to a composer, John Cage, who arranged a performance involving poets, artists and dancers at Black Mountain College in 1952. Cage's lectures at the New School for Social Research in New York in 1958 and his collaborations with Merce Cunningham and Robert Rauschenberg influenced a whole range of artists, besides musicians like the American La Monte Young, the Canadian Robin Page and the British Cornelius Cardew, all of whom challenged the formal definitions of what was and what was not music.

Happenings, which as we have seen, spread to Liverpool in 1962 and had such an exaggerated impact at Edinburgh in 1963, were central to the movement, but aspects of performance and environmental art already existed independently in Europe. The 'sTigma' of 1965 had grown out of the activities of Group H. Bruce Lacey (who also performed with the Alberts) showed his satirical robots, and John Latham his 'Skoob' (books spelt backwards) constructions/paintings. Latham, whose activities link the visual and verbal assaults on the word, started incorporating mutilated books in his work in 1955, and set light to his first skoob-tower – built of books and stuffed with fireworks – in 1958. His most notorious action, which caused him to lose his teaching post at St Martin's School of Art, was to chew up the school's copy of Clement Greenberg's *Art and Culture* and return it to the library in a bottle. The result, with its accompanying document-ation, now resides in a leather attache case in the Museum of Modern Art in New York.

Since one of the purposes of such art forms was to liberate art from the grasp of commercial dealers by producing works that were impossible to sell, its creators led a guerilla existence on the margins of the art world, and their efforts were generally ignored by the critics. Tomas Schmidt, a member of the international Fluxus group, remarked 'the traditional, neatly separated forms of presentation are no longer applicable. The newspapers always had big problems as to which of their critics should be the one for Fluxus – and often resorted to the gossip one.' The sole London gallery-owner to show interest in such work was the poet Victor Musgrave who had opened Gallery One in 1952. He had been a member of a surrealist group in Cairo in the 1940s, and gave the French neo-Dadaist Yves Klein his only London showing. In 1962 the movement in Britain towards performance art received a powerful stimulus when Musgrave showed eight Fluxus artists under the title *The Misfits* at Gallery One.

Fluxus was the creation of American event-artist George Maciunas, who had taken part in happenings in New York before debts forced him to move to West Germany in 1961, where he got a job with the American army. In Dada fashion he issued manifestos and published a periodical, *Fluxus*, which like the *Sigma Portfolio* and *My Own Mag* helped to establish an inter-national network of contacts: Ben Vautier in Nice, Dick Higgins in New York, Daniel Spoerri in Paris, the Korean Nam June Paik in Cologne and Josef Beuys in Dusseldorf. According to Maciunas,

FLUX ART – non art – amusement forgoes distinction between art and non-art, forgoes artists' indispensability, exclusiveness, individuality, ambition, forgoes all pretension towards a significance, variety, inspi-ration, skill, complexity, profundity, greatness, institutional and com-modity value. It strives for non-structural, non-theatrical, non-baroque, impersonal qualities of a simple, natural event, an object, a game, a puzzle or a gag. It is a fusion of Spike Jones, gags, games, Vaudeville, Cage and Duchamp.

Before returning to America in 1963 Maciunas organized a series of 'festivals' in Weisbaden, Copenhagen, Paris, Dusseldorf, Stockholm, Nice and London.

At Gallery One *The Misfits* 'included a labyrinthine black-out room, a fun-making machine shop and Ben Vautier living and sleeping in the window. Nothing was for sale, although small objects were given away.' At a Fluxus evening at the ICA Robin Page performed his 'Guitar Piece'; wearing a silver crash helmet. Page proceeded to kick a guitar out of the Dover Street gallery and, followed by the audience, punted it round the block of commercial art galleries in Cork Street and back into the ICA. (At a Fluxus 'Little Festival of New Music' at Goldsmiths College in 1964 Page performed his piece 'Shouting a Plant to Death'.)

Page, who taught for a time at Leeds College of Art, became a colleague of John Fox, one of the performers in the 'Festival of Anarchy' held by John Arden and Margaretta D'Arcy at their house in the Yorkshire village of Kirkbymoorside in 1963, a mixture of films, plays, poetry readings and concerts. Fox in turn came into contact with Albert Hunt, who taught at Bradford College of Art; there the performances became almost exclusively theatrical. Indeed, as we shall see in Chapter VI, two experimental theatre groups grew out of what was originally an art-directed movement: John Fox's Welfare State, and Mark Long's People Show, which began by performing material by Jeff Nuttall in the Better Books basement. By 1966 such cross-category developments seemed almost usual. The Filipino artist David Medalla, who had launched the Signals Gallery in 1964 as a centre for kinetic art, emerged as the leader of the Exploding Galaxy, a dance group.

Attempts to break down the formal categories of art (and by implication the social structures which exist to enforce them) must, as in the case of Burroughs's dislocation of the word with cut-ups, involve attacks on the materials of art themselves. One answer to the problem of producing unexploitable work was 'auto-destructive' art. The principle practitioner in London was Gustav Metzger, who published his first auto-destructive manifesto in 1959 and developed a technique for spraying acid on nylon: the result was an action painting that disappeared before your eyes. And if smashing a guitar sounds familiar, note that Metzger was Pete Townshend of The Who's most-admired tutor at art school. Metzger described auto-destructive art as 'a slow time-bomb to be placed in Bond Street and equivalent "*centres-de-luxe*". Autodestructive art is *public-art*. We want monuments to Hiroshima – where the material is squirming, writhing, where heat-bursts puncture the material.' Metzger – a founder member of the Committee of 100 – brings the avant-garde aspects of works like 'the sTigma' into direct relation with politics. 'Auto-destructive monuments [and his reference is to the monks in Vietnam who burnt themselves alive in protest at the war] contain the brutality, the over-extended power, the nausea and unpredictability of our social systems.'

Metzger was a leading spirit in the Destruction in Art Symposium, a month of meetings and performances that brought many of the exponents of event-art to London in September 1966: the ZAJ Group from Spain, Hermann Nitsch and the Viennese Institute for Direct Art, Wolf Vostell from Cologne, Al Hansen, Ralph Oritz and the American-Japanese artist Yoko Ono from New York. Yoko Ono's first show in New York in 1960 included the 'instruction' work 'Blood Piece: use your own blood to paint. Keep painting until you faint (A). Keep painting until you die (B).' It was at an exhibition of her 'Unfinished Paintings and Objects' at the Indica Gallery in 1966 that she met John Lennon. The notorious 'Bottoms' film – a montage of bare behinds – followed in 1967.

British contributors to the Destruction in Art Symposium included Cornelius Cardew and the artist Mark Boyle, whose work extended from exact reproductions of randomly selected square feet of the earth's surface, to creative archeology, and to performances such as *Son et Lumière for Bodily Fluids and Functions*, when Boyle and his wife 'extracted all the available fluids from ourselves on the stage and projected them onto ourselves and the screen to the accompaniment of the amplified sounds of our bodies.' DIAS got off to a bad start when the launching press conference, banned from the Jeanetta Cochrane Theatre, had to take to the streets, causing firemen and police to be called to the South Bank, where John Latham had fired a skoob-tower. (Ill. 10.) This event was mild in comparison with Hermann Nitsch's 'Abreaktionspiel', performed at St Bride's Institute.

The carcass of a lamb was ritually paraded, nailed, hit, manhandled. Its entrails were produced, offered to the audience: one performer put them inside his trousers and pulled them out by his fly buttons. Simulated blood was poured over the carcass and a film projected onto it. This showed a penis, with a cord attached to it, moving from side to side. Every now and then there was a cacophony of shouting, stamping, banging and trumpeting.

The performance was watched by the police. As organizers, Gustav Metzger and John Sharkey, gallery director of the ICA, were charged with mounting 'an exhibition of a lewd, indecent and disgusting nature' and fined £100. Plainly the authorities did not care for such monuments.

The first issue of *International Times* was as critical of the Destruction in Art Symposium as it was of Peter Brook's *US*, complaining that 'it should have been an historic occasion, instead it was riddled with bad planning and fear', and summing it up as 'embarrassment everywhere; blood and ego-mania'. As with *US*, it would appear that the Symposium had not proved radical enough. *IT* proposed to strike out in a new direction, and the first editorial warned against going down the old road.

A standard London process seems to be: things have to change . . . let's shake up this city . . . we'll start an avant-garde theatre (or bookshop, or gallery, or political group, or newspaper, and so on) . . . but first we need bread . . . try the Arts Council . . . try and find a backer . . . set up a charity, maybe. A year later, if he's lucky, the change-maker has his particular Round House. Now he has to spend maybe another year in getting over all the legal hangups before he can use it. Finally, once he's ready to start, having played the money-power game, what does he do? He starts to play the art game. Now that he's got a theatre, it must succeed as a theatre. Now that he's got a bookshop he must sell books. Further, he is likely to have committees, a board of directors, an endless stream of meetings to contend with . . . his project is caught in its own terms.

IT hoped to avoid such traps because, probably unconsciously, its founders had recognized that the economic and creative conditions were right for the paper to survive. The underground press was already flourishing in America; in Britain the youth market had reached such a size that a section of it, principally students, would be eager to sustain a newspaper that criticized the affluence in which they were sharing. Record companies in particular would be ready to advertise, and there was an increasing number of events, following the Albert Hall reading, which called for publicity among the constituency to which *IT* would appeal. The difficulty of advertising the London Traverse effectively and cheaply was one of the reasons for Jim Haynes to start discussions on launching *IT*.

The original editorial board of *IT* consisted of Haynes, Jack H. Moore, Barry Miles, John Hopkins, Michael Henshaw and Tom McGrath. Their past activities and inter-connections trace a typical map of the underground. Haynes and Jack Moore were Americans who had worked together at the Traverse (Moore's main interest was the theatre, later video, though he had once run a detective agency in Dublin). Haynes and Barry Miles had met even earlier, when Haynes was still running his paperback shop; later Moore would stay with Miles in London. Miles (who dropped his Christian name entirely) had continued to publish since he had first launched *Tree* in Cheltenham in 1959: *Hoard, Night Scene* (1963), *Darazt* (1965), *Long Hair* and *Long Hair Times* (1966). *Darazt*, a limited edition anthology, included a short story by William Burroughs and three collages by Miles which anticipate the graphic design of *IT*. It also carried photographs by John Hopkins, a photo-journalist who had worked for *Town* magazine and the *Observer*, who became *IT*'s first production manager. Hopkins and Miles collaborated on a number of projects using Miles's company Lovebooks; the company secretary was Michael Henshaw, a former tax inspector who became secretary to Centre 42, and the financial adviser to many leading figures in the underground. Lovebooks Ltd became the publishing company for *International Times*.

In October 1965 Miles, after a period as manager of Better Books, had opened a bookshop at the Indica Gallery in Mason's Yard, launched by the pop singer Peter Asher (whose sister Jane was Paul McCartney's girlfriend) and John Dunbar, husband of singer Marianne Faithful. In September 1966 the Indica Bookshop moved to Southampton Row, where the London Traverse had a script office, and in October the basement of Indica became the editorial offices of *IT*. All that was lacking was an editor. Tom McGrath, Glasgow-born, a former features editor of *Peace News* who was also a veteran of the Braziers Park meeting, the Albert Hall reading and the riotous Commonwealth Poetry Conference at Cardiff in September 1965 attended by the French Situationist

Jean-Jaques Lebel, was summoned out of rural retreat in Wales to take charge.

Although the development of offset photo-lithography had made printing relatively cheap, it was still necessary to play the 'money-power game'. Haynes was the expert fund-raiser, and he secured a personal loan of £500 from the 'underground' millionaire Victor Herbert, a former associate of the dubious American financier Bernie Cornfeld, and a regular patron of the counter-culture. The day after publication, on Saturday 15 October, *International Times* was launched with a huge party at the Round House. *IT* later reported

2,500 people dancing in that strange, giant round barn. Darkness, only flashing lights. People in masks, girls half-naked. Other people standing about wondering what the hell was going on. Pot smoke. Now and again the sound of a bottle breaking. Somebody looks as if he might get violent. There was a lot of tension about.

The participants and spectators trace another pattern. Paul McCartney was there, so was the record producer Mickey Most. Michelangelo Antonioni, the director of *Blow-Up*, came with Monica Vitti; Peter Brook was somewhere in the crowd. Bob Cobbing and the London Film Makers' Co-Operative projected Kenneth Anger's *Scorpio Rising* and William Burroughs's *Towers Open Fire*. A pop-painted American limousine from the Robert Fraser Gallery had been driven into the arena. The music came from the first 'psychedelic' bands, The Soft Machine (a Burroughs reference), and Pink Floyd. The group had started playing earlier in the year in Notting Hill Gate, where John Hopkins had organized two local festivals as part of an attempt to launch a London Free School. (The inspiration came from an American psychiatrist, Joe Berke, a contributor to the Destruction in Art Symposium who had been involved in the Free University of New York.) Mark Boyle, who was working with the light-and-sound workshop started at Hornsey College of Art in 1962, had devised a system of slides using a mixture of oil and coloured water which, activated by the heat of the projectors, threw constantly shifting patterns of light over the walls and the dancers. The audience was drowned in noise and colour; those who were not already drunk, stoned on pot or tripping on LSD found themselves transported into the magical atmosphere of an opium dream.

Thus in October 1966 the earnest solemnities of Arnold Wesker's Centre 42 gave way to the carnival of the underground.

'It was like an enormous party, night after night.' So Jim Haynes recalls the era heralded by *International Times*. In January 1967 *Oz*, glossy and printed in colour, appeared in London, its Australian editor Richard Neville committed to the revolutionary potential of sex, drugs and rock'n'roll: 'The most memorable experiences underground are when you connect to the music, to the light show, happening and movie simultaneously, while being stoned and fucking all at the same time – swathed in stereo headphones, of course.'

Opportunities for such multiple pleasures were themselves multiplying. In December 1966 John Hopkins's previously peripatetic 'spontaneous underground' settled on Friday nights at the Blarney Club in Tottenham Court Road as UFO (Unidentified Flying Object). Such profits as there were went to support *IT*. Arthur Brown and Jimi Hendrix joined Pink Floyd and The Soft Machine as regular attractions. In September 1967 an exposé in the *News of the World* forced UFO's flight to the Round House, but its magic evaporated in the face of the curious and hostile attention of television and the press, and it folded. A second, more commercial form of UFO opened as the Electric Garden in Covent Garden in June 1967; there was a fight on the opening night between supporters of Yoko Ono and the Exploding Galaxy who were booked to perform, and those who wished to carry on drinking. In August, under new management, it reopened more peaceably at the same address as Middle Earth. Alexandra Palace, the Round House and the Albert Hall were all the sites of festivals and celebrations: *The Fourteen Hour Technicolour Dream* at Alexandra Palace; *The Alchemical Wedding, A Gathering of the Tribes* at the Albert Hall.

As the underground surfaced, it boosted the commercial exploitation of the youth market. The summer of Swinging London was succeeded by the summer of 'flower power', its efflorescence the Beatles album *Sergeant Pepper*. The black and white of David Bailey's ruling images dissolved into fluid pools of colour and splashes of light. (Coincidentally, BBC2 started transmitting in colour in 1967.) Following the Beatles' conversion from hard-edge rock'n'roll to electronic transcendentalism, 'psychedelic' bands took off; all over Britain shops selling caftans, scarves, bells, candles and joss sticks proliferated in imitation of more up-market, down-the-King's-Road boutiques like Granny Takes A Trip. Designers Michael English and Nigel Waymouth, known collectively as 'Haphash and the Coloured Coat' were busy creating swirling, sensual patterns for record sleeves, posters and shop-fronts.

In the summer of 1967 Jim Haynes at last found a suitable building for the experiment in art-and-life-style that he had been dreaming of since the Traverse. His association with *International Times* had lost him the blessing of Lord Goodman, who disapproved of its pro-drug line. Haynes resigned from the London Traverse to set up on his own, without any official backing to constrain him. He rented a small, two-storey building at the north end of Drury Lane in Covent Garden, and called it the Arts Lab. On the ground floor a gallery led through to a tiny adaptable theatre designed by Jack Moore; in the basement there was a seatless cinema, the audience arranging themselves on tiers of foam rubber. The programming was as free-form as the events – concerts, dance, plays – continuing until one or two in the morning, and all night at weekends. Inevitably, as the wandering tribes of Europe found their way to Drury Lane, the Arts Lab also became a doss house. On the strength of Haynes's ingenuity, the fees from film crews and the donations from rich supporters, the Arts Lab lived from hand to mouth until the energy and goodwill ran out in the autumn of 1969. In spite of the eventual financial collapse, Haynes was unrepentant.

The thing that the bookshop, the Traverse, and the Arts Lab had in common was their humanity. There were not fixed hours of entering or leaving, people came in, and lingered and talked and met each other. I keep stressing this fact that love affairs began there but it's true. That's probably why the puritan elements in the country were against the bookshop, the Traverse and the Arts Lab. The ecstasy count, the sensuality count, was very high.

The Arts Lab gave a home to the growing fringe theatre: the People Show transferred there after the Better Books basement was closed down; David Hare and Howard Brenton launched their Portable Theatre, and Pip Simmons began performing there. The Arts Lab spawned imitators in Manchester, Birmingham,

Brighton and elsewhere. By 1969 there were fifty such projects. In the first *Arts Lab Newsletter* Jim Haynes explained 'A lab is a *non-institution*. We all know what a hospital, theatre, police-station and other institutions have in the way of boundaries, but a lab's boundaries should be limitless.'

Michael Kustow, the new director of the ICA, tried to introduce some of the Arts Lab's free-wheeling atmosphere into their new premises which opened in April 1968 in the unlikely setting of the Royal Mall. The sensuality count at the opening party was high, at least.

At one end of the gallery a wiry-looking avant-garde ballerina per-formed something erotic with a brass bed-stead, wearing a Napoleonic hat; in the centre, the African band had got into its swing, and a girl was undulating above people's heads, her belly-button drawing the lecherous gazes of esteemed public faces. It was a sight for the pen of Hogarth or George Grosz, had they been able to make the not-so-distant leap from raffish eighteenth-century Covent Garden or lush Twenties Berlin to observe the plumage and the motley, the hip gyrations and the greedy glances of this patchwork parade. As night fell, the wine took hold, and at 2 a.m. everyone – young, old, straight, freaky, stiff-suited or near naked – joined in a Bacchanalian dance to the electronic voodoo of an impassive rock group.

CHAPTER 4

The Dialectics of Liberation

'I'd love to turn you on.'

The Beatles *Sergeant Pepper's Lonely Hearts Club Band* (1967)

When Richard Neville came to sum up the salient features of the underground in *Play Power* (1970) he produced a list that follows Richard Hamilton's prescription for Pop, but emphasizes the anarchic at the expense of the creative: 'Alive, exciting, fun, ephemeral, disposable, unified, uncontrollable, lateral, organic and popular.'

In *International Times* No. 10 in March 1967, Tom McGrath editorialized: 'we have reached a stage at which it is now possible to talk about a "we" despite the multi-direction and anti-uniformity of our movement. . . . It is essentially an inner-directed movement – a new way of looking at things – rather than a credo, dogma or ideology.' The new way of looking at things was essentially permissive; 'the search for pleasure/orgasm covers every field of human activity, from sex, art and inner space, to architecture, the abolition of money, outer space and beyond.' All this was 'post/anti-political – this is not a movement of protest but one of celebration.' Above all, it was 'essentially optimistic. . . . The new approach is to make positive changes wherever you are, right in front of your nose. The weapons are love and creativity – wild new clothes, fashions, strange new sounds.'

McGrath's examples link the optimism of the underground to the commercialism of Swinging London and the King's Road. As

125

we saw in chapter II, the energy, 'classlessness' and even sometimes the rock'n'roll of the young was welcomed and exploited by
the Establishment. The apparently apolitical ideology of the
underground was the leading edge of a wave of liberalization that
– in the personal sphere at least – created a genuinely more
permissive society. This was assisted by government legislation
both in sexual and family matters – homosexual law reform and
the legalization of abortion in 1967, the Divorce Act of 1969 –
and in the sphere of self-expression, with the abolition of theatre
censorship in 1968 and the decrease in practice of censorship of
erotica. (The abolition of the death penalty in 1965 was another
long overdue humane measure.) The alleged sexual licence of
young people, assisted by the spread of reliable contraception
through the Pill, though it alarmed some people, was of little
concern to the Government. However, as Jeffrey Weeks points
out in *Sex, Politics and Society* (1981), 'there was no official
endorsement of hedonism. There was in fact a strong element of
negative utilitarianism in the legislation, more concerned with
removing difficulties, and minimizing suffering, than in positively
enhancing happiness.'

As the young began to take control of their own affairs, and
make more overtly political criticisms of their society, certain
aspects of the youth culture appeared more subversive. The
emergence of wild rock musicians like Jimi Hendrix seemed
positively threatening. George Melly detects a split within pop
music itself in the summer of 1967, between a bland and erotically
sublimated popular music and a form that still expressed cultural
aggression.

On the one hand it had severed the links between pop in the kiddy-
mum-and-dad-Eurovision-song-contest sense and hard pop. On the other
it had made it clear that hard pop was anti-Establishment. There was no
danger after that summer of pop becoming officially acceptable. It was
tolerated but only just, its heroes were harassed at regular intervals and
that, from the teenage viewpoint, was enough to endorse its continuity.

The way in which rock'n'roll worried the authorities can be
measured in the pronouncements of Lord Goodman in his successive reports as Chairman of the Arts Council from 1965 onwards.
In 1966 he was concerned that 'the pop groups are winning the
battle' against those who would promote the arts as a means of

'teaching people what are the worthwhile things in life.' The next year's report reproduces parts of his speech to the House of Lords in April 1967.

> I believe there is a crucial state in the country at this moment. I believe that young people lack values, lack certainties, lack guidance; that they need something to turn to; and need it more desperately than they have needed it at any time in our history – certainly at any time which I can recollect. I do not say that the arts will furnish a solution, but I believe the arts will furnish some solution. I believe that once young people have been captured for the arts they are redeemed from many of the dangers which confront them at the moment, and which have been occupying the attention of the Government in a completely unprofitable and destructive fashion.

Lord Goodman is referring obliquely to the Government's attempts to control an alarming spread in the use of the third of the subversive trio of pleasures of the young. Sex and rock'n'roll could be tolerated, but drugs could not.

Since their use is an illegal activity, it is impossible to give precise figures, but there is no doubt that there was an increase throughout the Sixties in the use of hard and soft drugs. The available statistics reflect police activity and changing legislation. The number of known heroin addicts in Britain increased steadily after 1953, when there were 290, and accelerated in 1961. By 1968 there were 2,782. The consequences of the use of heroin were recognized by the underground as serious; the drug most at issue was cannabis. In the early 1950s the smoking of pot was largely confined to the West Indian community and a few jazz musicians – a teenager was charged with possession for the first time in 1952 – but from 1965 onwards prosecutions for cannabis offences increased rapidly; in 1967 they doubled to 2,393 and in 1968 they reached 3,071. In 1970 there were 7,520. In 1965 the hallucinogenic drug LSD, which was not at first illegal, began to appear in significant quantities.

As important as the increased use of drugs was the changed attitude among the young (and not so young) leaders of the underground which encouraged their use. Heroin addicts no longer concealed their addiction – Trocchi's contribution to the Edinburgh writers' conference is a case in point. The use of drugs was a caste mark: it defined the user as an outsider, while attaching him to a peer group of similar outsiders with their own language, style of dress and internal economy. Drugs were the vehicle for inner-voyaging; radical psychiatrists used LSD as a rapid means of tapping the 'unconscious material' of the mind. One of the unwritten books of the Sixties is a projected collaboration between Trocchi, William Burroughs and R. D. Laing on a definitive anthology of 'Drugs and the Creative Process'. If on occasion LSD revealed inner-world horrors rather than visionary splendour, the unpleasant effects were associated with the idea of experience through suffering. *IT* promoted the use of LSD with articles such as this, reproduced from *The Oracle of Southern California*:

Man's need to surrender is helped by psychedelic sacraments. Psychedelics are more aphrodisiac than scientific studies of fucking can ever show. The sexual energy aroused on acid is general, god-like, cosmic. Hence most people are not interested in merely genital fucking on an acid trip; they are fucking the universe.

The Society for Mental Awareness, set up to 'examine without prejudice scientific, social and moral aspects of psychotropic drugs use', and directed by the American Steve Abrams, tried to give drugs some philosophical respectability, and campaigned for the legalization of cannabis.

Not everyone in the underground was convinced of the beneficial effects of LSD. Jeff Nuttall's account of the period is coloured by the sense of a noble venture going out of control. In *My Own Mag* No. 15 in April 1966 (Nuttall was soon to transfer his energies to a comic strip for *IT*) he warned against the temptation to 'sail off into areas of consciousness where experience of the self is substituted entirely for experience of the world.' The movement was being distracted from its task of subversion – 'revolution by infiltration rather than confrontation' – by 'literature, art, pornography, underground movies, heroin or other quaint rural handicrafts.' His conclusion in *Bomb Culture* was that

once Lysergic Acid was launched as something other than mere pleasure, as a ready window on the Zen eternal, as a short cut back to the organic life, religion and wonderment, as an open road to Laing's lost self, it left art and Timothy Leary standing and took protest and pop with it.

128

'Drugs are an excellent strategy against society', he writes later, 'but a poor alternative to it. The same can be said of the nihilistic element in the philosophy and religion accompanying the drug culture.'

The response of the Government to the spreading drug culture was, as we shall see, to curb it with increased legislation. And although the general direction was away from censorship, there were occasions when the purely cultural activities of the under-ground brought them into conflict with the law. In 1960 the *Lady Chatterley* case demonstrated that it was indeed possible to defend a book accused of obscenity – defined under the 1959 Obscene Publications Act as a 'tendency to deprave and corrupt' – on the grounds of its literary merit; in 1964 the successful prosecution of the eighteenth-century erotic novel *Fanny Hill* showed that the floodgates had not necessarily been opened. In February 1964 copies of John Calder's British edition of Trocchi's *Cain's Book* were seized in a raid on a Sheffield dirty bookshop, and declared to be obscene. Calder appealed against the judgement, but lost. Lord Chief Justice Parker ruled that *Cain's Book* was obscene because it appeared to advocate drug-taking. There was 'no reason whatever to confine depravity and obscenity to sex.' As John Sutherland comments in his study *Offensive Literature* (1982),

Parker's decision was highly significant. It marked a new phase of obscenity-hunting in which the primary target would not be the work's text (for instance its incidence of four-letter words) but the *lifestyle* it advocated, or that was associated with its author or even its readership. If it was risking 'obscenity' to be a junkie and a beat, it was also soon going to be similarly risky to be a hippy.

In October 1964 John Calder published an unexpurgated edition of Trocchi's fellow cosmonaut's *The Naked Lunch*. In spite of heavy advance disapproval in the *Times Literary Supplement*, no prosecution followed. From 1966 to 1968 however, Calder was involved in the lengthy and expensive defence, from magistrates' court to the court of appeal, of Hubert Selby's *Last Exit to Brooklyn* (first published in America in 1964). Calder won his case, and the authorities gave up the use of the Obscene Publications Action against works that might sustain a literary defence. Instead there were other legal means of exerting control. As early as December 1965 Dave Cunliffe, the founder of *Poetmeat* and Screeches Publications, had been charged with sending indecent material through the post, and publishing 'an obscene article for gain'. The article was an anthology, *The Golden Convulvulus*, prepared in collage-style by the poet Arthur Moyse. Cunliffe's liberal defenders were unable to say the anthology had very much literary merit, and Cunliffe's defence led him into the dangerous waters of opinion on the precise limits of sexual freedom. *The Golden Convulvulus* was judged to be indecent, but not obscene; accordingly Cunliffe was fined £50 on the first count and exculpated on the second. As John Sutherland points out, the publishers of *Poetmeat* were on trial as much for their social attitudes (Cunliffe: 'I advocate complete sexual freedom and the constructive use of mind-illuminating chemicals') as the precise issue of pornography.

Nor were artists, alive or dead, immune. In 1966 the police seized a number of Beardsley reproductions in a Regent Street bookshop while a major exhibition of his work was running at the Victoria and Albert museum (though five originals of the offending illustrations to *Lysistrata* were viewable at the V & A only on special request). In September 1966 the Robert Fraser Gallery was raided and twenty-one drawings by Jim Dine were taken away. Fraser was fined £20 under the Vagrancy Act. As we saw, Hermann Nitsch's performance at the Destruction in Arts Symposium in the same month led to prosecutions.

Though presented as an issue of public safety and the protection of legally established monopolies, the Marine Broadcasting (Offences) Act of 1967, which shut down the offshore pirate radio stations that had flourished since Radio Caroline began transmitting at Easter 1964, was interpreted by the young as an act of censorship. The BBC was itself about to be brought to heel under the chairmanship of Lord Hill.

The Establishment showed it could be petty and contradictory. At the beginning of 1967, eager to catch the tide of 'youth', the Arts Council decided that it would appoint two 'junior members' to each of its advisory panels. The Literature Panel accordingly invited Barry Miles to join them, but within days Lord Goodman intervened. Miles's association with the drug culture through *International Times* made him unacceptable. The novelist Brigid

Brophy, a panel member, enquired if, had this been the eighteenth century and Samuel Taylor Coleridge had been on the panel, he too would have had to resign. In spite of a protest motion from the panel, Lord Goodman had his way.

As the guardians of traditional culture became more and more alarmed, drugs were increasingly the issue over which the authorities and the avant-garde came into critical conflict. One person's psychic exploration became another's criminal investigation. The literary issues were of no interest to the police, whose job it was to enforce the law, or to the majority of politicians, who were prepared to accept a reduction in censorship, but supported a series of legislative measures to curb drug abuse. The competition between the legislators and the ingenuity of those who would use drugs can be measured by the number of substances that came under control: in 1950 there were 33, in 1960 65, in 1970 106. The 1964 Dangerous Drugs Act introduced new offences in respect of cannabis and the 1964 Drugs (Prevention of Misuse) Act increased control over amphetamines – the preferred drug of the Mods who were looking for a means to stay awake all night rather than spiritual enlightenment. This act was modified in 1966 to make illegal the use of LSD, mescaline and psilocybin. The 1967 Dangerous Drugs Act further limited the powers of doctors to prescribe to addicts, but more importantly it gave the police extensive powers to stop and search suspected drug users, powers which they did not possess in relation to other offences. Negatively, in 1968 the Government rejected the recommendations of an official enquiry chaired by Baroness Wootton which sought to reinforce the distinction between hard and soft drugs, and decriminalize the use of cannabis.

The extension of police powers to stop and search caused the greatest aggravation, for the long hair, beards, beads and caftans which announced membership of the alternative society inevitably attracted the attention of the police. One of the earliest police raids of 1967, and one of the most inflammatory, was not under the new act, but under the Obscene Publications Act, demonstrating a link that both sides perceived. On 9 March the police raided the offices of *IT*, and showed as much interest in the contents of the ashtrays as of the subscription lists and editorial files. The result was considerable disruption for *IT*, which was reduced to producing a number of single-sheet 'guerilla' issues, but no prosecution followed. The principal casualty was the editor, Tom McGrath, who went underground shortly after writing his optimistic editorial for *IT* No. 10.

Another of *IT*'s staff, John Hopkins, came to be treated as an underground martyr when in June 1967 he was sentenced to nine months imprisonment for the possession of cannabis, and for allowing others to smoke it in his house. (This was a new application of the 1965 Dangerous Drugs Act, which hitherto had been thought to apply only to public places such as clubs.) Hopkins had been arrested in February, and in the same month the Sussex police, oblivious to any theory of the long front of culture, arrested art dealer Robert Fraser, and Mick Jagger and Keith Richard of the Rolling Stones in a raid on Richard's house. The trial in July became a *cause celèbre*. Richard was sentenced to a year's imprisonment for allowing his house to be used; Jagger got three months for the possession of amphetamines legally acquired in Italy. Jagger and Richard were allowed to appeal, but Robert Fraser, who had pleaded guilty to possessing heroin, went to jail for six months. The trial took on symbolic significance, right down to the respective costumes of those in court. As Angela Carter wrote in *New Society*, it was 'an elegant confrontation of sartorial symbolism in generation warfare: the judge in ritually potent robes and wig, invoking the doom of his age and class upon the beautiful children in frills and sunset colours'.

This treatment of the leaders of the new cultural community aroused liberal protests, notably *The Times* leader 'Who Breaks a Butterfly upon a Wheel' and 'legalize pot' rallies and advertisements in the national press. The advice bureau Release and information service BIT were set up in self-defence. More arrests followed a demonstration led by Suzy Creamcheese (an American famous for being famous) against the *News of the World*, which had helped to instigate the raid. There was plainly an element of revenge in the sentencing. The judge declared: 'There are times when a swingeing sentence can be a deterrent.' Richard Hamilton, for whom Fraser was a dealer, responded with the screenprint *Swingeing London* (Ill. 5). Following an appeal, Richard's conviction was quashed, and Jagger got a conditional discharge.

The police continued to harass the underground: Middle Earth was raided; Finch's pub in Portobello Road, the Morning Star in Kingston, Tiles in Oxford Street, and the Tudor Bar in Brighton frequently attracted police attention. In October 1968 it was shown that even the Beatles were not immune, when John Lennon and Yoko Ono were arrested on drugs charges. Lennon was fined £150 for possessing cannabis.

After the initial enthusiastic welcome to Swinging London, the patronage and the MBEs, it appeared that 'square' society had now decided to draw the line, and with increasing firmness, as police handling of demonstrations against the war in Vietnam showed. 'Vietnam' is the most convenient symbol of the growing sense of violence, both on the part of governments, and of those that opposed them. As we saw in chapter III, destruction of one kind or another was a vital element in the art of the avant-garde: destruction of forms, elimination of categories and the breaking of limits. This destruction was seen as a necessary liberation of the creative spirit, but it also paradoxically conveyed the imprisonment of the artist within a culture where the individual's capacity for destruction is microscopic in proportion to that of governments. As Jeff Nuttall put it: 'We were eaten up by repressed violence and we were soured by the constant terror of inconceivable violence being committed on ourselves and the rest of man.'

This repressed violence came out in works like 'the sTigma' or the fantasies of William Burroughs, in the risk of self-destruction through heroin addiction, or in the destruction of the creative impulse through drink and drugs. The myth of the outsider merged with the myth of the heroic guerilla, so that posters of Che Guevara hung for sale beside rock stars and Beardsley reproductions. There was a pornography of violence. The extravagant layout of *Oz* was violent, erotic, and its editors were not above reproducing images of torture and execution of Vietcong prisoners (as in issue No. 10) to create an impact that transcended political protest. The noise and aggression of rock music could be used to similar effect: Tony Palmer's television documentary *All My Loving* (1968) made dangerous equations between pop music, protest and violent images from Vietnam. In reaction, Pamela Hansford Johnson's *On Iniquity* (1967) linked the new freedoms with the Moors murders, in which two children and a teenager were the victims. 'We may be creating an atmosphere in our life, in "London, the Swinging City", as *Time* magazine has it, and in other urban centres, which may result in grave infection to our social health.'

The violence was internal as well as external, but R. D. Laing for one argued that the responsibility for that violence lay with a distorted society. 'Only by the most outrageous violation of ourselves have we achieved our capacity to live in relative adjustment to a civilization apparently driven to its own destruction', he wrote in *The Politics of Experience and the Bird of Paradise* (1967). 'From the moment of birth, when the stone-age baby confronts the twentieth-century mother, the baby is the subject of violence, called love, as its mother and father have been, and their parents and their parents before them. . . . We are effectively destroying ourselves by violence masquerading as love.' This inversion of accepted meanings extended to more general authorities. Laing believed that those in charge of mental health services operated a 'police state' and a 'guerilla war' against the sick.

The people who do this are the danger, but they don't see it that way. They're divorced from reality, but they think they are sane. They're the violent ones but they think that they are maintaining sanity, peace, law and order. Those of us who have seen through this to some extent can see that we have a system of violence and counterviolence.

It was to explore such themes that Laing, together with other members of the Philadelphia Foundation's 'Institute for Phenomenological Studies' organized a grand conference at the Round House in July 1967.

'The Dialectics of Liberation – Towards a Demystification of Violence' took over the Round House from 15 to 30 July. (A week early the building had housed an 'Angry Arts Week' in support of protest against the Vietnam war.) It shows the distance the line of thought suggested by Burroughs and Trocchi had travelled since the Edinburgh writers' conference of 1962. It also shows the underground turning towards the political: the only artists to make significant contributions were Julian Beck of the Living Theater, and Allen Ginsberg. But the conference retained a characteristically carnival atmosphere. 'We rebelled, we organized, we talked, we learned how to get high on oxygen, how to get stoned on human communication. Several people brought sleeping bags and actually lived there,' wrote A. M. Fearon in the anarchist paper *Freedom*. 'A pedal organ in one corner was in constant use. Impromptu poetry recitals were held. Poems were pinned up on the wall, and were joined by a set of charcoal drawings. Someone discovered an old piano frame in the yard and began playing it with two sticks: others joined in with metal pipes, milk crates, tin cans and produced a mind blowing sound . . .'

This ecstatic description contrasts with that of *International Times*: 'Ronnie Laing and Stokely Carmichael drew crowds of over a thousand and Stokely's Black Power rally was a surprise; instead of demystifying violence, the crowd cheered frenziedly at every mention of violence. Non-violent actions were booed – racism was once again affirmed.' *IT* may have been soured by being banned from sale at the conference, but it had placed its finger on an essential contradiction that was never resolved. Even David Cooper had to admit that it was 'a curious pastiche of eminent scholars and political activists.' By the end of the first week there was evidently an ideological split between the activists who wished to apply the techniques of third-world revolution, and a minority of more scholarly thinkers who sought to explore the notion of 'state violence'. As Roger Barnard observed in *New Society*, the organizers themselves could be oppressive, and exercised 'a very effective tyranny of the microphone.'

The Trinidadian-born Black Power activist Stokely Carmichael, then at the height of his insurrectionary reputation in the United States, spoke most fiercely for 'counter-violence'. He quoted Guevara on 'hatred as an element of the struggle, the relentless hatred of the enemy that impels us into effective, violent, selected and cold killing machines.' He clashed with Ginsberg over the revolutionary potential of hippies – 'we see them as neutrals, not as friends', and when the disagreements from the floor became too loud, a fight nearly broke out. Ginsberg – whose principal contribution to this discussion was the chanting of a mantra – recommended Burroughs's writing as 'politically speaking one of the best analyses of the present consciousness existing in the West.' In other sessions John Gerassi, Paul Sweezy and Ernest Mandel followed Carmichael's line in supporting terrorism and sabotage. The rhetoric of violence runs through David Cooper's closing address, even though he recognized the inappropriateness of violent action.

When we become conscious of our oppression we have to invent the strategy and tactics of our guerilla warfare. We deracinated white intellectuals, we who are bourgeois and colonizing in essence, even though some of us wear the spurious label of 'working-class origin'; we must realize that we cannot pretend to engage in clandestine operations aimed at subverting the system because we have not been bred in this sort of struggle. Certainly we have to keep some secrets, but on the whole our scene is illuminated by all the forms of artificial lighting that issue from our culture. What we have to do quite simply is to deploy all our personal resources in attacking the institutionalization of experience and action in *this* society.

There were more considered and less romantic contributions, from the French Marxist literary critic Lucien Goldmann, from Jules Henry, author of *Culture Against Man* (1963) who demonstrated the deliberately depersonalized effect of the American cultural apparatus, and from the anarchist Paul Goodman. Goodman's theme was the danger of excessive centralization, be it urbanization or 'professionalization'. Centralization and regimentation of the young – 'compulsory miseducation' – had brought about the alienated international youth movement that was proving itself aware of the spiritual and ecological damage being done to the planet. Goodman received a standing ovation, but the loudest applause was reserved for the new father-philosopher of the underground, Herbert Marcuse.

Marcuse, an elderly German refugee teaching at the University of California seems an unlikely candidate for this role, but his book *One-Dimensional Man* (1964) had brought him to prominence with the argument that even the most liberal societies – and especially the United States – were intolerably repressive. His case was that affluence had created a freedom from want that left mankind as the passive instrument of a dominating system. This reinforces its power by the creation of false needs which link exploited producer and privileged consumer. (There is a clear parallel with William Burroughs's drug-dominated universe.) The mass media and the welfare state encourage passivity, and even 'permissiveness' is in fact repressive, because it does not lead to the realization of true sexuality. In these circumstances the Marxist conditions for revolution no longer exist: the conflict of capital and labour is over and we have reached the end of ideology. Western society is becoming increasingly totalitarian as

136

all subversive ideas are squeezed out by the corporatized culture of television, radio, newspapers and mass-market paperbacks. The long front of culture, it would appear, leads to one-dimensional man, where art and language, as well as social welfare and affluence are modes of oppression.

At the Round House, having praised the abundance of flowers around him, Marcuse spoke on the need for liberation from this affluent but repressive society. Revolution was impossible, since there was no mass basis for one, and anyway, revolutions tend to replace one form of oppression with another. What was needed was an *imaginative* change that of necessity had to appear extraordinary.

If this qualitative difference today appears as utopian, as idealistic and as metaphysical, this is precisely the form in which those radical features must appear if they are really to be the definite negation of the established societies, if socialism is indeed the rupture of history, the radical break, the leap into the realm of freedom – a total rupture.

Such a change would release the creative impulses in mankind, in spite of the system of repression which appeared to keep them so powerfully in check. Marcuse was adapting the language of inner space when he called for 'a break in the continuum of repression which reaches into the depth dimension of the organism itself, or, we can say, that today qualitative change, liberation, involves organic, instinctual, biological changes at the same time as political and social changes.'

The crux of Marcuse's argument – which essentially follows that of *One-Dimensional Man* – was a passage that was bound to appeal to his audience. As a result of social, and indeed biological change a new ideal man would emerge, incapable of war and working in a new collectivity that reconciled art and technology. There is something of the Situationist theory of surplus play in Marcuse's utopia.

No longer subjected to the dictates of capitalist profitability and efficiency, no longer to the dictates of scarcity, which today are perpetuated by the capitalist organization of society; socially necessary labour, material production, would and could become (we see the tendency already) increasingly scientific. Technical experimentation, science and technology would and could become a play with the hidden – methodically hidden and blocked – potentialities of men and things, of society and

137

nature. This means, unblocked, unrepressed, one of the oldest dreams of all radical theory and practice, it means that the creative imagination, and not only the rationality of the performance principle, that creative imagination would become a productive force applied to the transformation of the social and natural universe. It would mean the emergence of a form of reality which is the work and the medium of the developing sensibility and sensitivity of man . . . it would mean an aesthetic reality, society as work of art.

Marcuse was not explicit as to how this change would come about. He warned that cultural suppression and manipulation was likely to increase. But signs of awareness of new values were there, and he flatteringly linked his audience to the oppressed when he located this awareness in 'non-integrated social groups, and among those who by virtue of their privileged position can pierce the ideological and material veil of mass communication and indoctrination, namely, the intelligentsia.' Marcuse emphasized that intellectuals were not a revolutionary class on their own, but served a preparatory function. The hippies – though 'much of it is mere masquerade and clownerie' – were already showing a serious revulsion against the values of the affluent society; their more political elements, the Diggers and the Dutch anarchist 'Provos' indeed demonstrated the appearance 'of new instinctual needs and values'.

Marcuse's paper proved eminently satisfying to the majority of his listeners: it confirmed that the liberal bourgeois state, with its apparatus of 'repressive tolerance' was in fact as oppressive as Fascist or Stalinist totalitarianism. The exercise of censorship and police power – however mild – demonstrated that consent was still ultimately obtained by force, and that parliamentary democracy was in essence a fraud. Instead, Marcuse offered an image of creative society which would be brought about, not by participation in the ordinary democratic processes, but by an internal revolution in consciousness. His conception of 'society as work of art' was indeed appealing, and it was plain that Marcuse intended his hearers to be at the forefront of that society. But Marcuse did not offer any solution to the problem of violence.

Nor did the conference as a whole. Those, such as Laing and Cooper, who wished to demonstrate the violent premises upon which society was built were trapped in the logical bind of the 'counter-violence' of revolutionaries like Carmichael. (Though logic itself could be dismissed as part of the repressive cultural impositions of the state.) These were preparing for a campaign of terror that would have little time for David Cooper's 'transcendental network of expertise' which would transform 'each institution – family, school, university, mental hospital, factory – each art form, into a revolutionary centre for transforming consciousness'. In so far as the use of psychedelic drugs was involved in this transformation, Carmichael was contemptuous of it. Cooper had announced that the purpose of the conference was 'to demystify violence in all its forms'; its effect however was to increase the mystification of violence among the participants. At this particular point of convergence the only unity was opposition to the *status quo*, a negative position that produced no solution.

The political consequences are described in the following chapter; the problem here is to trace their effects on the arts. The issue brings us back to the theme of violence in the words and images that have been described, and indeed to the reason for the popularity of Artaud. In a review of the *Marat/Sade* Charles Marowitz commented:

Artaud's theatre has two great fascinations for us today. First it is – despite his aesthetic harangues – *more* realistic than the current theatrical output – by which I mean, closer to the genuine feel of violence and hostility which nourishes our contemporary behaviour and ambitions and second, it contains the seed of a new and viable aesthetic, an alternative to the low-keyed copycat styles which glut our plays, films and television programmes.

In November 1965 William Gaskill's first season as artistic director of the Royal Court presented Edward Bond's *Saved*, in which a group of thugs stone a baby to death in its pram. Bond defended his play in the ensuing controversy by saying that this violent action was necessary if we are to understand the consequence of violence. He returned to this theme in his preface to the text of his even bleaker and physically crueller play *Lear*, published in 1971.

The stoning of the baby, he explained, was a metaphor for the moralized aggression in society which exists to discipline and dragoon the child into an alienated adult. (The echo of Laing is clear.) 'This is not done by thugs but by people who like plays condemning thugs.' We live in a permanent state of aggression brought about by the systematic deprivation of our physical and emotional needs. 'The whole structure becomes held together by the negative biological response to deprivation and threat – it is an organization held together by the aggression it creates. Aggression has become moralized, and morality has become a form of violence.'

Bond is writing of a public morality, rather than one of individual responsibility. The difficulty of such a position is that it appears to justify the very state of aggression which he seeks to condemn. Julian Beck's contribution to the Round House conference illustrates the case in point. In 1963 Julian Beck and Judith Malina's Living Theater had been evicted from their New York base by the tax authorities, and rather than compromise their anarchist and pacifist politics the group – a fluctuating commune of some thirty people – had gone into exile in Europe, wandering from city to city mounting performances that pushed further and further towards Artaudian extremes. At the Round House he explained, 'we are trying to reach the creative moment itself. . . . not the enacting of it, but the action of it on the stage.' The theatre had become a holy place: 'The actor-priest does not find the answer himself, but in communion with the spectator-participant.'

The problem for spectator-participants, however, as they discovered when the Living Theater performed at the Round House in June 1969, was that while they might be invited to take part in the sexual rituals of the troupe (Beck explained that there was 'a great deal of free sex and inter-community sex . . . a reasonable amount of multiple-party sex' plus homosexuality and lesbianism) they were also likely to be screamed at and insulted. As Marowitz bserved, 'an anarchist revolution based on the tenets of non-violence is not achieved through organized bouts of aggression which inevitably muster intellectual resistance.'

Beck's ultimate goal, he announced in 1967, was to abandon theatre altogether, and simply live communally somewhere like the Round House. This, we may speculate, would be a version of Marcuse's 'society as work of art'. The tendency of all these art forms which sought to convey internal or external violence, from the Living Theater to 'Abreaktionspiel' was ultimately to abandon the forms of art altogether. But such radicalism towards the forms of art did not dispense with the need for art – or the need for artists. In consequence the artist became the material upon which the work of art was wrought. But there was a major flaw in this approach, as A. Alvarez pointed out in his easy 'Extremist Art' in 1968:

Perhaps the basic misunderstanding encouraged by Extremist art is that the artist's experience on the outer edge of whatever is tolerable is somehow a substitute for creativity. In fact the opposite is true; in order to make art out of deprivation and despair the artist needs proportionately rich internal resources. Contrary to current belief, there is no short cut to creative ability, not even through the psychiatric ward of the most progressive mental hospital.

The danger was that the artist would become the victim of the aggression that he or she was trying to reveal in society at large. If the forms and categories of art, as previously understood, were indeed part of a system of cultural oppression, then they had to be destroyed. This can be most fruitful (and illuminating of the categories that are challenged) but also risky. As Alvarez wrote in *The Savage God* (a study of suicide and attempted suicide, including his own), 'What is involved then, is an artistic intelligence working at full pitch to produce not settled classical harmonies but the tentative, flowing, continually improvised balance of life itself. But because such a balance is always precarious, work of this kind entails a good deal of risk. And because the artist is committed to truths of his inner life often to the point of discomfort, it becomes riskier still.'

One risk is of the self-destruction of artists, destroying themselves as they tear the cultural categories down around them. Another is more insidious: with the destruction of art, the artist is not destroyed, but elevated, and the personality of the artist become a substitute for the forms of his art. This can be as harmful as critical indifference. The tragic paradox is contained in Alexander Trocchi's quotation from Artaud in the *Sigma Portfolio*: 'And if there is still one hellish, truly accursed thing in our time, it is our artistic dallying with forms, instead of being like victims burnt at the stake, signalling through the flames.' It reached its tragic absurdity when Yoko Ono said that she and John Lennon took heroin in 1968 'as a celebration of ourselves as artists'.

* * *

The paradox was to be underlined in the following years, yet it would be wrong to over-emphasize the negative and destructive elements in the underground at the expense of aspects that were more colourful and joyous. The underground was itself a kind of collage, and though the context of each was altered by the other, it was possible to select one element rather than another. The summer of 'The Dialectics of Liberation' was also the summer of *Sergeant Pepper's Lonely Hearts Club Band*.

The release of *Sergeant Pepper* in June 1967 marks the apogee of the Beatles' influence. In 1966 *Revolver* had signalled that their music was extending its range, and, with the song 'Tomorrow Never Knows', that their minds had been chemically stretched. *Sergeant Pepper* is the culminating collage of the Sixties.

The album has its thematic roots in that perenniel source for English literature, childhood; in this case the Beatles' recollections of Liverpool in 'Penny Lane' and 'Strawberry Fields'. It had been decided, however, to break new ground by treating the LP as one brand-new continuous work, and when these two songs were prematurely released in February as singles, the autobiographical theme had to be modified, for the songs could not now be used. After some desultory recording at the end of 1966, the Beatles discovered their alter egos in the fantasy identities of four circus bandsmen. The conception echoes the nostalgic world of Peter Blake and his fictional wrestlers and circus performers, and appropriately, when the album was completed, Blake was called in to design the sleeve.

The music is closest to Pop Art collage in 'Being for the benefit of Mr Kite', for the words are a 'found' object, taken from an old music-hall poster, and the swirl of steam-organ sounds is an internal collage created by the producer George Martin from lengths of tape cut up, and then haphazardly spliced. The residual autobiographical elements of domestic allusion and Lancastrian good humour – 'Vera, Chuck and Dave' – are enclosed by hallucinogenic, shimmering curtains of sound, a decadent oriental-ism slashed with the 'tangerine trees and marmalade skies' of 'Lucy in the Sky with Diamonds', which points to the group's discovery of the imaginative advantages of LSD. There are songs expressing loneliness and nostalgia, but no love lyrics as such.

Blake's sleeve, which contained a do-it-yourself Sergeant Pepper cut-out kit, extended the musical collage into a joke group

5. *Swingeing London*: Richard Hamilton's comment on the Jagger drugs trial, 1967

6. Environmental anguish: part of the *sTigma* installation by Jeff Nuttall and others, Better Books basement, 1965

'Spontaneous planet-chant Carnival!': the first
International Festival of Poetry at the Albert Hall, 1965
7. (*above*) Michael Horovitz

8. Allen Ginsberg,
with (right)
Simon Vinkenoog

9. Alexander Trocchi

photograph which mixes the devices of Bailey's *Box of Pin-ups* with Adrian Henri's 'Me'. The exotic, mustachioed, satin-uniformed Beatles of 1967 stand ironically beside the wax-work images of their clean-cut 1963 selves. Behind them crowd a gallery of cultural heroes and villains, from Bob Dylan to Aleister Crowley, from Karl Marx to Laurel and Hardy. (The figure of Gandhi was excised on the advice of Lord Goodman.) A row of cannabis plants escaped the lawyers' eagle eyes, but the reference to drugs in the refrain 'I'd love to turn you on' in the final track, 'A Day in the Life' was unambiguous. The song is a pendant to the work, and comes after the Lonely Hearts Club Band's finale. The words are a surreal jumble of private allusions, but in the concluding forty-two instrument single chord travelling from the instruments' lowest to highest register, the Beatles publicly marked a turning, not just from black-and-white to extravagant, piercing colour, but from outer, to inner space.

As the underground celebrated the conquest of inner space, attitudes towards them began to change. For the Beatles, the BBC banned 'A Day in the Life' from the airwaves; in August, unable to cope with his private life, their manager Brian Epstein committed suicide, and his death began the train of events that led to the dissolution of the Beatles' partnership.

In November 1967 the psychedelic bubble of economic opti-mism burst when Harold Wilson conceded a 14.3 per cent devalu-ation of sterling. In spite of an immediate improvement in the balance of payments, the prospect of long-term economic decline was confirmed. In March 1968 *Life* magazine's Henry Luce disposed of the euphoria displayed by *Time* two years before.

For one who arrived in Britain two years ago, at a time when Wilson's 'consensus' Government was riding high, when there was much talk of the steady homogenization of the class system, when 'swinging London' was at its frenetic zenith, it is hard to observe any salutory underlying trend which might, even in the long run, counter the deep economic woes which are so often curtly passed off as 'cyclical'. Among other things, 'swinging London' is dead.

Similar epitaphs began to appear as the end of the decade drew near. Some, like Nick Cohn, pushed the moment of nostalgia back towards its beginning. In 1969 he wrote, 'I have a memory of two fat years, 1964 and 1965, when you did nothing but run loose and waste time, buy new clothes and over-eat and gab, when you never thought you'd ever have to work in your life again. It was futile, of course, pop has always been futile, but it seemed elegant, it was easy living, and English pop was better than it's ever been, than it's ever likely to be.' Others saw the Sixties moving towards an apocalypse. Jeff Nuttall's *Bomb Culture* begins: 'between the autumn of '67 when I completed this manuscript, and the summer of '68 when I am writing this preface, young people, under various pretexts, made war on their elders, and their elders made war on them. The war continues.'

CHAPTER 5

Goodbye Baby and Amen

*'A student revolt is
primarily a cultural
revolt assuming
physical form.'*

Hornsey Art Students in *The Hornsey Affair* (1969)

The 'war' of 1968 is now so thoroughly over that it is tempting to dismiss Jeff Nuttall's introduction to *Bomb Culture* as no more than a symptom of the apocalypticism to which he, like many others at the time, was prone. Yet there was a sense of impending crisis; the spread of student revolts, guerilla wars in the Third World, the violence in Vietnam, the rise and fall of hope for change in Eastern Europe following Czechoslovakia's 'Prague Spring', all promoted the idea that some cataclysm was about to occur; one that was violently to be encouraged, or resisted. In several instances the war between the generations was real enough.

Although it is possible to trace the origins of a long-term economic crisis and its consequent social strains to this period, the conditions in Britain were lacking for a true civil war, for the crisis was not deep enough to pull the whole fabric of society apart. There was none the less a sense that things were coming to a head. In 1971 the Marxist historian Eric Hobsbawm described the 1960s as a 'pre-revolutionary period'.

Until the end of the 1960s capitalism functioned splendidly as an economic institution, probably better than any alternative at that time. What seemed to 'go wrong' in some profound but not easily specifiable sense was the *society* based on a capitalist abundance, and nowhere more obviously than in its stronghold, the United States.

Hobsbawm went on to point out that because the crisis was experienced as a social one, 'the fashionable critique of society ceased for a time to be economic and became sociological: its key terms were not poverty, exploitation, or even crisis, but "alienation", "bureaucratization", etc.'

Though our economic problems have since become severe, sociology, with its attention to cultural and institutional, as opposed to purely economic and political, factors has continued to supply us with our chief terms for a critique of the events of 1968 and after. Sociologists, rather than literary critics or art historians, have produced theories to account for the cultural upheaval, and we must perforce use some of the theoretical language of their critiques. Two writers in particular have sought to provide explanations, Bernice Martin, whose *A Sociology of Contemporary Cultural Change* appeared in 1981, and Stuart Hall, who has contributed extensively to joint studies of the social and cultural history of the period. Hall and Martin approach the subject from quite different points of view, but they agree both on the nature and location of the crisis: it was within the post-war generation, and in particular its intelligentsia.

As a Marxist, Stuart Hall explains the crisis in terms of the conditions of late capitalism. Through the mechanism of a cooperative consensus between the classes (such as was established in Britain in the 1950s) society, culture and the economy are managed in the interest of capital, to the extent that capital establishes a 'hegemony' which masks the coercive nature of the control it exercises. But, as he points out in *Policing the Crisis* (with Chas Critcher, Tony Jefferson, John Clarke and Brian Roberts, 1978) there are periods when '*the whole basis of political leadership and cultural authority becomes exposed and contested.*' (Italics his.) This is not necessarily at a moment of economic collapse or political revolution, but it is a moment when the authority of the state (which represents the interests of capital) is sufficiently challenged for consensus to break down. The crisis is not overtly economic or political, but it is cultural, and a 'crisis of hegemony' occurs. Hall further argues that the state wards off the political and economic threats heralded by such a cultural crisis by acting repressively.

146

The masks of liberal consent and popular consensus slip to reveal the reserves of coercion and force on which the cohesion of the state and its legal authority finally depends; but there is also a stripping away of the masks of neutrality and independence which normally are suspended over the various branches and apparatuses of the State – the Law, for example.

It is in this context that Jeff Nuttall's perception of a state of war between the generations should be understood.

Bernice Martin is not a Marxist and has no ideological commitment to the idea of class warfare and revolution. Rather (though political considerations hardly appear) the ideological thrust of her study is conservative. Her argument is that the crisis provoked by the counter-culture was part of a much longer-term struggle between the needs of society to impose limits on its members in order satisfactorily to function, and the need of individuals to express their desires and enjoy their pleasures.

The so-called counter-culture was advance warning of the much wider and less spectacular thrust of the Expressive Revolution into the whole hemisphere of personal/cultural activities in advanced industrial society. It was a specialist and exaggerated form of a phenomenon which is affecting all spheres of society, though to different extents and at different rates.

Martin believes that the struggle over the limits to expression – literally, where society draws the line – was played out with special significance in the field of popular music, where rock'n'roll offered the image, but not the substance, of revolt. Indeed, she dismisses the revolutionary pretensions of the underground.

The counter-culture of the 1960s looked revolutionary in its first flowering (hence the 'counter') and indeed was experienced as such by many of its early innovators. The wider society too was initially convinced of the 'revolutionary' nature of the new phenomenon, both because of its evident outrage and because so many of the counter-culture's practitioners declared themselves revolutionary. Yet underneath the red clothing was a beast of a different colour, or perhaps a chameleon able to take on *any* political colouring.

It is on this point that Bernice Martin and Stuart Hall converge: the counter-culture could not produce a political revolution. Hall, however, has a more penetrating explanation. It does not contradict Martin's reasoning; instead, it is possible to absorb her

147

arguments within his analysis. The counter-culture was not, as it claimed, a revolution against contemporary society, but an upheaval within it.

This point of origin *within* the crisis of the dominant culture may help to explain why the 'counter-culture' could not stand on its own as a political formation. Its thrust could be better defined as a 'systematic inversion', a symbolic upturning, from within, of the whole bourgeois ethic. Some of its sharpest engagements were engendered, not by taking 'another', path, but by pushing the contradictory tendencies from within contemporary culture to their extremes – by trying to subvert them from the inside, through *a negation*. This may also account for why the 'cultural revolution' oscillated so rapidly between extremes: total 'opposition', and incorporation.

The upheaval, Hall argues, was caused by one of capitalism's contradictions: in order to maintain the full production and employment enjoyed in the late 1950s and early 1960s it was necessary to promote consumption as fiercely as it was once necessary to promote the thrift and deferment of gratification that stimulated investment for production. Yet the myth that 'you've never had it so good' and all the appeals to pleasure and consumption in the swinging Sixties undermined traditional bourgeois discipline and restraint.

Hall is not being original in this. From the early 1960s sociologists had been pointing out the intimate connection between work and play, that it was *necessary* to consume in order to produce. In *One-Dimensional Man* (1964) Marcuse analysed consumption as a sophisticated form of social control. 'Play' becomes 'leisure', and thus we have the paradox of a 'leisure industry'. Note that one of Bernice Martin's indices of social change is the question of where the line is drawn between work and play.

Such a conflict or contradiction will first find its expression at the point where no clear division is possible between work and play: in art. Art carries both social and expressive values; it is equally a vehicle for religious utterance and frivolous entertainment, and most serious art operates ambivalently between those extremes. Thus the conflict of values in the late 1960s was experienced primarily through culture. In the early 1960s anxiety about national identity had been expressed as the cultural debate between high art and mass communications; as the social and economic tensions at the root of that anxiety worsened, it is no accident that the rhetoric of the time became that of cultural revolution.

The notion that the crisis of 1968 was a crisis *within* the dominant culture helps to explain the paradox of the intimate relationship between the counter-culture and the values it opposed. The turning towards 'inner space', the anti-materialist idealism and would-be spirituality of the underground was a reaction against the excessive materialism of consumer society. But the very materialism and hedonism promoted by the official culture in the cause of consumption (overt or implicit eroticism in advertising, for instance) made that anti-materialism possible. The underground thrived at a moment not so much of surplus value, as of surplus play. The counter-culture for the most part engaged consumers rather than producers, and it has withered with the renewal of economic depression. It is a profound irony that one means of reaching inner-space, drugs, should have depended on dealers who operated as primitive entrepreneurial capitalists in an entirely unregulated economy. (At least until they were caught.)

In that the underground was an extension of the 'youth market', it was indeed the creation of the overground economy, but Stuart Hall argues that it was not recognized as such at the time. Instead it was perceived as a threat to traditional values, and suppressed accordingly. He does not make a direct connection between the economic crisis and devaluation of 1967 and the cultural revolution of 1968, but it is surely no coincidence that the hedonism that had been promoted as 'Swinging London' in 1966 should be given a bad press two years later. In a contribution to a group of essays he edited in 1976, *Resistance through Rituals*, Hall describes both 'youth' and the 'counter-culture' as images through which bourgeois society came first to articulate, and then resolve, the conflict – the cultural break – which it had itself provoked.

In the first flush of affluence, the guardians of the middle-class ideal first encountered the break in the shape of 'youth': first, working class, then its own. In the name of society, they resisted its hedonism, its narcissism, its permissiveness, its search for immediate gratifications, its anti-authoritarianism, its moral pluralism, its materialism: all defined as 'threats' to societal values springing from both aspirant working-class youth and malformed, badly socialized middle-class youth. They mis-recognized the crisis *within* the dominant culture as a conspiracy *against*

149

the dominant culture. They failed (as many members of the counter-culture also failed) to see the cultural 'break' as, in its own traumatic and disturbing way, *profoundly adaptive* to the system's productive base.

While agreeing on the cultural location of the crisis, Martin and Hall disagree on its consequences. For Bernice Martin the upheaval of 1968 was a means of 'cultural transmission and transformation' which

> drew attention to, and familiarized the wider society with, a range of expressive values, symbols and activities by showering them forth in their most extreme and dramatic form. The process of the 1970s has been to shift the various cultures and subcultures to accommodate an expansion of expressive possibility inside their various styles.

For Hall the cultural confusion is a symptom of a deeper political and economic crisis that remains unresolved. That resolution has been partially postponed by the reassertion of legal, economic, political and cultural controls which have held organized labour in check. The very 'accommodations' which Martin identifies in the 1970s are part of the means of control.

The idea that cultural accommodation or adaptation is in itself a means of control is vital to a third strand of argument about the nature of what occurred, one which had a direct influence on the character of events. As we saw in the previous chapter, the 'repressive tolerance' of capitalist society was a major theme of the 'Dialectics of Liberation' conference at the Round House in 1967. Marcuse in particular had argued that contemporary sexual permissiveness was merely a means of encouraging passivity, and that mass culture was a form of oppression. This point was made even more strongly in the literature of the Situationists, who since 1958 had been spreading their ideas through their periodical, *Internationale Situationniste*.

Following the publication of the 1960 manifesto (distributed in translation, as we saw, as part of Alex Trocchi's *Sigma Portfolio*), the Situationists' principal theorists Guy Debord and Raoul Vaneigem developed the idea of society as a 'spectacle', a false projection which masks our alienation from our true selves. Radical ideas which challenge this false projection are subjected to a process of 'recuperation', which renders the challenge harmless by appearing to shift ground and grant participation, without in fact altering the fundamental conditions of alienation and oppression. (This is an extreme version of the Marxist view of the operation of 'hegemony'.) Culture plays a vital role in this process of mystification; culture supplies the 'spectacle' which obscures the reality of exploitation, be it capitalist, or Soviet communist. In the West culture has become a product that is bought and sold and, with the apparent resolution of the problems of production, is indeed the primary means by which consumption is maintained. As Guy Debord says in *La Societé du Spéctacle* (1967), 'Culture turned into commodity must also turn into the star commodity of the spectacular society.'

It follows that the spectacle must be confronted where it is most spectacular: at the point of culture. The argument is essentially anarchist; the symbols of the state apparatus must be attacked in some way as to reveal their true meaning. Indeed, one of the objects of such attacks was to provoke the oppression which is normally masked by the spectacle. This was the strategy adopted at the University of Strasbourg when a group of Situationists deliberately bankrupted the students' union and provoked a confrontation with the authorities. Similar tactics at Nanterre in March 1968 sparked off the closure of the campus which in turn led to the student occupation of the Sorbonne and the subsequent *évênements* of May.

The important point here is that if society is to be attacked through its symbols, then it is quite justifiable for the attacks themselves to be symbolic acts against symbolic targets (as for instance the demonstration against the Miss World contest in London in 1970). Spectacle must be fought with spectacle. Political activity as it is normally understood is merely a diversion, a form of recuperation which allows the political activist to construct his own illusion of progress, while the mask of oppression remains intact. Instead, the Situationist philosophy encouraged what might be called a 'politics of theatre', where symbolic gestures were just as meaningful to the participants as real acts. Politics as theatre was a remarkably pervasive idea; Stuart Hall uses it almost unconsciously, for instance, when he comments that the student revolutionaries evolved 'an entirely novel *repertoire* of confrontation tactics, theatrical and dramaturgical in inspiration'. It could also be used negatively, as when the students who occupied Hornsey College of Art in 1968 complained that 'confined by inertia and hostility, our will to change the world was turned into

151

a theatrical event, a kind of demonstration.' (This is the ruling metaphor in David Caute's play, *The Demonstration* (1970).) One kind of political theatre could lead to another. John Barker and Jim Greenfield, who were later to be sent to prison as members of the Angry Brigade, began their revolutionary careers at Cambridge University, performing agitprop street theatre.

There are other, more ambivalent reasons for this theatre of politics. A generation that had absorbed the doctrines of Marshall McLuhan was aware that the news media demanded extravagant gestures if its message was to be heard. Once aroused, the media magnified events and gave a platform to relatively small groups of people. At the same time, as the students at Hornsey complained, the overwhelming inertia of the rest of society – if you like, its repressive tolerance – produced a frustration that could only be relieved by violent or absurdist acts. The media, as instruments of the spectacle, fed this frustration with objects for emulation. In his history of the New Left, *An Infantile Disorder?* (1977), Nigel Young comments that for youth culture 1968–69

is a period of songs such as 'Revolution' and 'Street Fighting Man', and for many the new violence of street-fighting appears more as expressive experience than political strategy. Many seemed to feel in this desperate discontent a need to emulate the dramatic violence of Tet and Paris; as revolutionary gestures, like the sporadic bombings and burnings, the street-fighting episodes were seen as part of a 'theatre of resistance', which extended into the verbal and symbolic violence of much rock music, reaching a climax in the actual murderous violence of the Altamont music festival.

Before examining in more detail how these gestures were made, there is a further feature of the apparent state of war to be discussed. The primary paradox is that the 'revolution' broke out not among the most oppressed (we are not here considering America, where blacks created a state of siege within their own cities) but among the most privileged: young, chiefly middle-class students.

A revolution of the privileged is a political nonsense (though a counter-revolution is not). It is true that the Education Act of 1944 had widened the social base of the university population, and that the expansion in higher education had proportionately increased its numbers. It is also true that the launching of new universities, such as Sussex and Essex had expanded academic disciplines, principally sociology, which encouraged a critical view of society, and that construction and expansion had placed a strain on physical resources, but the British university population was never big enough to be anything more than an élite, while its institutions never experienced the academic and physical stresses such as were felt at the Sorbonne. The reason for the student upheavals in Britain from 1967 to 1970 is, once again, that it was part of a crisis within the system, rather than a revolt against it.

If, as we can see, this crisis is experienced culturally rather than politically, it will be experienced most violently at the point of transmission of cultural values: the universities, polytechnics and art schools. Part of the rhetoric of student revolt was against a society based on mass production, yet higher education was primarily intended to train the managers of a technocratic society – the 'technical intelligentsia' celebrated by T. R. Fyvel in *Intellectuals Today*, published in the crucial year of 1968. Whether they eventually became teachers, doctors, lawyers – even in a few cases professional writers or artists – students in one way or another were destined to be the reproducers of the cultural values they inherited, though as transmitters of culture they were also in a position to alter its messages. This is another reason for the often symbolic nature of what occurred. Students were not alienated and oppressed workers, but they could act out the alienation and oppression that they saw in society.

We should remember, also, that this symbolism was not entirely self-generated. Since students and young people were the medium through which society experienced its crisis, they were liable to have symbols attached to them. Sociology has once more provided a conceptual framework, the so-called 'deviancy theory'. In a period of political consensus radical and oppositional groups, such as students, or the economically or socially excluded, such as blacks or homosexuals, are thrust further to the margins by being labelled as 'deviants'. This is firstly because during a period of consensus – for instance, when there is little difference in the overall policies of the major political parties – agitation for change can only take place on the margins. Thus Stuart Hall argues in a contribution to *Deviance and Social Control* (1974), 'the protests from students – the privileged but alienated *cadres* of the new society – and from blacks – the permanently *lumpen* strata of an

153

"affluent society" – are the *loci* of political conflict when the class agencies of change are temporarily contained inside the structures of the state.'

In *The Drugtakers* (1971) Jock Young suggested an elaboration of the deviancy theory. He posited a process of 'amplification' through which the deviant group, once it has been identified as such, takes on and amplifies the characteristics it has been ascribed. Thus the drugtaker, who originally adopts the habit as a solution to a sense of *anomie*, finds that his alienation is only increased by the activities of the police. Yet as society's image of the drugtaker is forced upon him, he achieves an identity as a result, even if at the price of being an outsider. This identity can be strong enough to attract others, and the use of drugs becomes an ideological gesture whose meaning is actually created by its illegality. 'The drug represents for him an alternative way of life; legalization, then, is irrelevant, for it is the deviant culture surrounding the drug which is important.' As we saw in the previous chapter, in 1967 the authorities had begun a determined policy of suppressing the use of drugs, but by that time these had acquired an ideological meaning for the underground. Drug raids and prosecutions for obscenity became emblems of a 'war' between the generations.

Thus 'straight' society helped to create the monster that appeared to threaten it. The very amorphous and contradictory nature of the counter-culture made it appear all the more conspiratorial and subversive, since it was not susceptible to the normal processes of negotiation or absorption. The view from within, however, was quite different. While the whole spectrum of authority, from liberal academics to right-wing politicians was fantasized into an oppressive establishment, there was very little unity within the underground, especially between the revolutionary Left and the counter-cultural hedonists.

The contradictory pulls of the underground proved impossible to contain. In April 1970, for instance, as a sense of disillusion and defeat began to spread, the exiled Living Theater, which had long practised a politics of theatre and a theatre of politics, announced that it was dissolving into separate 'cells'. One was to disperse to Paris to pursue political activities, one to Berlin to take up environmental issues, one was to stay in London and continue cultural work, and one set off for India in search of spiritual enlightenment. Only the group led by Julian Beck and Judith Malina, which undertook a fresh programme of agitational theatre in Brazil, survived into the 1970s.

However much the foregoing has suggested that we interpret the upheavals of 1967–70 symbolically, the student revolts were also a historical fact, and produced a real sense of shock in the older generation. But before tracing their course, it is worth examining the case of the Anti-University: it both exemplifies the ideology of anti-structure of the underground, and demonstrates the chaotic reality of trying to put it into practice.

As with so many aspects of the British underground, the Anti-University imitated an American example, the Free University of New York, which had been active since 1965. Two of its instigators, Allen Krebs and Joseph Berke, had been closely involved with the New York project; Berke had tried to establish a London Free School in Notting Hill Gate in 1966. The initiative for the Anti-University came from the 'Dialectics of Liberation' conference in 1967. In November of that year Krebs, Berke and David Cooper set up a group which shared their interests in radical politics, existential psychiatry and counter-cultural activities. The group – which included the poet Ed Dorn, a veteran of Black Mountain College, the feminist Juliet Mitchell and the poetry publishers Asa Benveniste and Stuart Montgomery – became an unofficial steering committee for the new alternative institution. With £350 lent by the Institute for Phenomenological Studies (part of the Philadelphia Foundation established by Cooper and R. D. Laing) a building in Shoreditch was rented from the Bertrand Russell Peace Foundation. (It had previously been occupied by the Vietnam Solidarity Committee.) A manifesto was issued stating that the Anti-University would 'destroy the bastardized meanings of "student", "teacher" and "course"', and 'do away with artificial splits and divisions between disciplines and art forms and between theory and action.' The advertised list of course-leaders is another roll-call of the underground, including R. D. Laing, Steve Abrams, Jim Haynes, David Cooper, Jeff Nuttall, Cornelius Cardew, Jim Dine, Barry Flanagan, Bob Cobbing, and Barry Miles.

The school opened in February 1968, but, as Harold Norse reported in *International Times*, 'the Anti-University got off to an anti-start. Within an hour the room, jammed with poets, painters, sculptors, publishers, novelists, psychoanalysts, sociologists, and just people was a howling underground cell of clashing ideologies and aims. The atmosphere was highly charged with dissension and mounting confusion.' The difficulty was similar to that encountered at Braziers Park in 1964. The cultural, the political and the psychotherapeutic, while sharing common ground, could not agree on common forms. 'Ronnie Laing pointed out that it was futile, as Adrian Henri had suggested, to pattern ourselves on aesthetic schools such as Black Mountain or the Bauhaus or any groups whose aims were centred around some aesthetic concern, but that we could form some kind of ashram . . .'

None the less courses did start, and a genuine attempt was made to create an inter-active form of teaching which challenged both the categories of art and the hierarchy of organization which they helped to support. But ironically, the Anti-University became one of the few academic institutions destroyed by the student revolts. Roberta Elzey, who was closely involved with its administration, describes the impact of May 1968.

. . . students the same age as Anti-University members paralysed France. This display of naked power made a few wild with envy, and they were determined to have a revolution, any revolution. Naturally, the Anti-University was a sitting duck, since its general meeting which allowed individual voices to be heard was vulnerable to filibusters or generally obnoxious speeches which bored and drove out most other members. Although this mini-revolt fizzled out after a few weeks, it left a bad taste in many mouths, particularly as the instigators never assumed any responsibility, did any 'dirty work', paid fees or contributed to the common cause.

At first the Shoreditch building had been occupied by a number of homeless students who formed a small commune and kept the building in order. But by July 1968 the Anti-University had degenerated into a mere 'crash-pad'. 'Soon the building had the aura of a Bowery flophouse: underwear thrown about, the toilet constantly blocked, and windows broken.' A similar degeneration had taken place in the Anti-University's finances. No salaries were paid after April 1968, and in the summer the building was reclaimed by its owners. Some courses lingered on into 1969, meeting in private homes, but the Anti-University had fallen victim to its own anti-structure.

The political leadership of the student revolts came from an array of extreme Left political parties, most of which hoped to fill the vacuum caused by the break-up of the Stalinist British Communist Party after 1956. The Communist Party remained in being, though it made less impact than the various Trotskyist groups who vied for dominance in the student movement: the International Socialists, founded in 1951 as a breakaway from the Revolutionary Communist Party; the Socialist Labour League, formed in 1959 and which ten years later became the Workers Revolutionary Party; and the International Marxist Group, which grew out of the journal *This Week*, launched in 1964. Besides Stalinists and Trotskyists, there were also Maoists, and a range of Anarchists and Situationists resolutely opposed to the more orthodox Marxist organizations. The existence of these groups demonstrates the marginalization of radical politics in the 1960s: the Labour Party was the party of government, and abroad there was no mass, disciplined revolutionary party which might set an example as the Russian Communist Party had done in the 1930s, until the Nazi-Soviet non-aggression pact. Such foreign models as there were were hardly appropriate to the British condition: the romanticized image of Cuba, third-world guerilla groups, the Vietcong, or China, whose propaganda about 'cultural revolution' and cult of youth in the Red Guards were for a time a completely misleading influence. Excluded by the consensus from influence on 'real' politics, these groups fought among themselves, further widening the gap between revolutionary ambition and achievement. An attempt by Raymond Williams, E. P. Thompson, Stuart Hall and others to regroup the elements of the New Left of 1960 around a *May Day Manifesto* in 1967 and a National Convention held in 1969 failed in the face of the political pressures at the end of the decade.

At heart, however, the political groups were trying to articulate an important social issue: people's pervading sense of isolation and alienation from mass, technocratic society. Charles Widgery – who as a member of the International Socialists and an occasional editor of *Oz* had a more comprehensive view of events

157

than most – has given a somewhat mocking account of the self-mystifications of student power in *The Left in Britain* (1976), but he does show that there was at least a temporary articulation of an alternative.

There was a new sense of what was possible. Students had changed the way they thought about themselves, they were no longer people to whom things just happened. The appalling conformity and petty competitiveness which is the reality of undergraduate life had been momentarily shattered. The student's life of postponed gratification and unacknowledged isolation for moments, at mass meetings or sit-ins, melted into an exultant recognition of solidarity, of human beings' uncrushable ability to climb out of the filing cabinets and computers and multiple-choice questionnaires and book lists they had been put into, and scream, 'I'm human.'

This sense of solidarity and community was precisely the aim of underground happenings, rock concerts and pop festivals.

Many of the student activists, like the initiators of the underground, had had their first glimpse of this new communality on the march with CND. The reversal of the Labour Party's commitment to unilateral nuclear disarmament in 1961 had served to increase frustration with orthodox politics. The arrival of a Labour Government in 1964 was some palliative so long as Wilson's small majority demanded loyalty, but Wilson's commitment to supporting the American war in Vietnam, his failure to resolve the problems created by Rhodesia's unilateral declaration of independence in 1965, and the lack of radical change after Labour's landslide victory in 1966 led to gradual disaffection among the politically active young.

By 1966 the focus of discontent was the war in Vietnam. Even if Britain was only giving tacit support, the issue was a far more bloodily visible one, thanks to television, than the hypothetical horrors of the Bomb. Emblematically, here were romantic guerillas pinning down the bureaucrats and technologists of the most powerful and affluent nation in the world. To readers of Marcuse the marches and sit-downs of CND appeared to serve as deliberate state safety-valves, while Vietnam offered opportunities for a far more radical critique of society than CND's single issue. Finally there was the active presence in Britain of American graduate students (some of them avoiding the draft) who introduced the more aggressive methods of the American New Left. Berkeley, in

California, had been in turmoil since 1964. Vietnam offered an umbrella-issue that could reunite the splinters of the extra-parliamentary Left, just as CND had done with the Bomb. The Vietnam Solidarity Campaign was launched in 1966, and the first convention of the Radical Students' Alliance met in January 1967.

The student revolt in Paris in May 1968 gave a further stimulus to activism, but it is important to remember that trouble had already broken out at British universities. The first tensions were experienced at the London School of Economics in 1966, following the announcement that Dr Walter Adams, then in charge of University College, Rhodesia, was to become the next Director. Adams was criticized for his alleged cooperation with the illegal and racist Rhodesian Government over the arrest of students and the expulsion of Lecturers. University College, Rhodesia was still linked to London University, and the appointment gave a focus to the more general demands for student participation in university government. There was a small boycott and sit-in, and then in January 1967 a minor riot over a banned anti-Adams meeting, during which a porter died of a heart attack. Disciplinary action was answered by a nine-day sit-in in March 1967.

A similar pattern of events was to be repeated at sixteen other colleges and universities by June 1968. Agitation by a small group would provoke disciplinary action which in turn called forth much wider protest from the student body. The theme of participation is important: having been encouraged by the general cult of youth to look upon themselves as a significant section of the population, young people responded with demands for a real say in their syllabuses and social organization, only to be rebuffed. The conditions were created for a theatre of politics. Colin Crouch, President of the Students' Union in 1967–8, observed the process at the London School of Economics.

The initial demands are for something on the lines of membership of committees. This is the only way, at least initially, that the demand for 'participation' can be given tangible organizational form. But the expectations linked to this idea of participation, the anger felt at its denial, and the way in which both the demand and the means of protest adopted to attain it are associated with a whole range of other political sentiments, are reasonable indications that discussion of numbers of students to sit on committees has really very little to do with the whole affair.

_* * *_

159

In the excitement of para-revolutionary events, with buildings occupied, the authorities in confusion, meetings in session day and night, and the press and police at the door, ordinary restraints collapse, and it is possible to experience a euphoria and release as profound as any catharsis provoked by the theatre of cruelty. 'In the charismatic situation, individuals attempt to break through the confining structures of an over-determined social world, to contradict the prevailing moral and social constraints and establish radically new counters to them.'

The same spirit made itself felt when broader issues were at stake. In October 1967 a threshold was crossed when fighting broke out between demonstrators and police during the Vietnam Solidarity Committee's first demonstration against the American Embassy in Grosvenor Square. At CND rallies demonstrators had sat down passively and allowed themselves to be arrested. This time they violently resisted. The American Embassy symbolized American power; the politics of confrontation turned Grosvenor Square into a symbolic Vietnam. In the autumn of 1967 and early 1968 there was a rash of student protests, demonstrations and occupations, either on the issue of participation, or against visits by politically unpopular speakers. In March 1968 the Vietnam Solidarity Committee organized a second demonstration in Grosvenor Square, attended by 25,000 people. This was much more violent than the first, police horses and truncheons were used, and there were 280 arrests. The violence was inevitably exaggerated by its selective re-transmission on television.

On 3 May in Paris a protest march by students at the Sorbonne turned into a riot and the Latin Quarter was taken over. This time what the revolutionary theorists had hoped would happen seemed to be taking place: a 'revolution from above' was acting as 'the little motor' for a much larger insurrection, as the students' protest set off a general strike. But the theorists had not reckoned with the French Communist Party, which was not ready for a revolution and called off the strike. Yet for a few weeks the situation in Paris seemed full of potential; the revolutionary euphoria was witnessed by British radicals who travelled to Paris and stayed there until the deportation of 'foreign agitators' was ordered. In May there were student demonstrations or revolts across the United States, and in Berlin, Rome, Geneva, Milan, Brussels, Vienna, Madrid, Tokyo and parts of Latin America.

In Britain there were serious disruptions at the universities of Hull and Essex, and troubles in the art schools, particularly Hornsey in North London, and Guildford in Surrey, both of which experienced long occupations. The sit-in at the main building of Hornsey, which ran from 28 May to 8 July is significant because a conscious effort was made to exclude political issues. What began as a dispute over control of union funds turned into a wide-ranging debate over the nature of art education, and the students rapidly came to the conclusion that 'in setting up a new educational structure at Hornsey one is creating the working model for a fundamental re-organization of the educational system, and thus, in effect, the value and priority system of our present society.' The values of the counter-culture were enshrined in the new system they proposed.

An open system whereby all individual demands can be taken into account whether specialized or comprehensive. Subjects to be set up in response to the need of an individual or group of individuals at any moment – thus the curricula will be in a continual state of flux. Within the operational curricula of any one moment there will be a total freedom of choice of options and combinations available to everyone. Complete freedom of individual or group research at any time with or without tutorial assistance.

While conducting their debate the Hornsey students, who had the active support of at least twenty of the staff, mounted an exhibition about the issues at the Institute of Contemporary Art, and took part in a Round House conference called by the Movement for Rethinking Art and Design Education. Sixty-two different colleges were represented, and they loudly supported Hornsey's calls for the abolition of O-level entry requirements and graded assessments, for full grants for all and joint government by staff and students. But there was no sympathy from the local authority responsible for the college. The occupation of Hornsey briefly became a siege, which only stiffened resistance. Eventually a bargain was struck by which the students would leave the building while their grievances were dealt with by a 'commission' of staff and students under the chairmanship of the politician and publisher Lord Longford. The commission sat throughout the

161

summer, but the students won little beyond representation on
college committees. When the college reopened for the autumn
term 28 students were not readmitted, and some 50 members of
staff (chiefly part-timers) were 'not re-engaged'. Similar tactics at
Guildford led to similar results: 35 part-time and 7 full-time staff
were dismissed.

In mid-1968 student ferment was at its height, and the Radical
Students' Alliance gave way to the Revolutionary Socialist Students' Federation, founded at a conference of the leading groups
at the LSE on 15 June. The conference was addressed by two
heroes of the Paris barricades, Alain Geismar and Daniel Cohn-
Bendit, who had been brought to London by the BBC for a
programme about the student revolts. Charles Widgery noted
that 'both looked exhausted and utterly unclear about where they
were', and that some of the British leaders were not pleased to be
upstaged by these international stars.

On 27 October a third march took place in London against the
war in Vietnam. Press and television were thoroughly alarmist,
but the Vietnam Solidarity Committee was divided over tactics. It
is evident that the majority of those who had been in Grosvenor
Square in the spring did not wish to see a repetition of the
violence, although a minority did. There were therefore contradictory appeals to follow the planned route to a rally in Hyde Park,
and to march on Grosvenor Square. While some 50,000 marchers
did indeed follow the urgings of Tariq Ali of the International
Marxist Group and demonstrate peaceably, some 3,000 led by
anarchists, ended up in Grosvenor Square and confronted the
police there. But the police, too, had decided on a change of
tactics, and there were only a few arrests. By 8.30 in the evening
the demonstration was over, and the television crews watching
the occasion were disappointed. Some far deeper cultural pattern
surfaced when police and demonstrators ended the day by singing
'Auld Lang Syne'.

Although the embers of student discontent continued to glow,
it was evident that there was going to be no 'revolution from
above' in Britain. The newspaper *Black Dwarf* might scream in
its issue for 15 October 'DON'T DEMAND. OCCUPY', but Fred
Halliday's editorial in the same issue admits that while everywhere
students were on the march, 'not in Britain. We are the only
major capitalist country which has not produced a comparable

162

student movement. There have been isolated cases of student insurrection, and students have been dominant in the anti-imperialist struggle, but there has not been a mass student movement.' The Vietnam Solidarity Committee finally fell apart at the end of 1969, when squabbles broke out between the factions, appropriately enough at a meeting to commemorate the death of North Vietnam's leader, Ho Chi Minh.

With the collapse of the temporary coalition over Vietnam, activism turned to single-issue campaigns over race, South Africa, the civil war in Nigeria and workers' control. But in one province of the United Kingdom student activism helped to supply, not so much the 'little motor' of revolution, as the detonator for buried conflicts whose roots and consequences were far beyond student issues: Northern Ireland. Relative affluence in the 1960s had obscured the deep divisions within the Ulster community; liberalization had increased the expectations of Roman Catholics, particularly those who had been enabled by the 1944 Education Act to acquire higher education at Queen's University Belfast. The Civil Rights Association formed in 1967 (heir to the Campaign for Social Justice) sought to end the political and economic discrimination against Roman Catholics, but it was not exclusively a Roman Catholic organization. The harsh response of the Ulster Government and the Protestant majority to the Civil Rights Association campaign drove them towards civil disobedience, while, as we saw in Grosvenor Square, demonstrators were more ready than before to resist the police.

In December 1968 a new and more radical grouping, People's Democracy, was founded at Queen's University, and the Civil Rights Association gradually lost control of events, while the Ulster police continued to attack demonstrations, driving the Catholic population towards their traditional 'protectors', the IRA. In August 1969 there was serious rioting in Londonderry and Belfast, and in conditions of near civil war between Protestants and Catholics the British Army intervened. A long period of attrition began, with the IRA split between 'Official' and 'Provisional' wings facing what it considered an army of occupation across a divide far deeper than the issues originally raised in 1967.

No such detonation occurred on mainland Britain, which, in

spite of bombing campaigns by the IRA, remained insulated by the psychological barrier of the Irish Sea. But such attacks and corresponding security measures contributed to the perception of a general increase in the level of political violence, both nationally and internationally. In Britain the theoretical violence of the underground and the rhetoric of its press was translated into much more aggressive action as the libertarian call for the end of restraints made itself heard. The squatting movement showed that campaigners for better housing were now prepared to take direct action, seize control of empty property, and if necessary defend it.

The 'official' squatting movement began after the BBC transmitted Jeremy Sandford's *Cathy Come Home* for a third time in November 1968. A long-term campaigner, Ron Bailey, decided to revive the tactics used by the homeless at the close of the Second World War, and the London Squatters Campaign was launched. 'Most were from the revolutionary libertarian Left.' This was a sincere attempt to provide housing for the homeless by occupying property left empty, often for redevelopment, by local authorities. The movement quickly spread to run-down areas of Hackney, Notting Hill, Brixton, Battersea, Hammersmith and Fulham, and similar city areas in other parts of the country, and by the end of 1969 it had won semi-legitimate status as a means of using 'short-life' property. The Lewisham Family Squatting Association, for instance, formed in October 1969, was able to make formal agreements with the local council.

Squatting, however, was also a convenient solution to the housing problems of the underground; the anarchist Left saw squatting both as an attack on property and the means of creating an alternative society. By March 1969 'official' squatters were having difficulty because of the activities of anarchist squatters who welcomed the siege mentality that squatting created. It is further evidence of the marginalization of protest that such groups abandoned orthodox politics altogether in favour of the 'politics of the street'. In March 1969 a group of twenty young people who had been using the Arts Lab in Drury Lane as a base broke into the empty and rotting Bell Hotel a few doors away and started to convert it into a free hostel. They were quickly driven out again by the Greater London Council, who rendered the place utterly uninhabitable; but the publicity aroused led to the formation of the London Street Commune, which went on to conduct far more spectacular squats at Endell Street in Convent Garden and, in September 1969, 144 Piccadilly. The occupation of a large mansion on one of London's principal thoroughfares by a representative selection of youthful sub-cultures, from Hell's Angels to skinheads, under the spray-painted slogan 'We are the writing on your walls' was thoroughly provocative, and was finally ended by the invasion of the police.

The squatters' movement, with its anti-authoritarian ideology of communal self-help, created an environment in which it was possible to believe that revolution was at hand, and the state must not only be resisted, but attacked. The 'urban guerilla' was an internationally known figure, from West Germany to Northern Ireland to Latin America, and Britain experienced its own version in the activities of the self-styled Angry Brigade. Following a wave of bomb attacks – which seem to have been aimed at property rather than people – ten were charged with 'Angry Brigade' offences in 1972, but it is difficult to be precise about the group's responsibility. Only five were found guilty, but some of their other activities, principally cheque frauds, involved many more people who could be said to sympathize with their aims.

John Barker and Jim Greenfield met at Cambridge, as we saw. Barker travelled to Paris in May 1968, and was one of the foreign students expelled by the authorities. In Cambridge they performed street theatre, and distributed agitational literature through the 'Kim Philby Dining Club', a typically Situationist joke against the social institutions of the university. Disappointed by the failure of the October 1968 Grosvenor Square demonstration Barker and Greenfield turned their attention to the repressive nature of the university itself, and in June 1969 they tore up their examination papers and left. They moved to London and ran a bookstall, and became involved in the busy underworld of radical politics and communitarian living. Greenfield met Anna Mendelson and Hilary Creek, future co-defendants at their trial in 1972, who had been at Essex University during the disturbances of 1968, and who were now active in the squatting movement. The group underwent a thorough political education in this and the Claimants' Union, formed to assert the rights of claimants to social security and other benefits from the Department of Health and Social Security. Early in 1970 they came into contact with Stuart

Christie, a British anarchist who had been imprisoned in Spain for smuggling explosives (and who was acquitted at the trial in 1972). Spanish anarchists had a long history of urban guerilla warfare and had carried out a number of bomb attacks against Spanish targets in London, and it is believed an alliance was formed between the two groups.

Although sporadic attacks on Spanish targets were joined in 1970 by attacks on the homes of the Metropolitan Police Commissioner and the Attorney General which, with an unexploded bomb at the site of a new police station can be read as symbolic attacks on the powers of the state, the Angry Brigade did not announce its existence until 5 December 1970, in a 'communiqué' sent to *International Times*. (A small bomb had been exploded beneath an outside broadcast van at the Miss World Contest in November and a machine gun fired at the Spanish Embassy.) In December 1970 Barker and Creek moved to Manchester, where they came into contact with Ian Purdie and Jake Prescott. Purdie was a former student who had been imprisoned for throwing a petrol bomb at the Ulster Office during a demonstration in 1969; in prison he had met a petty criminal and drug user, Prescott.

On 12 January 1971 a bomb exploded at the house of the Home Secretary, Robert Carr, and the Angry Brigade claimed responsibility. Later that month Prescott was arrested on a drug charge, and talked about his activities to other prisoners while on remand. The police raided a number of squats and communes, and discovered a massive cheque fraud which was being used to fund the group. In March Prescott and Purdie were arrested and charged with bomb offences, while the rest went into hiding. The bomb attacks continued, including one on a typically Situationist target, Biba's boutique on 1 May. Working through the underground press, the group tried to establish Purdie and Prestcott as underground heroes. Before their trial took place, however, the police raided a flat in Stoke Newington and discovered arms, explosives, and Angry Brigade material. Eight people were arrested. In November 1971 Purdie was acquitted on bombing charges, but Prescott was sentenced to 15 years; in May 1972 Barker, Greenfield, Mendelson and Creek were given sentences of 10 years. The judge commented: 'Undoubtedly a warped

166

understanding of sociology has brought you to the state in which you are.'

While the activities of the Angry Brigade and the London Street Commune provided the popular press with images of a monster that must be trapped and destroyed, the ideological divisions within the counter-culture were too great for it ever to have constituted a real threat. The values of 'peace and love' could not sit easily with the earnest endeavour of the political radicals. Thus at the time of the second Grosvenor Square demonstration in May 1968 *International Times* came out strongly against the violence, and even went so far as to reprint reports from the right-wing press which suggested that the leaders personally avoided confrontation with the police, while urging others on.

Bernice Martin, as we have seen, does not consider that the student revolutionaries were revolutionary anyway.

The student revolutionaries of 1968 saw the gestures of symbolic anti-structure with which they attacked that 'formal and grammatical' base of education as inherently revolutionary. Of course, they were nothing of the kind. Their origins, like those of the students who wielded them, lay in the tradition of privileged classical humanism. The educational axioms of the counter-culture were simply logical extensions of the principles which had long been enshrined in élite education in Europe.

None the less, a small proportion of student activists took their politics very seriously indeed. The problem was how to retain the interest of the rest of the student body, who were less dedicated to the cause. As Eric Hobsbawm has commented, 'though there is no intrinsic connection between sexual permissiveness and social organization, there is, I am bound to note with a little regret, a persistent affinity between revolution and puritanism.'

While the events of 1968 did, as we shall see, reintroduce a strong political element into the arts, the more hedonistic elements in the counter-culture were incapable of the discipline necessary to achieve revolution. As Richard Neville put it succinctly in *Play Power* (1970), the underground was not prepared to accept the New Left's doctrine of work. 'Nor do its members accept the other axiom of the old New Left that repressive institutions can only be exterminated by "immense sacrifice, dedication and responsibility". It is this opposing construct within the Movement which causes so much conflict. The sober, violent, puritan Left extremists versus the laughing, loving, lazy, fun-powder plotters.'

The response of the puritan radicals was a reassertion of political discipline that both emphasized the sectarian splits, and cut off the spontaneity released by the expressive attitudes of the underground, which had given events such exhilarating drive. Meetings became more manipulative, agendas replaced free debates, and the respective groupings retreated into small cells which enforced a rigid conformity on its members. The underground itself began to be dismissed as a form of recuperation. 'An Open Letter to the Underground from the London Street Commune', circulated in 1969, deplored 'the ideological split between . . . political and cultural "sectors".'

Up till now, the function of the so-called underground has not been to accelerate the growth of dissent among kids, which would involve finding out what its different forms have in common, but rather to obscure any real perception of these concrete problems of communication and interaction in a stifling haze of hashsmoke and Amerikan hipculchur.

The anonymous Situationist street paper *Arson News* denounced 'The middle-class drop-out scene (beatniks, Provos, students, flower power)' as the 'latest product of a consumer society only too glad to market the latest shit.'

Such denunciations would not much concern those who believed that they could achieve 'inner space' by a thoroughgoing retreat into the private world of the hippy. Political activity, even of a kind with whose aims they sympathized, was only one more obstacle on the path towards spiritual goals, goals which could not be reached, but which drew them on none the less. As Paul Willis remarks in his study of hippies in *Profane Culture* (1978), at one level their self-contained lifestyle, with its emphasis on creativity and individual enjoyment, constituted a critique of the radical Left, who had 'no programme for the detailed and every-day.' But precisely because of their inner directedness and emphasis on the personal, the hippies could never constitute a political force. 'The dazzling world of changes they made in their immediate lives and in their own proper cultural fields left unchallenged the larger world of political and social institutions which were the material base for the experience of the classes from which they came. Though stupendously outmanoeuvred and embarrassed at a day-to-day level, the dominant class remained supreme in its control of the most basic patterns of life for the majority.'

The more violent gestures of the underground, meanwhile, played into the hands of those in the 'dominant class' who wished to reassert the authority of traditional political and moral values. Radical sociologists have invented the term 'moral panic' to describe the process by which all the spontaneous and discon- nected disturbances of 1967 onwards grew into the image of a threatened social breakdown. In 1968 the pendulum of permissive- ness began to swing back, with the Government's rejection of Baroness Wootton's report on drug abuse, followed by the 1970 Misuse of Drugs Act, which consolidated the earlier legislation aimed at curbing the drug culture.

In the view of Stuart Hall, it is to this period that we can trace the development of a 'Law and Order' society which has continued to harden its position to this day.

The resolution of the state to resist, and the panic and fear of the 'silent majority' at having their routinized way of life threatened and shattered, made a fateful *rendezvous*. Out of this convergence the drift into reaction and authoritarianism was born. In Britain the greatest casualty was the disintegration of liberalism. Outflanked on its student left, intellectual liberalism threw in the sponge without a fight, and many of its outstanding stalwarts, eloquent about academic freedom in general only up to the point where some actual, particular freedom was threat- ened, emigrated speedily to the extreme Right.

Bernice Martin takes a narrower view of the consequences for higher education.

The student radicals helped to explode the myth that unrestricted university expansion was a prerequisite of economic prosperity: they drew the attention of the political paymasters to all those purely express- ive activities which, in the past, had been a luxury of the gentlemanly class, but which, in the era of mass higher education, had looked set fair to become part of the new rights of the common man. It is hardly surprising that governments of all political colours responded by tighten- ing the financial strings, by sharpening the insistence of the instrumental functions of education and by encouraging a shift away from subjects which in the late Sixties were troublesome, 'useless', and vocationally irrelevant.

The first sign of a more restrictive attitude on the part of the Government was the decision early in 1968 to halve a proposed increase in student grants. In May the university Vice-Chancellors met to discuss university discipline, and prepare a common policy to deal with disturbances. As the third Grosvenor Square demonstration showed, the police had improved their techniques for handling the new style of protest. At the London School of Economics – where the Director, Walter Adams, had taken up his post in spite of the protests – internal security gates were installed, and this time the authorities were ready to deal with the expected protest. When the gates were torn down the school was immediately closed, and the radicals found that they were unable either successfully to spread the issue to the rest of London University, or to prevent the expulsion of leaders and the sacking of the only two lecturers who had supported them.

The last flare of student protest (though sit-ins have never entirely disappeared from the repertoire) came early in 1970, when students at the University of Warwick occupied the Registry over plans for the student union and discovered that there were secret files on their political activities. At Warwick the dispute grew into a debate over the nature of the 'business university', encouraged by the presence on the staff of the Marxist historian E. P. Thompson, who questioned the links between Warwick University and local industrial interests. The 'files' issue spread to other universities, including Oxford and Cambridge. And it was at Cambridge that the new attitude to student activism was roundly demonstrated. In February 1970 a group of students had invaded a Greek business dinner at the local Garden House Hotel, claiming that it constituted an honour to the military dictatorship in Greece. The university authorities cooperated with the police in identifying the ringleaders, and in July 6 students were sent to jail for up to 18 months, and a further 2 sent to borstal. Cambridge University had drawn the line between a rag and a riot.

It is significant that in 1968, at the height of the counter-cultural revolution, the publisher John Calder should launch the Society for the Defence of Literature and the Arts, precisely because he believed that a reaction against permissiveness was setting in. Following the final, ambiguous Appeal Court ruling in June 1968

170

which allowed Calder to publish Hubert Selby's *Last Exit to Brooklyn* after a two-year battle, the Arts Council convened a conference on the obscenity laws, which in turn set up a working party to produce a report. Although the report, published in 1969, quoted the Arts Council Chairman Lord Goodman's view that the 1959 Obscene Publications Act had become 'a total nonsense', the Arts Council was careful to distance itself from its conclusions, stressing that it was an *independent* investigation, in spite of the fact that it was conducted by the leading liberal figures in the arts with whom the Council was entirely sympathetic.

The report concluded that 'to shock has always been one of the beneficent social functions of art, an inevitable by-product of the fresh vision which characterizes a good artist.' These eminently progressive sentiments contrasted the merits of expressiveness with the dangers of repression. 'The so-called permissive society may have its casualties: the repressive society almost certainly has a great deal more. Repressed sexuality can be toxic both to the individual and to society. Repression can deprave and corrupt.' The report therefore recommended that the obscenity laws be repealed, as they had been in Sweden, or at the least suspended for five years. But the tide of permissiveness had definitely turned. When the report was offered to the Labour Government, its recommendations were ignored.

The opening of the 1970s saw a definite reaction, both public and from private pressure groups, against the freedoms of expression won in the previous decade. Mrs Mary Whitehouse was now a national figure, courteously received by politicians and the Chairman of the BBC. In 1967 the writer and broadcaster Malcolm Muggeridge, who now made something of a profession out of his distaste for the decline in moral standards, addressed the annual convention of the National Viewers' and Listeners' Association, and it was he who in 1969 suggested to Mrs Whitehouse that there should be a nationwide 'Festival of Light'. The organization that grew out of this held its first rally in Trafalgar Square in 1971. In that year Mrs Whitehouse served on the independent commission on pornography set up by Lord Longford, whose report in 1972 came to quite the opposite conclusions to the Arts Council working party in 1969. The police meanwhile, were conducting their own concerted campaign against pornography through the Obscene Publications Squad. The campaign coincided with a boom in the availability of hard-core pornography which became easier to account for when it emerged that the so-called Dirty Squad had been massively corrupted, to the point that it was virtually farming the trade for bribes, and even reselling seized material to favoured dealers. Owners of alternative bookshops and publishers of radical newspapers were not so lucky.

The prosecutions of *International Times*, *Oz* and other publications in 1970 and 1971 must be seen against the expansion of the underground press. It was believed in the underground that the prosecutions were brought precisely because of its success. At its height in 1968 *IT* was selling 50,000 copies an issue; in 1970 *Oz* was selling 40,000 (rising to 70,000 after the trial.) These figures compare very favourably with those of magazines subsidized by the Arts Council, or indeed the *New Statesmen* or the *Spectator*, but the style of underground publishing was such that they could never become commercial ventures. The one exception is *Time Out*, begun by Tony Elliot in 1968 after he had noticed the usefulness of the free listings in *International Times*. At first only a listings magazine that supplied the capital with the sort of information that *What's On in London* did not, *Time Out* gradually took on the task of reviewing the cultural activities of the underground, and reporting the events and attitudes that concerned it. By 1971 it was producing 100-page issues, and, while still adhering to the ideology of the alternative society, it had become a successful business.

A more typical example of underground newspaper enterprise is the history of *Idiot International*. In 1969 Douglas Gill, who had edited some issues of *Black Dwarf*, was given £50,000 by a South American millionairess and left-wing sympathizer to start a left-wing press and publishing house. Equipment was bought and the Larcular Press started, with plans to publish English, French and Italian editions of *Idiot International*. Only the French and English editions ever appeared. A number of issues of other alternative papers were printed, but the operation was ridden with faction and inefficiency, and the press was mainly used to print pornography. *Idiot* was defunct by 1971.

Ink, launched in May 1971, was an attempt to link underground and overground styles of journalism. It was the brainchild of Richard Neville, and was originally edited by Neville and another colleague on *Oz*, Felix Dennis. The idea was to create a British version of the New York *Village Voice*, and exploit the big market that *Time Out* was beginning to develop. Some £20,000 in capital was raised from investors like John Lennon and Germaine Greer (Lord Goodman was reported to have subscribed £50) and a number of Fleet Street journalists were engaged, including Andrew Cockburn and Anna Coote. Thanks to the new interest in the launch, 45,000 copies of the first issue were sold, but shortly afterwards Richard Neville and Felix Dennis were obliged to concentrate on their forthcoming trial over *Oz*, and the running of affairs passed to the publisher, later literary agent, Ed Victor. There was dissension among the journalists, and the venture was thrown into disarray by the result of the *Oz* trial. *Ink* folded at the end of February 1972.

In 1969 there were eleven British alternative newspapers registered with the Underground Press Syndicate, ranging from *Peace News* (founded 1936) to *King Mob Echo*, a fleeting production of Notting Hill Gate Situationists. Nearly all of them were run on a cooperative basis, and consequently were prone to internal disputes. In August 1968 the original founders of *International Times* were ousted by employees siezed with the spirit of Paris, and the paper was re-registered as a cooperative in the name of Knullar Ltd. ('Knullar' is the Swedish for 'fuck'.) Some of the original *IT* team, including Jim Haynes and Bill Levy, moved to Amsterdam and launched the 'international sex paper' *Suck* in 1969. In October 1969 there was a second coup at *IT*, when staff rebels took control of the offices with the help of members of the London Street Commune. The largely rock-music-oriented *Rolling Stone*, launched in San Francisco in November 1967, experienced similar vicissitudes with its British edition. In November 1969, after splitting from the parent company this became *Friends*, and after *Friends* went into liquidation in May 1971 lingered on as the alternative newspaper *Frendz*. In May 1968 *Black Dwarf*, edited by Tariq Ali, had been launched as an attempt to unite the political and counter-cultural wings of the underground, but in March 1970 Ali and four other members of the staff left to found *Red Mole* (later, in May 1973, *Red Weekly*) as a newspaper for the International Marxist Group. The surviving editorial collective was only able to keep *Black Dwarf* alive until September 1970.

In November 1970 *Friends*, itself on the way towards trans-mogrification into *Frendz*, reported that it had just lost its third distributor in a year. '*Cyclops* has died. *Strange Days* has died. *Idiot International* has died. *Black Dwarf* has died. *Grass Eye* and *Zig Zag* ail. *IT* struggles on. The "alternative" press is in trouble all round.' It was in particular trouble with the police, who did not need to go to the lengths of a prosecution to discourage printers, distributors and newsagents from handling its pro-ductions, though both the Unicorn Bookshop in Brighton and Compendium Books in London were taken to court. In November 1970 three directors of *International Times* were tried at the Old Bailey on a charge of conspiring to corrupt public morals and public decency by printing personal advertisements placed by homosexuals. They were given eighteen-month suspended sen-tences and the paper was fined £1,500 plus £500 costs, which successfully wrecked its finances. (In January 1971 *IT* was again raided, this time by the Special Branch, on the trail of the Angry Brigade and looking for explosives.) While *IT*'s appeal (partly upheld) made its way up to the House of Lords, similar charges were brought against *Oz*.

The *Oz* trial, which opened at the Old Bailey in June 1971, ran for six weeks, the longest obscenity trial in history. The offending issue was *Oz* No. 28, a 'School Kids Issue' that had been put together with the help of a group of schoolchildren exercised about 'children's rights'. The issue contained its usual personal small-ads, and was decorated with a number of sado-masochistic cartoons, including Rupert Bear apparently violently raping the American comic character Gipsy Granny. (The cartoon was a collage produced by one of the children.) Richard Neville, Jim Anderson and Felix Dennis were charged with conspiracy to corrupt young children, publishing an obscene article, posting an obscene article, and possessing obscene articles for gain.

While Richard Neville defended himself, the other two engaged the liberal barrister (and author) John Mortimer, who was simul-taneously conducting the defence of Richard Handyside, a young publisher who had produced an English edition of the Danish *Little Red Schoolbook*, which contained advice on sex and contra-ception. The prospects for the *Oz* defendants did not look good when the magistrate at Clerkenwell Crown Court decided that the *Little Red Schoolbook* was indeed obscene. In the event the

10. Destruction
in art:
John Latham
and burning
skoob towers,
on the site
of the future
National Theatre,
1966

11. A fringe theatre farewell: Welfare State's Sir Lancelot Quail
leaves England at the end of his pilgrimage, 1972

12. Three-dimensional hard-edge: Anthony Caro *Homage to David Smith* 1966

13. Conceptions in space: Roelof Louw *40′ × 20′* 1969

three were found not guilty of conspiracy, but guilty on all other counts. *Oz* Ltd was fined £1,000 plus £1,250 costs; Dennis was sentenced to 9 months imprisonment, Anderson to 12 months, and Neville to 15 months to be followed by deportation. The case immediately went to appeal, and the sentences were reduced to 6 months suspended. But members of straight society had already exacted a symbolic revenge: while held in prison for seven days awaiting probation reports before sentencing, the trio had their long hair forcibly cut by prison warders.

The trial hearing itself was not as enlightening about social attitudes as the *Lady Chatterley's Lover* case had been a decade before. The defendants tried to present themselves as being on trial for their politics and lifestyle, but the prosecution stuck doggedly to the sordid details of *Oz* 28, and easily picked holes in the woolly philosophical assertions of defence 'expert' witnesses. The wisest words came from the philosopher Richard Wolheim, who was asked by Neville what the consequences of the trial might be.

The bringing of this prosecution against *Oz* could be socially damaging. It does seem to me, in some ways, to endanger, or be a threat to, an attack upon the morality of toleration which is a large part of the morality of a society like ours. And second, I do think it might do something to produce the kind of polarization in our society which we already see in existence in other societies such as America. And this seems to me to be extremely damaging to society.

When the defendants escaped most of their penalties on appeal, Mrs Whitehouse, who had attended the trial and pronounced herself pleased with the original result, launched a 'Nationwide Petition for Public Decency'. The Festival of Light and the Viewers' and Listeners' Association collected 1,350,000 signatures, which were duly presented to the Prime Minister, Edward Heath, in April 1973.

Edward Barker's and Mick Farren's *Watch Out Kids* (1972) shows the anger that was felt in the underground at the new attitude being displayed by the authorities. It also demonstrates the extent to which fantasy and paranoia had penetrated the counter-culture, now that 'the feeling of community that was about to emerge three years ago has scattered and split.'

Flower power's failure convinced nearly all of us that society could not be changed by simple example. It was also apparent that society was not even prepared to tolerate the existence of any minority who attempted to live according to other principles, no matter how peaceful or self-contained their culture might be.

Some had tried to fight back politically, but 1968 had changed nothing, and more violent methods seemed necessary. Building on the rhetoric (though not the sentiment) of *Bomb Culture*, which since its publication as a paperback in 1970 had become almost an Old Testament history for the underground, Farren and Barker claim: 'The war has already started. The bombs of the Angry Brigade and the freaks out on the street are part of the first offensive. So are the supply lines that carry dope; they can handle anything from guns to people. So are the rural hippies growing their own food.' Their idealized vision of an unpolluted, unexploitative, communal and freely creative society turns into a fantastical and nightmarish opposite when they conclude that this new Jerusalem

will require guns and bombs to defend it against a civilization that, as it falls, would rather destroy everything with it than admit that it was wrong. When we have to fight we will fight like crazies. Killer acid-freaks turning up where they are least expected, destroying property and structure, but doing their best to save minds.

Mick Farren, a former news editor on *International Times*, and a leader of the so-called White Panthers, a pale British imitation of the *enragés* of Paris or Watts, found himself in court in January 1973 for his editing of *Nasty Tales*, a paper launched in 1972 to exploit the temporarily profitable ambiguity between counter-cultural ideology and pornography. The paper introduced itself with such lines as 'Hi, kids. Don't forget your *Nasty Tales* out today. Packed to the brim with drugs, sex and violence comix.' Though the judge in his summing up said that many people thought 'the pendulum of permissiveness ' had swung too far, *Nasty Tales*, its editors and distributors, were acquitted. Landed with costs however, *Nasty Tales* folded in 1974.

As John Sutherland wisely observes in *Offensive Literature*, 'one reason that *Nasty Tales* was cleared was that its kind of protest was, by 1973, out of date and irrelevant'. The return to power of a Conservative Government in 1970 had reanimated political as opposed to cultural debate. *International Times* had virtually ceased publication by the end of 1973, in June *Oz* had gone into liquidation owing £20,000. In its last issue Charles Widgery, who had edited the magazine during the *Oz* trial, wrote this epitaph:

The truth of the matter is not that the-leaders-sold-out or that-something-greatly-beautious-grew-cankered, but that the underground got smashed, good and proper by those forces of which it stood in defiance. It was smashed, because it could not, by 1968, be laughed at or ignored or patronized any longer. The underground was able to make really painful attacks on the system's intellectually based forms of power. Of all the intellectual property speculators of the Sixties, it made the most sizable incursions into capitalism's real estate, the family, school, work, discipline, the 'impartial' law courts and the British Broadcasting Corporation. Unlike previous movements of radical critics, it actually transmitted its mood of indiscipline to young people of all classes.

By the time of the collapse of *Oz* the mood of the underground had changed from euphoria to disillusion. Economic and political conditions no longer encouraged utopianism; instead there was a need to hold on to such gains as had been made. Circumstances favoured a disengagement and retreat into private concerns. The exploration of inner space had always been important in underground ideology, and sects offering the mystical solace of Eastern religions, together with fundamentalist Christian groups, appear around 1968, in parallel with the political militants. A lead was given by the Beatles, who first indicated their approval for transcendental meditation by joining the Maharishi Mahesh Yogi on a course at Bangor in Wales in August 1967, and then spending eleven weeks at his ashram in India in 1968.

The cults that prospered – Krishna Consciousness, the Divine Light Unification Church, Scientology, the Jesus People – tended to cut their followers off from the world, and then, like the militant sects, reinforce this retreat with a rigid internal discipline that forbade normal social contacts. The hippy trail to India combined the romantic tradition of the *wanderjahr* with a search for enlightenment outside Western society. At home there was a move to withdraw from urban communities to the remoter areas of Scotland and Wales, where life could be led as far as possible without engagement in straight society. The commune movement, whose individual groups exercised varying degrees of discipline, had 300 subscription-paying members in 1971, and their journal sold 2,500 copies. At that time there were estimated to be at least fifty serious communal ventures of differing types under way in Britain.

A sense of withdrawal became widespread: Arnold Wesker's play *The Friends* (1970) evokes the mood among a group of young people who have created, and then abandoned, a design enterprise that has made them rich and fashionable. Wesker is plainly critical of the *Time* magazine and King's Road values that have undermined the group. The one middle-aged character shouts at them:

'The Trend-makers.' Huh! The habit of discontent was all your lot ever created. Making the young feel that the world belonged only to them. Real little class terrorists you were, intimidating everyone over the age of twenty-five with your swinging this and your swinging that. You never thought you'd grow old or die. Even the politicians and the poets were frightened of you, you screamed so loudly about your squalid backgrounds.

By the end of the decade several of the leading lights who owed their success to London's rise to fashion left the city. Peter Blake moved to the West Country in 1969, where fellow artists Richard Smith, Joe Tilson and Howard Hodgkin had already settled. (In 1975 Blake formalized his withdrawal with the creation of the Brotherhood of Ruralists, a retreat in all senses of the word.) The move marks the closure of the era of Pop Art. Blake said, 'One of the things one sort of subconsciously hoped for was that Pop Art would have a new public. I hoped that if I painted a picture of Elvis Presley, Elvis Presley fans would enjoy the picture. But they didn't go to the galleries, they didn't look at the art magazines, they didn't even see the picture.'

Blake is quoted from *Goodbye Baby and Amen: A Saraband for the Sixties*, a collection of David Bailey's photographs published in 1969 that is as deliberately elegaic in tone as the *Box of Pin-Ups* was provocative. The 'cast of characters' is much larger than in 1965, models and restaurateurs are outnumbered by pop stars, actors and directors; artists and writers remain in the minority. The all-embracing nature of the spectacle is summed up by photographs of John Lennon and Daniel Cohn-Bendit (taken from a television screen) facing each other across the page. Peter Evans's text is written emphatically in the past tense. 'To the older generation critics, it was a shallow and irrelevant epoch in British history. To the cast, it was a long, long happening in a no-man's land, both elusive and energetic and inevitably evaporative in the end.'

Though it marks a genuine transition from one period to another, the tone of *Goodbye Baby* might have been less elegaic if it had been published at any other time than 1969. The end of every decade invites a miniature millenarianism, and Christopher Booker's *The Neophiliacs*, also published in 1969, is no exception. Booker, who was deposed from his editorship of *Private Eye* in 1963, spent the next six years working on this 'Study of the revolution in English life in the Fifties and Sixties'. He has presented it as an external account – 'there seemed to be no one standing outside the bubble, and observing just how odd and shallow and egocentric and even rather horrible it was' – yet it is striking how much the book is of a piece with the events described.

Booker's argument is that the period from 1956 to 1966 was a distinct episode in British history, a kind of collective dream, and then nightmare, inspired by unparalleled affluence. Politicians and pop singers alike were seized by a 'psychic epidemic' that could only be understood in terms of group psychology. From the perspective of 1968 and 1969, for Booker the turning point is 1966, the year of Swinging London which fascinated and appalled him. After that the dream fades into reality. As 'the particular collective fantasy which had so dominated English life between 1955 and 1966 continued to subside, the climate was one of aftermath, disillusionment, exhaustion, even of reaction. . . . by 1967–8, many people were beginning to feel to a more or less conscious degree that, in the previous five years, they had come through some kind of shattering experience.'

There is a buried element of autobiography in Booker's argu-ment, for in 1965 the former satirist had had a religious awaken-ing, and the psychological pattern he imposed on events was to some extent his own. Influenced by Malcolm Muggeridge, with whom he stayed while working on the book in 1968 and who had experienced a similar conversion, his conclusion is conservative and religious: the fantasy that had seized society was an expression of the fundamental evil against which man's better nature was set to struggle. He called not only for a revival of Christianity, but

179

for an organic, hierarchical social structure that would revive man's 'orderly' instincts. This may seem quite the opposite of the anarchist views that have been quoted, yet it is, once again, an appeal to a lost sense of community. 'It is this ideal unity from which, by his condition, man has been exiled. And it is this ideal unity which he either attempts to work towards and re-establish, or to dissipate and destroy.'

Bernard Levin's *The Pendulum Years: Britain in the Sixties*, published in 1970, shows a similar conservative reaction. Like Booker, Levin used the imagery of the psychiatrist's couch.

Britain, in the Sixties, can fairly, though cautiously, be compared to a patient undergoing psycho-analysis, and reaching the stage of being brought by the therapist to face the truth about the blocks with which he had protected himself from self-knowledge. The self-knowledge that Britain had been hiding from implied that she had lost her once-commanding position in the world, that the days of her glory were no more, that she was no longer in a position to command obedience, admiration or danegeld from the rest of the world.

Both Levin and Booker interpret the period as one of illusion, giving way to reality – the rhetoric of 'realism' was to become popular on the political Right. It is true that the country's underlying economic problems were ignored, and that the ephemeral expansion of the mid-Sixties helped to obscure them, but what these accounts really tell us is that by 1969 the decade was once more being re-interpreted. The anxiety of the early years and the brief optimism that followed gives way to an altogether grimmer mood. The appeal to social order coincided with a perceptible change in the political and economic climate which helped to reinforce the feeling that a period of excess had to be brought to an end.

As for the psychiatrists, whose language had been so freely borrowed by the journalists, there too was a sense of public defeat and private withdrawal. The anti-psychiatrists' community at Kingsley Hall was dissolved in 1970. In 1971 R. D. Laing put aside the campaigns he had been waging in the Sixties and travelled to Ceylon to study at a Theravada Buddhist monastery. He returned in 1972, and resumed his work for the Philadelphia Foundation, but he did not publish again until 1976. His colleague David Cooper gave up his practice, and in 1971 was living in alcoholic squalor in worse conditions than some of his former patients.

> He does not think there is anything the matter with him
> because
> > one of the things that is
> > the matter with him
> > is that he does not think that there is anything
> > the matter with him

CHAPTER 6

The Party

*'Shocking the bourgeois is,
alas, easier than overthrowing
him.'*

Eric Hobsbawm 'Sex and Revolution' (1969)

In September 1972, assisted by an Arts Council grant, the alternative theatre company Welfare State made a month-long ceremonial pilgrimage from Glastonbury to St Michael's Mount. They travelled in a caravan of converted vehicles, including a hearse, an ambulance, and an army rocket launcher to carry the circus tent used by the twenty-five performers. According to an observer, 'They followed in reverse a route of magical significance previously travelled by Phoenician tin traders, Joseph of Arimathea and King Arthur. It was not a Second Coming, but a First Going Away. Welfare State could not see that there was anything left to come for, but there good reasons to leave the barbaric and insensitive culture.' Under protest, the counter-culture was stealing away. (Ill. 11.)

There were indeed good reasons for wishing to go into retreat in the early 1970s. With the Conservative Government of 1970–4 came a period of increasing political and economic unrest. Unemployment was steadily on the increase, until it reached its first million in 1975. Inflation, which like unemployment had begun to be a problem in the last years of the Labour Government, appeared to be taking off beyond control. The Heath Government's economic policies fuelled inflation by releasing quantities of credits which were supposed to create industrial investment, but which instead set off a doubling in property prices and fostered the creation of dubious fringe banks. Such policies were a provocation to the Trades Unions, whose powers were curbed by the 1971 Industrial Relations Act. In 1970 and 1971 British industry had the worst record for strikes and stoppages since 1926. Some of these were in response to the pressure for higher wages spiralling upwards with inflation, but after the introduction of the Industrial Relations Act in August 1971, followed in November by a system for controlling pay and prices, the political and economic battle became the same. In January 1972 the miners struck in support of their claim for an increase three times greater than the sum permitted by Government policy, and won. In June the dockers imposed a similar defeat. Wages and prices continued to rise until a freeze on both was imposed in November.

Inflation continued to rise as the value of the pound, which was allowed to float in June 1972, was driven down by trade deficits. Then in October 1973 the Arab-Israeli war led to a boycott by oil producers and a massive increase in the price of oil, which quadrupled by the end of the year. The oil crisis played into the hands of the miners, who were preparing for a second battle with the Government over wage policy. An overtime ban caused the Government to declare a state of emergency, and on 1 January 1974 British industry was put on a three-day week to save power. At the beginning of February the miners decided to go on all-out strike, and the Government decided it had no option but to call a general election.

The result of this extraordinary and bitter election – for the three-day week continued until 8 March – was that no party had an overall majority. However, on 4 March Harold Wilson once more became Prime Minister. Inflation continued to soar and the stock market to slump. In October a second general election gave the Labour Government a majority of three. The world-wide recession continued to drive unemployment upwards. In February 1975 Margaret Thatcher became leader of the Conservative Party; although the Conservatives did not return to power until 1979, a new political era was opening.

The period 1970–5 was one of intense activity on the radical Left, but it did not lead to the breakthrough that was hoped for – in fact, quite the opposite. The new era has proved to be one of political reaction and economic depression. Yet if 1968 produced no political results, we cannot entirely dismiss the rhetoric of cultural revolution. The campaigns of the late Sixties made a number of gains in personal and artistic freedom that opened the way for further campaigns to assert the rights of women, homosexuals and blacks. The theatre experienced a second revolution after that of 1956, and rock'n'roll has managed a transition in cultural status from that of a minority entertainment limited to one age-group and excluded from serious consideration as an expressive medium, to one where it holds an equal place with other arts of the avant-garde. Rock reveals the extent – and the limits – of the cultural shift that followed the upheavals of 1968.

Rock both shaped and mirrored the values of the cultural revolution. It enacted violence, it was expressive, it attempted the transcendental, and it had the great technical advantage of being enjoyed both in private, through recordings, and *en masse*, at concerts and festivals. In both cases the individual listener could identify with a community of fans who felt the same emotional appeals as he or she did. Its primary effect was indeed to transmit feeling rather than thought. This is not to denigrate feeling, but it helps to explain why the political ideology of rock – and by extension that of the counter-culture – remained almost entirely personal. Writing in 1969, George Melly recognized this limitation. 'Its only revolutionary value is in its insistence on personal freedom. This is certainly important, but the right to smoke pot or strip naked in public are not going to affect the structure of society. This is not to deny the pop world a political bias. It is almost totally anarchist because, alone among the schools of political thought, anarchism defends total freedom.'

It is important to remember that, as in other art forms, there was a cultural 'break' in the pattern of popular music around 1968. While much popular music remained blandly commercial, groups that had risen on the first wave of general popularity – the Beatles, the Rolling Stones, the Who – turned to more experimental and critical work, while a new generation of 'underground' groups concentrated on the avant-garde audience who liked music not acceptable to the average listener to what in 1967 had become the BBC's Radio 1. The distinction hardened between 'rock' and 'pop'. In *The Sociology of Rock* (1978) Simon Frith points out

184

that there was an important economic relationship between rock and the underground – after all, rock was the most fruitful source of income – and this had important consequences for the way rock was perceived.

Rock turned out to be the basic form of underground culture, but in becoming so it was imbued with an ideology that was at marked variance with previous notions of pop. Rock was valued for its politics, its freedom, its sexuality, its relationship to cultural struggles. The music that was most despised and distrusted by the underground press was precisely the commercial, successful, teenage pop that had been essential to the development of the British music press. Rock was defined as the music that articulated the values of a new community of youth, it was opposed to the traditional values of show-biz; and as the appeal of the underground spread from its original bohemian roots so did this notion of rock.

Thus nurtured by the underground, and nurturing it, rock became the means of transmission of counter-cultural values to a far wider audience. Bernice Martin concludes that rock has been the most important factor in the enlargement of personal (as opposed to political) freedom.

The fact that rock is play, leisure-time self-expression for the kids, does not make it trivial. Human beings persistently experience the frivolous and the profound, the ephemeral and the elemental, in the *same* activities. This is as true of rock music as of sex itself, and it is this fact which renders it such a powerful medium of cultural communication in contemporary society. It has certainly acted as the single most important vehicle for the spread of the hedonistic messages of the Expressive Revolution, passing them up and down the age and class hierarchies in ways in which have become so normal that we no longer even notice the radical nature of the change which has occurred in our cultural presuppositions over these last three decades.

Rock, it seems, has achieved a 'long front of culture' in the way that fine art has not.

One of the reasons for the success of rock was of course that its subversive and hedonistic messages were being transmitted with the aid of a powerful and profitable communications industry. The capitalist nature of the industry was a further constraint on the capacity of rock to influence political thinking as opposed to personal feeling. But there were moments when both inside and outside the rock world the movement took on a quasi-political nature, either as a hint of what was possible, or as a symbol of the menace to order that rock contained. At rock festivals the conflicting elements of the counter-culture could come together in mutual celebration. As Michael Clarke points out in *The Politics of Pop Festivals* (1982),

> music was there to celebrate common areas of values: anti-authoritarianism, sexual relationships without marriage, drug consumption, togetherness. The pop festival became the venue at which these values and feelings could be celebrated *en masse*, with the minimum of interference from straight society, without at the same time involving a total and permanent rejection of that society: the perfect location for the weekend hippy.

Inevitably the sight of so many young people enjoying themselves in their own manner to their music provoked hostility among those who feared such freedom. They disguised their feelings as anxiety about 'drugs, sex, disorder and squalor'.

The history of pop festivals goes back, appropriately enough, to the *annus mirabilis* of 1956, when a jazz festival was held in the grounds of Lord Montagu's country house at Beaulieu, but the Aldermaston marches of CND undoubtedly contributed to a tradition of physical discomfort and communal joy. The Beaulieu Jazz Festivals had ended in 1961, victim of their own popularity which attracted the disturbances press and police predicted. But in that year the promotor Harold Pendleton launched his series of festivals, first at Richmond and then Windsor Race Course. In 1967 a 'festival of the flower children' was held at Woburn Abbey. In 1968 8,000 people attended a festival on the Isle of Wight mounted by a new commercial enterprise, Fiery Creations. By then summer festivals had become an established part of the rock culture and economy. In 1969 – the year of both Woodstock and Altamont in the United States, the apogee and nadir of such events – Fiery Creations drew 100,000 people to the Isle of Wight, while 250,000 attended the free concert in Hyde Park during which the Rolling Stones marked the death of their guitarist Brian Jones.

By 1970 the size and commercialism of the festivals were attracting criticism both from the authorities and the underground. Fiery Creations fought a hard legal battle with local interests to mount a third Isle of Wight Festival in August. They invested £1.5 million and 200,000 people came, but the festival site with its double row of 10ft-high security fences was besieged by some 60,000 who had occupied a hill overlooking the stage. Among them were the former performance artist and hero of the Paris barricades Jean-Jaques Lebel, leading a group of French and Belgian Situationists, and Mick Farren, leading the White Panthers, who were determined to contest the spectacle. In July Farren had helped to organize a festival known as Phun City near Worthing in Sussex, originally intended to raise funds for *International Times*. Legal difficulties left them unable to charge entrance money, and the 'free festival' movement was accidentally born. Moving on from this 'model of the alternative society' to the Isle of Wight, it seemed to Farren 'more as though a concentration camp was being built than a rock festival.'

The struggle between security guards and gate-crashers went on for four days, until Fiery Creations capitulated and allowed the festival to be taken over. After the débâcle, local politicians brought in an Isle of Wight Act which made it impossible for such events to be repeated, and in 1971 Fiery Creations went into liquidation. The same lobby then introduced a Night Assemblies Bill which would have severely restricted all rock festivals, but the proposal was defeated, and a system of voluntary regulation was set up instead.

At midsummer in 1971 the free festival movement held its most successful event, the Glastonbury Fayre. This was a festival of the alternative lifestyle as much as of rock music: the ancient mystical associations of Glastonbury, supposedly the resting place of Joseph of Arimathea, had become reinforced by more recent cosmological calculations that the area had been visited by Unidentified Flying Objects. The Guru Maharaj Ji addressed 10,000 from a specially constructed pyramid aligned to attract the beneficent forces of the region. It was unlikely, however, that the dedicated anarchism of the movement would be tolerated for long, or that its leaders would be content with toleration. In 1972 a 'Rent Strike People's Festival' was attended by 700, held without permission in Windsor Great Park. 8,000 came to its sequel in 1973, sufficient to deter the police from punitive action, but in 1974 220 were arrested when the police moved in to clear the site. In that year Stonehenge became the focus for a summer solstice festival that was held in the face of increasing official harassment until a last stand in 1985.

By 1975 rock and rock festivals were part of national culture, and the form was about to receive fresh stimulus from a second, or even third generation educated in the traditions of the 'youth culture', with the emergence of punk. Simon Frith notes that the youth market has had its corresponding effect on its exploiters. 'In the last ten to fifteen years students' use of rock – whether for relaxation or as a form of art – has transformed not just the predominant sound of universities and colleges but also the music and marketing policies of the record industry.' The specialist newspapers, such as the *New Musical Express* and *Melody Maker*, which at the beginning of the 1960s were content with little more than recycling the publicity material fed to them, underwent a parallel transformation. Peter York writes in *Style Wars* (1980), 'In three definable periods (Class of '68, Class of '72, Class of '76), they hired successive waves of young journalists from the avant-garde margins – the underground press, the fanzines etc. – who were anything but hacks. These personality writers became celebrities within their milieu, and major reputation brokers. Their first duty, just like a real critic, was to the reader, to Art, to their political commitment.' In the same way the quality press also began to review rock concerts and records alongside theatre and dance.

Although generally capable of carrying political meaning only at the level of myth and imagery – 'Streetfighting Man', 'Are you going to San Francisco?', 'Revolution' (the songs of Bob Dylan are an exception) – rock music did convey values of personal freedom promoted by the underground to a wider constituency. This did not amount to a complete transformation, but it did significantly alter the cultural pattern by changing the categories and hierarchies of taste.

Though rock found acceptance as a new cultural form, its largely emotional appeal limited its critical impact on the popular culture that was gradually absorbing it. Those who wished to demonstrate the possibilities of revolutionary change needed a more articulate medium. Given the awareness of spectacle both as mask and manifesto, and the theatrical nature of so many gestures of the underground, there were sound reasons for the theatre to become the principal form through which the politics of the counter-culture found their most lasting expression. The theatre that was created was not merely the framing of a particular message in a chosen art form; the form itself, and the theatrical practice behind it, was a laboratory for the social change its creators wished to bring about. As the playwright Howard Brenton put it in 1974, 'My generation shares an idea that the theatre not only describes but actually shows new possibilities, that you can write so force-fully that a possibility of a new way of looking at the world, a new way of living, can actually be found through the theatre.'

To achieve this, the new theatre tried to be revolutionary both in its politics and its aesthetic. It was the product of an urgent need to find new forms with which to convey the cultural and political conflict. Some of the earliest manifestations were indeed crude agitprop street events where the political message was primary: posters, street plays and radical newspapers were all called forth as means to communicate the new ideas that the upheavals had released. But the new ideas demanded new means of expression. The theatre, once it was broken free of the social and economic conventions that structured it and surrounded it, offered a medium that was both flexible and, since its technologi-cal requirements can be very small, direct.

These were the pressures that generated the astonishingly rapid expansion of 'fringe' theatre between 1968 and 1975. The term derives, as we have seen, from the visiting groups that clustered round the official programme of events at the Edinburgh Festival, but it also suggests a marginalization of the new theatre groups' work. This exclusion from the official theatre was part handicap, part advantage. Until 1978 performers in fringe theatre groups could not qualify for membership of the actors' union, Equity. On the other hand, the cooperative basis on which most fringe companies were run, and the fragile economics of their operation, would have been completely impossible if even the minimum wage required by Equity contracts had been imposed. As the fringe developed, the issue of its status became more acute, particularly for writers who wished to be heard by as large an audience as possible. The need for subsidy – which the general economic conditions of the 1970s made it increasingly difficult to do without – called into question the new groups' relations with its patrons, be it the Arts Council or the subsidized theatres that began to open their doors to them. As with rock, the fringe gradually became absorbed and systematized, so that in the 1980s it is doubtful that a special category of 'fringe' theatre truly exists at all. That had not occurred by 1975, however, and in the period up to the effective stop on expansion caused by the Arts Council's difficulties in that year, it was not at all clear whether the recognition and then absorption of the fringe would be a victory or a defeat.

The new forms created in the agitational atmosphere of 1968 did not spring out of thin air. Joan Littlewood's Theatre Workshop had been pointing a way forward since 1945, not simply in terms of a political commitment implicit in the choice of plays presented and how they were done, but in terms of the different relationships within the company and between the company and its audience. Though her directorial methods were ultimately autocratic, Joan Littlewood had shown that it was possible to develop both script and production collectively, so that actors felt that they had a part in creating the play. Given the right themes and the right company, it was possible to appeal to a working-class audience in its own terms, and it was logical to try to base this theatre within a community, as Littlewood did at Stratford in East London, and Peter Cheeseman did in Stoke-on-Trent when he became director of the Stephen Joseph Theatre Company at the Victoria Theatre in 1962. Littlewood's ensemble work was regularly dissipated by transfers to the West End, but Cheeseman has developed a strong tradition of creating plays with specific local appeal.

Though subsequently dismissed by radical playwrights like John McGrath as 'bourgeois' and 'élitist' (in spite of the early training McGrath received there), George Devine's creation of a writers' theatre at the Royal Court was also an attempt at an alternative theatre practice, an attempt to resist the devouring monster of commercialism in the West End and on Broadway by allying actors and writers. But both Littlewood and Devine were working within traditional buildings that imposed certain forms. John Arden, the Royal Court writer whose career took a definite new direction after 1968, has commented:

The so-called *revolution* at the Royal Court and Theatre Workshop in the late Fifties had been largely a revolution of content. Playwrights were at last handling a whole range of material hitherto unacceptable to

190

critics and managements, to say nothing of the Lord Chamberlain. . . .
But this new (or renewed) public was still expected to submit to exactly
the same actor-audience relationships that had obtained at least since the
start of the century.

These relationships could not obtain during a CND rally, at a
rock concert, or in a poorly ventilated basement in the middle of
the day. The Little Theatre movement, with its small but committed following, supplied one precedent for a different audience
relationship. David Halliwell's peripatetic writers' collective,
Quipu, had begun experimenting with lunchtime theatre – a
subtle but significant change in theatre-going – in 1966. The visits
in 1967 of the American Café La Mama Troupe to the Traverse
in Edinburgh and the Mercury Theatre in London and of Joe
Chaikin's Open Theater to the Royal Court were further encour-
agements to develop new theatrical forms and a different audience
relationship.

Though their aims were finally the same, the two British groups
that were already active had begun from opposing aesthetic
positions. Historically, the Cartoon Archetypal Slogan Theatre,
launched by Roland Muldoon and Claire Burnley in 1965, can
claim to be 'the first rock'n'roll theatre group', but CAST draws
on a long tradition of agitprop theatre, and indeed its founders
worked at the Communist Unity Theatre, where political drama
had had a home before the Second World War and whose
members had performed agitprop in shelters during the Blitz.
Expelled for deviationism, the Muldoons performed their first
show, *John D. Muggins is Dead* – an anti-Vietnam war play that
anticipates Brook's *US* – in folk clubs and pubs, adopting a music-
hall style that could retain the attention of their audience while
driving their political message home with vigour and humour.

By contrast, the People Show has been described as 'pre-
political'. The phrase is Jeff Nuttall's, who encountered the other
founding elements of the troupe at the Abbey Arts Centre in
New Barnet, Hertfordshire in 1966, where the former cells of the
Brethren of Antioch were let to artists and writers. The people he
met there – Mark Long, Syd Palmer, John Darling and Laura
Gilbert, who had already begun some theatrical experiments –
formed the cast for a poetry and jazz event Nuttall scripted for
the musician Mike Westbrook at the 1966 Notting Hill Gate

Festival. Encouraged by their success, Nuttall introduced them to the basement of Better Books. 'The number of studio theatres that have subsequently attempted the efficiency of that filthy cellar are numerous. The way in which they have all failed is significant. The inevitable black walls, lighting unit, architect-designed seating define the studio theatre. Better Books basement was just a fucking cellar and could be redefined for every piece.'

As we have seen, Nuttall's concerns were part-poetic, part-sculptural; though they were a significant application of Artaud's theatre of cruelty, they were not theatrical in the accepted sense. The closest equivalent was Dada-cabaret. 'I was interested in the fact that absurdity in language doesn't just make people laugh, it also strips language of sense and leaves the bare bones of syntax showing; reveals linguistic structures by paring away the clouding of emotive communication. Far from the chaos which the prosaic mind takes it to be, Dada is the way to a very lucid constructivism.' Such methods eschewed the bald slogans of agitprop. Instead, surreal juxtapositions created 'a clouding reference, a masking of meaning, to compel the poem, music, painting to be perceived as poem, music, painting, not as a description of a nightingale or a treatise on the state of the working class.' The social concern at the root of political theatre is none the less present – as for instance in Nuttall's script on the Moors murders, *A Nice Quiet Night* (1967) – but the aim was 'to take crucial anxiety and turn it upside-down in creative play.'

The People Show escaped from both the physical definitions of a theatre building, and from the conventional meaning of what a piece of theatre was. New physical relations and a new aesthetic pointed the way to a non-theatrical theatre that, developing from the New York happenings, has become known as performance art. Their first event in the Better Books basement was literally a people show, in that the performers stood as living sculptures, parts of their bodies exposed through cut-outs in screens, while they spoke their lines. The fine-art tradition of visual as opposed to verbal communication encouraged an exploration of process rather than product – product that in any case could not be treated as a commodity on the art market. Dada, collage and found objects contributed an element of chance; both the performers' bodies as kinetic sculptures, and the space in which they happened to be, called for responses that lay outside the control

192

of any writer or director. Yet the abandonment of theatrical conventions of illusionism, narrative or plot opened up new possibilities for theatrical performance, just as the unfamiliar spaces radically altered the relationship between performers and audience.

The People Show, which continues in being, spawned ideas that escaped the confines of theatre altogether. Though he continued to write for them on occasion, Jeff Nuttall broke with the group in 1968, and was replaced by Roland Miller, who in turn left the People Show in 1971. At the end of 1968 Nuttall moved to Yorkshire and taught first at Bradford Art School and later Leeds. He introduced the People Show to a region which, as we saw in chapter III, had been a busy centre for theatrical experiment ever since John Arden's Festival of Anarchy at Kirkbymoorside in 1963. At Bradford Art School Peter Brook's former assistant on *US*, Albert Hunt, had mounted such events as a restaging of the Russian revolution in the streets of Bradford in 1967, and Hunt went on to develop (in this context) more orthodox theatre pieces such as *John Ford's Cuban Missile Crisis* (1970). Meanwhile one of his collaborators, the Bradford Art School's librarian, John Fox, had laid the foundations for a form of theatre that has abandoned conventional notions almost entirely.

John and Sue Fox founded the Welfare State in 1968 as a pop group to present theatre in dance halls; their thrust was towards street theatre, circus and devising handmade ceremonies, namings, memorial services, performances, processions and dances, constructing sideshows, environments and landscape sculptures and arranging workshops and teaching courses for any sympathetic space, situation or season.' The 'performance' includes a long period of preparation, preferably with as much inter-action as possible with the local community for whom it is intended, and a similar period afterwards. In 1972, when the Foxes moved to Leeds, the Welfare State itself became a commune. In February 1973 it took up temporary residence on a scrap-heap in Burnley, and performance for a time became virtually indistinguishable from an eccentric everyday life.

The Welfare State – which also continues to function – sought to serve the community through ceremonies that would revive a lost sense of magic; their communitarian aims are not as distant from those of the agitprop groups as might at first appear. 'Community theatre' attempts to reconcile the political aims of the performers and the social needs of the audience; its difficulty is that the theatrical form itself becomes secondary. This was the experience of the founders of the Brighton Combination in 1967. Three London University graduates, Jenny Harris, Ruth Marks and Noel Grieg, inspired by the example of Jim Haynes's work in Edinburgh, the People Show and Theatre Workshop, opened a cooperative community venture in Brighton. According to Jenny Harris their converted schoolhouse was more a café and dance hall than a theatre. 'The crucial thing was to find a new audience. We were trying to create a new context. We were trying to create something that wasn't a theatre, but which was a place where you could put on plays.' Plays were in fact only one element in a programme of films, discos, exhibitions and readings, and the focus was the community. Howard Brenton and the director Chris Parr staged some of his earliest plays there, but for them the theatrical experiment did not work out. Harris commented, 'none of them actually stayed because we weren't interested in what they were interested in – which was a literary field. . . . We were more interested in the *process* and the young people that were coming in.' The Combination's founders themselves became disenchanted with the atmosphere in Brighton. In 1971 they began a community arts project for the Albany Trust in South London, and two years later opened the Albany Empire, where (in spite of an arson attack for which the National Front were suspected, and which destroyed their original building) theatre has found the relation they intended it to have with the audience they have created.

In the spring of 1968, just as external events were reaching their peak, there was a remarkable conjunction of radical talent at the Unity Theatre. John Arden, having devised a one-day Vietnam event while he and his wife Margaretta D'Arcy were teaching at New York University in 1967, wrote a play for the Cartoon Archetypal Slogan Theatre, *Harold Muggins is a Martyr*. It was a fairly crude parable about Britain in the 1960s, but it was the first of Arden and D'Arcy's explicitly propagandist plays. While making a significant gesture by choosing to work with CAST, Arden also brought down John Fox from Yorkshire to build settings for what had originally been intended as an

environmental play. Arden and Margaretta D'Arcy also performed, and by all accounts the mixture of talents and attitudes
proved explosive. Accustomed to improvisation and anarchic
humour, the Muldoons had difficulties with Arden's crafted lines,
and relations broke down before the opening night. Neither the
fans of Arden nor CAST were satisfied, but the performance
and the discussions that followed them each night became a
spontaneous conference, in Arden's words, 'of many left-wing
artistic groups and individuals who, maybe for the first time, were
made aware of each other and their respective work.' One of the
longest-running political theatre groups, which had to take the
theatrically acceptable name Red Ladder in order to qualify for an
Arts Council grant in 1975, grew out of the Agitprop Information
Service that resulted from the 1968 discussions.

1968 was the turning point for the fringe theatre, and we should
not neglect the impact of Paris and the student revolts. Howard
Brenton has said

> May 1968 was crucial. It was a great watershed and directly affected
> me. A lot of the ideas in *Magnificence* came straight out of the writing of
> that time in Paris, and the idea of official life being like a screen. . . .
> May 1968 disinherited my generation in two ways. First it destroyed any
> remaining affection for the official culture. The situationists showed how
> all of them, the dead greats, are corpses on our backs – Goethe,
> Beethoven – how gigantic the fraud is. But it also, secondly, destroyed
> the notions of personal freedom. Freaking out and drug culture, anarchist
> notions of spontaneous freedom, anarchist political action: it all failed. It
> was defeated. A generation dreaming of a beautiful utopia was kicked –
> kicked awake and not dead. I've got to believe not kicked dead. May
> 1968 gave me a desperation I still have.

Yet in spite of Brenton's dismissal of the 'official culture', it was
changes in the attitudes of the guardians of that culture that
allowed the emergent elements of the fringe theatre to become a
significant force. The developments of the following years would
have been impossible without the benevolence of the Arts Council
and the abolition of theatre censorship.

Pressure for the abolition of stage censorship had been mount-
ing ever since the relaxation of literary censorship by the Obscene
Publications Act of 1959. In 1966 a joint committee of both
Houses of Parliament was set up to consider theatre censorship.

By law, every play performed in public had to be licensed by an officer of the Queen's household, the Lord Chamberlain, who employed a team of readers to consider scripts, and even on occasion to visit theatres to check on their production and performance. The accepted means of circumventing the Lord Chamberlain was the 'club' production, but this loophole was declared illegal in 1965 when the Royal Court was prosecuted for its club première of Edward Bond's *Saved*. There were later club performances at the Royal Court and elsewhere (another encouragement to the development of fringe theatre venues), but in November 1967, in spite of having recommended his own abolition to the Parliamentary Committee (which concurred) the Lord Chamberlain banned outright any performance of Bond's new play *Early Morning*, for it showed in an unfavourable light two classes of person about whom he was particularly sensitive: politicians, in the shape of Gladstone and Disraeli, and the Royal Family, with a lesbian Queen Victoria. The Arts Council, caught on a legal hook, threatened to withdraw the Royal Court's grant if it went ahead with the production; the British Council later sent the play on a foreign tour. Two Sunday-night performances of *Early Morning* were scheduled for March 1968. The first was attended by police, whose presence sufficiently frightened the Royal Court into cancelling the second and substituting an afternoon 'critics' dress rehearsal', a no-charge, invitation-only event with entrance by a side door.

Fortunately these absurdities were ended, and the Royal Court spared from prosecution by the passing of the Theatres Act on 27 September 1968, which abolished the powers of the Lord Chamberlain. On the 28 September *Hair*, an American musical which used stage nudity and four-letter words to celebrate draft evasion and the dawning of the age of Aquarius, opened at the Shaftesbury Theatre to enormous commercial success. Managements were still cautious however, and in 1970 Kenneth Tynan's sex revue *Oh Calcutta!* had to open at the Round House, transferring to the West End only after the Attorney General had indicated that he would not prosecute.

It is important to appreciate that the Theatres Act merely placed drama on an equal footing with literature by removing pre-censorship. It was still an offence to present an obscene performance in public or private, the test being that of the 1959

Obscene Publications Act. As the Arts Council pointed out in its theatre report in 1970, 'the position, therefore, now is that plays, like novels, are subject to an Act which is far from satisfactory.' Censorship can be exercised through patronage and control of access as much as by legal means. As John Arden pointed out in 1977, 'The abolition of the Lord Chamberlain's function . . . has by no means resulted in a Theatre of Free Speech, let alone Free Opinion.'

The principal point of patronage is to stimulate performance, and in the mid-1960s the Arts Council paid particular attention to the state of the theatre. The spate of theatre building and restoration helped to create demand and opportunities for fresh work. In the autumn of 1967, having already surveyed the subsidized theatre in London and the provinces and decided on increased spending in those areas, the Council began a two-year enquiry which led to the publication of *The Theatre Today in England and Wales* (1970). Its conclusions about the commercial theatre were understandably gloomy. In London, 'the situation causes a good deal of concern. Most of the producing managements and the theatre owners are worried. . . . Outside London the theatre of private enterprise is on its last legs, physically run-down and morally disheartened.' The network of companies and directorships which as 'the Group' had held British theatre back in the Forties and Fifties (see *In Anger* p. 66) had become 'the Octopus', dominated by Associated Television's acquisition of the Stoll-Moss theatres. Lew Grade's ATV and his brother Bernard Delfont's EMI were shown to have control over large sections of the theatre industry, though their profits were plainly made elsewhere. 'Outside London, commercial theatre is generally speaking no longer viable, and in London it is becoming decreasingly so.'

The Arts Council's answer was enhanced public subsidy, both in London to the Royal Shakespeare Company, and to the National Theatre – then operating in the Old Vic while its new building was rising very slowly on the South Bank – and in the provinces, where it was decided to construct a network of a dozen large-scale touring theatres out of the remains of the old pre-war touring and variety circuit. At the same time subsidy was steadily increased to provincial repertory companies, from 24 in 1960 to 52 in 1970. In that year the total Arts Council subsidy to the theatre was just over £2 million, of which £375,000 went to the National, and £275,000 to the RSC.

The Arts Council's theatre report gave only a page to consideration of the fringe, and in its forecast of the 'Panorama of the Theatre' its rise is not foreseen. Yet from the 6 part-time companies in existence in 1968 (the first year that grants were given to the fringe) by 1970 the number in London alone had increased to 32. By the end of the 1970s the fringe was getting £2 million in public subsidy on its own account, divided among some 60 companies.

The Arts Council found it difficult to come to terms with the new forms of art that were being submitted for subsidy, for they did not conform to the old academic disciplines of form or practice. That, after all, was the point about them, to mix media and confuse categories. In October 1968 the Arts Council gingerly approached the problem by forming a New Activities Committee under the chairmanship of Lord Boyle, and including such luminaries as Lord Harewood, Peter Hall and Professor Frank Kermode. With the exception of its chairman and deputy chairman, the committee enthusiastically recommended that a New Activities and Multi-Media panel should be set up, with £100,000 to spend. What they liked was the new movement's 'apparent opposition to established art forms and methods of presentation.'

Lord Goodman thought otherwise, however, and in 1969 gave the committee under its new chairman, the art collector Michael Astor, £15,000. The Arts Council's earnest endeavours to come to terms with the counter-culture merely raised expectations that it was unwilling to satisfy. The incomprehension that the committee showed at an early meeting at the House of Lords led to the formation of the Friends of the Arts Council Cooperative, which in 1969 began regular meetings of up to eighty interested activists, who wished to democratize the distribution of funds by handing the decisions over to the artists involved. The meetings of the New Activities Committee became targets for disruption and invasion. Astor countered by inviting six FACOP members onto the committee, but when these tried to act as delegates for their excluded colleagues, relations broke down.

In February 1969 FACOP held five days of meetings to discuss what applications it could support for the £15,000 available, and arrived at a grand total of £125,000 worth, including £10 to pay the fine of a demonstrator outside the American Embassy. Some applications did get through, notably to support the Hebden Bridge Festival in May 1970, and the work seen at *Come Together*, a fringe festival at the Royal Court later in that year, but the Arts Council decided that the New Activities Committee had not been a success, and it was wound up. A downgraded Experimental Projects Committee lingered on until 1973, and community arts began to receive subsidy in 1974, but in the main the Arts Council preferred to maintain the traditional categories of art. Lord Goodman revealed the difficulties the official culture had with the new art in his report for 1968–9. The New Activities Committee

has discovered that the major myth is the belief that it is employing a common language. It has, to some extent, underrated the resentment arising from the very fact of its intrusion. It has also underrated the self-contained and palisaded character of the 'activities', and the fact that the occupants of the palisades regard themselves as a community requiring nothing from the Arts Council, except possibly its premises and its funds.

Goodman's patronizing attitude was met with equal incomprehension on the other side. Jeff Nuttall, who served briefly on the committee, wrote later,

It was exactly what Marcuse calls containment and what the Situationists call 'the creation of spectacle'. The ironic thing was that the very art that they were buying up for spectacle with their first trickle of grants belonged to the Dada, Surrealist, Beat tradition whose declared purpose was a deep-seated revolution of the sensibilities.

In spite of these vexed relations – the Arts Council ever censorious, the artists always suspicious and always demanding – a new theatrical economy emerged, with its own network of theatres and performance spaces, each with its individual policy. Although the fringe received only a small proportion of the total Arts Council budget for theatre, there was a rapid expansion up until 1975, when inflation and government policy brought the steady increase in general subsidy to an end. By that time there were over a hundred alternative theatre companies, some with their own base, but for the most part constantly on the move round some two hundred small-scale touring venues. The new companies had in turn created opportunities for a new and sizable generation of writers. Arts centres had sprung up all over the country, presenting dance, theatre and exhibitions, and undertaking a great deal of local community work which blurred the distinction between amateur and professional, between cultural and social. In London the free listings in *Time Out* provided a vital information service; in 1970 *Theatre Quarterly* was launched as the equivalent of *Encore* (1956–64), which had provided a critical context for the first revolution in British theatre.

The pioneer ventures had been the Traverse and Arts Lab in Drury Lane; when that folded its place was taken by the Oval House in Kennington, officially a boys' club, but whose director from 1961 to 1973, Peter Oliver, had converted the gym and chapel into theatre spaces. The Oval House became an important venue for meetings and conferences, as well as performances. In 1968 Verity Bargate and Frederick Proud began mounting lunchtime performances at the Soho Theatre in a small building next to Better Books. When they moved to a basement in Riding House Street, provided rent-free by the London Polytechnic, this became the Soho Poly. Also in 1968 a developer allowed Charles Marowitz and Thelma Holt to open their Open Space Theatre in another basement in the Tottenham Court Road. The entertainment rooms of pubs became temporary and sometimes permanent small theatres: the King's Head in Islington started a supper theatre in 1970; the Bush Theatre opened above a pub in Shepherd's Bush in 1972, and rapidly gained a reputation for its commitment to presenting new plays. Again in 1972 Maurice Colbourne, Mike Irving and Steve Gooch converted a disused synagogue in Half Moon Street in Aldgate; in 1979 the Half Moon moved to new premises in the Mile End Road, and subsequently built an entirely new theatre on the site, which opened in 1985.

One of the most remarkable progressions was that of Ed Berman's Inter-Action Trust. Berman, an American Rhodes scholar, began as a resident dramatist and director at the Mercury Theatre in Notting Hill Gate in 1967. His chief interest, however, can be described as creative play in the community. After leaving the Mercury he set up Inter-Action as a cooperative charity to mount game sessions on play sites and at carnivals. Theatre work continued in parallel with this. In 1968 he launched into lunchtime theatre, first at the Little Theatre in St Martin's Lane, then at the

Ambience restaurant in Queensway, and later at the Green Banana in Soho. There was sufficient demand for such work for there to be a touring company, The Other Company, run by Naftali Yavin, and a children's theatre group, Dogg's Troupe. After a period of homelessness, in 1972 Berman opened the Almost Free Theatre – so called because the audience were invited to pay what they could – just off Piccadilly Circus. Berman took advantage of the new attitude in local government towards the use of short-life property and formed the Inter-Action Housing Trust in 1970, so that its members could live as a commune. In 1977 they moved into their own purpose-built property in Kentish Town. Although theatre, as 'creative play' has always been an important element in Inter-Action's work – Tom Stoppard's *Dirty Linen* (1976) for instance, which had a long run at the Arts Theatre – it has been essentially subordinate to its communitarian projects. An environmental play about farming, *The Last Straw* led to the creation of a real farm, City Farm No.1, in 1972, and since then Inter-Action's urban farming projects have been, if anything, more prolific than its theatre.

The new theatre spaces inevitably broke away from the old hierarchical architecture of traditional theatres: there were no longer numbered seats with differential prices and separate access to the auditorium – indeed there might be no seats at all; there was no imaginary 'fourth wall' between actors and audience, often there was no stage and the actors took their action right into the audience's laps. Yet these small theatres, rarely with more than 250 seats, created an exclusivity of a different kind, and they could not serve as popular theatre in the way Joan Littlewood would have understood it. Though inexpensive to run, the constraints of size meant that they could not be commercially profitable, and would always require subsidy of some kind. The lunchtime theatres, of which there were at least ten in the early Seventies, extended the subversion of traditional theatre by being cheap, accessible and blurring the distinction between work and leisure, but the brevity of the playing time and practical economic considerations severely limited what could be done.

This does not depreciate what was achieved: in 1972–3 the Soho Poly managed to première 30 plays in 38 weeks of lunchtime performances and 18 weeks of evening shows, on a grant of £3,000. Writers got £50, actors a mere £5, which shows that the chief subsidy came from the artists themselves, but the season none the less included performances by Colin Blakely, David Warner and Julia Foster. In 1979, after the fringe had been put on an official footing and had secured agreements with Equity, it cost the Soho Poly £60,000 to mount 15 shows.

The flexibility and freedom discovered in fringe theatres did not go unnoticed by established organizations. In 1968 the Royal Court converted the former night-club at the top of its building into a studio, and opened it to the public in 1969 as the Theatre Upstairs. Heathcote Williams's *AC/DC* was an early commission. In the autumn of 1970 the seats were temporarily removed from the main auditorium to make way for *Come Together*, a 16-day festival of fringe work from 21 different groups, from electronic music to rock'n'roll, and performance art to Peter Terson's *1861 Whitby Lifeboat Disaster* from the Victoria Stoke-on-Trent and the Brighton Combination's *N.A.B. Show*, a popular play with the Claimants' Union.

The Royal Shakespeare Company already had its own 'fringe' in the shape of Theatregoround, a small touring group set up in 1965 and largely staffed by junior company members who visited schools, colleges, factories and village halls with educative anthologies and demonstration pieces. Theatregoround grew in size and prominence within the RSC, and in 1970 and 1971 Theatregoround productions were included in the Stratford seasons. However, it was not part of the RSC's subsidized activities, and it was wound up in 1971. There was still a call from within the company for the opportunities it had created, and in the autumn of 1971 the RSC rented a small London dance-theatre, the Place, off the Euston Road, and mounted a season of new work which allowed the company to break out of some of the constraints imposed by its own tradition.

The season was an important opportunity for Buzz Goodbody, the first woman director to work for the RSC, who had joined as John Barton's assistant in 1967, having graduated from the radical ferment of Sussex University. At the Place Buzz Goodbody directed Trevor Griffiths's *Occupations*, an early example of a fringe-writer moving towards the centre, even if the Place was itself considered a fringe venue. The RSC mounted further seasons at the Place in 1973 and 1974, and under pressure from within the company it was decided to convert a tin warehouse at

Stratford, formerly used by Michel Saint-Denis for his company classes, into a permanent studio theatre. Buzz Goodbody was appointed artistic director, and the Other Place opened as a 140-seater in April 1974, 'a first step towards ending the economic and social barrier between the RSC and the society that partly finances it.' Sadly, Buzz Goodbody committed suicide just as the second season opened with their production of *Hamlet* in April 1975. The fresh work and new writing produced first at the Place, the Other Place, and then the Warehouse, which opened as the RSC's studio theatre in London in 1977, did much to revitalize the RSC energies and maintain its reputation during the 1970s. The National Theatre mounted its own 'experimental' season at the Jeanetta Cochrane Theatre in 1969, and opened the Young Vic in 1970. By the end of the decade no subsidized theatre in the country considered itself complete without a studio in which to present experimental work, while local touring and schools projects became a standard part of their repertoires.

Though none of the fringe companies had anything less than a critical attitude to the politics and aesthetics of orthodox theatre, there was an evident spectrum of intentions in their work. The shortage of money and facilities universally discouraged elaborate effects or illusionistic naturalism, and imposed simplicity of means and direct address, but within the movement there is a distinction to be made between those whose aims were primarily political, and those whose concerns were still primarily theatrical. The most politically committed groups virtually rejected the use of theatres altogether, preferring working men's clubs, meeting halls or community centres, but even those using theatres found that their aesthetic was affected by new working methods.

The conception of a performance 'devised by the company' combined the desire to arrive at a collective, 'democratic' text and production with a general suspicion of words as masks to meaning. In such productions the writer was downgraded, replaced by various forms of 'physical theatre' that sought to make an emotional rather than an intellectual impact. The Freehold, founded in 1969 by Nancy Meckler, who had worked with the La Mama company, developed the disciplines of the Living Theater and Jerzy Grotowski by reworking classic texts such as *Antigone* or *The Duchess of Malfi*. The Pip Simmons Theatre Company,

203

which like the Freehold was first seen at the Arts Lab, developed a Pop-art approach to words that deliberately exploited their banality in a context of music and dance. In these circumstances the writer was supplanted by the director, who edited both the physical and verbal aspects of the performance: in the case of Steven Berkoff's London Theatre Group, another beneficiary of the existence of the Arts Lab, Berkoff combined the roles of writer, director and performer.

The formal and aesthetic experiments of the fringe could be – and were – exploited in mainstream theatre, as for instance in Peter Brook's production of *A Midsummer Night's Dream* for the RSC in 1970. Brook's International Centre for Theatre Research, which he then established in Paris, is an example of the desire to achieve a 'pure' theatre that speaks a universal language of experience unhindered by verbal interference. The conception has been attacked by John Arden.

> . . . in the end the international theatre-group, swooping by jumbo-jet from one cultural function to another all over the world, has ceased to attempt to communicate specific ideas about anything to anybody – a non-verbal compost of currently-received physical images which can mean all things to all men is trundled from stage to stage between Tokyo and Nancy, Zagreb and Singapore. 'Controversy', if aroused at all, is set afoot by such classless generalizations as naked bodies, cursorily motivated violence, and a broad demonstration of 'compassion for the human condition'.

At the same time, the notion of a company-devised play could lead to the most minute naturalism. Here the cast would research the backgrounds and putative experiences of their chosen characters for weeks before encountering each other or beginning to improvise on the circumstances chosen for the play. Once again the director became the editor of the final script. The technique was pioneered by Mike Leigh with *Bleak Moments* at the Open Space. One of his performers, Mike Bradwell, settled in Hull in 1971 and launched the Hull Truck company by advertising for actors in *Time Out*. Their first show, *Children of the Lost Planet*, set in a commune in Hull, began a series of plays that sought to address a generation of young people Bradwell felt had been neglected by playwrights.

A third option was adopted in 1974, when William Gaskill,

former artistic director of the Royal Court, Max Stafford-Clark, former artistic director of the Traverse, and David Aukin, who had managed such groups as the People Show, the Freehold and Foco Novo (launched 1972), set up Joint Stock. The writer, director and cast would meet for a period of research and workshop investigations of the subject, and then temporarily disperse while the author wrote a script that was then produced in the normal way. After adapting Heathcote Williams's book *The Speakers*, Joint Stock engaged David Hare to work on an adaptation of William Hinton's account of collectivization in revolutionary China, *Fanshen*, first seen at the Crucible in Sheffield in 1975. Howard Brenton's *Hitler Dances* (1972) had been evolved in this way with the Traverse Theatre Workshop, which anticipates Joint Stock.

Although pressed on the one side by companies that rejected the authority of words, and on the other by *auteur* directors and casts, writers benefited from the opportunities that the rise of the fringe created. Catherine Itzin calculates in her study *Stages in the Revolution* (1980) that by 1978 there were at least 250 playwrights working in the alternative theatre. A great many of them submerged their identities in the group work of community theatre and the Theatre-in-Education companies that had begun to develop after 1965, but given the essentially literary nature of the British theatrical tradition, it was through its writers that the fringe made a lasting impression on the culture it sought to criticize.

The nearest group to a 'writers' theatre' on the fringe was the Portable Theatre, founded by Tony Bicât and David Hare in 1968. The literary emphasis of Portable appeared only slowly; both Bicât and Hare saw themselves as directors, and their original intention was, as their name implied, simply to take theatre to places where it normally did not go. The mobility of the fringe was one of the reasons that it created an audience very different from conventional theatre-goers, and this desire to escape conventional theatre buildings was common to many fringe groups, but the first Portable Theatre work at the Arts Lab, Genet and adaptations of Kafka and Strindberg, did have a markedly literary character. Hare recalls 'after the first Portable production two of the actors started saying it would be much more interesting to use bodies than these dull words. . . . So they went off and founded the Freehold.' The idea of a writers' theatre took firmer shape when David Hare found he had to write a play in order to fill a gap in the programme, and Howard Brenton joined the group.

After his period of work at the Brighton Combination in 1969 Howard Brenton followed the director Chris Parr to Bradford, where Parr had taken up a theatre-fellowship at the university, and wrote a number of short plays performed at student rock concerts. Brenton also benefited from the local interest in performance art and street theatre by writing *Wesley* for a Methodist Chapel, and *Scott of the Antarctic* for Bradford ice rink, both performed at the Bradford Arts Festival in 1970. In the meantime the Royal Court had put on his *Revenge* at the Theatre Upstairs, and while still running Portable David Hare had become the Court's literary manager. Brenton's first play for Portable, *Christie in Love*, opened at the Oval House in November 1969.

Brenton's resurrection of the multiple sex murderer Christie and his attempt to switch sympathy towards him and away from the monstrous and amoral police was intended 'to give an audience a sense of moral vertigo.' David Hare has said, 'What we had in common was that we thought we were living through a period of extreme decadence, both socially and theatrically. We just couldn't believe that the official culture was incapable of seeing the extreme state of crisis that we thought the country was in.' Brenton's *Fruit*, written to tour during the general election campaign in June 1970 explored the crisis in terms of a thalidomide victim who attempts to blackmail the Tory Prime Minister for having had homosexual relations with a member of the Labour opposition. The Prime Minister is unconcerned, confident that the public does not care, and Brenton offers a different approach to ending the corruption of power by demonstrating how to make a petrol bomb.

The deliberate provocation of Brenton's plays, their oppressive sense of disgust and fear and loathing of authority was echoed by other Portable writers. At the 1971 Edinburgh Festival (by which time they had an Arts Council grant of £8,000) Portable presented Snoo Wilson's *Blow Job*, Chris Wilkinson's *Play for Rubber GoGo Girls*, and their first collective work *Lay-By*, written by Brenton, Hare, Brian Clark, Trevor Griffiths, Snoo Wilson,

Steven Poliakoff and Hugh Stoddart. *Lay-By* plays on the public prurience exploited in *Christie in Love* by presenting a particularly nasty alleged rape on a motorway carried out by a pornographer and his mistress. For Hare the play 'got the authentic stink of pornography . . . there's something about the ugliness and perverse excitement of pornography in the play, something about the battering of minds of working-class people.' For Brenton this battering extended to the whole social environment: 'it raised a lot of – not so much issues as the landscape of the people up the M1. And it seemed like this extraordinary suppurating artery up England.'

The horror and repulsion of *Lay-By*, in particular the final scene when the naked corpses of the three main characters are washed down prior to being made into jam, severely limited the play's ability to tour. Portable experienced even greater difficulty with its next collective work, *England's Ireland*, written by Brenton, Hare, Tony Bicât, Brian Clark, Francis Fuchs, Snoo Wilson and David Edgar during a week-long retreat in Wales in 1972. *England's Ireland* was almost the first attempt by British theatre writers to come to terms with the near civil war in Northern Ireland. It proved almost impossible to find anywhere outside London that would accept it for performance, and Portable discovered that it was no longer in favour with the Arts Council.

According to Brenton, Portable went bankrupt because of *Lay-By* and *England's Ireland* but there were also other pressures which by 1973 caused the dissolution of the group. Collective writing is a demanding process; there was discontent among the actor members of the company, who had established themselves as Portable Workshop in 1971, and under Malcolm Griffiths broke away completely in 1973 to form Paradise Foundry. But the needs of political theatre – or theatre that had *become* political through the experience of the fringe – called for something more than what Portable had been allowed to create or was able to provide. David Edgar, a contributor to *England's Ireland*, had had a parallel experience with his work with the Bradford-based group, General Will. Edgar, a journalist who had graduated with a degree in drama from Manchester in 1969, was another beneficiary of Chris Parr's presence at Bradford University. Edgar produced an almost continuous series of agitprop plays for General Will from 1971 to 1973, but by then his writing had developed to a point where 'I was fed up with seeing agitprop plays that were messy, and also I was increasingly thinking that the politics you could get across was very crude, whereas the world about us was getting more complicated.' Edgar was facing a dilemma that confronted many of his colleagues, both within and outside the fringe movement.

By 1970 the position of writers who wished to comment on the condition of society in the public arena of the theatre had become a vexed one: on the one hand the upsurge of radical feeling had brought political issues much closer to the surface; on the other those writers whose political position had been implicit rather than explicit in their work found it difficult to come to terms with the fashionable agitprop sloganizing. David Mercer's play *After Haggerty* (1970) conveys the predicament of a Northern working-class intellectual such as himself whose position was fundamentally Marxist but who could not join any Marxist organization 'because I have not encountered one in my lifetime which I could give my allegiance to without abdicating my critical intelligence.' The Russian invasion of Czechoslovakia in 1968 had only served to underline the lessons learnt by those who had witnessed the effect of the invasion of Hungary in 1956.

For Arnold Wesker the practical failure of Centre 42 and the critical failure of *The Friends* left him stranded on the reputation for radical socialism of his earlier plays which his current work no longer seemed to support. Wesker did not believe that Britain was facing a potentially revolutionary situation, and he found that as a 'simple, old-fashioned humanist' he was obliged to convey his suspicions of state socialism just as much as his criticisms of capitalism. Edward Bond, on the other hand, responded by steadily intensifying the political thrust of his plays. *Lear* (1971) shows that revolutions may indeed replace the cruelties they have overthrown with even greater ones, but this does not remove the obligation to struggle against the violence institutionalized by governments. Bond evidently felt the difficulty of his position as a radical writer within an essentially bourgeois culture, however, for both *Bingo* (1973) and *The Fool* (1975) portray artists trapped by the contradictions of their society. In *Bingo* Shakespeare's renaissance humanism is contrasted with his participation in the economic exploitation brought about by the enclosures of common land; in *The Fool* the eighteenth-century poet John Clare is driven mad by the demands society puts upon him.

John Arden's experience of this dilemma was an embittering one, for his was not a case of having to find an accommodation with the established theatre, but of being expelled from it. *Harold Muggins is a Martyr* had marked his rejection of his earlier pacifism in favour of revolutionary socialism, and his discontent with more orthodox theatres like the Royal Court. He and Margaretta D'Arcy had had a dispute with the ICA in 1968 when it proved impossible to mount *The Hero Rises Up* there, and the production went on at the Round House instead. During 1972 John McGrath's company 7:84 presented the Arden's play attacking Britain's presence in Ireland, *The Ballygombeen Bequest*, but performances were stopped halfway through the tour by a writ for slander.

Simultaneously with these legal difficulties, the RSC were in rehearsals of *The Island of the Mighty*, a reworking of television material on the Arthurian legend commissioned by the BBC but never used. While the play was in preview the Ardens concluded that the director, David Jones, had unfairly cut their text, and reduced its political force, and, having been refused a meeting they requested with the cast, declared an industrial dispute, although Equity refused to make it official. They stood with placards outside the theatre, until one night one of their supporters disrupted the performance. Although the audience voted for the play to continue, the Ardens occupied the stage. D'Arcy tore up the carpet. David Jones offered a post-performance discussion of the play, but during the uproar Arden asked the audience, 'Look, are you actually saying to me that you wish me to leave this theatre?' The audience roared their assent, and Arden replied, 'In that case I will leave this theatre and never write for you again.' The Ardens have kept their promise to the official theatre, and no new work was seen in London until the fourteen hours of *The Non-Stop Connolly Show*, created in Dublin for the Irish Transport and General Workers' Union, were performed section by section at the Almost Free Theatre in 1976.

Ironically, while the Ardens were doing battle with the RSC, Arnold Wesker was also in dispute. The RSC's artistic director Trevor Nunn had agreed that they would produce *The Journalists* in the same season as the Arden's play, also to be directed by

David Jones. However the production was cancelled when it proved impossible to get sufficient actors in the company to agree to be cast. David Jones fought hard for the play, but the upshot was another lawsuit that dragged on until 1980, when Wesker was forced to settle out of court. Wesker has commented that it was a time 'when the influence of the Workers' Revolutionary Party was at its height among the actors, and my play would seem to have committed the cardinal sin of having four Tory cabinet ministers who were intelligent', but it is equally an example of the actors' assertion of their right to a say in production matters.

Whatever the reason, the attitude displayed by the management of the RSC towards these writers would seem to justify John McGrath's deep suspicion of the large theatrical institutions which he likened to 'nationalized industries, i.e. they are capitalist structures but without the need to make a profit.' McGrath had worked at the Royal Court, in television and films, and had a conventional success with *Events While Guarding the Bofors Gun* in 1966, but a visit to Paris in May 1968 convinced him of the need for a thorough reappraisal of his responsibilities. During the election year of 1970 he wrote, 'in this country, the time is ripe for revolutionary socialism to make itself known as a real alternative to the failed "pragmatism" of the Labour leadership. . . . we have to oppose bourgeois theatre by creating a truly revolutionary theatre, in order to help bring about a change in society and in our own art.'

McGrath's search for a suitable form led him first to the Everyman Theatre in Liverpool, where he worked with Alan Dossor on shows that sought to forge a link between the theatre and the surrounding working-class community, but at the same time he was able to use the precedent of groups like the Portable to obtain an Arts Council grant to found his own company, 7:84 (meaning, in Britain 7 per cent of the population own 84 per cent of the wealth). Beginning with *The Trees in the Wind* at the Edinburgh Festival in 1971, it has taken McGrath some time to achieve the popular style whose aesthetic he describes in his book *A Good Night Out* (1981): directness, comedy, emotion, immediacy, localism. In 1972 *The Ballygombeen Bequest* ran into legal difficulties, and McGrath is convinced that his reworking of Arden's 1959 play as *Serjeant Musgrave Dances On*, to reflect the shooting of civilians by the British Army in Derry on Bloody

210

Sunday in January of that year, cost him the chance of a substantial annual grant from the Arts Council. In 1973 part of the company split away to become the agitprop Belt and Braces Roadshow, but in Scotland McGrath had a success with a semi-documentary on the exploitation of the Highlands, *The Cheviot, the Stag and the Black, Black Oil.*

Although 7:84's exile from the traditional theatre has been in part enforced by the limited patronage of the English and Scottish Arts Councils, McGrath has established his company by working almost entirely outside the customary systems of management. The segregation has been an ideological point of honour. In 1974 7:84 was one of the fringe companies approached by the National Theatre with an invitation to perform there when the new theatre complex opened. The political theatre companies were adamant in their refusal. McGrath told *Theatre Quarterly* 'I would run about twenty-five miles from the National Theatre'. Their argument was that by 1975 the fringe already constituted a national theatre, rooted in the community and far more deserving of subsidy than the theatrical nationalized industries. But there was also a different case to be made.

The dilemma facing young writers who had learnt their craft on the fringe, and were then given an opportunity to write for larger theatres, is comparable to that facing political activists who had believed in the possibility of revolutionary change in 1968, but had had to appreciate that the practical, if compromised, route to change lay through orthodox politics. Should they re-enter the Labour Party, or remain with an ideologically correct but ultimately impotent fringe party? Both political and cultural circumstances changed after 1970: the Labour Party, uncompromised by power, was in a position to lead resistance to the industrial and economic policies of the traditional party of capital. At the same time the counter-culture was losing its glamour, as it proved a totally impractical way of life. As Howard Brenton has said, 'freaking out and drug culture, anarchist notions of spontaneous freedom' were defeated. David Edgar has described the new conditions.

. . . people of my generation of the late Sixties went through a kind of counter-cultural experience, based politically very much on the assumption that working-class revolution in the West was dead, and that one

211

had to look elsewhere – the Marcusian line. Then, in Britain, working-class militancy showed this sudden and unexpected revival in the early Seventies. That led to a rejection of the cultural revolution, particularly in the International Socialism group I was close to at the time.

The hardening of this political line can be seen in Howard Brenton's *Magnificence*, produced while he was writer-in-residence at the Royal Court in 1973. (Brenton's connection with the Court is an example of the 'entryism' being discussed.) As Brenton has said, *Magnificence* is a product of 1968, and its hero Jed followed a trajectory from squatting to bombing parallel to the Situationists of the Angry Brigade. The play, which shifts in style between naturalism and caricature with the freedom won by writing for the fringe, plainly sympathizes with the anarchist Jed, but in the end his murderous gesture is shown to be futile. In 1974 Brenton declared that 'the fringe has failed'.

Its failure was that of the whole dream of an 'alternative culture' – the notion that within society as it exists you can grow another way of life, which, like a beneficent and desirable cancer, will in the end grow throughout the western world, and change it. What happens is that the 'alternative society' gets hermetically sealed, and surrounded. A ghetto-like mentality develops. It is surrounded, and, in the end, strangled to death. Utopian generosity becomes paranoia as the world closes in. Naive gentleness goes to the wall, and Manson's murderousness replaces it. The drift from the loving drug scene in Amsterdam in the late Sixties to the speed and wretchedness five years later illustrates the process. The truth is that there is only one society – that you can't escape the world you live in. Reality is remorseless. No one can leave. If you're going to change the world, well, there's only one set of tools, and they're bloody and stained but realistic. I mean communist tools. Not pleasant. If only the gentle, dreamy, alternative society *had* worked.

A similar conclusion had been reached by Trevor Griffiths. 'One of the reasons I wrote such a short time for the fringe is because I realized how impotent it was as a mouthpiece to the whole of society.' Of an older generation than the other contributors to *Lay-By*, Griffiths had had his political education in the era of the New Left and CND, and though the emergence of the fringe, in particular the Stables Theatre in Manchester, gave him his chance as a dramatist, his aim was the 'strategic penetration' of bourgeois culture, not only by accepting a commission from the National Theatre, but also by writing for the other national theatre, television.

Occupations, an exploration of revolutionary strategy played out through Gramsci's leadership of the strikes in Turin in 1920, was as we saw presented by the RSC at the Place in 1971. (It was also taken on tour in a different production by 7:84.) On the strength of its success, he was then commissioned to write a play for the National Theatre.

The Party, which opened at the Old Vic in December 1973, angered the Left both with what it said, and where it said it. The choice of the National's artistic director Laurence Olivier to play the old Trotskyist Tagg seemed as offensive as the play's demonstration of the apparent impotence of the revolutionary Left. Yet *The Party* was not intended as a satire; it was written to show the 'lack of candour that people offered, for example in relating their life-roles to their abstracted revolutionary role – the lack of connection between what they did day-by-day and what they did night-by-night'.

Set in London in May 1968, it reveals in almost diagrammatic form the perplexity of those faced by the seemingly revolutionary situation in Paris. Called together by a television producer (the model was Tony Garnett) whose own *déclassé* guilt is represented by his working-class brother down from the North, a group that ranges in views from street-theatre anarchism to Tagg's hard-line Trotskyism debates the possibility of joint action. A sociology lecturer and journalist argues the intellectual *New Left Review* line that revolution will only come from the Third World; Tagg pours contempt on the radical intelligentsia for their distraction by emotional causes while the only proper course is to concentrate on building a party in the industrial working class. Both conclude, for different reasons, that the events in Paris will not lead to the desired revolution. Trevor Griffiths's sympathies seem to lie with the least rational character in the play, the drunken playwright Sloman (modelled to a certain extent on David Mercer) whose self-destruction reflects the frustration of his position as an ex-member of Tagg's party who has realized that his political contribution can only be made through his craft. Yet it is he who asserts that revolution will occur, and in the process will throw up the leaders that *The Party* shows the Left conspicuously to lack.

It was not Griffiths's intention to offer a neat solution to the dilemma of the Left: he resumed the theme in a different form in his television series about a Left-wing MP, *Bill Brand*, transmitted in 1976, and examined the reformist and revolutionary traditions through a play about an evening-class for stand-up comics in *Comedians* (1975). As Howard Brenton said in 1972, 'the theatre is a dirty place. It's not a place for a rational analysis of society – it's there to bait our obsessions, ideas and public figures.' The point is that these are public issues that, for all of the criticisms of the institutions concerned, had to be presented in larger theatres.

Practical reasons for leaving the fringe cannot be ignored. The collapse of Portable Theatre showed that it was almost impossible to construct an independent political theatre. David Edgar has acknowledged that there was an element of personal ambition in wanting to reach a larger audience. There were also the creative possibilities offered. 'Howard Brenton and David Hare and I and a number of other people wanted to write plays about subjects which required large numbers of people, and also about public subjects which did not take place in rooms but in *areas*, which it is nice to have the space to represent.' For all these reasons, from 1973 onwards younger radical writers began a determined move into the 'official' theatre. *Brassneck*, co-written by Brenton and Hare for Richard Eyre at the Nottingham Playhouse, opened in September of that year, a first exercise in what Brenton called 'epic' theatre analysing the corruption of a commercial family over three generations. Brenton's *The Churchill Play*, forecasting internment camps for dissidents on mainland Britain by 1984 (they were already in place in Northern Ireland) followed at Nottingham in 1974. David Hare was commissioned by a commercial manager, Michael Codron, for whom he had written *Slag* in 1970, to write *Knuckle* (1974). His *Teeth'n'Smiles* was presented by the Royal Court in 1975 and had a commercial transfer. David Edgar began work on his play about the National Front, *Destiny*, which eventually appeared at The Other Place and then the Aldwych in 1976. Howard Brenton accepted a commission from the National Theatre; in 1976 *Weapons of Happiness* was the first new play to be premièred on the Lyttleton stage.

The final influence of these and other new writers on the theatre they so successfully infiltrated is a question that falls outside the end-date of this study, but it is clear that they have become a major force. As Trevor Griffiths said in 1979, 'Who would have thought in 1956 that I or Brenton or Edgar or Hare would be having work – very committed work – on television. We must not only read it as repressive tolerance, we've got to see ourselves as agents in the struggle, because it is a struggle.' Of course, the issues raised by political theatre were not the exclusive property of the fringe. In 1974 the RSC presented Tom Stoppard's *Travesties*, which specifically 'asks whether the words "revolutionary" and "artist" are capable of being synonymous, or whether they are mutually exclusive, or something in between.' Stoppard explored the question by farcically interlocking the lives of James Joyce – the pure artist, Lenin – the pure revolutionary, and Tristan Tzara – the Dadaist who believes that 'an artist is someone who makes art mean the things he does' – in Zurich in 1917. There is no firmer conclusion than there is to Griffiths's *The Party*. The narrator's closing speech suggests that in the theatre the synthesis is less important than the dialectic.

> I learned three things in Zurich during the war. I wrote them down. Firstly, you're either a revolutionary or you're not, and if you're not you might as well be an artist as anything else. Secondly, if you can't be an artist, you might as well be a revolutionary . . .
>
> I forget the third thing.
> BLACKOUT.

The fringe, as we have seen, threw out a challenge to orthodox social structures by adopting an alternative practice and mode of production. What was done and said in performance constituted a demonstration of the new possibilities offered by the cultural and political upheavals of the Sixties. It is logical that the fringe should play an important part in the evolution of the sexual, as well as political, liberation movements that got under way in the wake of 1968. Within the theatre women had to challenge all the structural and cultural male dominance that the theatre reflected from the rest of the world. Self-expression in the theatre was an essential part of claiming a voice elsewhere. One of the most powerful early feminist statements took the form of a play, Jane Arden's *Vagina Rex and the Gas Oven*, presented at the Arts Lab in February 1969, almost before the movement had begun.

As Jeffrey Weeks has pointed out in *Sex, Politics and Society* (1981), there was no common origin for the sexual liberation movements that emerged in many Western countries in the early 1970s.

Much of the rhetoric of the sexual radicals came from the counter-culture; their political pre-histories were often in the civil rights movements and student radicalism; their political commitments remained radical and frequently revolutionary, as sexual oppression came to be seen as an indispensable aspect of all social oppression. But the fundamental elements generating a sexual politics were the contradictions experienced in a culture which increasingly stressed the sexual, but commercialized and trivialized the human body, denied the validity of homosexuality, and generally still subjected sexual autonomy and pleasure to the demands of heterosexual monogamy.

These contradictions were acutely felt in the theatre, where women were literally being cast in the roles demanded of them by a male-dominated society.

The first indications of a revival of concern for women's rights in a British context came in 1967, when reports began to circulate of the discontent among women in the radical movement in the United States, both with their general exploitation as handmaidens of the movement, and because of the exclusion of women's issues from the 1967 National Conference for a New Politics in Chicago. In 1966 Betty Friedan, author of *The Feminine Mystique* (1963) had helped to launch the American National Organization of Women, but radical women perceived its orthodox liberal objectives in the same terms that Black Power activists viewed white liberals in the civil rights campaign. A number of provocative marches and demonstrations in 1968, notably the disruption of the Miss Universe contest and Valerie Solanas's shooting of Andy Warhol on behalf of her Society for Cutting Up Men (gestures entirely in keeping with the politics of spectacle), drew the attention of the media and gave the movement distorted but useful publicity.

In Britain a different political culture meant that women were seen more in terms of an exploited class than, as in America, as an exploited race. As early as 1966 Juliet Mitchell had published an influential Marxist analysis of the exploitation of women in the *New Left Review* 'The "true" woman and the "true" family are images of peace and plenty: in actuality they may be sites of violence and despair,' she wrote, but it is noticeable that women's liberation did not appear on the agenda of the Dialectics of Liberation conference in 1967. Two political campaigns involving women, Lil Ballocha's campaign for trawler safety in Hull, and

Rose Boland's campaign for equal pay for women machinists at the Ford Plant in Dagenham, placed the issue in an industrial and employment context, and intensified the demands for the Equal Pay Act, introduced in 1970 to take effect in 1975.

During 1968 women's issues began to be raised within the small British revolutionary socialist parties, while at the same time women's groups and workshops began spontaneously to follow the example of a women's group in Tufnell Park in North London that had strong links with the American radical movement. In January 1969 *Black Dwarf* introduced a special women's rights issue with the headline '1969, Year of the Militant Woman?' In February the International Marxist Group Launched *Socialist Woman*. The first signs of the tensions that an exclusively feminist critique could create appeared at the 'Festival of Revolution' at Essex University in the spring, where women's discussions were opposed and disrupted by men. A loose confederation of women's groups had begun to evolve into the London Workshop, and in May it produced the first edition of a women's liberation newsletter, *Shrew*. The culmination of this almost undirected activity was a conference at Ruskin College in Oxford in February 1970 on women's history which spontaneously became the first national conference of the women's liberation movement.

As one of the movement's leading theorists, Sheila Rowbotham, has said, 'it was really from the Oxford conference in February 1970 that a movement could be said to exist.' The conference passed what became known as the four demands: equal pay, equal education and opportunity, 24-hour nurseries, and free contraception and abortion on demand. But it was a feminist principle that the movement should avoid the authoritarian and hierarchical structures of male organizations, and an autonomous system of 'networking' was preferred to the creation of a single organization. A Women's National Co-ordinating Committee was established, but abandoned in 1971 when it fell victim to the sectarian squabbles of the Left and the unsettled issue of lesbian participation in the movement. Women's Liberation had emerged just as the student militancy of 1968 was on the wane, and as Sheila Rowbotham said in 1972, 'We found ourselves caught between being a new movement which is still essentially for mutual education and propaganda and, at the same time, a

217

movement trying to organize without any explicit theory of where our strength lies within capitalism and of thus how we can act.'

In 1970 public awareness of at least some of the issues was greatly increased by the publication of Germaine Greer's *The Female Eunuch*. Greer, an Australian who combined teaching in the English Department of Warwick University with appearances in *Oz* and participating in the editing of *Suck*, recognized that 'the most telling criticisms' of her work 'will come from my sisters of the Left', for *The Female Eunuch* did not follow the developing socialist-feminist line. Drawing on Simone de Beauvoir's *The Second Sex*, (1949 translated 1953), it was more a feminist reading of the sexual politics of the counter-culture, and was as concerned to liberate men as women from the sexual roles that society has imposed upon them. 'The emphasis should be taken off male genitality and replaced upon human sexuality.' Women are eunuchs in that they have been forced into a passive version of the male role, and their active libido has been repressed by education and 'the civilizing process'. 'The chief means of liberating women is the replacing of compulsiveness and compulsion by the pleasure principle.' Following the anti-Freudianism of Wilhelm Reich, she wished to see 'the redeployment of energy, no longer to be used in repression, but in desire, movement and creation.' Though women must cast off the stereotypes imposed upon them by men, she was not in favour of aggressive rebellion, for this only emphasizes the male-female polarity. Instead, in the optimistic mood of the early years of the counter-culture, she hoped to replace violence and separation with mutuality and community.

Though an important contribution, *The Female Eunuch* looks back to the lost innocence of the underground rather than to the sharper struggles that were to be provoked by and within the women's liberation movement. In the following years a distinction developed between socialist-feminists, who traced the roots of oppressive sexism to the class divisions of capitalism, and the radical-feminists, who saw sexism as the source of all social antagonisms. Socialist-feminists sought to practise their feminism within the context of a general political struggle to end oppressions; radical-feminists envisaged some kind of revolution by women against men, or, particularly in the case of lesbians, total separation from them.

218

These distinctions helped to ensure that no national organization or strategy emerged, though, as we saw, there were also ideological reasons for retaining collective autonomy. However, the debate helped to create a specifically women's press, of which *Spare Rib*, launched by a collective of women journalists who had worked on underground newspapers, has proved the most long-lasting. The publishing house Virago, whose first title appeared in 1975, was to prove very influential in the following decade, both by publishing contemporary women writers, and rediscovering voices from the past. The coming into force of the Equal Pay Act, together with the Sex Discrimination Act, in 1975 was an ambivalent tribute to the success of the first stage of the women's movement. It showed that their point had been made, and that feminism was now firmly on the cultural agenda, but the legislation was criticized by more militant feminists on the grounds that the modest, and unfulfillable reforms would serve as a justification for nothing more being done, as has turned out to be the case.

In the theatre, Jane Arden's Holocaust Company had pointed the way with *Vagina Rex*, following it up with *Holocaust* at the Open Space Theatre and *A New Communion for Freaks, Prophets and Witches* in 1971, but the most immediate result of the Ruskin conference of 1970 was the formation of the Women's Street Theatre Group. The group's history follows the path of other agitprop groups formed after 1968, but it is symptomatic of the cultural contradictions experienced by many activists on the fringe that some of its founder members should also be members of the RSC, including the director Buzz Goodbody. It was not enough to work within an organization in the hope of changing it (though Goodbody was very useful in educating the RSC); it was also necessary to endure the arduous – and almost deliberately unprofessional – conditions of street theatre. Their main aim was to prepare material for the first Women's Day march in London in March 1971, but there was an early demonstration outside the Miss World Contest in November 1970. The group parodied the sexual display of the contest with electrified costumes as 'The Flashing Nipple Show'. The group also tried to disrupt the 1971 Festival of Light rally with a pram and placard saying 'Fuck the Family', and had to be taken into protective custody. (A simultaneous demonstration by the all-male Gay Street Theatre

219

Group survived longer by passing among the crowd dressed as nuns.)

Later in 1971 the Women's Street Theatre Group transmogrified into the all-female 'Punching Judies' and produced their first agit-prop play, *The Amazing Equal Pay Show*. Red Ladder and other agitprop groups also began to take up feminist issues. In 1973 Ed Berman approached members of the 'Punching Judies' with the offer of a special season of women's theatre at the Almost Free. Following the principles of feminist collectivism, the programme was evolved over six months of Sunday discussions, which became a standing conference on the status of women in the theatre. There was considerable dissension within the meetings, and the ten-week season of lunchtime plays was finally presented by two groups, the Women's Company, consisting of professional actresses, and an 'alternative' group who took the name the Women's Theatre Group in 1974. Plays by Jennifer Phillips, Pam Gems, Michelene Wandor, Sally Ordway, Dinah Brooke and Jane Wibberly were presented. The Women's Company was short-lived, but the Women's Theatre Group won an Arts Council grant in 1974, and took its place on the alternative theatre touring circuit. In 1975 Monstrous Regiment was formed as an explicitly socialist-feminist theatre group. The 1973 season at the Almost Free acted as a catalyst for women's theatre, which in turn opened up further opportunities for women writers such as Caryl Churchill and Pam Gems, who were already working in the theatre, but having to contend with discrimination against their sex.

In 1975 Ed Berman performed a similar service for the homosexual community with a season of plays on homosexual themes. The Gay Liberation movement had emerged at the same time as the feminist, with the formation of the Gay Liberation Front in 1970. *Gay News* was founded in 1972, the same year as *Spare Rib*. The first National Conference of Gay People was held in Leeds in 1971, but there was a clash of views between the GLF, which advocated aggressive tactics, and the more conservative Campaign for Homosexual Equality. The Gay Liberation Front was itself divided between the majority males and minority females, and dissolved after 1972. Gay Sweatshop, the umbrella title of the season at the Almost Free, became a touring company with Arts Council subsidy in 1975.

* * *

Few individuals or institutions were immune to the political and economic upheavals of the first half of the Seventies, and, as we shall see in the following chapter in greater detail, the Arts Council, which had created the fringe almost in spite of itself, was no exception. When Lord Goodman retired as chairman in 1972 the Council's grant-in-aid had trebled from just under £4 million in 1965 to just under £12 million. The incoming Conservative Government had agreed to return to a system similar to that of the mid-Sixties, by which the Council would know in advance what to expect for the next three years, and so could plan its budget accordingly. In his report for 1973–4 Lord Goodman's successor Lord Gibson had to announce that 'this system of trienniel funding has been abandoned before the end of the first triennium.' The grant it was to receive for 1974–5 was £21,335,000, which was calculated to be an increase of 14.3 per cent, but inflation was running at at least 17 per cent.

The effect of inflation on wages and other overheads now threatens the survival of many of our supported companies. Several have made it clear that they cannot continue to exist without larger grants than we have been able to allocate to them.

With no idea of what the budget was to be for 1975–6, 'It hardly needs saying that in present circumstances it will be extremely difficult to find support for new activities to which the Council has not already pledged funds.'

The Arts Council's clients and would-be clients on the fringe had responded to the renewed industrial militancy at the beginning of the decade with renewed industrial militancy on their own behalf, often directed against the Arts Council. The spontaneous outflow of creative energy began to harden into pressure groups and committees as the fringe realized that the period of expansion was over. Increasingly the Arts Council's bureaucratic and secretive ways of reaching decisions were called into question by groups who saw that they were being discriminated against in favour of the 'official' culture.

In 1972 the Association of Lunch Time Theatres was formed to press for increased Arts Council subsidy, and to counter pressure from Equity, which claimed that the fringe was exploiting actors and undercutting the legitimate theatre. This was followed in 1973 by the London Association of Community Theatre Groups, which

221

became a nationwide organization in 1974. The Association of Community Theatres, as it became known, was the forum for the forty or more political theatre groups which saw themselves as taking part in the resistance to the Conservative Government, and its context was always political. In 1975 the broader-based Independent Theatres Council was formed as an umbrella organization for the entire fringe, and cooperated with TACT in demanding more money from the Arts Council and seeking an accommodation with Equity. Equity was itself riven by political disputes over the decision to comply with Conservative industrial legislation in 1972, and the efforts to make the union more representative through a branch and delegate structure. In 1975 Equity's fringe committee recommended that the fringe should be unionized, and a fringe contract was introduced in 1978. The dramatists had meanwhile formed their own Theatre Writers' Union in 1975.

The growing economic difficulties in which artists found themselves gave other groups not normally associated with unionization a taste for self-organization. The campaign for a Public Lending Right, a proposal to reward authors for the use of their books by the public library service, which had first been made in 1951, took on a new vigour when the Writers' Action Group was formed by Brigid Brophy, Maureen Duffy and others. The initial failure of the Society of Authors to support WAG led the more militant writers to leave the 'gentlemanly' society and join the industrially-minded Writers' Guild, which was affiliated to the TUC, and which had until then only represented film and television script writers. After a long campaign, the first PLR payments were made in 1984. The Poets Conference, first convened in 1970, with Bob Cobbing as secretary, became an unofficial trades union for poets, and led a successful *putsch* by radical members of the Poetry Society, who won control of its general council and the *Poetry Review*, and honoured Basil Bunting as their president.

In May 1972, after preliminary attempts to affiliate with the Association of Technical and Managerial Staff, a group of politically committed painters and sculptors formed the Artists' Union. A statement read:

The confused and desperate condition in which artists now find themselves is of course symbolic of a wide state of affairs. Over the past years the situation of art and artists has become more and more critical.

222

The Party

The aims of artists are under severe constraint by the structures both economic and associal under which we work. On several levels art is being controlled and dictated by people and conditions which are neither answerable nor responsive to the real needs and aspirations of artists.

1974 and 1975 were, as Lord Gibson had warned, very difficult years for Arts Council clients. The combination of recession and inflation hit the repertory theatres just as badly as it hit the fringe, and the RSC was in constant financial crisis. In the middle of 1975 the Arts Council had to find the RSC an extra £200,000 to keep it afloat. The Royal Court went dark for several months. In October, halfway through the financial year, the Council decided that it had to make cuts. This was presented as a 'freeze' of 50 per cent of the Council's unallocated money; established companies who had already committed themselves to projects, though they had not received the money, were protected, but individual artists and the smaller groups suffered.

There was to be no new money for touring, for writers' bursaries or guarantees to make up royalties on new plays, or for any community arts projects. The fringe were the first to feel the chill winds of a changed economic climate for the arts which has meant that since then public subsidy has at best only been maintained at the equivalent of the 1975 level.

What particularly galled the fringe was the favoured treatment being given to the National Theatre; yet if it was the purpose of such an institution to play out the dramas of the national psyche on its stage, then the National was doing its job very well – before the doors of its new building were even open. While the National Theatre company launched under Sir Laurence Olivier in 1963 soldiered on at the Old Vic, work on the new building – moved downstream and shorn of a matching opera house – began in 1969. As an architectural conception its scale and concrete mass reflected the civic confidence and faith in technology and planning of 1965, when its design was agreed.

The building was to be completed by 1973, for a fixed sum of £7.5 million. But the property boom provoked a labour shortage, while inflation and revived industrial militancy encouraged labour disputes. In 1972 a further £2.3 million was allocated to the project, and the anticipated opening postponed to 1974. In 1973 the oil crisis completely changed future estimates of the cost of running the building, while a disastrous season of plays at the New Theatre put the performing company into deficit by £80,000 and forced cuts to the company just when it should have been expanding. The building was still not ready by the end of 1974 and plans for an opening in April 1975 had to be abandoned when it was discovered that the elaborate new stage technology could not be installed in time, and in some cases did not work. The costs of construction rose above £10.5 million, and in November 1974 Parliament agreed to an open-ended commitment to complete the building at whatever cost. By 1975 the property market had collapsed, and there was less incentive to subcontractors to complete the work, for there was little prospect of any more.

These uncertainties and delays inevitably had a demoralizing effect on the acting company, as plans were laid and actors hired for opening productions in the new building that never came off. In April 1972 it had been announced that the successor to Olivier – now Lord Olivier – was to be Peter Hall, the former artistic director of the RSC. Hall had insisted that Olivier should approve of his appointment, but it was none the less a *fait accompli*. Olivier was still intended to lead the company into the new building, but in March 1973 Olivier, along with his literary manager Kenneth Tynan, decided to resign. Inevitably, as a director rather than an actor, Hall had different views on the policy and management of the National, and the senior team that Olivier had created began to disappear. The fiercest rows were with Jonathan Miller, who resigned as an associate director early in 1975, and Michael Blakemore in 1976, both of whom criticized Hall's personal dominance of the National as both director and administrator.

The first of the National's three stages to be ready, the Lyttelton, came into use in March 1976, but there was not a grand opening until the first night of *Tamburlaine* in the Olivier auditorium in October. Before then industrial militancy outside the building had made its way within, and there was a strike by stage hands in August. Although the National Theatre's grant for 1976–7 had risen to £2 million, it still faced a deficit of £540,000, and there would have to be fewer productions than planned in the following year. The final cost of the building was £20 million, and some of its technical problems had still not been solved ten years later.

* * *

When Howard Brenton said in 1974 that 'the Fringe has failed', his comment has to be seen in the context of his own success in carrying the political debate into the concrete citadel of the National Theatre with a commission to write *Weapons of Happiness*. Neither the fringe nor the National Theatre can be said to have failed in that the one produced a new generation of writers, and the other put them on stage. Where the fringe had failed, as Brenton pointed out, was in establishing an autonomous, alternative way of life, let alone carrying through the political revolution whose intimations made their chimerical appearance in 1968.

The reasons for this political failure are both practical and theoretical. The theoretical reason was, as we saw, that the upheavals of 1968 were a cultural rather than a material crisis. In practical terms, when the economic crisis of the 1970s (and after) became manifest, it was fought through at a directly political level, while the means of support for the counter-culture more or less evaporated. At the same time the counter-culture, in heralding that crisis, had given sufficient provocation to the authorities to ensure that steps were taken to suppress it, through legislation and active and passive censorship. By its attacks on liberal values, which it dismissed as mere forms of recuperation, the counter-culture had partly invited its own suppression.

Yet the cultural crisis was genuine enough, and if, like Bernice Martin, we think in terms of an expressive, rather than political revolution, then it is clear that the fringe, and the rest of the counter-culture, has not failed. It never had a coherent programme or a single identity, which is why single issues – feminism, ecology, community art – have become individual themes, rather than part of some overall strategy for change. But that does not detract from their significance. Individual freedoms, in fact, have advanced further than collective ones. There is greater freedom of expression and choice of lifestyle in Britain than there was at the beginning of the Sixties, even if that freedom is not without limits. The greater limit to freedom is material rather than legislative: the social and cultural impoverishment that results from long-term economic decline. Of that decline the National Theatre, just as much as the counter-culture, has become a prisoner. In the first half of the 1970s all the arts were confronted by conditions for which the Sixties had left them unprepared.

CHAPTER 7

The Arts in Hard Times

*'All we have left is the
English language. Can it
be salvaged? That is my
question.'*

Spooner to Hirst in Harold Pinter's *No Man's Land* (1975)

As, on the one hand, inflation eroded the value of Arts Council subsidy, and, on the other hand, recession made it impossible for the Government to compensate for inflation's effects, the Arts Council's weakened financial position made its decisions more, not less important for its would-be clients. As we saw in the last chapter, subsidy was as vital to fringe theatre as it was to the 'official' culture of the National Theatre which the counter-culture opposed. The Arts Council, just as much as the art forms it supported, was badly affected by the economic difficulties of the early Seventies: before examining what happened to the arts after 1970 – and tracing some of the developments that were taking place away from the arena of the counter-culture – it is important to take stock of how the Arts Council had itself changed since the early 1960s.

At the beginning of the decade the Arts Council had a somewhat patronizing attitude to its clients, but the policy of 'response' indicated a willingness primarily to assist the arts when called upon to do so, rather than a desire directly to intervene. In his report for 1962–3 the then secretary-general, Nigel Abercrombie, wrote, 'we can sometimes enjoy ourselves in the role of sugar-daddy to the arts, but we are at present more often, better and more characteristically employed as match-makers, midwives and nannies.' (This was the period when the BBC was fondly referred to as 'Aunty'; it is revealing that a secretary-general should suggest that the Arts Council was 'nanny'.)

The increase in the Arts Council's budgets under Labour led to an expansion in the arts and inevitably of the Council's own importance. We can see a more interventionist attitude under the chairmanship of Lord Goodman, as he sought to use the arts to distract the young from the dangerous pleasures of sex, drugs and rock'n'roll. As we saw in the previous chapter, around 1970 there are signs of a 'closure' on the part of the Arts Council towards the more troublesome aspects of the avant garde.

The history of the New Activities Committee demonstrates it most acutely. Having failed to come to satisfactory terms with these manifestations of the counter-culture, the Arts Council decided to keep in force the old categories and academic divisions of the arts, both structurally, in its system of departments and advisory panels, and financially, in its dispensing of subsidy. It was just this 'grading, sorting and packaging of artistic activities' that the Friends of the Arts Council Cooperative objected to.

In 1970 the political and economic situation conspired to reinforce this tendency. The Conservative Government was unable to sustain the Council's funds at a satisfactory level, a condition which increased competition for subsidy among its clients. At the same time the Government had its own views on how the arts should be financed. Museums are not the responsibility of the Arts Council, but the decision by the Minister in charge of the Department of Education and Science, Margaret Thatcher, to introduce museum charges (immediately rescinded by Labour in 1974) showed that they were concerned that culture could do more to pay its way. Nor, officially, has the Minister for the Arts any say in the running of the Arts Council, but in a debate in the House of Lords in February 1971 the new Minister, Lord Eccles, spoke of his disquiet at the use of Arts Council money to fund 'works which affront the religious beliefs or outrage the sense of decency of a large body of tax-payers.' There was no direct outcome from these remarks, but Lord Goodman found it prudent to pass on a general 'reminder' to clients.

Regardless of the precise sums at its disposal, however, the central issue for the Arts Council as an institution, had become the question of how it took its decisions. Constitutionally, it was governed by a Council whose members were appointed by the Government, but from which they were entirely independent, once the necessary grant-in-aid had been awarded. The Council was advised by the specialist staff it employed, together with panels of unpaid experts, but these panels had no control over the Arts Council's ultimate decisions. It was, in fact, a law unto itself. Throughout the 1960s the Arts Council was being urged to become more representative, to democratize its procedures and become less of a metropolitan oligarchy of interlocking interests.

A democratization of a sort was achieved by the spread of Regional Arts Associations, part-funded through the Arts Council and partly through local interests, chiefly the local authorities. The Regional Arts Associations did have an elective membership, and were empowered to assist 'amateur' activities in a way that the Arts Council was not. The twelve English Regional Arts Associations founded between 1958 and 1973 brought a measure of devolution (together with the Arts Councils of Scotland and Wales) but that did not create any democracy at the centre. In 1968 an investigation by a House of Commons Estimates Committee recommended that the Arts Council should find ways to have artists more 'fully and directly' represented in its deliberations, and that this should be done in conjunction with 'bodies representative of artists', by which was meant organizations like Actors' Equity.

There were voices within the Arts Council that favoured such a development, but the majority was against it. The loudest voice for reform was that of Hugh Jenkins, a former Equity official who had become a Labour MP, and who was a member of the Arts Council from 1968 to 1971.

Lord Goodman and I disagreed totally about democracy. Relations between the Arts Council and other bodies in the arts were by this time [1968] much closer than in earlier days [1962], partly as a result of the work of the Theatres Advisory Council, but the Council as a whole still believed in the curious proposition that to retain its independence *from* government it was necessary for it to be appointed *by* the government. There was also a more rational objection. Appointment ensured that the Arts Council consisted of persons dedicated to the arts. When the Arts Council emerged from the Council for the Encouragement of Music and Arts there was no demand for democratic control. . . . It was not until the Council had grown into a great influence in the land and government patronage was taken for granted that complaints began to be heard that this enormous power, this decisive influence, was exercised by a small group of appointees answerable to no one but themselves. By that time the Council had become a part of the Establishment and tradition had converted defect into virtue.

In March 1974 Hugh Jenkins found himself in a better position to argue with the Arts Council, when Harold Wilson appointed him Minister for the Arts. Thanks to Jenkins, the Labour Party had a manifesto commitment 'to make the Arts Council more democratic and representative of workers in the arts and entertainment', and Jenkins proceeded to try to fulfil it. He did not succeed, and was outmanoeuvred by Lord Goodman's successor as Arts Council chairman, Lord Gibson. The issue upon which he fell was not directly that of the Arts Council, but the Labour Government's proposal for a wealth tax. Lord Gibson supported the powerful lobby of country-house owners, art collectors and dealers who argued that a wealth tax would inevitably force the dispersal of private collections, almost certainly abroad. The argument that a wealth tax was a threat to the nation's artistic heritage (this is the moment when 'heritage' becomes a significant issue in cultural debates) was a convenient means of heading off a wealth tax altogether, and in the face of the difficulties raised by the problem of collecting the tax, the proposal was abandoned in December 1975.

Having made himself thoroughly unpopular with what he called 'the snobbocracy in the arts scene', and frustrated in his attempts to move the Arts Council towards greater democracy, in August 1975 Hugh Jenkins tried to engineer Lord Gibson's resignation. However, as he wrote in a letter to his superior minister in the Department of Education and Science, Fred Mulley, 'now at the moment when I am beginning to undermine them, I find myself being undermined.' Harold Wilson had asked his adviser, Harold Lever, Chancellor of the Duchy of Lancaster, to conduct his own investigation into the arts, and Jenkins found himself circumvented. His position had already become untenable when in 1976 Wilson resigned as Prime Minister. In the reshuffle James Callaghan replaced Hugh Jenkins with the socially more acceptable Lord Donaldson.

The episode reveals the complex relationship between the Arts

229

Council and government: Hugh Jenkins was hardly operating the official policy of non-interference when he moved against Lord Gibson. That Lord Gibson was able to resist him shows that, regardless of its economic dependence on government, the Arts Council is a powerful institution, almost another unenfranchised estate, like the fourth estate of the press. It has continued resolutely to resist pressure to democratize itself, while on the other hand it has proved unresistant to the promptings of government. The situation might have been different if the Arts Council could have absorbed the pressures on it through a steady expansion of its subsidies, but the 1975–6 report ended a chapter in the Council's history when it declared that the arts were entering a period of restraint. The report was titled 'The Arts in Hard Times'; the effect of hard times has been an economic as well as a cultural closure.

The Arts Council of Great Britain has played a key role in sustaining three art forms which represent the arts at their most traditional and at their most avant-garde: grand opera, painting and sculpture. These forms, in their dependence for survival on Arts Council support, have been institutionalized. Opera, through the Royal Opera House, Covent Garden (which also maintains a ballet company) and Sadlers Wells, which became the English National Opera in 1974, has always absorbed a significant proportion of the subsidy available, simply because it is an extremely expensive art form that would never survive without it. But it has retained a privileged position that reflects the privileged positions of its supporters. Its status and function is institutional by nature. Painting and sculpture have had less money at their disposal than opera, music or theatre, and their activities have been much more diffuse. But the effect of Arts Council patronage, plus the educational system which supplied the part-time employment that enabled many people to survive as professional artists, has been to produce an avant-garde with an orthodoxy almost as rigid as that which used to be associated with the Royal Academy.

This situation has developed in some measure because of the collapse of the traditional private patronage on which members of the Royal Academy (which had no government subsidy) depended before the Second World War. Since latterly there have been so few private patrons who buy paintings for themselves, traditional ideas or taste have ceased to have much influence on what should or should not be produced, as Andrew Brighton has argued.

The collapse of traditionalism as a publicly defensible body of assumptions was partially caused by its institutional erosion. The post-war growth of state patronage administered by staff virtually invulnerable to inexpert public taste saw the rise of the patronizing power, via the State, of the 'highbrows' and 'experts' belaboured by Munnings [President of the Royal Academy at the end of the war]. By the early Sixties, the historical view of British painting which lay behind state patronage was broadly one that devalued Sickert, John and the Slade tradition to the level of a provincial backwater.

The new orthodoxy preferred to see art constantly renewed by an avant-garde of painters and sculptors who were struggling with problems of form and expression that posed fresh problems requiring fresh solutions. This view of art as a constant forward march towards some indefinable goal was reinforced by the writings of Clement Greenberg, Michael Fried and other American critics who regularly decided where art should go next, sometimes before the painters they promoted had got there. Thus there developed an unconscious process by which critics manufactured schools of painting with their own built-in obsolescence. This view coincided with the interests of dealers and museum officials, for it gave them an opportunity continually to add to public collections, and arrange exhibitions that displayed their knowledge of new trends. In Britain, where critical battles were fought with less ferocity than Paris or New York, the artist was seen as a heroic problem solver, often as interesting for his personality – say, Francis Bacon or David Hockney – as for the critical context of his work.

As we saw in chapter II, the boom in art sales in the early Sixties was chiefly in works that had secured a gilt-edge value which escaped the vagaries of contemporary public taste – the French Impressionists and Picasso were historically the most recent to transcend purely art values – but there was also a lively market in contemporary art, where paradoxically the work acquired value not because it was traditional, but because it was new. The change in the economic climate was quickly felt by the dealers in new art. In March 1968 Christopher Finch reported in *Studio International*, 'I do not think that I am alone in detecting symptoms of atrophication in the London art scene.'

Certainly some dealers have done their best to bring the atmosphere of their activities into line with present-day life as it might be lived; but the fact that they are involved in running art galleries goes against them. It involves them in an obsolete social network on which, ironically, they depend for their existence. No amount of hip hangers-on sipping vodka at private views can alter this. The unhappy fact is that London galleries – ostensibly dealing in Culture at the highest level – are heavily mortgaged to what is, in fact, a crushingly boring sub-culture.

By the following year the market for contemporary art was in crisis, as Edward Lucie-Smith wrote in his survey *Art in Britain 1969–70*: 'it is clear that commercial art galleries are struggling to survive. In 1969, for the first time, one began to feel their days were numbered.' Galleries close their doors for many reasons, but there is a correlation between the ending of certain operations and the passing from fashion of the artists they promoted. Two galleries associated with the 1950s realists, the Beaux Arts and Zwemmers, shut down respectively in 1964 and 1967; Indica, and McRoberts and Tunnard, both specializing in kinetic art, closed in 1967. The Pop art galleries were the next in difficulties: Robert Fraser shut down in 1969, Kasmin in 1972; an attempt to revive his business through the Garage Gallery in 1973–4 also failed. At the time of the second failure, Lynda Morris reported:

'Sixties collectors' no longer purchase new works, but what is important, they want to realize the value of earlier purchases. It is common for paintings to be bought under a gentleman's agreement that the dealer guarantees the price paid. This clause has affected many dealers, particularly with the limited market for native work. The great names of British art in the Sixties no longer have a reliable market outside our enchanted isles.

As a result artists – and this time also dealers, who hoped to survive as middlemen – were forced to rely more and more on the Arts Council, the Tate Gallery, and other public galleries not only for sales, but also for approval and authentication of the worth of their work through public exhibitions. Since 1968 the walls of the Arts Council's Hayward and Serpentine Galleries have been as bitterly contended for as those of any besieged city.

In these conditions it is not surprising that artists became dissatisfied with the gallery system. The purely aesthetic question of what constituted a work of art anyway, first raised by

Duchamp's bottle-rack and urinal, joined with a more directly ideological objection to art as an item of commodity exchange. As we shall see, the art-object never escaped the cash-nexus, but that it was possible for the attempt to be made at all was the result of state patronage, through teaching and the public gallery system.

One of the ways in which resistance to the traditional structure manifested itself was in a new collectivism among artists. This ran directly contrary to the artist-as-individual-hero promoted in the early Sixties. One of the earliest collective ventures was the Artists' Placement Group, launched by John and Barbara Latham in 1966, and by 1970 including in its membership Keith Arnatt, Stuart Brisley, Garth Evans, Barry Flanagan, Leonard Hessing, Ian Munro, Jeffrey Shaw and others. Stuart Brisley has described their dissatisfaction with the economic coils in which art was trapped.

There was a situation where the financial structure virtually controlled the forms of art, that is, into 'painting', 'theatre', and so on. It had done so because collection of cash required it in those forms. The shops, the gallery market, box office and doors, these devices all led to a belief that there was such a thing. Now, the artists' decision to make something interesting happen regardless of whether it would pay off – always a key element – has become part of the facts of life, an essential in the structure of a total, in contrast to the purely monetary economy.

Brisley's escape route was 'environmental art', in which the artist became the central performer in a series of obscure and often arduous rituals. Environmental work, he wrote, 'evolves as a challenge to the use of art as a commodity. It validates other relationships between art, people and the artist.'

APG's policy was to create a new relationship between the artist and industry, and companies were approached with a view to 'placing' an artist within a commercial enterprise, not to design projects, but simply to conduct his own artistic enquiries in a new context. There were a number of successful placements, and APG was given a small grant by the Arts Council, and an exhibition at the Hayward Gallery in 1971. But relationships with the Arts Council soured, for APG was simultaneously following a Dadaist course, parodying the structure of commerce with collages from the business sections of newspapers, tipped into issues of *Studio*

233

International, or through John Latham's 'Report and Offer for Sale', a prospectus for the work of APG displayed at the Hayward show. Latham has given this account of his more subversive intent.

In 1965 the art gallery appeared to be folding, or to be no longer relevant in London except in so far as it could further the series one called art – which went along by pressure of anti-art. The APG (Artists Placement Group) probe . . . was never a scheme for helping artists, or for raising money for that matter. . . . Art was to scrub off – all kinds of stuff, systems, things, science, painting, ideas, love, boredom, politics, whatever it was, art was to defy it – maggots. Art was your actual opposition.

Latham's absurdist techniques also caused dissension within the group. In March 1972 Stuart Brisley attacked Latham's predominance in APG. 'The structure of the company is that of a tightly knit, highly autocratic family business, with a poor record of human relations, particularly with artists.'

APG has continued to function, but organizations with more bureaucratic structures had more success. In 1967 the Art Information Registry was launched, initially as a means by which artists who could not get a gallery to represent them could use AIR to promote their work. The Arts Council gave financial support, and in 1969 SPACE followed, as an agency to help artists solve the vexed problem of finding somewhere to work. SPACE began in disused warehouses in St Katherine's Dock, let on short leases by the GLC, which was waiting to redevelop the area. SPACE, and the ACME housing trust, have continued to negotiate living and working conditions for artists in London.

Dissatisfaction with the commercial gallery system is one thing – particularly if you cannot get a gallery to represent you anyway. The attempt to escape the confines of the gallery through the production of ephemeral, 'unsaleable' art is in line with a more thorough-going objection to capitalism. But if there are doubts about the validity of art as a 'commodity fetish' there must also be doubts about the validity of the producers of that commodity, artists. Peter Fuller, a Marxist art critic who began writing professionally in 1968, a year that gave him a glimpse 'of an alternative political and social future', has argued that the artist has lost his traditional function. Photography, television and advertising have made the artist 'no longer *necessary* for the bourgeoisie'. In these circumstances the artist has lost his way.

... dispossessed of his authority and expertise as the professional representative of the bourgeois visual tradition, the artist has diminishing cultural effect. Because there was *nothing* for him to do, he was allowed to do anything he liked: his enforced marginality was presented to him as emancipation into full artistic freedom.

The first response to this enforced freedom was to assert the independence of art from any obligation to represent the real world, and concentrate on solving the problems of painting that painting posed. The second was the non-art, or anti-art, of the 1970s.

The aesthetic problems of abstraction (and the institutional commitment to their exploration) were large enough to ensure that abstract painting continued. John Hoyland, Gillian Ayres, John Walker and Howard Hodgkin were prominent among those who were still preoccupied with registering coloured marks on a flat surface. The economic and critical dominance of New York over the international art market ensured that British artists continued to look in that direction, and that developments in London occurred at best in parallel, and usually a little behind, those in New York.

For painters on both sides of the Atlantic, the problem was that once the veteran modernist Ad Reinhardt had produced his all-black paintings at the beginning of the 1960s, the aesthetic quest for 'pure' painting and 'objectness' appeared to have reached a dead end, and investigation had to take a different direction. Thus by 1969 a British painter in the New American manner, David Sweet, found himself in the paradoxical position of defending abstract works that would have been considered outrageous or incomprehensible in 1950 for their 'conservatism' against the radicals who had moved into minimalism and conceptual art.

Pop art (which, as chapter II showed, did have indigenous British as well as American sources) suffered the fate of its own fashionability. Lawrence Alloway commented in July 1969: 'English pop culture has prospered (music and clothes) but English Pop Art has not.' Tim Hilton wrote that 1969 'quite clearly marked the end of the English Pop scene'. The David Hockney retrospective at the Whitechapel (after which he did almost no painting for three years), and *Pop Art Redefined* at the Hayward Gallery in 1969, helped to suggest that the end of a particular period had been reached; we have seen the change in atmosphere away from the optimism that first promoted Pop. Richard Hamilton has spoken of the pessimism of the 1970s: his *Swingeing London* prints and his paintings of excrement in the manner of advertising art (1973) graphically demonstrate the change of mood.

One of the routes out of the apparent impasse in abstract painting was to work out the problems through the three-dimensionality of sculpture. A leading figure was Anthony Caro, who had worked as an assistant to Henry Moore in the 1950s, but after a visit to America in 1959 adopted the American David Smith's method of welding sculpture. The effect was to move away from the closed, bulky forms of Moore and sculptors of the Fifties towards an openness of structure that suggested the open aesthetic of American colour field-painting. In this he won the important approval of the American critic, Clement Greenberg. His welding together of 'found' scrap materials echoes the collage method, although he gave them a uniform appearance with coloured paint which contributed to the lightness and playfulness of the completed works, emphasized by simply placing their freely articulated abstract limbs directly on the ground, without a plinth. (Ill. 12.)

Caro's influence was felt strongly by those who worked around him as teachers and students in the sculpture school of St Martin's School of Art, where he had taught since 1953. Caro's one-man show at the Whitechapel in 1963 was followed by a 'New Generation' show in 1965 that suggested that the line taken by Caro had released a vigorous new school of abstract sculpture: David Annesley, Michael Bolus, Phillip King, Tim Scott, William Tucker, Isaac Witkin, all of whom had been at St Martin's. Caro's international status was confirmed by a one-man exhibition at the Hayward Gallery in 1969, for which Michael Fried wrote the catalogue.

Developments from the sculpture school at St Martin's did not rest there. Conscious of the stimulus they had received from the intense activity and argument within the school, a number of graduates moved into a disused brewery in Lambeth in 1967, known as the Stockwell Depot. Here they were able to work on a large scale, and within the collective identity of shared premises, continue their research in a mutually competitive and critical atmosphere. This meant that there was only one group show, in 1968, (Roland Brewer, Roelof Louw, Roger Fagin, Peter Hide, David Evison, Gerard Hemsworth, Alan Barclay, John Fowler) but the Stockwell Depot, like the SPACE studios in St Katherine's Dock, meant that a new solution had been found both to the problem of working-space, and of exhibition outside the normal gallery situation.

Although sculpture has traditionally been perceived as the most solid of objects, it is through sculpture that what has been called a 'dematerialization' of art forms began to take place. The process can be seen in the work of a sculptor like Roelof Louw, a student at St Martin's from 1961 to 1965, and then a part-time teacher there. By the time of the 1968 Stockwell Depot show his work consisted of thin rods whose main function was to define large areas of empty space. He subsequently moved into creating works with rope (Ill.13), or simply laying out iron poles in a pattern on Hampstead Heath. Barry Flanagan, at St Martin's from 1964 to 1966 and a teacher there from 1967, decided that working in metal produced results that were too predictable, and changed to making shapes out of canvas filled with plaster, or suggesting designs in rope. For his first show in 1966 he wanted the work to appear 'as if in my normal working situation' and so created a piece in the gallery by pouring out a hundredweight of sand onto the floor. Richard Long, who had begun to explore the possibilities of a new interaction between the artist and his natural surroundings even before he went to St Martin's in 1966, spent three days in December 1967 creating a sculpture that consisted of 'sixteen similar parts irregularly surrounding an area of 2401 square miles. Near each part was a notice giving the information. Thus a spectator could only see one part (no information being given to locate the others), but have a mental realization of the whole.' These separate developments all point in the direction of minimal, and then conceptual, art.

Although these new approaches are in part a reaction against the materialism of Pop, there are also continuities. There is a common source in Dada, and the anti-aesthetic, or no-aesthetic

237

of Marcel Duchamp. Duchamp said that he wanted to get away from the physical aspects of painting; conceptual art did that entirely. Minimalist art still offered some physical object for contemplation, but the 'information' it carried was as limited as possible. In *Studio International* for May 1968 an interview with John Latham is illustrated by a blank area of page captioned *'Minimal Event.* The white surface is defined as white and as surface by the incidence of a minimal black on it.' The information might be of an abstract, mathematical kind, as in the sculptures of the American Sol Lewitt, which are based on grid forms, as with the self-explanatory *46 three-part variations on three different kinds of cubes*, or the arrangements of bricks or sheets of steel by Carl Andre.

A cross-over point between minimalism and purely conceptual art was the realization that minimal pieces were not necessarily constructed by the artists themselves, but by technicians following their instructions. This tendency was noted by Lucy Lippard and John Chandler in *Art International* in February 1968.

As more and more work is designed in the studio but executed elsewhere by professional craftsmen, as the object becomes merely the end product, a number of artists are losing interest in the physical evolution of the work of art. The studio is again becoming a study. Such a trend appears to be provoking a profound dematerialization of art, especially of art as object, and if it continues to prevail, it may result in the object's becoming wholly obsolete.

This principally American development does have precedents in Europe, in the work of the Fluxus Group (chapter III) and some of the ideas raised by auto-destructive art. John Latham told the Destruction in Art Symposium in London in 1966: 'in borrowing from physicists the idea of non-existence as part of the structure of events and applying it to art, many of the apparent characteristics of time, space and continuity are contradicted and it is clear that language abounds with pseudo-entities. In proposing some new terms in the context of Event structure, or NOIT, a rationale emerges.'

By 1969 it was evident that the dematerialization of art was well advanced. Two exhibitions of American work in London in that year revealed the tendency to a wider public. 'The Art of the Real' appeared at the Tate Gallery under the auspices of the

Museum of Modern Art in New York, and featured paintings by Ad Reinhardt, Frank Stella, Jasper Johns, Kenneth Noland and Jules Olitski, and sculptures by Carl Andre, Donald Judd, Robert Morris and Sol Lewitt. This was followed by an even more radical show at the ICA, 'When Attitudes Become Form', a travelling exhibition (sponsored by the cigarette company Philip Morris) which in London included four British artists; Roelof Louw, Richard Long, Barry Flanagan and Victor Burgin, a graduate of the Royal College of Art who spent 1965 to 1967 at Yale. Barbara Reise wrote of the American minimalists 'Their work involves ontological questionings of matter, of the relation between ideas and physical form, of "art" as material object, space or place, or concept. One must *think* to get the full effects of their work, which unfolds over time in conceptual richness.'

Two other events in Britain in 1969 mark the arrival of conceptual art. In May 1969 two former students of St Martin's, Gilbert Proesch and George Passmore, invited David Hockney to dinner in a house rented for the occasion. One hundred numbered and signed invitations were issued at three guineas each, offering a chance, not to share the meal, but to watch its consumption. Thirty people arrived to observe the trio eat seven courses served by Lord Snowdon's butler. Hockney said he found that the conversation at table was 'rather banal', but 'I think what they are doing is an extension of the idea that anyone can be an artist, that what they say or do can be art. Conceptual art is ahead of its time, widening horizons.' Gilbert and George had given their first performance of their 'singing sculpture' at St Martin's in January, in which, their faces gilded so that in their trim suits they looked like tailors' dummies, they mimed to a recording of 'Underneath the Arches'. This became a famous act, performed at such places as the Plumpton Jazz Festival. Gilbert and George (at this stage in their work) placed themselves at the centre of whatever 'art activity' they were engaged in, and logically developed into the production of video performances.

The jokey, satirical attitude of Gilbert and George – it was no accident that they invited the master-publicist of Pop to share their table – had a celebratory ring to it. 'With the tears streaming down our faces, we appeal to you to rejoice in the life of the world of art.' The magazine *Art-Language*, which first appeared in May 1969, represents conceptual art at its most serious, not to say dour. Here too was a collective activity, one that appeared to defy all possibility of exploitation through the gallery system.

The concept of 'declaration' (employed by Duchamp when he signed ready-made objects, thus declaring them to be works of art) had been used by Terry Atkinson and Michael Baldwin in 1967 in their collaborations that developed at Coventry School of Art. Their first productions included works with a residue of visual content, such as a rectangle with linear depictions of the geographical outlines of the state of Kentucky and Iowa, entitled *Map not to include: Canada, James Bay, Ontario, Quebec, St Lawrence River* . . . etc., and the *Air Show* (1967) whose basic tenet 'was a series of assertions concerning a theoretical usage of a column of air comprising a base of one square mile of the earth's surface.' Such work existed principally through document-ation, and in May 1968 the Art & Language Press was founded in Coventry by Baldwin and Atkinson, together with David Bain-bridge and Harold Hurrell.

Although these developments were taking place independently of what was going on in America, Michael Baldwin and Terry Atkinson had had contacts with Sol Lewitt, whose 'Sentences on Conceptual Art' appeared in the first number of *Art-Language*. Their most important American colleague was Joseph Kosuth, who contributed three articles on 'Art and Philosophy' to *Studio International* in 1969, and became American editor of their journal. They also had a useful ally in Charles Harrison, the assistant editor of *Studio International*, who had arranged the British version of 'When Attitudes Become Form', and in 1970 organized the first Art & Language group exhibition in London, 'Idea Structures' at the Camden Arts Centre. In 1971 Harrison became editor of *Art-Language*. *Studio International*'s publicity for the group proved invaluable.

The Art & Language group took minimalism to its logical conclusion, by producing not objects, but documentation of concepts of objects that might possibly be. Yet the purpose was not a reduction to point zero, but an expansion to infinity, as *Art-Language* No. 1 explained.

Painting and sculpture have physical limits and the limit of what can precisely be said in them is finally decided by precisely those physical limits. Painting and sculpture, *et al*, have never been out of the service of the mind, but they only serve the mind to the limits of what they are. The British conceptual artists found at a certain point that the nature of their involvements exceeded the language limits of the concrete object, soon after they found the same thing with regard to theoretical objects, both put precise limits on what kind of concept could be used.

In the traditions of the avant-garde. however, this did not solve anything, as Charles Harrison acknowledged in 1972:

> once the possibility of a paradigm had been envisaged – in crude terms once it was possible to envisage an activity in art which was not *a priori* directed towards the production of objects – it became obvious not so much that new possibilities were open (though, heaven knows, there have been lemmings enough only too ready to hurl themselves into a sea of 'post-object art') as that new problems, a new genera of problems lay in the path of any assertion making.

Thus the group found themselves far from the material world of art, exploring the outer reaches of linguistic philosophy. It was axiomatic of Art & Language that what you can formulate in language is what you understand, but the language they adopted proved almost impenetrable to the understanding of many outside the group. Their activity became the process of recording and indexing the progress of discussions within the group, in order to reveal the difficulties they themselves had. The difficulties were part of the process, hence the 'Mapping and Filing Project' they displayed at the Hayward in 1972.

Trained philosophers, however, such as Sue Stedman-Jones, writing in *Studio International* in 1973, found it difficult to take their philosophical speculations seriously. She located them firmly in the field of art rather than language.

> Whatever the intentions of this group . . . are, they are not philosophical. Having swallowed wholesale the works of such monsters of abstraction as Whitehead, Russell, Frege and Quine, they remain, despite their intellectual indigestion, artists. The approach to ideas is not analytic, discussive or explicatory. The basis for the choice of philosophical ideas is at best eclectic, intuitive and inspirational. The feeling one gets is that this is a collage of ideas. A world of Dadaist or surrealist nature arises from the pages of conceptualist art writing.

This association with the post-Duchamp tradition might appear to give conceptual art just the validation that the critical procedures

241

of avant-garde art require, but Stedman-Jones points to the insecurity this search for validity betrays. Art is

a type of activity which is not tied to any states of affairs (therefore is not empirical) nor to any logical laws (therefore is not 'logical') for validation. To search for this kind of validation is an indication of ontological and epistemological insecurity. To try to tie it to logical necessity is to imply that this is the only kind of necessity it can have and similarly it is to deny art a unique kind of freedom. The only reason for such an attempt is that the artist is unsure of his intentions or the validity of his action.

As was the case of the cultural theorists of the Left – and Art & Language was conscious that 'the pursuit and analysis of the implications of the art work as such ('the theory of art') . . . may/ will have relevance in the long term in the cultural/political context' – conceptual artists were divided among themselves. One of Art & Language's fiercest critics was the equally theoretical John Stezaker, who sought to reverse the process of thought that made the art-object disappear altogether, by beginning with an abstract theory as to what kind of art-object might be possible. Bruce Maclean (another former St Martin's student) worked with Gilbert and George before forming 'Nice Style: the World's First Pose Band', which was 'not theatre, not dance, not mime, not rock or art, but pose, a context of its own.' In 1972 Maclean reversed the declaration process, by officially renouncing his status as an artist. Conrad Atkinson's 'Strike at Brannons' at the ICA in 1972 and 'Work, Wages and Prices' in 1974 followed the exhibition procedures of conceptual art-shows by displaying charts, computer print-outs, photographic and video-document- ation, and using the gallery as a location for discussions. Later, Mary Kelly's 'Post-Partum Document', first exhibited in 1975, applied the documentation principle to feminist issues of child- rearing.

In spite of their criticism of the traditional structures of the art world, conceptual artists were remarkably successful in manipulat- ing them to their advantage. A mere three years after the term had acquired any currency it was being promoted by an exhibition at the Hayward Gallery and at a parallel *Survey of the Avant- garde in Britain* at the short-lived Gallery House. The Arts Council followed up 'The New Art' at the Hayward in 1972 with a touring exhibition, 'Beyond Painting and Sculpture' in 1974, and 'Art as thought process' in 1975. The introduction to 'The New Art' noted that the artists involved had won 'notice and acclaim abroad while meeting with little or no interest at home', and the organizer, Anne Seymour of the Tate Gallery, commented 'instead of being quite unusable within the sinister structure of the art market, an enormous amount of money has been made out of conceptual art.' Commercial art galleries were prepared to follow the avant-garde where it led: the Rowan, Lisson, D'Offay, Situation and Nigel Greenwood galleries all invested in aspects of conceptual art.

Thus any idea that conceptual artists had somehow dismantled the bourgeois conventions of art as an ideological representation and reproduction was contradicted by the fact that they were entirely dependent on bourgeois institutions of patronage, especially the state-subsidized gallery. Writing of the American European movement in general in 1972, Lucy Lippard commented:

> It seemed in 1969 . . . that no one, not even a public greedy for novelty, would actually pay money, or much of it, for a xerox sheet referring to an event past or never directly perceived, a group of photographs documenting an ephemeral situation or condition, a project for work never to be completed, words spoken but not recorded; it seemed that these artists would therefore be forcibly freed from the tyranny of a commodity status and market orientation. Three years later, the major conceptualists are selling work for substantial sums here and in Europe; they are represented by (and – still more unexpected – showing in) the world's most prestigious galleries.

Lippard also noted that the looked-for 'interactions between mathematics and art, philosophy and art, literature and art, politics and art, are still at a very primitive level.' What is also evident is that the conceptual artists had almost completely ceased to interact with their audience. Some, like Richard Long, produced an aesthetically pleasing art-work almost as a by-product – in this case photographs of the landscape through which he passed and in which he left his discreet marks. But a gallery lined with neatly typed and framed statements offered little to a public which obstinately insisted on looking for an artist's material response to a material world.

This insistence was directly felt when Coventry School of Art, the home of Art & Language, was absorbed into Lanchester Polytechnic. Under the influence of their tutors, students in the 'art theory' course introduced in 1969 were producing no painting or sculpture at all, and several found that they were in danger of not being awarded degrees. The 'art theory' course was terminated in 1971 when a new dean of studies declined to renew the contracts of the part-time teachers who were servicing it, and only Terry Atkinson and one part-timer survived. (The policy of merging art schools with technical colleges under the polytechnic scheme announced in 1966 (see chapter II) had the effect of reducing the autonomy of art schools in general.)

Looking back in 1984 on the challenge to the orthodox notion of avant-garde painting and sculpture that *Art-Language* and other forms of conceptual art posed, Charles Harrison and Fred Orton concluded,

The authority of Modernism was subject to some considerable scrutiny and opposition in the later 1960s, as was the authority of many other intellectual, cultural and political régimes. During the 1970s the dust settled again upon a surface apparently little changed. The supposed revolution in thought has left the institutions of cultural and intellectual life relatively untransformed. Those who have attempted to persist with the work of redescription and criticism have had to do so either outside those institutions or in an uneasy relationship with them, a relationship in which the learning of tolerances is not always easy to distinguish from their exploitation, or the critical exercise of competences from their effective disablement.

In art, as in politics, radical theorists have reached an uneasy compromise with the dominant institutions.

In his *The Art of the Sixties* (1977) Hugh Adams lays the blame for the compromised art of the Seventies at the door of the Arts Council, and its counterpart abroad, the British Council.

. . . as a result of the movement away from the art object, due to its perceived status as an item of commodity exchange, the Arts Council has emerged with an apparent corner in righteousness. The misconception that it somehow commissions, buys, and displays art in a 'neutral' way for the public good, has gained it a false moral edge, allowing the artists, for whom the commercial system is repugnant, to become increasingly ensnared by it. The situation is dismaying, because it developed largely unrecognized, creating the illusion of a healthy free art, when there was no such thing but a form of subtle self-censorship resulting in a soft-core British aesthetic.

Hugh Adams condemns 'the divorce from realities' of Sixties art in general.

Roaring young lions of the early Sixties became sleek, purring, sedentary ones later, their art consequently soft, and sufficiently accessible for the manipulators and middlemen to be able to package producer and bland product alike. Mainstream art of the Sixties: Pop, Post-Pop, Minimalist, Op-Shaped Canvas, Colour-Field, and all the others can be seen as having indulged in a giddy ten-year dance, often very colourful, often quite sensual; sometimes heady, sometimes tasteful. Predominantly it was self-indulgent, a dance behind thick glass, sealed in from the great forces moving and affecting society.

This is an exaggerated view: the developments in painting through the decade and a half since 1960 follow, in their own terms, the material changes that were taking place in society, as this study has tried to show. The attempt by conceptualists to escape the system upon which they depended acutely conveys the double-bind in which the would-be artist found himself. And just as there is evidence elsewhere of a reaction against the more revolutionary proposals of the late Sixties, there was a contrary response to the apparent success of conceptual art. In 1974 and 1975 the Hayward Gallery surveys were explicitly devoted to more orthodox forms.

The painter and critic Andrew Forge used just these reactive terms when speaking in 1974 of his selection (and the further selection made by those artists he had invited to participate) for 'Aspects of British Painting'. 'Since the late Sixties painting and sculpture as autonomous activities have been under a great deal of critical pressure. I'm interested in the repercussions, the backlash if you like. It's already clear that one aspect of the backlash has been a huge efflorescence of painting.' In his introduction to 'The Condition of Sculpture' that followed at the Hayward in 1975, the sculptor William Tucker wrote, 'if this exhibition is "about" anything, it is about the persistence of sculpture in the face of avant-garde theory and the lack (in this country at least) of serious economic support.' One of the exhibitors was the American Carl Andre, whose 'Equivalent VIII' was bought by the Tate in 1976. The anger provoked when this row of 120 firebricks went on display shows that even William Tucker's view of what constituted sculpture still puzzled many people.

In spite of the general increase in visual awareness during the 1960s, Britain continued to have a predominantly verbal rather than visual culture. Public taste and institutional patronage had a quite opposite effect on literature to that on painting and sculpture: in the visual arts the emphasis was on the avant-garde, in the novel and poetry conditions favoured naturalism and traditional forms. A return to strict forms in poetry and a retreat from experimental fiction had been a feature of the 1950s; this came both from a desire to assert traditional values, and from the sense that, in literature at least, modernism had reached the limits of its development in the novels of Virginia Woolf and James Joyce, and in the poetry of Ezra Pound.

There was also a strong economic inhibition to experiment, especially in the novel, for while institutional funds, through education and the public library system, were vital to the economics of literary publishing, public taste in books exercised itself without the mediation of the 'experts' of the art world. Even though as many as 80 per cent of the copies of a new novel were bought by public libraries, the buying was done by individual librarians on behalf of just those people who otherwise would have bought them through a bookshop. Book buyers, and the far greater number of book borrowers, were predominantly middle-class, and their preference was for the naturalistic novel that told a story through the actions of fictional characters who lived in a recognizably real world. Novels that challenged their perception, either by abandoning the usual methods of chronology and narration, or by emphasizing the irrational and the erotic, appeared with far less frequency on public library shelves. At the same time the libraries' insistence on hardback books discouraged the first-time publication of literary fiction in paperback. While fringe theatres attracted a new audience with the cheapness of their seats, new novels were out of reach of many young people who might have formed a new constituency. During the 1960s the number of novels published annually fell back, their prices rose, and their print runs became shorter. These factors conspired to make the experimental novel an even riskier proposition than it was already.

In his aptly named *The Reaction Against Experiment in the English Novel 1950–1960* (1967) Rubin Rabinovitz suggests another reason for the difficulties in which experimental writing found itself.

The successful novelist in England becomes, too quickly, a part of the literary establishment. Between novels, he supports himself by reviewing for the weeklies and quarterlies and giving broadcasts over the BBC. All too often he uses his position as a critic to endorse the type of fiction he himself is writing.

The reviewing Establishment changed very little during the 1960s. Cyril Connolly and Raymond Mortimer were the chief reviewers on the *Sunday Times*, Philip Toynbee (though an experimental novelist himself) was on the *Observer*; V. S. Pritchett continued his weekly *causeries* for the *New Statesman*. Other periodicals tended to use the same small number of writers over and over again.

The Arts Council's patronage of literature was of quite another order to that of painting or sculpture. It did indeed support some experimental writing through grants to particular writers, but it was in no position to have a decisive influence on the literary economy. A separate Literature Department only came into being in 1966, and it never disposed of more than 1 per cent of the Council's total funds. Between 15 per cent and 20 per cent of that went in the form of direct aid to writers. In 1968–9 109 writers received grants, out of a total allocation to literature of £66,000, but by 1973 the number had fallen to 50 awards from a total of £150,000. The Literature Department (which perforce had to draw its advisers largely from the more traditionally minded literary Establishment) never succeeded in evolving a clear policy to which it could commit itself, and with few funds at its disposal it was content to fend off piecemeal the competing demands of writers, publishers and editors of literary magazines, who all asserted their right to subsidy. In 1969 the novelist and publisher Giles Gordon, who had served on the Literature Panel, declared that the panel was 'rapidly, completely, and utterly failing in every single respect. On the whole, the money goes to the wrong people for the wrong reasons.' John Sutherland concludes in his study *Fiction and the Fiction Industry* (1978), 'the Arts Council seems to have done badly by the writer and not really to have advanced beyond tokenism.' The situation since then has become even worse.

The contributors to *The Writer in the Market Place* (1969) paint a picture of the utmost bleakness: the literary agent Michael Sissons had 'a feeling of very considerable gloom' about 'a dwindling market'. The publisher Michael Dempsey declared 'the whole atmosphere is very gloomy' and 'the very worst kind of novel is invariably the one that reaches the largest scale'. The novelist Joe Martindale claimed 'the market place and its minions are slowly castrating literature.' The Death of the Novel had long been pronounced by critics like Cyril Connolly and George Steiner, as a result of the collapse of the bourgeois society that sustained it. But with between 2,000 and 3,000 fiction titles being published every year, it was premature to speak of the death of the novel as such. What was worrying was the British novel's lack of distinction.

Most British novels seemed limited and provincial in comparison with the linguistic richness and formal invention of leading contemporary American novels, and positively backward in relation to the *nouveaux romans* of Alain Robbe-Grillet and Nathalie Sarraute. This sense of insufficiency was heightened by a new interest on the part of American and British academics in the novel as an art form, as for instance in Wayne Booth's *The Rhetoric of Fiction* (1961), *The Nature of Narrative* by Robert Scholes and Robert Kellogg (1966), David Lodge's *The Language of Fiction* (1966), Frank Kermode's *The Sense of an Ending* (1967), and Robert Scholes's *The Fabulators* (1967). Although it comes from a later date, Peter Ackroyd's polemical *Notes for a New Culture* (1976), which shows a high regard for the *nouveau roman*, sums up the criticism levelled at English naturalism. Ackroyd concludes with this attack on the 'paucity' of theoretical speculation which,

with certain honourable exceptions, manifests itself in English creative writing. Our own literature has revealed no formal sense of itself and continues no substantial language. Our writing has acquiesced in that orthodoxy which has already been described, resting as it does upon a false aesthetic of subjectivity and a false context of realism. And it is this conventional aesthetic which has been reified into the English 'tradition'.

248

The public for this literature is similar in most respects to the recipients of popular culture, and the writing of our time – specifically that which is constantly being described as 'new' – confirms a similar set of values. Since there is no properly responsive public, there are only literary groups dominated by the popular media and by the fashionable concerns of the metropolis. England has insulated itself from the development of modernism.

In *The Situation of the Novel* (1970) Bernard Bergonzi links the decline of the novel as an art form to a more general decline: 'in literary terms, as in political ones, Britain is not a very important part of the world today.' In the depressed state of twenty years' decline, followed by the failing of hopes raised by the Wilson era, 'I do not think it surprising that many English writers, and some of the best among them, have exhibited the classical neurotic symptoms of withdrawal and disengagement, looking within themselves, or back to a more secure period in their own lives or the history of their culture, making occasional guesses about a grim and apocalyptic future.'

Bergonzi believes that that 'there is a crisis in the English sense of cultural identity is obvious.' An essay by David Lodge, 'The Novelist at the Crossroads', published in the *Critical Quarterly* in 1969, relates such self-questioning to the debate about the nature of narrative. His metaphor is that of a writer who has followed the main route of naturalistic fiction but now finds himself at a crossroads:

> the pressure of scepticism on the aesthetic and epistemological premises of literary realism is now so intense that many novelists, instead of marching confidently straight ahead, are at least considering the two routes that branch off in opposite directions from the crossroads. One of these leads to the non-fiction novel, and the other to what Mr Scholes calls 'fabulation'.

Lodge describes his essay as 'a modest affirmation of faith in the future of realistic fiction'. (Although he himself uses self-conscious literary parody in *The British Museum is Falling Down* (1965) and switches to a filmscript format to supply an ambiguous sense of an ending to *Changing Places* (1975).) The terms in which he defends realism show that the crisis is a crisis of liberalism.

If the case for realism has any ideological content it is that of liberalism. The aesthetics of compromise go naturally with the ideology of

249

compromise, and it is no coincidence that both are under pressure at the present time. The non-fiction novel and fabulation are *radical* forms which take their impetus from an extreme reaction to the world we live in – *The Armies of the Night* and *Giles Goat-boy* are equally products of the apocalyptic imagination. The assumption behind such experiments is that our 'reality' is so extraordinary, horrific or absurd that the methods of conventional realistic imitation are no longer adequate. There is no point in carefully creating fiction that gives an illusion of life when life itself seems illusory.

Significantly, the authors he quotes as examples, Norman Mailer and John Barth, are both American, though, as Morris Dickstein points out in *Gates of Eden* (1977), there was a price to be paid for the new American novel's gift of fantasy and imaginative excess', in that its obscurity caused it to lose 'its wide and loyal audience, its status as the royal road to cultural success.'

The idea that the novel is a liberal form, and that liberalism is under threat, is a view shared by Lodge's fellow academic and novelist, Malcolm Bradbury. In an interview in T. R. Fyvel's *Intellectuals Today*, he gave this description of the liberal dilemma.

I don't have a strong sense that anything I value or do will survive for very long. By this sense I don't necessarily mean that the world will come to an end but that we are moving into a world of anarchy where the values I'm most attached to have little chance of surviving. Are they the values of an élite culture? Well, one could call them liberal humanist values. I feel very much more identified with a notion of art as order, of art as growth, than with art as indulgence or as mere self-expression. To take this point further, what is also worrying me is the apparent exhaustion of the written word.

Subsequent events can only have increased this pessimism. We see it underlying the comic satire of new-university politics in Bradbury's *The History Man* (1975). In *The Situation of the Novel* Bergonzi directly links the crisis of liberalism with the upheavals of 1968. 'The recent wave of student-power movements, with their instinctive belief in the rightness of violence and their contempt for tolerance and free speech, indicates that among a powerful segment of those who are young, articulate and highly educated, "the gradual death of liberalism" . . . is no longer very gradual.' Even those who spurned the naturalistic novel as a refusal to face reality shared the dilemma. The dedicated experimentalist B. S. Johnson wrote in 1973, 'today what characterizes our reality is the probability that chaos is the most likely explanation; while at the same time recognizing that even to seek an explanation represents a denial of chaos.'

The link between the world as portrayed in the naturalistic novel and the liberal world view has a long pedigree: in 1961 the terms of the debate were restated in an essay by another novelist and academic (though this time a philosopher rather than a teacher of English literature), Iris Murdoch. 'Against Dryness' has as its starting point just that awareness of anxiety and disillusion that was pervasive in the early years of the decade. She detects a sense of imaginative failure.

The Welfare State has come about as a result, largely, of socialist thinking and socialist endeavour. It has seemed to bring a certain struggle to an end; and with that ending has come a lassitude about fundamentals. If we compare the language of the original Labour Party constitution with that of its recent successor we see an impoverishment of thinking and language which is typical. The Welfare State is the reward of 'empiricism in politics'. It has represented to us a set of thoroughly desirable but limited ends, which could be conceived *in non-theoretical terms*; and in pursuing it, in allowing the idea of it to dominate the more naturally theoretical wing of our political scene, we have to a large extent lost our theories.

The theory looked for here is an adequate account of the nature of human personality that gives sufficient place to individual freedom. 'What we have never had, of course, is a satisfactory Liberal theory of personality, a theory of man as free and separate and related to a rich and complicated world from which, as a moral being, he has much to learn.' This rich and complicated world Iris Murdoch defines as 'contingency'. The novel is a valuable way to come to terms with this world, but few novels manage to comprehend it in its totality; they tend to be 'either crystalline or journalistic', either about the individual, or the grand social background, but not both. The crystalline form, with its use of symbolism, has a dryness against which she is writing.

Reality is not a given whole. An understanding of this, a respect for the contingent, is essential to imagination as opposed to fantasy. Our

251

sense of form, which is an aspect of our desire for consolation, can be a danger to our sense of reality as a rich receding background. Against the consolations of form, the clean crystalline work, the simplified fantasy-myth, we must pit the destructive power of the now-so-unfashionable idea of character. Real people are destructive of myth, contingency is destructive of fantasy and opens the way for imagination. . . . Too much contingency of course may turn art into journalism. But since reality is incomplete, art must not be too much afraid of incompleteness. Literature must always represent a battle between real people and images; and what it requires now is a much stronger and more complex conception of the former.

Iris Murdoch's argument is both liberal, in that it respects the individuality of human beings over against dry theory, and humanist, in that it suggests that man is free to improve his own circumstances. But it is also pessimistic. Murdoch's 'contingency' suggests that if the world is 'not a given whole', it may be ultimately unknowable, just as characters are not completely knowable – she writes of the 'opacity of persons'. Thus the late twentieth-century liberal novel will not share the certainties of Arnold Bennett. And in practice the characters in Iris Murdoch's novels often have 'opaque' motivations in their sexual or psycho-logical struggles for power. At the conclusion to *A Fairly Honour-able Defeat* (1970) a character remarks, 'human beings set each other off so. Put three emotional fairly clever people in a fix and instead of trying quietly to communicate with each other they'll dream up some piece of communal violence.' This describes the world of Iris Murdoch's novels very well, where sex or violence of an unpredictable nature are the mainspring of plots involving 'emotional fairly clever people in a fix'. Malcolm Bradbury has called her books 'a mythic enquiry into the status of character'. These are not 'social' novels, for, as she remarked in the *Listener* in 1968, the circumstances of the novelist have changed, 'the nature of society having changed, and one's confidence in it having so largely evaporated.'

This loss of confidence affected even the most dedicated exponent of the public novel, C. P. Snow, although the pessimism of *The Sleep of Reason* (1968) and *Last Things* (1970) which brought his *Strangers and Brothers* sequence to a close may have been due to a sense of his own mortality, and the critical disrepute into which his novels had fallen. Bergonzi called him 'the most

deeply backward-looking and nostalgic of living English novelists.'
The Sleep of Reason includes a thinly disguised account of the
Moors murders case which his wife Pamela Hansford Johnson
had also used in *On Iniquity* as evidence against the counter-
culture. The world of the new universities, and the radical
activities of the narrator's son in *Last Things*, suggest that after
1968 the senior common room of a Cambridge College or the
committees of the great and the good in which the narrator has
spent most of his working life no longer represent the ideal state,
where rational enquiry will lead to a reasonable compromise.

The conclusion to Anthony Powell's parallel sequence *A Dance
to the Music of Time*, *Hearing Secret Harmonies* (1975), has
darker themes than the social comedy of the earlier novels in the
sequence, devoted to the pre-war years. In the penultimate
novel, *Temporary Kings* (1973) the anti-hero of the sequence,
Widmerpool, is suspected of dubious dealings with the Russians,
and of involvement in sexual scandal. The introduction of a new
character, Russell Gwinnett, significantly an American, enables
Powell to rewrite some of the lives of his leading characters
through the perspective of Gwinnett's research for a biography of
X Trapnel. Gwinnett's involvement with Pamela Widmerpool
becomes a disturbing case of sexual and emotional dominance:
the 'secret harmonies' of the last novel, though foreshadowed in
The Kindly Ones (1962), suggest that there is more to the
contingencies of the encounters and re-encounters of the characters in the sequence than the accidents of the picaresque. Powell's
ruling image implies that time is circular, that there is no such
thing as progress, but change and decay are inevitable.

The later novels in *A Dance to the Music of Time* confirm Malcolm
Bradbury's argument in his essay 'The Post-war English Novel'
that the idea that English writers refused to penetrate beyond
surface realism at all is too simple. Many writers – Iris Murdoch,
Muriel Spark, Angus Wilson, Anthony Burgess – moved towards
a more metaphysical form in their later books. 'One has only,
indeed, to inspect a sufficient range of works and careers to see
that in various forms mythic, symbolist, and grotesque styles of
writing, which might be thought of as non-realist styles, have
been constant in post-war fiction.' Even the resolutely anti-
experimental Kingsley Amis (whose novels in the Sixties are also

darkened by themes of death and sexual unease) side-stepped into experiment through his interest in science fiction with *New Maps of Hell* (1960), or by adopting the mask of Ian Fleming to write a James Bond story *Colonel Sun* (1968, under the pseudonym Robert Markham).

Since *The Lord of the Flies* (1954) William Golding had been recognized as a 'fabulator', where the naturalistic surface concealed a metaphysical allegory. The medieval church builder in *The Spire* (1964) discovers the earth-bound, egotistical roots of his spiritual ambition to complete the spire of his cathedral: the building is treated as a symbol both of religion and the soul of man. Golding said in 1963, 'I am becoming more and more convinced that humanity – the people we are, those we meet – is suffering from a terrible disease. I want to examine this disease, because only by knowing it is there any hope of being able to control it. And when I look around me, to find examples of this sickness, I seek it in the place where it is most accessible to me, I mean in myself.' Thus the social is tested within the context of the personal, and the personal is treated in terms of symbols that reach towards the universality of myth.

The theme of evil – a version of Golding's disease of humanity – runs through the fiction of Angus Wilson. Bernard Sands, the homosexual hero of his first novel *Hemlock and After* (1952), says of his own novels that they proceed 'from an irrational preoccupation with evil that was probably the result of nervous anxiety.' Wilson combines the panoramic social view that he admires in nineteenth-century writers such as Dickens with a twentieth-century self-consciousness about the artificiality of the fictional form. *No Laughing Matter* (1967) spans a period from 1912 to 1967, and depicts change and decay through a dozen related characters. But the movement of history as it affects the Matthews family is conveyed by the use of writing styles that parody the changes in literary and theatrical fashion, from Ibsen and Shaw through to Beckett. *As if by Magic* (1973), in which nearly every act of goodness has evil results, opens with a pastiche of Dickens and maintains a constant level of literary self-awareness that mirrors the search for a secure identity by the younger characters, whose perception of themselves is indeed shaped by the novels of the past, from Jane Austen to D. H. Lawrence.

The novels of Angus Wilson or Anthony Burgess contradict George Orwell's principle that good prose should be like a windowpane, but parody and games with the nature of fiction reveal a self-consciousness about the authorial 'I' that can mean there is uncertainty about the value of writing fiction at all. This dilemma may itself become a novelist's subject-matter. In *The Golden Notebook* (1962), which interrupts the more 'realist' sequence of the Martha Quest novels *The Children of Violence* (1952–1969), Doris Lessing breaks up the conventional structure of a short novel with four notebooks kept by the central character in the framing story, which indicate the fragmentation that she experiences. (The fifth, 'golden' notebook presents a dream-like synthesis of their themes.) Doris Lessing's preface to the new edition of 1972 makes it clear that she was using this form as a means of discussing the novel itself, and that she considered this more important than the feminist themes of personal freedom that preoccupy her central character. None the less the 'fear of chaos, of formlessness – of breakdown' which contributes to the writer's block that drives the narrator to her notebooks is a product of the social and psychological oppression she experiences. The exploration of the writer's doubts about the validity of her craft (and we may understand both Lessing's and her fictional narrator's) becomes, as Lessing says in her preface, an attempt to shape 'a book which would make its own comment, a wordless statement: to talk through the way it was shaped.'

In other hands, the idea that the author of fictional characters is himself a fiction can become merely arch games-playing for its own sake. In *The French Lieutenant's Woman* (1969) John Fowles writes as a twentieth-century author writing a nineteenth-century novel; the 'I' of the novelist who intervenes and comments on the story is an invention. In his preparations to write the novel Fowles noted, 'if you want to be true to life, start lying about the reality of it', but this paradox only conveys the author's lack of confidence in his ability to reproduce reality – reality having been undermined by just those epistemological uncertainties that cause David Lodge's novelist to hesitate at the crossroads.

B. S. Johnson had tried to resolve the problems of the artificiality of the novel by emphasizing its material nature with typographical eccentricities, blank pages, holes and, in *The Unfortunates* (1969), by leaving the book unbound, but grouped in twenty-seven sections which could be shuffled as the reader wished. This was not a complete subversion of the normal chronological reading of a text however, for the reader was still given specific sections to read at the beginning and the end. Johnson's first novel, *Travelling People* (1963), begins with a first-person introduction in which the writer concludes, 'it was not only permissible to expose the mechanism of a novel, but by doing so I should come nearer to reality and truth', but Johnson seems to have been trapped in his own perception in *Albert Angelo* (1964) that 'telling stories is telling lies'. Alan Burns, who used a cut-up method similar to William Burroughs in *Babel* (1969) and *Dreamerika!* (1972), found that it led to a dead end. 'I had fragmented myself out of existence.'

By 1975, the liberal world view, both inside and outside the novel, was at breaking point. The new writers that had begun to emerge found their material in the fantasy, eroticism and personal violence released by the counter-culture, for instance Angela Carter's *The Magic Toyshop* (1968); Martin Amis's *Dead Babies* (1975); and Ian McEwan's short stories in *First Love, Last Rites* (1975). The shift away from naturalism has since released new energies into the novel, but there was less confidence about the future of the form in the early Seventies. As Malcolm Bradbury observed in 1977, 'fiction has conspicuously grown more provisional, more anxious, more self-questioning, than it was a few years ago.' Six years earlier, in 1971, Bradbury had offered a sociological explanation for this in his study *The Social Context of Modern English Literature*. The sub-text is that anxiety about the future of the written word that he had confessed to T. R. Fyvel.

Bradbury's study, which begins with the emergence of the literary self-consciousness of modernism at the end of the nineteenth century, concludes that economic and cultural conditions are no longer in the writer's favour, and that the decline in imaginative writing is a measure of the disappearance of a social context for writers. Fragmentation has taken place in the audience as well as the novels: 'the writer has lost a coherent literary community to appeal to'.

. . . writing tends now to become part of the bland overall environment of the mass-culture situation itself – even when its final appeal is that it

256

be *not* assessed in those terms. The new environment and the new relationships of literature are a good deal more fluid and evanescent, less open to the impact of the individual creative identity. The consequences are not quantitative, affecting the *amount* of writing; they are qualitative, affecting the *excellence* of writing. Writers are uncertain about their values, their audience and their chances of survival as remembered artists; and literary art now tends to become either a version of history or documentary or a fictive game.

In 1971 Bradbury was expressing alarm about the economics of book production, as prices rose and print-runs fell. The oil crisis of 1973 and the world recession that followed had a severe effect on the book trade. In 1973 the price of novels rose by as much as 50 per cent, and there followed cut-backs by stock-holding bookshops and libraries. The volume of titles did not fall, but the situation of the literary novel became even more precarious than it was already. An intervention by the Literature Department of the Arts Council in 1974 in the shape of the New Fiction Society proved a failure (by 1977 it had sold only 13,000 volumes, at a cost to the Arts Council of £60,500). In 1978 John Sutherland concluded that 'erosion rather than collapse seems to be the danger, though in the long run the result could be the same.' As an industry, publishing has generally recovered from the slump of 1974, but with the usual print-run for a first novel in hardback at 1,500 and an ever-widening gap between the average novel and the bestseller, the social context of literature seems to have fragmented even further.

The economics of poetry are such that it is possible to sustain a lively poetic culture without large subsidies or large profits. The fact that no one expects to make a living from poetry allows poetry a freer life. In comparison with the 1950s, the 1960s were a boom period for poetic activity, for little magazines, readings, and even commercial publications. The Penguin Modern Poets Series begun in 1962 included a bestseller, *The Mersey Sound*; Cape moved significantly into poetry publishing in 1963, Macmillan in 1968. By the end of the decade there were over a hundred small poetry presses active; a poetry-reading circuit was well established, and the Arts Council Literature Department was providing grants both to poets and poetry publishers. All but a few sustained themselves with teaching jobs or journalism, but poets found that their status became recognized in a way that it had not been before.

This was true both of the poets who were published by established magazines and commercial houses, and the many voices of the underground. In his introduction to a survey-anthology *British Poetry Since 1945* (1970), Edward Lucie-Smith acknowledged the achievement of the underground's 'dissident voice' in reaching a strong position outside the official culture. The cause had been

the immense growth in the popularity of poetry with the young; the new fashion for poetry readings, the return of poetry to its prophetic role. Poets suddenly found themselves the spokesmen of a real community – a community which took its standards from the art schools rather than the universities, which identified itself with a kind of political protest which rejected politics, with the new music of the groups (it is worth remembering how many popular musicians began their careers as art students) and which was eager, it seemed, for more wholly radical attitudes than the poets themselves could provide.

Fresh little magazines continued to spring up: *New Measure* (1965–9), *Second Aeon* (1966–74), *Samphire* (1968–81), *Grosseteste Review* (1968–), *Oasis* (1969–), *Good Elf* (1970–77), *Earthship* (1970–2), *Little Word Machine* (1972–9) and, an important medium of exchange between the small presses and reviews, *Poetry Information* (1970–9). In 1967 the public poetry event, such as had been so spontaneously and chaotically successful at the Albert Hall in 1965, received official recognition when the Arts Council launched its first 'Poetry International' festival.

In 1973 Jon Silkin – whose Newcastle-based *Stand* had maintained an honourable independence from metropolitan orthodoxies since the 1950s – celebrated the current pluralism that was such a contrast to the struggle for ascendency between *New Lines* and *Mavericks* in 1956. He wrote in his introductions to the anthology *Poetry of the Committed Individual*:

This change, in which no set of criteria may now be said to dominate, permits the *variety* of good poetry; and whatever may be said about the amount of bad poetry, given the comparative rigidity of English society and its culture, at a time when a revaluation of Britain's position threatens to harden and shrink our responses, we have to accept, gratefully I think, such relative openness.

But he also warned that the 'sentimental tyranny' of there being only one acceptable form of poetry might return. Such a closure has since taken place.

In the mid-1960s those in what might be called the mainstream of British verse, members of the Movement and its successors, felt themselves externally threatened, and domestically challenged. As in the case of the novel and the visual arts, the external threat came from America. The examples of Robert Lowell, John Berryman and Sylvia Plath were held up in contrast to the 'lack of scale and ambition; a timid refusal to whip up some experimental vigour; a failure to seize chances, tackle the big themes, and face up to brute realities' of English verse, as Alan Brownjohn wrote resentfully in 1972. As we saw, this view was being promoted by the influential English critic A. Alvarez, in the editions of his Anglo-American anthology *The New Poetry* (1962) and his essays on Extremist verse. The success of Ted Hughes, and the general acknowledgement that Lowell, Berryman and Plath, had indeed written major poetry increased the pressure on British poets to accept what Brownjohn called 'a state of demoralized inferiority.'

The domestic challenge came from the underground, whose models were essentially American, but who had evolved their own styles through *New Departures*, the Liverpool poets, and the Mordern Tower group in the north-east. Michael Horovitz's anthology *Children of Albion* (1969) contained work by sixty-two poets in a wide range of free-form verse and 'protest' poetry. Their popularity was the result of their appeal beyond the canons of accepted poetic taste – which is why it was so resented in certain quarters. In 1970, however, a number of these poets, including Pete Morgan, Lee Harwood, Tom Pickard, Ken Smith and Barry McSweeney were elected to the general council of the Poetry Society. This institution, with premises in Earl's Court Square, had been in existence since 1909, and was the nearest thing to an academy of poets that existed within the informal structure of poetry. Under the editorship of Derek Parker, the Society's *Poetry Review* had begun to take note of the poetic revolution going on around it, but when Eric Mottram succeeded as editor in 1971 the takeover by the underground seemed complete. *Poetry Review* changed 'from a mansion of grand-motherly amateurism into the outpost of American and European modernism', wrote Douglas Dunn in 1977.

At the same time the Poetry Society, which was already receiving subsidy from the Arts Council, pre-empted the Literature Department's plans to establish a National Poetry Centre by launching its own appeal for funds, and in 1971 the Department reluctantly increased its grant to the Society from £3,000 to £11,500 in order that the Centre should be established at Earl's Court Square. In 1973 a National Poetry Secretariat, an agency for arranging and grant-aiding poetry readings throughout the country, was given an office in the Poetry Society's building. The takeover of the general council by the radical wing was not complete, however, and the Poetry Society became the focus of a factional struggle in which poetic principles and personalities became inextricably mixed.

The mainstream of British poetry, that is, those who followed in the direction suggested by *New Lines* in 1956, was represented by 'The Group', which traced its origins to the private poetry seminar organized by Philip Hobsbaum while still a student at Cambridge in 1952, and chaired by Edward Lucie-Smith from 1959 onwards, following the seminar's move to London in 1955. It was never the intention of the Group to impose a particular orthodoxy, though inevitably regular meetings of a collection of friends produce a harmony of opinion. In the case of the Group their critical procedures tended to enforce a formal discipline, though the inclusion of Adrian Mitchell, Peter Redgrove and George Macbeth in *A Group Anthology* (1963) shows that a wider range of political and personal emotions was permissible, and there was never the insistence on decorum associated with the Movement.

In 1962 the poet and critic Ian Hamilton launched *The Review*, which continued intermittently, and later with Arts Council support, until 1972. (Hamilton also held the influential position of poetry and fiction editor at the *Times Literary Supplement* from 1965–72). *The Review*, with contributions from Hamilton himself, Peter Porter, David Harsent, Hugo Williams and Colin Falck continued to explore the area of emotion opened up by the Group, but always on a modest and individual scale. Alan Brownjohn, a long-serving member of the Group, including in its later revival as the Poets' Workshop, defended this caution about grand statements. 'Reticence, as a quality, is about at the same time possessing yet withholding, the features of extremity.'

itself by one class over against another in Tony Harrison's *The Loiners* (1970).

In Northern Ireland, the use of language and the cultural traditions in which the words were framed had potentially dangerous resonances for their users. Although it is tempting to make a direct connection between the social conflict in Northern Ireland after 1968 and the emergence of a considerable group of poets in the province (a connection regarded with suspicion in Belfast, where it is less easy to see poetry as a consolation for the fear, oppression and disruption that has resulted), it is important to remember that several of the poets were writing and publishing before the conflict became open.

When James Simmons launched the poetry magazine *The Honest Ulsterman* in 1968 as a 'handbook for a revolution', he was thinking of 'the revolutionary process inside a man produced by literature making him see the world fresh and new'. In 1960 Philip Hobsbaum, the originator of the Group, took up a post at Queen's University, Belfast, and a Belfast version of the Group developed. Seamus Heaney, a Queen's graduate who joined the teaching staff in 1966, took over chairmanship of the Belfast Group in 1967, when Philip Hobsbaum moved on. Heaney published his first collection, *Death of a Naturalist* in 1966, and *Door into the Dark* in 1969. Derek Mahon published *Night Crossing* in 1968, and Michael Longley *No Continuing City* in 1969. But as Seamus Heaney has said, 'by then the curtain was about to rise on the larger drama of our politics and the writers were to find themselves in a play within the play.'

Seamus Heaney, a Roman Catholic, campaigned for civil rights in the early stages of the deepening crisis in Northern Ireland, but spent 1970–1 on the campus at Berkeley, California, where he witnessed a different kind of cultural struggle between radicals and conservatives. His first collections had shown him as a poet of nature working in traditional forms who celebrated in particular the complex cultural geology of Northern Ireland, and comparisons were made with Ted Hughes. Education had taken him from the farming community in which he was born, and he was conscious of having a voice that could speak for that traditionally 'silent' community – all the more silent because of the hostility to Roman Catholics in a Protestant-dominated province. (There are parallels between Heaney's experience of the effects of education and Tony Harrison's in England.) But at Berkeley Heaney learned that 'poetry was a force, almost a force of power, certainly a mode of resistance.'

When Heaney returned to Belfast the sectarian divide was even wider than it was when he had left. There was terrorism on both sides, the British army was on the streets, and internment had been introduced. In March 1972 the Government took over direct rule of the province. Heaney's sympathies were republican; he wrote in 1972, 'I speak and write in English, but do not altogether share the preoccupations and perspectives of an Englishman, I teach English literature, I publish in London, but thc English tradition is not ultimately home.' At Easter 1972 he resigned from his post at Queen's and travelled south to County Wicklow in the Republic of Eire, finally moving to Dublin in 1976.

Heaney's reputation continued to grow, with the publication of *Wintering Out* in 1972, and he was regarded as the most prominent of a group of Northern Irish poets (both Protestant and Catholic), all of whom had to cope with the expectation that they would 'say something' about the conflict in the province. (In 1974 the Blackstaff Press, launched in 1971 in Belfast with help from the Arts Council of Northern Ireland, published an anthology, *The Wearing of the Black*, which revealed the extent of the revival of poetry-writing.) Heaney, however, sought to protect himself from this pressure:

You have to be true to your own sensibility, for faking of feelings is a sin against the imagination. Poetry is out of the quarrel with ourselves and the quarrel with others is rhetoric. It would wrench the rhythms of my writing procedures to start squaring up to contemporary events with more will than ways to deal with them. I have always listened for poems; they come sometimes like bodies come out of a bog, almost complete, seeming to have been laid down a long time ago, surfacing with a touch of mystery.

Heaney is borrowing the imagery of 'The Tollund Man' in *Wintering Out*, inspired by the discovery of long-preserved corpses in the peat bogs of Denmark, apparently the victims of ritual sacrifices or executions. There is a clearly Jungian reference in the imagery of dredging poems from the subconscious, but in the same poem he draws a parallel between the bog-corpses and the victims of sectarian killing in Northern Ireland.

These links are drawn closer in *North* (1975), in poems such as 'Punishment' and 'The Grauballe Man'. *North* was indeed treated as a direct statement about Northern Ireland, though it was greeted with more reserve in the province itself. Heaney's ambiguity about the violence comes through in such poems as the concluding 'Exposure', set in Wicklow, where the price of poetry appears to be a kind of exile.

> I am neither internee nor informer;
> An inner émigré, grown long-haired
> And thoughtful; a wood-kerne
>
> Escaped from the massacre. . . .

What Heaney's poems have achieved is a development away from the strict rationalism and formality of the Movement which none the less preserves control of language (enriched by his ambiguous cultural location) and of emotion (his situation is his subject-matter); his work has become a major example to other poets.

In the early 1970s the gang-warfare (to use a phrase of A. Alvarez in his introduction to *The New Poetry*) between *Children of Albion* poets and the Group became more intense. In 1973 Anthony Thwaite, then literary editor of the *New Statesman*, warned in the *Listener* that

we seem to have reached a state of deadlock or separatism in poetry, with, on the one side, a belief in the transparent virtues of spontaneity, immediacy, and energy released by both poet and audience in an instant flash of communion; and, on the other, a conviction that art has a great deal to do with shape, form, control, and that a good poem shouldn't reveal all its facets and depths and resonances at a single hearing or reading.

Thwaite was concerned by the 'basic instability' this revealed and, probably with the *Black Papers* controversy in mind, he continued:

In an educational set-up torn between syllabus demands of a traditional and too-often irrelevant sort and vaguely permissive gestures towards self-expression and undifferentiated creativity, I can see a future coming when there will be two poetries: one the preserve of school-teachers and dons who go on talking in a lecture-room vacuum about form and interpretation, and who manipulate people through exams, and the other a blurred area dominated by sensation and fashion, and having the popular and fluent transience of the record charts.

In the 1970s it was the turn of the Children of Albion to feel threatened by twin pressures, this time from above and below.

From above, as Grevel Lindop has noticed, an older generation was able to bear down from the positions of status and influence that they had reached. The Movement no longer existed, but

during the 1970s a number of like-minded writers, several of them former 'Movement' poets, have quietly taken over many of the symbolically important positions in the outer world of public poetic business. One might say that a certain generation of poets – or a certain phase of poetry – has come into its inheritance. John Wain, for example, was Professor of Poetry at Oxford from 1973 to 1978; a friend and admirer of Larkin's, he devoted his fifth lecture to Larkin's work. Another friend and former 'Movement' poet, Kingsley Amis, as well as remaining one of the leading English novelists, was entrusted with the editing of a *New Oxford Book of Light Verse* to replace Auden's 1938 anthology. Oxford Books of this and that are felt to have a kind of canonical status, embodying the doctrine of their generation on whatever genre they represent, and Larkin was honoured in his turn by an invitation to edit the *Oxford Book of Twentieth-Century English Verse*, which appeared in 1973.

Larkin's selection was fiercely attacked by his former Movement colleague Donald Davie, who had switched his allegiance to Pound and modernism, but the publication of Larkin's collection *High Windows* in 1974, which was a considerable commercial success, confirmed his authority as a poet who addressed a non-specialist audience in tones that echoed its nostalgia, frustration and disenchantment.

From below, a slightly younger generation of mainly academic poets was beginning to react against the experimentalism and indulgence of the free-form poets, just as these had reacted against their predecessors' formal restraint. The young editor Michael Schmidt, who had begun publishing in pamphlet form while still at Oxford, was a key figure in the new conservatism, and his imprint Carcanet became increasingly influential as its list grew with Arts Council support. Schmidt looked back with some regret to the Movement as 'the last moment when a residual literary consensus existed.' This is clear from Carcanet's first volume in a critical series launched in 1972. Edited by Michael Schmidt and Grevel Lindop, *British Poetry Since 1960* deplores the pop poets and modernists of that decade, and presents the Group as the only significant movement to emerge. Schmidt found an ally in C. B. Cox, editor of the *Black Papers*, who joined Schmidt to launch *Poetry Nation Review* in 1973, (later to become *P. N. Review*). Schmidt's 1976 anthology *Ten English Poets*, among them Alistair Elliot, Grevel Lindop, Gareth Reeves, and Olive Wilmur, presents an alternative to the 'droves of unspeakable epic poets, tearful lyricists, rhetoricians of a political kidney, adolescent angst-peddlers, geriatric lovers, spineless satirists, sinless confessional writers, pasticheurs of modernism, and even the occasional down-market pornographer' who seemed to deluge Carcanet with submissions.

This critical counter-attack coincided with an intensifying struggle for resources and access to patronage as the poetry boom began to fade. The fragile economics of commercial poetry publishing suffered from the huge rise in the cost of paper and printing after 1973. Literary societies lost grant support and cut back on poetry readings, while the circuit became monopolized by a few specialist performers. The Arts Council Literature Department failed to increase its meagre budget; many small publishers suffered from the bankruptcy of Better Books in the early Seventies, and reliable outlets shrank to virtually two bookshops, Compendium and Turret Books (which was also a small publisher). The arguments on the general council of the Poetry Society became even more heated, for *Poetry Review*, the printing facilities of the Society, and even access to rooms for meetings, seemed to be restricted to the radical group that had taken over in 1970. Following an angry public meeting, the Arts Council, as the Society's paymaster, began to exercise stricter control in favour of the more reticent school, and in 1976 ordered a special investigation. This recommended that funds to the Society should be increased, but the price was that there should be a change of policy. In 1977 the liberals staged a successful counter-coup on the general council: Eric Mottram ceased to be editor of *Poetry Review*.

Towards the end of the decade a situation was developing not unlike that of the mid-1950s. Though himself a major beneficiary of the prevailing system, Michael Schmidt complained in 1980:

'the academy – schools and universities alike – has modern poetry by the throat. The market for books of poems is now pre-eminently academic. No new poet is safely established until he is on a syllabus.' (The leading syllabus poets also happen to consti-tute what is regarded as the mainstream tradition in contemporary poetry: Philip Larkin, Ted Hughes, and Seamus Heaney.) In his contribution to Carcanet's *British Poetry since 1970*, from which Schmidt is quoted above, Blake Morrison links the younger poets of the 1970s with the clerical poets of the Movement.

Our 'typical young poet' today is likely to come from a professional middle-class background, or if it is working-class we are less likely to hear about this than we would have been in the Sixties. He – or she: but if I fail to add this qualification from here on that is because 'he' is still more likely to be the case – attended grammar school and then went to university, probably Oxford or Cambridge. He will almost certainly have read English Literature, and there is a good chance that he will now be teaching it at a higher education level. His politics are on the whole quietly conservative, and where they intrude into poetry at all it is as a kind of nostalgic liberal humanism. Our poet belongs to the tradition of the poet as *clericus*, and is out of sympathy with Sixties Romantic notions of the poet as risk-taker, 'mad genius', or bard.

The situation has not changed since Blake Morrison wrote this description in 1980. However, today's *clericus* lives in a very different world to that of his poetic parent in the 1950s, whether he is a dissident or a conformer. All artists, not just poets, are even more dependent on the institutions of the state or the great corporations that dominate journalism, broadcasting and much of publishing. Personally, however, he – or she – is freer in his choice of means of expression, he is less bound by social codes of dress and behaviour, he is freer in his sexuality and how he chooses to express it. He will have travelled further and enjoys a greater and faster range of communications. In spite of inflation and recession, as a member of the professional class he has a higher standard of living than his father did, with more material goods and intellectual pleasures available to him. It is, quite literally, a more colourful world than the grey flannel, black-and-white images and grimy austerity of the mid-1950s.

Although education and the cultural apparatus generally main-tain a hierarchy of taste that still places grand opera in a superior position to pop, the distinctions are less rigid. There has been a

267

levelling up, as well as a levelling down, and the emphasis is on the multiplicity of choices available. The idea of modernism, of an avant-garde in the arts devoted exclusively to the difficult problems that art poses to itself has gained far wider acceptance, though one branch of 'post-modernism' seems to be in reaction to this. In his *Notes for a New Culture* (1976) Peter Ackroyd asked,

How is this modernism to be best expressed? Perhaps it can be described as a sense of freedom. We no longer invest created forms with our own significance and, in parallel, we no longer seek to interpret our own lives in the factitious terms of art. Artistic forms are no longer to be conceived of as paradigmatic or mimetic. Our lives return to their own space, outside interpretation and extrinsic to any concern for significance or end.

Ackroyd none the less seems to be conscious of the dangers such a radical separation between art and life implies, for he continues, 'I might put this differently by suggesting that it is the ability of literature to explore the problems and ambiguities of a formal absoluteness which we will never experience. For these forms seem to proclaim the death of Man.'

In the 1960s the emphasis of the Fifties on challenging the mandarin hierarchy of taste was continued to the point where there was not only a 'long front' of culture, offering a choice of categories, but a deliberate confusion of categories altogether, which is why collage became such a significant style for all art forms. It is the most eclectic of modes, imposing a form by its refusal to adopt one. The mixed-media events of the Sixties tried to find a way round and through the established cultural channels as defined by what was permissible in theatre, dance, music and so forth. We may see the community arts movement as an attempt to use cultural styles as means of political expression which circumvent the established forms of institutional representation.

A long front of culture is, however, the result of the development of a mass society, where the old pyramid model of a minority and majority culture is replaced by a series of separate audiences identified by their lowest, rather than highest, common factor. In *The Social Context of Modern English Literature* Malcolm Bradbury concluded that what was taking place was

a levelling *out*, a flattening away of cultural distinctions and differentiations. The idea of an improving standard has certain evidence to

268

support it – the greater provision of books at all levels, increased borrowing from libraries, the growing range and variation of titles, the greater spread of educational and serious non-fiction reading. But sensational, popular and routine reading has also grown. Perhaps a more accurate portrait is of a growing flexibility of taste: an increased crossing of the lines among some readers, especially young ones, in both directions. In terms of the fortunes of literature, this seems to have caused a certain displacement: indeed the evidence is clear that the centrality of imaginative literature – that is, in other than its most popular forms – has declined, becoming just one factor in the vastly growing output of communications, rather than representing a central association of the very idea of the book.

This has not been beneficial to literature, as most professional writers will acknowledge, and imaginative writing, as opposed to writing for information, education or debate, does seem to be less significant than it used to be, though the sheer production of fiction of all kinds as entertainment makes this relative decline from the Edwardian era difficult to quantify. As we have seen, it was the project of F. R. Leavis and his followers to assert the existence of a hierarchy within imaginative writing – the great tradition – and to assert literature's moral ascendancy in culture generally. Literature is no longer seen as central in this way, and the very development of cultural studies in higher education has found social (and, if only by implication, moral) significance in a much wider range of activities.

Cultural history is only one of a number of approaches which substitute the less loaded concept of 'areas' of study for the old system of 'disciplines'. Inter-disciplinary studies, forms of sociology and history have broken down the categories previously enforced in higher education. The best example of this is the methodology of the Open University – a much more revealing title than the projected 'university of the air' – which began operations in 1971. This suggests new possibilities at all levels, not only in the use of the American system of course credits and the flexible choice available, but its open admissions system, the second chance it offers to those who have missed university education, and the use it makes of radio and television to create a 'global campus'.

Television remains, of course, the dominant cultural force that it became after 1956, and this has tended to reinforce both a long front of culture through the hunt for mass audiences, and an emphasis on narrative, naturalistic art. Single plays reach huge audiences, but they do not have the influence of long-running serials, be they *Coronation Street* or *The Forsyte Saga*. In both cases what emerge are characters who correspond to recognizable social types, who reflect a cultural climate and set of values rather than act upon them. Television has plundered nineteenth- and twentieth-century English fiction, and its own narrative structure has reinforced the traditional novel's emphasis on character and plot.

What television has done is increase the amount of information available to people, though, more significantly, it has also increased the amount of people a single piece of information can reach. The arts have benefited, at one level, from the mass audiences that have been created. In September 1973, introducing a series in the *Observer* colour supplement (itself part of the phenomenon he describes) Richard Findlater declared:

Never before in British history have the arts (taken in the widest sense) been accessible to so many people: the evidence is in the record-breaking attendance figures at major exhibitions; the sale of LPs, prints and paperbacks; the viewing statistics for opera, ballet and drama on television. Never before has so much money (both public and private) been invested in art institutions, objects and events: witness the level of Sotheby's auction prices, and the millions spent on new theatres. Never before have so many impresarios, critics, middlemen, apparatchiks and salesmen lived off the professional artists and their work. Never before has there been so much do-it-yourself art – amateur acting, music-making, Sunday painting.

This mass enthusiasm would seem to contradict F. R. Leavis's conception of cultural history as an inevitable process of decline, but there remains the question of what kind of art has been so enthusiastically consumed. Inevitably, the bulk is the art of the past. Museums and galleries may have become the centres for the performance artists of the avant-garde, but their principal job is still to display the glories of avant-gardes now safely overtaken. Throughout the 1960s and 1970s there was a series of revivals, more or less nostalgic, of the visual styles of the past, from Art Nouveau to 1950s kitsch. Bernice Martin has pointed out that this obsession with styles has become a matter of conservatism, as well as curatorial conservation.

. . . in all cultural spheres there is a passion for tracing the history of the constituent elements in the currently popular packages. The London art galleries and the popular booksellers run highly successful retrospectives on expressionism, symbolism, surrealism, and so on. A similar process occurs in both popular and avant-garde film, in the cinema and crucially on television. So the media become pre-occupied with the *history* of styles: it is all very classical and academic, this recontextualization of all that had been deliberately *de*-contextualized in the cultural jumble sale of the Sixties.

A classic example of the historicizing process was Kenneth Clark's hugely popular television series *Civilization* in 1969, which had its own regretful subtext and a theme of decline and fall. The very title carried a reassuring message, as Christopher Booker points out. 'It was as if, out of the dark night of the late Sixties, with all its frenzied contemporaneity and hideous confusion, people saw in the urbane figure of Clark and the magnificent array of agreeable images he presented, a kind of icon – an emblem of stability and eternity in a world which had become a nightmare.'

Christopher Booker, as we have seen, is no friend of the Sixties, but he is no friend of the Seventies either. He wrote in 1980, 'in the past ten years, our culture in the widest sense – architectural, artistic, scientific, philosophical – has reached the most dramatic dead end in the entire history of mankind.' From across the political spectrum, Raymond Williams shares this view. In his 'Retrospect' to the 1975 edition of *Communications* (1962) he declared:

It is clear, looking back, that the period from the late Fifties to the early Seventies in Britain was a time of evasion of all the structural problems of the society. But this was not, as it is now at time represented, the result of general inattention. The evasion was systematic, and the communications institutions were one of its central agencies. From about 1958 until the economic crisis of the winter of 1973–4 a social and cultural phase, articulated if not led by the media, deflected attention from all the long-run structural problems of the society, and offered a lively series of short-term definitions and interests. The celebration of the 'affluent' society, and of happy consumption, looks sick enough now, from a time of deep economic crisis and a million and a half unemployed, but it was always sick, beyond its lively cosmetic effects.

In 1986 we must amend the figure to three million unemployed.

The most evident 'evasion' was the myth of Swinging London, a false image that disguised the reality of economic and political decline. But even Williams cannot deny that one of the hopeful signs of the period was the development of an 'alternative' culture. But while it loosened the bonds of conformity and self-repression of the 1950s, the alternative culture was parasitic upon the affluence and indulgence of Swinging London, and was blocked when it moved into overt opposition to the institutions and economic system upon which it ultimately depended. Its existence as a wild and uncontrollable alternative proved a useful myth to those who wished to reinforce the authority of the interests they represented, but if the alternative society was to be effective as anything more than a marginal form of social protest (and self-indulgence) then its values had to be at least partially absorbed by the rest of society, so that its 'alternative' nature was dissolved.

After the evasions of Swinging London and the illusions of the counter-culture, by 1975 a world recession had produced a grim economic reality. In her novel *The Ice Age* Margaret Drabble describes that year in terms of a national calamity.

The old headline phrases of freeze and squeeze had for the first time become for everyone – not merely for the old and unemployed – a living image, a reality: millions who had groaned over them in steadily increasing prosperity were now obliged to think again. A huge icy fist, with large cold fingers, was squeezing and chilling the people of Britain, that great and puissant nation, slowing down their blood, locking them into immobility, fixing them in a solid stasis, like fish in a frozen river: there they all were in their large houses and their small houses, with their first mortgages and second mortgages, in their rented flats and council flats and basement bedsits and their caravans: stuck, congealed, amongst possessions, in attitudes, in achievements they had hoped next month to shed, and with which they were now condemned to live. The flow had ceased to flow: the ball had stopped rolling: the game of musical chairs was over. *Rien ne va plus*, the croupier had shouted.

At the National Theatre – still waiting to enter into the concrete heaven they had been promised ten years before – audiences could observe John Osborne's allegory of Britain in terminal decay, *Watch it Come Down*, or listen to two elderly men of letters who had not met since 1939 revive ancient antagonisms that reached back beyond the days of Fitzrovia.

SPOONER. No. You are in no man's land. Which never moves, which never changes, which never grows older, but which remains forever, icy and silent.
Silence.
HIRST. I'll drink to that.
He drinks.

SLOW FADE.

CHAPTER 8

The Poverty of Theory

*'Never has an intellectual class
found its society and its culture
so much to its satisfaction.'*

Edward Shils *Encounter* April 1955

The period 1970–5 brought to an end, not just the brief flowering
of the counter-culture and the economic illusions of the Sixties,
but the long period of accelerating expansion in material benefits
and material consumption that followed post-war reconstruction.
After the excitements of the second half of the 1960s, and all the
opportunities they offered both for greater self-expression and
grosser self-indulgence, nothing could be quite the same. But it is
important to recognize the way in which things were different,
and the extent to which the morning-after-the-night-before
revealed, not the rosy dawn of revolution, but a scene of exhaustion, disillusion and discontent. The Swinging Sixties passed so
rapidly into myth that even within the period covered by this
book, the recriminations and the search for explanations had
begun. To complete the story, and to draw this account of the
arts in Britain since 1939 to a close, it is necessary to test some of
the explanations that have been offered, and to try some of our
own.

In February 1975 the radical journalist Peter Sedgwick sat down
to write an introduction to David Widgery's *The Left in Britain
1956–68*, an anthology that documents the rise of alternative
politics. He was forced to a deflating conclusion.

274

Most of the people whose middle-class manifestations are described in this book are now leading very quiet lives. And the apparently radical alignment of their actions and beliefs from march to sit-down, college occupation to insurrectionary newspapers, was a temporary excitement within a liberalism whose subsequent career was to be indistinguishable from that evoked in the least militant of their generation.

He was not alone in thinking that somehow 1968 and all that had turned out to be a non-event. Peter York's article for *Harpers and Queen* in 1978, 'Recycling the Sixties', identified the confusion in people's minds about what had actually taken place. 'The "revolution in English life in the Sixties" [Christopher Booker's phrase] had more to do with getting things for the first time than with barricades. Revolution was the name of a night-club, and, later Che Guevara that of a boutique.'

Certainly there was no political revolution, yet there are marked social differences between 1964 and 1975, as Bernice Martin's *A Sociology of Contemporary Cultural Change* set out to investigate in 1981.

One may, of course, wonder how deep the transformation has been and whether isolated and specialist items of expressiveness have been inserted in peripheral, private and interstitial niches or used in mass culture for the same old purposes of profit and easy titillation. Yet a shift in cultural norms has undoubtedly occurred and one needs to explain why things which the market would not take in the 1950s now form the staple fare of the mass-communications industry.

Martin notes that 'what was shocking in 1968 is often too common-place today to require comment.' Yet an almost identical observation had been made by Brian Inglis in 1964: 'the permissive community already exists, to a great extent – notably in connection with the arts. In the theatre, in the cinema and in print, a latitude of theme and expression is now accepted which would have been inconceivable even ten years ago.'

If 1968 was a watershed, so too was 1956, as the previous study in this series, *In Anger*, tried to show. These comments illustrate the power of the arts to manifest changes of attitude in advance of their acceptance by the bulk of society. The arts are, in this sense, genuinely avant-garde, but they are shaped by the material conditions in which the whole of society finds itself. It is the dynamic relationship between the imaginative arts and the wider

275

institutions of culture (which include politics and the law) which causes 'revolution' to mean at once a night-club, a political programme, and a pop song.

The fact remains, however, that while 1968 brought about significant cultural changes, the political consequences were few. In both cases, the reason is that the crisis of 1968 was experienced most acutely within the intelligentsia. As we saw in chapter V, the paradox was that 1968 appeared to be a revolt not of the oppressed, but the privileged. It was precisely the lack of connection (especially the cultural differences) between the young, mainly middle-class students and the working population that caused the 'little motor' of their marches and sit-ins to splutter feebly, and then stall. There may have been, as Jeff Nuttall claimed, a war between the generations, but in spite of the increased industrial militancy of the early 1970s, class war did not ensue. Instead, we have to recognize that 1968 was an upheaval within the middle-class that ultimately found an accommodation, partly through absorption, partly through coercion, and, most important of all, through changes in the economic conditions that had helped to bring the crisis about. This was by no means the first occasion on which such an upheaval had occurred.

In a lecture on the Bloomsbury Group in 1978, Raymond Williams offered a useful conceptual tool that can be applied not only to the counter-culture of 1968, but to the other cultural groupings which preceded it. Williams pointed out that the Bloomsbury Group was numerically too small to be subjected to the usual methods of sociological analysis, but too large and – having no explicit manifesto – too diffuse to be analysed in terms of biography. What was most important about the group, and the hardest precisely to analyse, was first the mechanism of interaction of its members, and then, through that, its profound collective influence on the rest of society. In this wider relationship, the Bloomsbury Group were part of a certain class, but opposed most of its values, especially its cultural ones. Thus they constituted 'a true *fraction* of the existing English upper class. They were at once against its dominant ideas and values, and still willingly, in all immediate ways, part of it.' The function of such class fractions, Williams argues, is not to *cause* political or cultural change, but to prepare the rest of its class for it. He applies this theory to a nineteenth-century English avant-garde, the Pre-Raphaelite Brotherhood, who were

not only a break from their class – the irreverent and rebellious young – but a means towards the necessary next stage of development of that class itself. Indeed this happens again and again with bourgeois fractions: that a group detaches itself, as in this case of 'truth to nature', in terms which really belong to a phase of that class itself, but a phase now overlaid by the blockages of later development. It is then a revolt against the class but for the class, and it is no surprise that its emphases of style, suitably mediated, became the popular bourgeois art of the next historical period.

If we look back over the period covered by the three volumes of this study, we can see in succession three separate class fractions experiencing (to different degrees) first opposition, and then accommodation. They are also three successive generations: the class of 1945, the class of 1956, and the class of 1968. Although there is clearly a social difference between the mandarins of 1945 (the direct heirs of the Bloomsbury Group) and the meritocrats of 1968, they are all, by virtue of their function and education, if not always by birth, middle-class. The emphasis shifts, with the sort of nuance that only British society permits, from upper-middle to lower-middle class, but they are all members of the bourgeoisie. To complicate matters, there is not only a dialogue going on between the individual fractions and their respective contemporaries, there is also a dialectic between the successive generations.

In *Under Siege* we saw how the successors to the Bloomsbury Group, many of whom had anticipated in the 1930s the need for the sort of social changes that war brought about, were absorbed into the bureaucracies of the Government and the BBC. Much of the intelligentsia spent its war in intelligence. Gradually, however they turned away from – as it was later called – commitment, either by adopting the oppositional style of bohemian Fitzrovia, or by asserting 'personal values' over against those of the state machine. This retreat, together with a post-war reaction that asserted the upper-class, mandarin values described in chaper III of *In Anger*, contributed to the imaginative failure of the Labour Government of 1945, and helped to create the intellectual climate of the Cold War.

Yet for all of its nostalgia, the class of 1945 did not resist change altogether; thanks to the experience of wartime, the arts, which previously had been largely a private activity supported by those who could afford it, became a much more bureaucratized affair, symbolized by the establishment of the Arts Council in 1946. The BBC had also become an important national institution, and as a result of the Butler Act of 1944 higher education ceased to be a private responsibility. The values of these institutions were not noticeably populist or progressive – the most significant cultural failure of the Attlee Government was to abolish the public schools – but they were certainly not those of the Conservative Party in the 1930s.

The 'moment' of the class of 1945 was the Festival of Britain in 1951, when the authority of institutions like the Arts Council was confirmed. Michael Frayn described 'Festival Britain' as the Britain of 'the radical middle classes – the do-gooders; the readers of the *New Statesman*, the *Guardian*, and the *Observer*; the signers of petitions; the backbone of the BBC. In short, the Herbivores, or gentle ruminants.' The do-gooders were only one section of the middle-class; another positively enjoyed evocations of the seemingly lost world of the country house in plays, novels, and in reality, as the revival of the upper-class rituals of the London season testified. With the ending of austerity in the early 1950s, the Herbivores were challenged by a new tribe, the Carnivores, the property speculators, the founders of commercial television and glossy magazines and – though their politics might seem to belie this – the Angry Young Men.

The Angry Young Men were the beneficiaries of the Herbivores' creation, the Welfare State, but that did not make them grateful. By origins provincial and lower-middle class, they were opposed to the aristocratic values of the pre-war Tories who had appeased Hitler and permitted the disaster of Dunkirk. Following their mentor, the angry old man F. R. Leavis, they despised Bloomsbury and the metropolitan élite, but they were also dissatisfied with the Welfare State and the bland neutrality of the early Fifties, if only, to quote John Osborne's Jimmy Porter, because 'there aren't any good, brave causes left.' The Suez débâcle provided a cause for anger, but it was as much a rage of frustration at the country's impotence (over Hungary, as well as Colonel Nasser) as disgust with the Conservative Government's

278

exercise in gunboat diplomacy. At the same time the climate of the Cold War kept radical left-wing politics at a distance from the parliamentary consensus that agreed on the need for full employment and a close alliance with America.

What the class of '56 shared with the entrepreneurs of the Macmillian years was ambition, literally, for room at the top. In their novels and plays they sought to replace nostalgia with realism; in their poetry they substituted a careful accountancy for the emotional self-indulgence of the neo-romantics of the Forties. Once they had established themselves the political radicalism with which they were originally associated evaporated; once they were in a position to defend, rather than attack, their inherent conservatism became manifest. Yet the meritocratic thrust of the Angry Young Men did assist in the replacement of a predominantly upper-class culture by a lower-middle-class technocratic one. Elements of the older mandarin values lingered on, but the new men were described as 'classless', though more accurately, in the mass society that was emerging in the early 1960s, they should be described as *déclassés*.

In spite of the later political shift of many prominent former Angry Young Men, the moment of the class of '56 was the Labour victory of 1964, won on terms completely different from those of 1945. It was won by appealing to sufficient numbers of the middle class with an image of technological change that satisfied their taste for ambition. The failure of that image to materialize as genuine change contributed to the dissatisfactions of the class of '68.

This broad sketch uses generalizations that do not take into account some of the detailed contradictions they contain, and employs clichés such as 'the Angry Young Men' which are open to dispute (although terms like 'Bloomsbury' and 'the Angry Young Men' *are* useful, in that this is how the groups were conceived of at the time). Within a time-span of forty years different sections will be dominant within different parts of the culture almost simultaneously.

A class fraction like the Bloomsbury Group is only part of a larger unit which is itself part of a broader social class. The common factor to the post-war generations in this study is that they are all members of the intelligentsia. The word is a nineteenth-century Russian coinage used to describe dissatisfied and unplaced intellectuals who led the opposition to the Tsar (another example of a class fraction at work). In Britain, however, the intellectual since the late nineteenth century has been seen to have a quite different relationship with his society. This was the theme of Noel Annan's essay of 1955, 'The Intellectual Aristocracy', which described the alliance between the political and intellectual leadership of the country that produced 'the paradox of an intelligentsia which appears to conform rather than rebel against the rest of society.' Annan was in part viewing the past in terms of the conditions of his present. In that same year 1955 the sociologist Edward Shils wrote in *Encounter*: 'Great Britain . . . seems to the British intellectual of the mid-1950s to be all right and even much more than that. Never has an intellectual class found its society and its culture so much to its satisfaction.' Shils failed to anticipate the fulminations of 1956, yet it is clear from T. R. Fyvel's study of a decade later, *Intellectuals Today* (1968, see chapter II, page 59) that that revolt had been absorbed, and that the essential unity between the intelligentsia and British society was believed to be intact.

But just as Shils failed to anticipate 1956, Fyvel failed to anticipate the far more serious disruptions of 1968, and it would seem that at least initially the counter-culture was not so easy to contain. In the July/August 1968 number of the *New Left Review*, Perry Anderson analysed the traditions of the 'intellectual aristocracy' from a radical point of view. In his editorial he described the *New Left Review*'s central preoccupation with 'forging a revolutionary and internationalist political culture' and welcomed the students as 'a potentially insurgent force'. In an article, 'Components of the National Culture', Anderson demonstrated the difficulties the students faced as a result of their intellectual heritage. Briefly, there is no revolutionary tradition in Britain because Britain has never experienced a revolution.

Before discussing Anderson's analysis of the consequences of this, it is important to note the parallels between this argument, and an almost contemporary one coming from quite another source. In three talks on the Third Programme, reprinted in the *Listener* in January 1967 (the medium conveys the mandarin message) John Holloway, reader in Modern English at Cambridge, discussed 'English Culture and the Feat of Transformation'. Holloway argued that even the upheavals of the Second World War had 'failed to make up a great and transforming experience. The national life went on as it would have done without them: just, indeed as it goes on in spite of deaths and mutilations on the roads, which are on a quite comparable scale.' Holloway celebrated the 'trained-mind amateurs' of the Civil Service, the public schools and the 'intricate continuity' they create in public life. 'The amateur, the personal, the intangible inclines to be dominant: instead of abstraction and principle we have individualism and variety.'

Yet in spite of the suggestion that 'what impedes self-transformation may not be our weakness but our strength', Holloway was ambivalently aware that 'somehow a long partial holiday period is coming to an end for us as a nation, and that because of this we must be ready to rethink our position in fundamental terms, and perhaps transform our life in fundamental ways.' Holloway's difficulty is that the very cultural tradition that he describes, 'something of an avoidance of the abstract-analytical on the one hand, and the visionary daemonic on the other – that distinctive double withdrawal into sense and sobriety, with a down-to-earth manipulation of the usual' makes the transformation called for almost impossible. Holloway was at an impasse.

Anderson, who saw the distrust of 'the intellectual or the theoretical' that Holloway describes as one of the crippling obstacles to radical change, believed that the absence of a transforming experience was responsible for the failure of British intellectuals to develop any universal theory of society, one that might cause them to question its values. 'British culture has never produced a classical sociology largely because British society was never challenged from within: the dominant class and its intellectuals consequently had no interest in forging a general theory of its total structure.' Instead, British intellectual disciplines developed piecemeal and empirically, and with the decline in quality of the native intellectual aristocracy in the 1930s, became dependent on Central European, mainly Austrian, emigré intellectuals who favoured tradition rather than revolution: Namier, Wittgenstein, Popper, Berlin, Gombrich, Eyseck, none of whom produced a general theory but who each resisted the revolutionary

281

sociology of Marx. (In fairness, they were exiles thanks to a general theory of society, Fascism.)

In the absence of any general ethical theory in philosophy (where logical positivism questioned whether such issues could even be discussed), the study of English literature, as defined by F. R. Leavis, filled the gap. Yet Leavis's refusal to discuss his ideas in terms of a general system meant that 'empiricism here found its strangest expression'. Leavis's only unifying element was the myth of a previously organic society, now in decline as a result of the materialistic pressures of mass communications. Leavis was aware of the tensions in society, but, virulently anti-Marxist, he could articulate no general theory to account for them. Yet precisely because the study of English literature as practised by Leavis required a sociological approach and an attempted overview, it led to the cultural criticism developed by Raymond Williams and Richard Hoggart, which had been so influential in the formation of the New Left. Paradoxically the culture which (as Holloway also demonstrates) is one of the prime obstacles to change, also supplies the locale in which analysis as a prelude to change can take place. Anderson concluded that British culture

is a deeply damaging and stifling force, operating against the growth of any revolutionary Left. It quite literally deprives the Left of any source of concepts or categories with which to analyse its own society, and thereby attain a fundamental precondition for changing it. History has tied this knot; only history will ultimately undo it. A revolutionary culture is not for tomorrow. But a revolutionary practice within culture is possible and necessary today. The student struggle is its initial form.

Here is the argument of another cultural fraction at work. But the experience of the class of '68 was to be rather different from that of its predecessors.

One of the reasons for the effectiveness of the intellectual aristocracy was, as Perry Anderson's colleague on the *New Left Review*, Tom Nairn, has pointed out, that 'the English civil machinery under-produced its intelligentsia. They were relatively few, they knew each other, and they enjoyed community with the other members of the new ruling-class. They were, in the familiar phrase, an "old boy network" as opposed to a democratic crowd

of equally stamped graduates.' In the 1960s, however, the expansion of education meant that Britain was in danger of over-
producing intellectuals. As we saw in chapter II, as early as 1963
Anthony Hartley was warning in *A State of England* about the
'irritation' of British intellectuals with the bureaucracy of the
Welfare Sate.

What would be much more significant (and alarming) would be if
there were any clear signs of the development of a body of intellectuals
placed outside society and inspired by a nihilistic hatred for it and its
traditions. For the moment the nihilistic sentiments expressed by English
intellectuals seem to run skin-deep, and a divorce between them and the
British state would become a reality only if there were to be serious
intellectual unemployment – a possibility which educational expansion
and our precarious economic situation does not allow us to exclude.

Writing the following year in *New Society* (a magazine launched
in 1962 as a forum for the new intelligentsia) Malcolm Bradbury
argued that the uncertainties of British intellectuals were indeed
due to this cause.

One might say there has been an over-production of intellectuals, in
that society now contains many who feel their training and their intellectual powers are in excess of the jobs they hold. This creates a characteristic pattern of frustration and irritation which was, for instance, clearly
evident in the writings of the Angry Young Men of the 1950s. . . .
evident, in fact, is the tendency for those who are potentially intellectuals
to put their talents to purveying a culture to which they are not themselves
fully committed. This modern version of the *trahison des clercs* is
characteristic of the relationship between an intelligentsia worried and
uncertain about the character of its intellectual commitments and its
relationship to the society in which it acts. It becomes, therefore, more
and more likely that the intelligentsia will be defined in terms of its
protest, its refusal to conform.

The upheaval of 1968 was just such a protest, and, as Bernice
Martin is quoted as saying in chapter IV, 'governments of all
political colours responded by tightening the financial strings.'
The economic difficulties of the 1970s gave a justification for
doing so. Writing in 1975, Tom Nairn concluded that Hartley's
nightmare had arrived. 'Rash State-sponsored reforms of Higher
Education, in the context of steeper economic decline, have

produced something more like the detached and restive intelligentsia of other nations. Over-production and under-employment may at last be reaching English shores.' The 'at last' is revealing.

By 1975 a class fraction had emerged that found it less easy to reach an accommodation between itself and its nominal class. This fraction – sometimes called the 'polytocracy', after its predominance in the new polytechnics – has had its political impact, as Anthony Sampson describes in *The Changing Anatomy of Britain* (1982):

> The new graduates in sociology and political science emerged into an unwelcoming world, feeling very separate from the traditional university élites. The rapid expansion of higher education, followed by recession, contraction and graduate unemployment, provided the classic conditions for intellectual revolt: the armies of young post-graduates and teachers had the time and the zeal to spend long evenings in local Labour Party organization, outlasting their more moderate rivals.

In the meantime, as Sampson later remarks, 'the road to most top jobs in Britain remains almost as narrow as ever', that is, it still runs via the public schools and Oxbridge.

It has been shown that the crisis of 1968 was a crisis within the intelligentsia, and that for a number of reasons it was without a significant political outcome. Yet because it was a political failure, there were cultural consequences for the participants. If we accept – as we should – Perry Anderson's argument that effective revolutionary theory in Britain is almost impossible because there is no revolutionary experience to draw upon, then 1968 acquires special significance as an experience, not of revolution, but of a revolution that failed. This explains first of all why, for a section of the intelligentsia, the search for a theory of revolution became all the more urgent, and secondly, why these theories became more and more remote from any possibility of application.

1968 was not a complete failure; the success of the fringe theatre in evolving its own economy and its subsequent cultural integration, both at national level and in the genre of community theatre that it created, shows that at least one medium was found for the messages of 1968. But there was still a search for the system of 'concepts and categories' whose absence Perry Anderson had lamented in 1968. The obvious area for this search was sociology, and sociology departments were indeed blamed for the student unrest. 'Sociology is the bastion of this barbarism' is Robert Conquest's typical comment of 1969. But the radical sociologists did not find it easy to persuade their departmental colleagues of the revolutionary potential of their discipline. In his editorial for *Working Papers in Cultural Studies* No. 2 in 1971 Bryn Jones complained that 'mainstream sociology is dominated by official or authoritarian perspectives at the service of the present organization of interest and privilege.'

Working Papers, produced by the Centre for Contemporary Cultural Studies at Birmingham University, is one of a number of groups gathered around a magazine that took up the project already announced by the *New Left Review*, to forge 'a revolutionary and internationalist culture'. Prominent alongside *Working Papers* are *Screen* (1969–) and *Radical Philosophy* (1972–) and we may add the annual 'Sociology of Literature' conferences at Essex University. The interlocking membership of the groups that contributed to and supported these journals constitutes a sizable class fraction that has yet to be fully assimilated into the general culture.

The individual groups and their reviews followed separate courses appropriate to their specific interests, but there is a common urge to expose the ideological underpinnings that support the British cultural tradition of empiricism and liberalism – the two least popular words in their journals. Both empiricism and liberalism were castigated for their lack of methodological unity: their appeal to common sense was dismissed as merely following the practical interests of the dominant class; the open-mindedness of liberalism merely concealed that class's commitment to the division of labour and the alienated consciousness of late capitalism. At all points the hegemony of empiricism and liberalism and the view they imposed on the world had to be rigorously contested. Because, as Perry Anderson had shown, the British cultural tradition was fundamentally conditioned by these concepts, a unifying theory had to be found that would produce a coherence absent in British philosophy. To do this, it was necessary to look outside, principally to European theorists.

The first of these was Marx, and his followers Lukács, Gramsci and Lucien Goldmann, who had supplied Marxism with the cultural theory that Marx himself had neglected to elaborate.

Marx's principle of 'base' and 'superstructure' was developed to a point where it was understood that all non-materially productive activities (such as the arts) were part of an ideological superstructure that was conditioned by its economic base.

A second source of general theory was structuralism. The linguistic philosopher Mongin-Ferdinand de Saussure (1857–1913) had argued that language was in itself the universal organizing principle of thought. Working from this the anthropologist Claude Lévi-Strauss (1908–) developed the theory that there was a universal system of signs, a discoverable semiology that revealed a structure (for which language was the model) that underlay whatever cultural system was under discussion. Combined with Marx, structuralism provided a theory of satisfying universality, although it is noticeable that the more comprehensively its schemes developed, the less comprehensible the language of its theorists became.

An important figure in the British perception of structuralism and subsequent post-structuralism was Roland Barthes (1915–80). His influence on cultural practice, in the shape of the *nouveaux romans* written by Alain Robbe-Grillet and Nathalie Sarraute meant that his theories were susceptible to empirical testing by English critics. Dick Hebdige, whose brief introduction in *Subculture: The Meaning of Style* (1979) is one of the clearest expositions available, explains Barthes's significance.

Barthes' application of a method rooted in linguistics to other systems of discourse outside language (fashion, film, food, etc.) opened up completely new possibilities for contemporary cultural studies. It was hoped that the invisible seam between language, experience and reality could be located and prised open through a semiotic analysis of this kind: that the gulf between the alienated intellectual and the 'real' world could be rendered meaningful and, miraculously, at the same time, be made to disappear. Moreover, under Barthes's direction, semiotics promised nothing less than the reconciliation of the two conflicting definitions of culture upon which Cultural Studies was so ambiguously posited – a marriage of moral conviction (in this case, Barthes' Marxist beliefs) and popular themes: the study of a society's total way of life.

The problem for cultural investigators was that as structuralist theories developed to the point where they could be termed post-structuralist, their connection with the real world of cultural activity became more and more remote. Meaning was dissolved either into impenetrable structures which demonstrated that the connection between words and things was at the very least arbitrary, or indeed that there was none at all; or into 'ideology', which meant that everything that was said or written was so conditioned by the ideology of economic production that it had no significance except as an expression of the 'structure' of that ideology. Man either had no connection with the objects around him in the world (as in the novels of Robbe-Grillet), or simply had no individual existence, as in the theories of Louis Althusser (1918–). The logic of Althusser and Michel Foucault (1926–1984) was that man had no control over the ideological structures which formed his perception of the world, and which he existed solely to reproduce. Ideology does not come from forms, but forms from ideology. All 'signs' were equal in an idealist philosophy which ultimately contradicted the materialism of Marx. But even the philosophical journals in which these ideas were expressed must be called into question, for the conclusion to be drawn from the post-structuralism or deconstruction of Jacques Derrida (1930–) was that a text *never* meant what it said.

This account underestimates the value of the concept of ideology to cultural analysis. There is a connection (as this study has tried empirically to demonstrate) between what is written or painted or performed, and the material conditions under which they are produced. But the extremities reached by post-structuralist theories are unsettling: they suggest that the world of experience is in fact unknowable, and that human agency – free will – does not exist, or at least is powerless against supervening ideological structures. This conclusion – which is in truth the ultimate denial of empiricism and liberalism – must be especially problematic for those who have entered the labyrinths of theory in order to find a universal explanation for human creative activity, that is, for culture.

The removal of the possibility of effective human agency undoubtedly shocked British Marxists who held on to the idea that society is improvable by the intervention of the principle of social justice and the equitable redistribution of wealth. This is the burden of E. P. Thompson's attack on Althusserianism and its exponents in the *New Left Review*, in his book *The Poverty of Theory*, published in 1978. What is significant here is Thompson's association of these theories with a particular section of the intelligentsia and his stress on their separation from practical influence, while at the same time exposing their material distance from the ideas they expound.

This particular freak . . . has now lodged itself firmly in a particular social *couche*, the bourgeois *lumpen-intelligentsia*: aspirant intellectuals, whose amateurish intellectual preparation disarms them before manifest absurdities and elementary philosophical blunders, and whose innocence of intellectual *practice* leaves them paralysed in the first web of scholastic argument which they encounter; and *bourgeois*, because while many of them would *like* to be 'revolutionaries', they are themselves the products of a particularly 'conjuncture' which has broken the circuits between intellectuality and practical experience (both in real political movements, and in the actual segregation imposed by contemporary institutional structures), and hence they are able to perform *imaginary* revolutionary psycho-dramas (in which each outbids the other in adopting ferocious verbal postures) while in fact falling back upon a very old tradition of bourgeois élitism for which Althusserian theory is exactly tailored.

For Thompson the important point is that 'in the much-publicized "revival of Marxism" in Britain in the last two decades, a mountain of thought has not yet given birth to one political mouse.'

If we step back from the intense in-fighting on the Left (and each of the names mentioned here has passionate friends and enemies) we can see that some kind of breakdown has occurred, between theory and practice, between authors and audience, even between language and meaning. There is a parallel between the retreat into philosophical sectarianism of the intellectuals and the separation into factionalism of the revolutionary parties of the Left after 1968. It is also possible to see a parallel between these developments and the loss of an audience by the avant-garde. In some sectors at least, the transmission and reception of ideas was interrupted, and not reconnected within the period covered by this book. We are too near to the events to appreciate their ultimate consequences, but the efforts of sociologists, Marxists, structuralists and cultural historians have been directed to discovering a satisfactory methodology that as yet does not appear to have been found. In this sense, here is a class fraction that is still attempting a revolt; whether it is against the class, or for the class, is still open to question.

* * *

The break in communication, the retreat into theory, clearly has implications for the arts, and it is useful to examine the case history of one of the new radical journals, for it demonstrates particularly clearly the point that is being made. At first it might seem paradoxical that cultural critics opposed to the ideology of capitalism should choose to concentrate on the most capitalist of cultural enterprises, the cinema, but this is what the film theorists of *Screen* did. It is possible that the crisis in the British film industry evoked unconscious parallels with the hoped-for crisis of late capitalism, but it is more likely that a mass art form, relatively free of acquired orthodox critical values, was particularly appealing to cultural critics.

Between 1960 and 1975 the number of cinemas in Britain fell from 3,034 to 1,530, and annual ticket sales shrank from 500 million to 116 million. Throughout this period American domination of the industry increased, both in terms of films shown and American participation in British productions. The domestic market continued to be largely controlled by Rank and ABC, until ABC was taken over by EMI in 1969. Independent production was still possible, but it was risky and arduous. As a result, by 1968 Britain had in effect developed a majority and a minority film culture. The majority was in decline, but still commanded larger resources than the minority 'art-house' culture that was mainly interested in European films, including the few independent British productions. This culture depended on a few cinemas, chiefly in London, the Academy, the Hampstead Everyman, the National Film Theatre, the New Cinema Club and the Electric Cinema Club, on cinemas in university towns, on film societies, and on distributors like Contemporary and Connoisseur. Attempts to build an effective cinema circuit by Parallel Cinema, backed by Joseph Losey, Tony Garnett, Ken Loach, David Mercer and Albert Finney failed, and in 1970 the company became simply distributors, Other Cinema Ltd. Film criticism was sustained by the British Film Institute's mainstream *Sight and Sound*, and by more ephemeral independent efforts: *Kinema*, *Cinema Rising*, *Monogram*, *Movie*, *After Image* and *The Silent Screen*.

An underground film culture of a sort developed during the Sixties, but ironically it also was heavily dependent on American resources. The American film-maker Steve Dworkin, for instance, lived in London, but made all his early films in America. In 1966

289

Bob Cobbing, who had shown films in the Better Books basement during his period as manager, founded the London Film Makers Co-Op with John Collins, Philip Crick and the critic Ray Durgnat. The Co-op later found an outlet at the Arts Lab. When a second Arts Lab opened in Robert Street in 1969 it was able to build up a library of films drawing on the agitprop Cinema Action, the Berwick Street Collective, Politkino and Liberation Films. On the closure of Robert Street in 1971 the Co-Op took over a disused dairy in Kentish Town, where it established film facilities and a small cinema.

Central to all these activities was the British Film Institute, the first cultural institution to be government subsidized when it was founded in 1934. Its function was to stimulate film education and criticism through *Sight and Sound*, by hiring out films from its archive, and with the screenings of the National Film Theatre, opened in 1951. When the 1964 Labour Government decided on a policy of arts expansion, the BFI's budget was increased and it set about establishing a chain of regional film theatres with programmes similar to those of the NFT. Unfortunately these regional cinemas did not attract a large enough audience for their 'quality' films, and from 1963 onwards there was a series of financial crises at the BFI. At the same time there were policy disputes within the governing body, when the film-makers Karel Reisz and Lindsay Anderson (pioneers of the Free Cinema Movement in the 1950s, see *In Anger* p. 153) became dissatisfied with the lack of critical acumen in *Sight and Sound* and the NFT programmes.

The British Film Institute's education department had expanded along with the rest of the Institute, and had developed an intricate relationship with the supposedly independent Society for Education in Film and Television, which was subsidized by the BFI, and had offices in its building. The Society's original interest was in the expanding area of film studies in schools, and it published a journal, *Screen Education*. In 1969, edited by Kevin Gough-Yates (who taught film studies at Hornsey College of Art) and Terry Bolas (who was the Society's secretary), the journal became simply *Screen*.

The editors declared that they were anxious to investigate the new field of semiology, stimulated in part by Peter Wollen's *Signs and Meanings in the Cinema* (1969) and the post-1968 line being taken in Paris by the influential *Cahiers du Cinéma*. But a palace revolution appears to have taken place in 1970, and by the end of the year the two editors, along with the Society's chairman and treasurer, had resigned. In the spring of 1971 *Screen* became a quarterly with a new editor, Sam Rohdie, and a new editorial board. Their policy statement reveals that the critical avant-garde had taken over. '*Screen* will aim to go beyond subjective taste-ridden criticism and try to develop more systematic approaches over a wider field.' This process would be fed by seminars, indeed 'the editorial board itself functions as a seminar.' *Screen*'s financial security through its support from the British Film Institute 'must be seized by *Screen* to develop theories of film study.' One of the first exercises in this was an article attacking the 'bourgeois ideology' of *Sight and Sound*.

Screen's seizure by the semiologists coincided with the climax of the internal crisis at the BFI. Reisz and Anderson resigned as governors, and the film producer Denis Forman succeeded Sir William Coldstream as chairman. The Institute's education department was subjected to a rigorous investigation by the governors, and six of its staff resigned. *Screen* and the Society for Education in Film and Television were also disciplined. It was proposed that the BFI's subsidy to *Screen* should be cut from £6,000 to £500 on the grounds that it was too 'theoretic and academic', and the seminars were ordered to cease. A compromise was however reached. The Society found new premises, and was given a grant of £9,994 for 1972–3. *Screen* retained its commitment to what it called 'cinesemiotics'. In 1974, when Sam Rohdie left to take up a teaching post in New York, he was succeeded as editor by Ben Brewster, who was also on the editorial board of the *New Left Review*.

The British Film Institute's attitude to *Screen* reveals in unusually naked form the hostility that the critical theorists encountered. (One of *Screen*'s contributors and guest editors, Colin MacCabe, was to be the subject of a fierce controversy over the role of structuralism in the English Faculty at Cambridge in 1981.) But more significant is that the theories they developed – or reprinted, in their regular translations from *Cahiers du Cinéma* – operated in a vacuum. As Alan Lovell (who also wrote on film for the *New Left Review*) admitted in the pages of *Screen* itself in 1972, the theorists were interested in semiology and the role of ideology but 'outside the magazines this tendency has virtually no existence.' There simply were not the films that turned theory into practice. Fewer than a dozen of the 120 film-makers contributing to the first London Festival of Avant-Garde Film in 1973 were British.

When, as in the British Film Institute's dispute with *Screen*, the normally tolerant controllers of access to patronage and communication took exception to what was being done, the radicals could claim that the authoritarian basis of liberalism had been unmasked. But if there was resistance to their activities, the 'illiberal' attitude this displayed was at least partly the radicals' own creation. As Stuart Hall (an influential voice in Birmingham University's *Working Papers in Cultural Studies*) commented in *Policing the Crisis*,

> The counter-culture did not arise from the experience of repression, but rather from the 'repressive tolerance' of the liberal-capitalist state. It *redefined* this liberalism, this tolerance, this pluralism, this consensus as *repressive*. It renamed 'consensus' as 'coercive'; it called 'freedom' 'domination'; it redefined its own relative affluence as a kind of alienated, spiritual poverty.

The radicals' attack on liberalism had a dialectical effect on those who would defend it. Defined as repressive, the state then sheds any moral responsibility for maintaining the welfare and education of its people – an argument that chimes with today's conservative libertarianism. If even medicine and psychiatry are part of the ideological structure of the state, what faith could be retained in the hope that life can get better and people helped by any kind of social improvement?

Alaistair MacIntyre, who had seen some of the nihilistic aspects of the new radicalism surface at Essex University, warned against the dangerous situation that was being created, in the conclusion to a short (and highly critical) study of Marcuse in 1970.

> . . . there is continuous pressure upon universities and other institutions to make the process of rational enquiry merely instrumental to the purposes of government. These assaults upon rational enquiry in the interests of the established social order have to be resisted. The new Marcusian radical case against tolerance makes those radicals who espouse it allies in this respect of the very forces which they claim to

attack, and this is not just a matter of their theory, but also of their practice. The defence of the authority of the university to teach and to research as it will is in more danger immediately from Marcuse's student allies than from any other quarter.

If some of the actions of those in authority became more overtly repressive, the radicals had themselves to blame.

One effect of the new radicalism was to drive an older generation of intellectuals further to the Right. As we saw, the radicalism of the Angry Young Men had included hostility to the Welfare State; there had been a kind of neutralism about their politics that underlay the aggression towards the cultural attitudes they criticized. In his study of the Movement, Blake Morrison comments, 'fear of the Left seems to have been a dominant part of the Movement ideology in the 1960s, with Amis, Conquest, Davie, Larkin and Wain being affected by it.' Philip Larkin and Robert Conquest had been politically conservative from the beginning; Donald Davie was pushed to the Right by his experiences as Professor of American Literature at Essex from 1965 to 1968. Morrison continues, 'until 1956, Movement texts had been divided between a desire for social reform and a desire to preserve the status quo; the tension was energetic and enriching. Now the conservative element in the Movement began to assume control.' By the mid-1970s other radicals of the 1950s had declared new allegiances: John Osborne, the historian Hugh Thomas, the journalist Richard West and Paul Johnson, who edited the *New Statesman* from 1965 to 1970, but became increasingly critical of the Labour Party before declaring for the Right. In 1975 the former young meteor, Jonathan Aitken, now a Conservative MP, founded the Conservative Philosophy Group with the businessman Sir Hugh Fraser. The participation of John Casey, an editor of the *Cambridge Review*, and Roger Scruton, editor of the *Salisbury Review,* has helped to create a vigorous *salon* for the exchange of right-wing views.

The best documented shift in political allegiance is that of Kingsley Amis, and it usefully demonstrates the cultural issues involved. In October 1959 he announced that his vote in the General Election would be for Labour, even though 'nobody, in Swansea West at any rate, hates the Labour Party as much as I do.' His vote would be 'anti-Tory, not pro-Labour'. Amis still voted Labour in 1964, but he was increasingly alarmed by the effects of the expansion of higher education. He wrote in 1960, 'nobody who has not seen it in all its majesty – I speak as a university lecturer – can imagine the pit of ignorance and incapacity into which education has sunk since the war.' And he warned that 'MORE WILL MEAN WORSE.'

Amis's temper was not improved when he left University College Swansea in 1961 to take up a fellowship at Peterhouse, Cambridge. In 1963 he became a full-time writer. (As chapter II of *In Anger* shows, the new writers of the 1950s had found university expansion very useful to them when beginning their careers.) Amis's essay 'No More Parades: On Leaving Cambridge' shows that he too was concerned about the possibility of an overproduction of intellectuals, though from a different point of view. 'When (or if) in due course people start noticing that we have more university graduates than we know what to do with and that their standard is low, I shall enjoy saying "I told you so" at a comfortable distance from the débâcle.'

Amis voted Conservative for the first time in the GLC elections of 1967, and the fact was recorded in an article for the *Sunday Telegraph*, 'Why Lucky Jim turned right: confessions of an exradical'. This was followed by a lecture to the Conservative Political Centre summer school at Oxford, a slight piece of work, but useful propaganda for the Political Centre, who reprinted it as *Lucky Jim's Politics*. Throughout, Amis asserts his essentially anti-political stance. 'Growing older, I have lost the need to be political which means, in this country, the need to be Left. I am driven into grudging toleration of the Conservative Party because it is the party of non-politics, of resistance to politics.' But this resistance now meant resistance to the politics of the Left, to progressive education and comprehensive schools, to the Left's failure to resist Soviet communism and its lack of support for the Americans in Vietnam, and indeed to anyone 'who buys unexamined the abortion-divorce-homosexuality-censorship-racialism-marijuana package.'

The trajectory of Amis's cultural politics traced a similar path to that of the founder-editors of the *Critical Quarterly*, C. B. Cox and A. E. Dyson. Both had studied at Cambridge under Leavis, and their journal was intended to fill the gap left by the closure of

Scrutiny in 1953. But their values were those of the class of '56, and they wished to break out of the 'puritanical narrowness of spirit in the Cambridge English School', which under Leavis's influence seemed to have no room for contemporary literature. Accordingly, although their 5,000 or so readers were chiefly academics and school teachers, they sought to base their policy on the 'assumptions of Philip Larkin, Donald Davie and the Movement poetry of the 1950s.' Richard Hoggart and Angus Wilson were among their literary advisers.

Launched in 1959, the *Critical Quarterly* sought to engage in contemporary literature, and published poems by Ted Hughes, Sylvia Plath and Anne Sexton, as well as those by former members of the Movement. They also published articles by the rising generation of academics, among them Bernard Bergonzi, Malcolm Bradbury and David Lodge. Bergonzi had edited the last group of Fantasy Press poets in 1956–7; Bradbury and Lodge had published their first novels in 1959 and 1960. Yet by the mid-1960s a certain disenchantment had set in. This was partly with the 'thinness of content' of the ex-Movement poets, but more especially,

as editors we could no longer feel optimistic that by promoting rational discussion of new literature we were contributing to a gradual and inevitable enlargement of the civilized community. We had to accept that we were increasingly in the position of a beleaguered minority, and that our duty in the future would involve more emphasis on the transmission of great literature of the past into the consciousness of the present-day reader.

The editors were both Labour voters in 1966 (and were not yet forty) but then came the demonstrations and sit-ins of 1968. Since 1962 they had also been producing a second journal, *Critical Survey*, aimed principally at school teachers. In March 1969 this became the vehicle for their first *Black Paper on Education*. 'We had observed in the schools the growing influence of progressive education in breaking down faith in high culture, in reason and disciplined learning. Emphasis on activity and self-expression easily became associated with the immediacy and sensationalism of neo-modern art.' It was later claimed that the *Black Papers*, with contributions from Kingsley Amis, Robert Conquest, John Gross, John Sparrow, Angus Maude, Rhodes Boyson, Philip Larkin and G. H. Bantock, had 'broken the fashionable Left-wing consensus on education.'

Although the editors disclaimed any political motivation for the *Black Papers*, the decision to send a copy to every Member of Parliament hardly showed political innocence. They were attacked by the Labour Minister for Education, Edward Short, and the *Black Papers* became an overnight bestseller. Two further issues appeared, in 1969 and 1970, and having begun by attacking the student militants as a threat to traditional academic freedoms, they concentrated increasingly on the dangers of comprehensive education. *Black Papers* No.3 was called 'Goodbye Mr Short', for the change of government in 1970 meant that he had been replaced as Minister by Mrs Margaret Thatcher, who withdrew the Government circular imposing comprehensivation on the education authorities. A fourth *Black Paper* appeared in 1975, edited by Cox and Rhodes Boyson, a former comprehensive-school headmaster who had become a Conservative MP. Contributors included Max Beloff, Amis, Conquest, Bantock, Ronald Butt, H. J. Eysenck, and Iris Murdoch.

Black Paper 1975 also included Bernice Martin's 'The Mining of the Ivory Tower', an essay that anticipates the arguments of *A Sociology of Contemporary Cultural Change*. The rival interpretations of the effects of 1968 that were discussed in chapter IV now come into clearer perspective: Bernice Martin was writing in *Black Papers*, Stuart Hall in *Working Papers in Cultural Studies*. There comes a point when sociologists who work in the field of ideology must be themselves tested for ideological bias.

Bernice Martin's conclusions are certainly a long way from Theodore Roszak's call for the rediscovery of magic as a protection against technology in *The Making of a Counter-Culture* (New York 1969, London 1970) (see page 82). Her theme is the 'self-defeating inner logic of pure anti-structure'. Not only must we 'conclude that the romantic crusade was always an impossible Utopian dream: it mistook the nature of liminality', but 'in the media of pure expressiveness the indispensable basis of order has been rediscovered.' Her argument is in the tradition of cultural conservatism. She acknowledges some of the counter-culture's liberalizing effects, but seeks to contain or absorb them, by allowing their legitimacy at a personal level, while ignoring the fact that attempts to work out their implications at a political level have been vigorously opposed. Her dismissive attitude to the 'Utopian dream' is itself part of that opposition.

Both Bernice Martin and Stuart Hall are responding to the cultural crisis of 1968, and the ensuing sharpened industrial struggles of 1970–4. Committed to the dominant culture, Martin argues for absorption: committed to supplanting that culture and the economic system on which it rests, Hall in his contributions to *Resistance through Rituals* (1976) and *Policing the Crisis* (1978) interprets the movement of the dominant culture since 1968 as one of 'closure'. As the counter-culture acquired a political dimension, it began to be characterized as 'a moral conspiracy against the state: no longer simply getting and spending, clothes and records, fun and games – but drugs, crime, the withdrawal from work, rampant sex, promiscuity, perversion, pornography, anarchy, libertinism and violence. It became a source of moral-political pollution, spreading an infection in its every form: the conspiracy to rebel. In a profound sense, the dominant culture – face to face with this spectacle – felt itself out of control.'

Thus for Hall 1970 becomes 'a watershed, a breaking point', the near civil war in Northern Ireland a dramatic manifestation of the profound disruption in the rest of society.

In response, the balance in the control culture began to swing, slowly at first, then sharply, towards a more openly repressive position. Then what had been simmering and festering not far below the surface, erupted into its very centre, and transformed and redefined the whole balance of the relations of force in society. What commands the transition from this tightening of control at the end of the 1960s into the full repressive 'closure' of 1970, presiding over the birth-pangs of a British version of the 'law-and-order' society, and redefining the whole shape of social conflict and civil dissensions in its wake, is the re-entry to the historical struggle in a visible, open and escalating form. A society careering off the rails through 'permissiveness', 'participation' and 'protest' into the 'alternative society' and 'anarchy' is one thing. It is quite another moment when the working class once again takes the offensive in a mood of active militancy.

Hall, it should be remembered, was writing in the period of a Labour government. In the longer perspective of 1986 we can see that when the industrial battles of 1970–4 were refought in the 1980s, this time they were a defeat for the militants, and the 'law-and-order' society has been substantially strengthened. The consequences of the recession since 1975 have reinforced this tendency by curbing the expectations of trades unions, and, for the economic optimism of the counter-culture, substituting a dole-culture where nihilism rules.

It would be wrong to force a conclusion on a situation which remains unresolved, but Raymond Williams's idea of class fractions may be useful in explaining what has happened to the graduates of '68. As Bernice Martin's study confirms, the counter-culture was successful in enlarging the area of personal freedom: in sexual matters, the family and artistic expression. In that sense the cultural revolution was a revolution 'for the class'. But as for overthrowing the institutions which tended to support the dominant culture – the universities and the education system generally, the BBC, the Arts Council and its institutional clients – the revolution did not take place. This was partly because of the strength of those institutions (which, ironically, were reinforced by the economic difficulties of 1975) and partly because, as members of the intelligentsia, the radicals were dependents of these institutions. Since alternative institutions, such as the underground press, had proved unviable, a compromise had to be found. While criticizing these institutions, the radicals continued to work within them. This contradictory position has not been resolved, and its very contradictory nature helps to explain the theoretical obscurities and sense of *anomie* of much Seventies art.

Meanwhile the divisions in our culture widen: on the one hand the institutions of official patronage glorify a past that never was, softening its hard edges in a syrup of nostalgia; on the other, a new generation has emerged that has abandoned even the hopes of the 1960s, and which can only replay the past in terms of pastiche, parody or irony. Neither has a good word for the present.

CHAPTER 9

Afterwords

*'We can study files for decades,
but every so often we are tempted
to throw up our hands and declare
that history is merely another
literary genre: the past is
autobiographical fiction pretending
to be a parliamentary report.'*

Julian Barnes *Flaubert's Parrot* (1984)

The research for the first volume in this series began in 1975. When *Under Siege* was being prepared for publication in 1977, the decision was taken not to write in the first person. For the sake of uniformity, and because this has been a history, albeit of very recent times, *In Anger* and *Too Much*, apart from their introductions, have not used the first person either. Until now. After ten years' restraint, I feel entitled to break my own conventions.

Readers have complained of the earlier volumes that they lacked some personal note. I do not myself regret this. To begin with, I have been writing a critical survey, a narrative of the period that has not been attempted in this form before, and I offer it as the point from which more polemical discussions can start. Secondly, I was only three when the period covered by *Under Siege* ended, and my experience of the 1950s was nothing to write home about. (Though, in a moment of self-indulgence, I did allow myself as 'the author' of *In Anger* to record my disappointment at the discovery at the Festival of Britain that the

Skylon was held up by wires.) Obviously, I have been privileged to experience a great many more of the cultural events of the Sixties, but since my first book was not published until 1976, it was very much in the role of spectator. And, as I explained in the introduction to this volume, there are many different views of the Sixties, and one eye-witness will be as unreliable as any other. Even more so if he is also trying to establish a general overview.

But if writing what I now call 'cultural history' has taught me anything (ten years ago I felt more hesitant about the genre, and leaned too much towards literary criticism), it is that every work of literature, every piece of art, is conditioned in some way by the cultural climate in which it is produced. The reason for writing about literary life in London during the Second World War was not just that it had not been done before (except in memoirs), but that my generation in particular feels the need to understand the circumstances of an event which we have not really witnessed, but which has conditioned the rest of our lives. (I hope that *Too Much* may perform a similar service for the generation that is now reaching adulthood.) Having seen how important the social and cultural changes were during the war – which seem to make 1939 a much more significant date than 1914 – it was essential to follow them through into the crucial post-war years, and then bring them as near as I could to the present without abandoning the idea of a history altogether.

As the study developed, I began to realize that something in British culture had gone wrong. Since 1939, nearly all the developments in literature have been negative responses of one kind or another. 1939 marked the end of what, for convenience, I must call modernism – that series of developments in the arts which began at the end of the nineteenth century which seemed to propel themselves forward in an investigation of the nature of art itself, and which in the process offered new possibilities of understanding and enjoyment. Since then, there have been successive phases of romanticism and revivalism. The war years saw the period of neo-romanticism in poetry and painting, and were succeeded by a regressive reassertion of what I have called mandarin values. In the 1950s both mandarinism and modernism were the subject of a 'negative feed-back' of an essentially conservative kind. In the 1960s there was another phase of romanticism, which reached back to the Dadaism of nearly fifty

300

years before. Since then we have once more entered a period of cultural conservatism.

British cultural life has been crippled by nostalgia: for the innocence of childhood, for pastoral life, for the world of the country house, for some moment in the not-too-distant past when the community seemed whole. And I now see that this sequence of books also began in that spirit. When I first read Julian Maclaren-Ross's *Memoirs of the Forties* in 1966, I was impressed by the picture he painted of a community of writers, sharing common difficulties and deprivations, but aware that their function as writers was respected, and that even, in a sense, it was one of the things the war was being fought for. To a would-be writer, Fitzrovia sounded like a marvellous place.

I realize now that this was a fantasy, probably as much Maclaren-Ross's as my own. As I discovered while writing *Under Siege*, Fitzrovia was a violent, drunken and despairing milieu, and, with possibly the exception of the poetry of Louis Macneice, produced little good work. But what the romanticism of the war years showed was that people were searching for some kind of healing and reintegrating myth, 'a myth', as John Lehmann put it in 1944, 'which we in England felt we were about to recapture for one moment of astonishing intensity in 1940, when everything seemed to be falling into place.' Though this is a myth to which both Right and Left have subscribed, things did not stay in place very long, and writers and artists must accept their share of responsibility for the consequences of resisting engagement, for turning inwards towards 'personal values', or looking backwards to pre-war life.

The backward glance became almost a fixed stare by the early 1950s, but even those whose politics inclined them to be progressive were hindered by a hankering after a past period of communal solidarity that probably never was. George Orwell seemed to regret the passing of Edwardian England, Richard Hoggart and Raymond Williams the working-class communities of their childhoods. And there was the ruling example of the cultural pessimism of F. R. Leavis. In *Scrutiny, A Retrospect* (1963) Leavis even managed to make the life of the magazine itself appear to have been a sober Arcadia.

Its large connection of very varied critics, serving an ideal of living perception and real judgment, came to form, in respect of sensibility and criteria, a community, out of whose essentially collaborative work a consistency emerged, so that *Scrutiny* established, for those concerned, in the face of contemporary confusion, with value and significance and the movement of life, something like an authoritative chart.

But not only was this an embattled minority, its value to its members seemed in part to be confirmed by their minority status. To believe in the past existence of an ideal state, now dissolved – and this applies to Hoggart's Leeds just as much as Evelyn Waugh's Brideshead – is to think in terms of conservation, and to be suspicious of all change.

The justification for writers in particular to withdraw from engagement and retreat into private concerns, a withdrawal that began during the war and contributed to the failure of the post-war Labour Government, was that the writer must resist totalitarian systems of all kinds. The warning was given by Orwell in 1940 when he wrote 'the autonomous individual is going to be stamped out of existence', but, unlike Orwell, who conducted active resistance to all orthodoxies, the majority of writers preferred an inner emigration. Resistance to totalitarianism was allowed to justify withdrawal from political responsibilities, just at the time when another kind of totalitarianism, the fear, conformism and intolerance of the Cold War, was tightening its grip.

As for what Orwell called the 'immediate, practical enemies' of intellectual liberty, 'monopoly and bureaucracy', British writers offered them little resistance. He wrote in 1946

Everything in our age conspires to turn the writer, and every other kind of artist as well, into a minor official, working on themes handed to him from above and never telling what seems to him the whole of the truth. But in struggling against this fate he gets no help from his own side: that is, there is no large body of opinion which will assure him that he is in the right. In the past, at any rate throughout the Protestant centuries, the idea of rebellion and the idea of intellectual integrity were mixed up. A heretic – political, moral, religious or aesthetic – was one who refused to outrage his own conscience.

But since the war British writers have become what Cyril Connolly called 'culture-diffusionists', in the BBC, the British Council, the Arts Council, journalism and higher education. The only alternative has been an increasingly marginalized, negative community of bohemians.

Not that the diffusionists showed much confidence in the culture they broadcast, as the essays in *The Craft of Letters in England* (1956) showed. The English novelist, for instance, according to Philip Toynbee, is 'on his own, struggling in a collapsed tradition, uncertain of his intractible medium and uncertain of his constantly changing material . . . the last quarter of a century has transformed his society, transformed his language, transformed his intellectual and emotional climate.' No wonder the past seemed a safer, kinder place. The new novelists and poets of the 1950s did seem to have a more robust attitude, but they were unwilling to admit that they had any collective viewpoint, or to accept the significance that the myth of the Angry Young Man thrust upon them. As I wrote in *In Anger*, 'the worst of the caution of the Movement was the caution about itself, the disclaiming of any responsibility for what it was doing.'

In the 1960s the consciousness and the tempo was one of change: Pop was affirmative and celebratory, the long front of culture offered the possibility of greater choice for a wider range of people. But it was also a fantasy, since it was based on the illusion of unending economic expansion. The counter-culture released a great deal of potential – and some monsters of violence and self-destruction as well – but dissipated it almost as quickly, as bohemias tend to do. The combination of economic recession and cultural reaction has, in the place of change, substituted decay.

If I have to choose one example of the ruling mood of the 1970s, it would be Philip Larkin's poem, 'Going, Going'. There are good reasons for treating this as more than just one utterance among many. At his death in 1985, Larkin enjoyed the status of our leading contemporary poet. He might have succeeded Sir John Betjeman as Poet Laureate, had it not been for his Movement caution and lack of production since *High Windows* in 1974. 'Going, Going', which is reprinted in *High Windows*, also has the status of an 'official' poem, for it was originally written as the prologue to a Department of the Environment report of 1972, *How do you want to live?* (The version in *High Windows* is more bitter, and contains a passage on industrial pollution not included in the original, which was printed over a photograph of ICI's plant on Teeside.)

Larkin's theme is disillusion and disappointment with the

303

elements of the modern world, be they new buildings, new people, new money. All are pollutants, but whereas before he had always felt that the England he loved would at least last long enough for his own purposes,

> For the first time I feel somehow
> That it isn't going to last,
>
> That before I snuff it, the whole
> Boiling will be bricked in
> Except for the tourist parts—

At a first reading, Larkin's poem seems a condemnation of certain contemporary values with which we can all agree.

> And that will be England gone,
> The shadows, the meadows, the lanes,
> The guildhalls, the carved choirs.
> There'll be books; it will linger on
> In galleries; but all that remains
> For us will be concrete and tyres.

But what are the values that are being lamented? First of all there is regret for a pastoral vision of England that has inspired English poets for 250 years – for the period of the Industrial Revolution that has produced the urban society which Larkin deplores, but upon which he has actually depended. The regret is understandable, but it is based on a fantasy. Secondly, 'the guildhalls, the carved choirs'; Larkin's image is of burgher virtue and Christian art, but we know from his poem 'Church Going' that he was not motivated by religious belief. Agnostically, he is going to 'snuff it'. What is most disturbing, however, about Larkin's poem, is the combination of nostalgia with resignation. He despises those who profit from pollution, and the people demanding a share of those profits, but there is no conviction in the values with which he opposes them. Somehow, 'it isn't going to last.'

There is no doubt that the oil crisis of 1973 and the recession that followed was a cultural, as well as an economic shock, coming as it did on top of the student upheavals of 1968, and contributing to the industrial troubles that brought both the Heath Government down in 1974 and the Callaghan government down in 1979. While the value of money was being eroded by hyper-inflation, the idea of continual growth, such as had taken place ever since 1945, was replaced by the perception of recession and decline.

In these circumstances, there is unsurprisingly a return to conservatism and conservation – the return to 'Victorian values' which can be understood only at the level of myth. People look to their culture for reassurance, they do not want art that is difficult, or even formally innovative. It is noticeable that in recent years there has been a revival of figurative painting, narrative poetry, and a re-emphasis on conventional naturalistic fiction. And above all, we have had a return to the past. As Bryan Appleyard says in a recent polemic, *The Culture Club* (1984), the past 'has offered stability and a system of codes and meanings which provide the illusion of an understandable world.' The imaginary past is deployed to make bearable the unbearable present and the unimaginable future.

The past has also prevented improvements to the present. In *The Changing Anatomy of Britain* (1982) Anthony Sampson attributes what I can only call the entropy of the past twenty years to the inertia of institutions. 'Each reforming Prime Minister was confronted by the limitations of his power as the bureaucracies, unions, and autonomous institutions closed their ranks against innovation.' In particular the cultural élites have survived through that 'intricate continuity' that John Holloway celebrated in 1967. And as Sampson points out, 'the rule of the Eton and Winchester tribes seem to reflect a degree of regression: a fear of disruptive forces and the preoccupation with controlling and containing people from the centre.'

One of the themes of this study has been the bureaucratization of arts patronage through the Arts Council, which is just one of those autonomous institutions – with strong representation from Winchester, if not Eton – which maintain the network of élites. In comparison with other European countries, state patronage of the arts is small, but the Arts Council's *attitude* has been as important as the actual funds it disburses. And for all that it is prepared to tolerate aspects of the avant-garde, its approach has been essentially conservative, and is becoming more so.

Partly because I wished to avoid the sort of arid speculations and obscure language of some of the cultural theorists I have quoted in this book, and partly because all three volumes have constituted

305

a pragmatic exercise in evolving my own cultural theory, I have never stated my abstract view of what culture is. I have been largely concerned with the 'high arts', because that is how culture was defined in the 1940s and 1950s; in the 1960s the 'long front' offered a different model, and I have followed that, though not as far as resolute anti-élitists might wish. 'Culture' is the medium of ideas in society, if you like, its language. Its relationship with politics and economics is always dynamic. As Stuart Hall has written, 'Culture is the way the social relations of a group are structured and shaped: but it is also the way those shapes are experienced, understood and interpreted.'

There are essentially two views to be taken of the role of culture in society: one is passive, the other active. The active view, which is the traditional English one, from Coleridge and Ruskin to T. S. Eliot and F. R. Leavis, is that culture is a moral force that shapes and reflects the best values in society. The passive view, which derives from Marx, and has much more recently gained ground in Britain, is that culture is the product of economic forces that it has no power to control. Its supposed moral values are the expression of an underlying and supervening ideology.

My own view, which derives from Ruskin, is that the relationship between culture and society is dialectical: in Ruskinian terms, the health of a nation is indicated by its art, but a sound art can have a healthy influence on the nation. In more modern language, there is no doubt that culture is a product, like everything else, of economic, social and political forces. But if culture is the language of society, then it is possible to argue in that language in more than one way. After all, if the content of culture were entirely determined by economic forces, it would be difficult for views which entirely oppose the present distribution of wealth to be proposed. (I suppose I am being naive, but Marcuse never came up with a satisfactory answer to his position as an American professor either.) Thus while I am a materialist, in that I hold that culture must be understood in terms of the conditions in which it is produced, my view is empiricist. The effect of paper rationing on British publishing during the war gave me the first insight into that approach. Thus, to me, the post-structuralist view that art and literature have no meaning other than their own self-referential structures reveals, not that art and literature are meaningless, but that contemporary society has reached a new level of alienation and *anomie*.

The irony is that those who would be least likely to accept Marx's base-and-superstructure view of culture are the ones who have, in Richard Hoggart's phrase, turned culture into a commodity. It is not for nothing that at present administrators habitually refer to writers' and artists' work as 'product'. Richard Hamilton's celebrated list of 1957 has become more than a prescription for Pop art: increasingly, culture is conceived in terms of marketing and management exercises. In its latest document, *A Great British Success Story* (1985), the Arts Council sets out to 'sell' the arts and prove their 'investment potential'. Business sponsorship of the arts, whose growth has been fiercely promoted by the Conservative Government since 1979, has been described by the Secretary-General of the Arts Council, Luke Rittner, as 'a civilized vehicle for furthering business activity'. The arts have become an adjunct to the business lunch – and at such occasions, who would risk serving up anything indigestible?

While I insist on the importance of the material conditions for the production of works of art – which is why I believe that the bureaucracies that support the arts could have a positive rather than a negative effect – I still believe in the autonomy of the individual artist. Regrettably, an approach such as the one I have taken since *Under Siege* often excludes the nuances of the individual imaginations, as well as the detailed experiences, of many people. It is the inevitable consequence of writing a work of cultural history, which describes the overall context in which works of art are created, that it is very difficult to do justice to each individual creative achievement, but if I did not believe in the autonomy of the artist – or at least his or her capacity to act upon the climate of culture, as well as be conditioned by it – I would not bother to write at all.

I have criticized the miasma of nostalgia that clouds our present perception of the past. But I must make it clear that in my rejection of nostalgia and pessimism I am not therefore arguing against a respect for cultural tradition. Unfortunately, the word 'tradition' has been almost as thoroughly appropriated by cultural conservatives as the word 'heritage'. As Seamus Heaney – a poet as respected as Larkin, and who in Ireland has faced the realities of the contemporary world to the benefit rather than detriment of his art – has said, poetry can be 'a restoration of the culture to itself . . . an attempt to define and interpret the present by bringing it into significant relationship with the past.' The problem of most contemporary cultural activity is that it seems to place the present in an *in*-significant relationship with the past.

The distinction I am making is between two cultures: a heritage culture which beautifully preserves the past, but which is nostalgic and, ultimately, ideologically conservative, and a critical culture, which, again in Heaney's words, 'keeps open the imagination's supply lines to the past', but which does not turn away from the present. I am calling for an open culture, which does not depend upon a minority to select the particular meanings and values that they cherish, and which encourages the individual, independent – even heretical – voice to put into question the inherited tradition, the determined present, and the unstable future.

Notes on Sources

I refer here only to material that has been quoted in the text, except where a general reference (and acknowledgement) to a secondary source is appropriate. Where the source of the quotation is clear in the text, I have not repeated it here. (N.Y.) means New York. Page references to *Under Siege* and *In Anger* are to the first editions, *Under Siege* 1977, *In Anger* 1981.

FOREWORD
Peter York is quoted from his article 'Recycling the Sixties' for *Harpers and Queen* in 1978, reprinted in his *Style Wars*, Sidgwick & Jackson, 1980. Morris Dickstein's *Gates of Eden* was published by Basic Books (N.Y.) in 1977.

CHAPTER ONE
The epigraph comes from *The Honest to God Debate*, edited by D. L. Edwards, SCM Press, 1963. *Honest to God* was published by the SCM Press earlier in the same year; the *Church Times* is quoted from *The Honest to God Debate*. Anthony Sampson's *Anatomy of Britain* was published by Hodder & Stoughton in 1962 and Harper & Row (N.Y.); the quotations here are from the first edition. Anthony Hartley's *A State of England* was published by Hutchinson in 1963 and Harcourt, Brace & World (N.Y.). Brian Chapman's *British Government Observed* was published by Allen & Unwin in 1963, W. L. Guttsman's *The British Political Elite* by MacGibbon & Kee in 1963. Raymond Williams's *The Long Revolution* was published in 1961 by Chatto & Windus and Columbia University Press (N.Y.).

Harold Macmillan made his speech at Bedford on 20 July 1957. *Suicide of a Nation?*, edited by Arthur Koestler, was a special

309

number of *Encounter* for July 1963. Sampson is quoted from *Anatomy of Britain*. Arnold Wesker's *Chips with Everything* was published in 1962 by Jonathan Cape and Random House (N.Y.). Williams is quoted from *The Long Revolution*. Martin Green's *A Mirror for Anglo-Saxons* was published by Longmans and Harper (N.Y.).

Burton Paulu's *British Broadcasting in Transition*, published by Macmillan in 1961, is a useful account of developments to that date. *Television and the Political Image*, by Joseph Trenaman and Denis McQuail, was published by Methuen in 1961; Richard Crossman's *Labour in the Affluent Society* was Fabian Tract No. 325, published in 1960. F. R. Leavis is quoted from *Scrutiny: A Retrospect*, Cambridge University Press, 1963. *Discrimination and Popular Culture*, edited by Denys Thompson, was published by Penguin in 1964. *The Modern Age: A Guide to English Literature*, edited by Boris Ford, was published by Penguin in 1961. Raymond Williams's *Communications* was first published in 1962 by Penguin. The Pilkington *Report of the Committee on Broadcasting 1960*, Cmmnd 1753, was published by HMSO in 1962.

Frank Parkin's *Middle-Class Radicalism; The Social Bases of the British Campaign for Nuclear Disarmament*, published by Manchester University Press in 1968, has a helpful account of CND's difficulties with the Labour Party. David Widgery's *The Left in Britain* was published by Penguin in 1976. Perry Anderson is quoted from *New Left Review* No. 29, 1965, and *New Left Review* No. 50, 1968. The account of the history of Centre 42 is based on Arnold Wesker's essays *Fears of Fragmentation*, published by Jonathan Cape in 1970, and *Arnold Wesker's Centre 42*, a D. Phil. thesis for the University of Ghent by Frank Coppitiers, 1972. I am very grateful to Arnold Wesker for making this available to me. I first quote Arnold Wesker from the *New Statesman* for 30 July 1960. Joan Littlewood's career is described in *The Theatre Workshop Story*, by Howard Goorney, Methuen, 1981.

Robert Holles is quoted on the closure of *John Bull* from *Encounter* August 1960. John Whale's *The Politics of the Media* (revised edition, Fontana, 1980) is a useful survey of press and television history. David Mercer is quoted from an interview in *The New Priesthood: British Television Today* by Joan Bakewell and Nicholas Garnham, Allen Lane, 1970. Graham Greene is

310

quoted from his *The Third Floor Front: A View of Broadcasting in the 1960s*, published by the Bodley Head in 1969. Jonathan Miller's article for the *Observer* is reprinted in Roger Wilmut's *From Fringe to Flying Circus*, Methuen, 1980, which is a very useful account of the recent history of British broadcast comedy. Patrick Marnham's *The Private Eye Story*, André Deutsch, 1982, is the semi-official history of the magazine.

Grace Wyndham Goldie's *Facing the Nation: Television and Politics 1936–1976*, Bodley Head, 1977, describes the development of *TW3*. Mrs Mary Whitehouse is quoted from her biography by Michael Tracey and David Morrison, *Whitehouse*, Macmillan, 1979. Irene Shubik's *Play for Today*, Davis Poynter, 1975, has a useful account of British television drama in the Sixties and early Seventies. Martin Esslin is quoted from his *Mediations*, Methuen, 1980, McGrath is quoted from *New Theatre Voices of the Seventies*, edited by Simon Trussler, Methuen, 1981. Nicholas Garnham denounces *Cathy Come Home* in an article for *Screen*, summer, 1972. *The Least Worst Television in the World* was published by Barrie & Jenkins in 1973.

The chief sources for the account of the Profumo scandal were *Scandal '63*, by Clive Irving, Ron Hall and Jeremy Wallington, published by Heinemann in 1963 and Brian Inglis's *Private Conscience – Public Morality*, André Deutsch, 1964. The song is quoted from Ned Sherrin's autobiography, *A Small Thing – Like an Earthquake*, Weidenfeld & Nicolson, 1983.

Marshall McLuhan's *Understanding Media* was published by Routledge & Kegan Paul in 1964 and McGraw Hill (N.Y.). Jonathan Aitken's *The Young Meteors* was published by Secker & Warburg in 1967. Anthony Hartley is quoted from *A State of England*, Hutchinson, 1963 and Harcourt, Brace & World (N.Y.). R. D. Laing's *The Divided Self: A Study of Sanity and Madness* was published by Tavistock Publications and Quadrangle Books, Chicago, in 1960. The political history of the period is recorded in *Post-War Britain*, by Alan Sked and Chris Cook, Penguin, 1979. Harold Wilson is quoted from *Purpose in Politics: Speeches 1956–1963*, Weidenfeld & Nicolson, 1964.

CHAPTER TWO
The epigraph is from Philip Larkin's 'Annus Mirabilis', in his collection *High Windows*, published by Faber & Faber in 1974.

Richard Hamilton is quoted from his *Collected Words*, Thames & Hudson, 1982, which gives a very helpful account of his life and work. The principal sources for the account of Pop Art are Lawrence Alloway's contribution to *Pop Art*, edited by Lucy Lippard, Thames & Hudson (revised edition), 1970; Mario Amaya's *Pop as Art: A Survey of the New Super Realism*, Studio Vista, 1965; Michael Compton's *Pop Art*, Hamlyn, 1970; John Russell and Suzi Gablik's *Pop Art Redefined*, Thames & Hudson, 1969; Dick Hebdige's 'In Poor Taste', *Block* No. 8 1983, and Anne Massey and Penny Sparke's 'The Myth of the Independent Group', *Block* No.10, 1985.

Barbara Rose's 'The Politics of Art', *Artforum* 1968 (I) and January 1969 (II), and Eva Cockroft's 'Abstract Expressionism: Weapon of the Cold War' in *Artforum* June 1974 describe MOMA's cold war connections. Richard Smith is quoted from Michael Compton's *Pop Art*, 1970; the catalogue of the Peter Blake retrospective at the Tate Gallery in 1963, edited by Michael Compton and published by Tate Gallery Publications, gives a full account of his work.

Lawrence Alloway's *Cambridge Opinion* article is reprinted in *Pop Art Redefined*; Richard Hamilton is quoted from 'Popular Culture and Personal Responsibility', and then 'For the Finest Art try POP' in his *Collected Words*. McLuhan is writing in *Understanding Media*. Edward Lucie-Smith is quoted from *The Social Context of Art*, edited by Jean Creedy, Tavistock Publications, 1970.

Kitaj is quoted from *Pop as Art*, John Russell from *Pop Art Redefined*. Hockney's exit is described by Guy Brett in the *London Magazine*, April 1963. The activities of Fine Artz Associates are described in the Royal College of Art magazine *Ark*, Nos 35 and 36, 1964.

The description of Centre Point is quoted from an article by Reyner Banham in *New Society*, 28 April 1966. Oliver Marriott's *The Property Boom*, Hamish Hamilton, 1967, gives a good account of the speculators; David McKie's essay on 'The Quality of Life' in *The Decade of Disillusion: British Politics in the 1960s*, edited by McKie with Chris Cook, Macmillan, 1972, describes some of the results.

Harold Baldry's *The Case for the Arts*, Secker & Warburg,

1981, has useful statistical information on the arts; the prime source is the Arts Council of Great Britain's annual reports. T. R. Fyvel's *Intellectuals Today: Problems in a Changing Society* was published by Chatto & Windus in 1968.

Stuart Hall and Tony Jefferson's *Resistance through Rituals*, Hutchinson, 1970, has useful material on youth cults. George Melly's *Revolt into Style* was published in 1970 by Allen Lane and Anchor Books (N.Y.). Thom Gunn's 'Elvis Presley' appears in his *Fighting Terms*, Faber & Faber, 1962.

Nick Cohn's *AWopBopaLooBopALopBamBoom: Pop from the Beginning* was published by Weidenfeld & Nicolson and Stein & Day (N.Y.). Jeff Nuttall's *Bomb Culture* was published by MacGibbon & Kee in 1968 and Delacorte Press (N.Y.). His *Performance Art Memoirs*, John Calder, 1979, and the Riverun Press, Dallas, continue his account into the 1970s. Colin MacInnes's *Absolute Beginners* was published by MacGibbon & Kee in 1959; Tony Gould's biography of MacInnes, *Insider/Outsider* was published by Chatto & Windus in 1983.

Anthony Burgess's *A Clockwork Orange* was published by Heinemann in 1962 and W. W. Norton (N.Y.). Ray Gosling's *Sum Total* was published by Faber & Faber in 1962.

The account of the career of the Beatles is based on Philip Norman's *Shout!*, Hamish Hamilton, 1981, and *The Love You Make*, by Peter Brown and Steven Gaines, Macmillan, 1983. Paul Willis's *Profane Culture* was published by Routledge & Kegan Paul in 1978. Pete Townshend is quoted from George Melly's *Revolt into Style*, Allen Lane, 1970. Liverpool poetry is discussed and reprinted in Edward Lucie-Smith's anthology *The Liverpool Scene*, published by Donald Carroll in 1967. Adrian Henri is quoted from his *Environments and Happenings*, Thames & Hudson, 1974; his poem 'Me' is quoted from *The Mersey Sound* (with Brian Patten and Roger McGough), Penguin, 1967. Brian Patten's 'Prosepoem . . .' was first published in his *Little Johnny's Confession*, Allen & Unwin 1967.

William Mann's review appeared in *The Times* on 27 December 1963. Jonathan Miller was writing in the *New Statesman* for 29 May 1964. Mary Quant's autobiography *Quant by Quant* was published in 1966 by Cassells and Putnams (N.Y.). This and *David Bailey: Black and White Memories*, the catalogue of an exhibition of David Bailey photographs at the Victoria & Albert

Museum in 1983, help to describe the early 1960s. Jonathan Aitken's *The Young Meteors* was published by Secker & Warburg in 1967 and Athenaeum (N.Y.). Peter Hall is quoted from David Addenbroke's *The Royal Shakespeare Company*, Kimber Press, 1974. David Bailey's *Box of Pin-Ups* was published by Weidenfeld & Nicolson in 1965.

Philip Larkin's 'Annus Mirabilis' is reprinted in *High Windows*, Faber & Faber, 1974. John Osborne's *Inadmissible Evidence* was published by Faber & Faber in 1965. The writer for the *Time* magazine article was Piri Halasz; the editor was Ed Jamieson. Peter Calvocoressi's *The British Experience 1945–75* was published by the Bodley Head in 1978; *The Decade of Disillusion: British Politics in the 1960s*, edited by David McKie and Chris Cook was published by Macmillan in 1972.

CHAPTER THREE

The title of this chapter acknowledges the assistance of Jeff Nuttall's *Bomb Culture*, MacGibbon & Kee and Delacorte Press (N.Y.), 1968, in tracing the early history of the underground. The epigraph is from Geoffrey Skelton's translation of Peter Weiss's *The Persecution and Assassination of Marat as Performed by the Inmates of Charenton under the Direction of the Marquis de Sade*, published by John Calder in 1965 and Athenaeum (N.Y.). Theodore Roszack's *The Making of a Counter-Culture* was published by Doubleday (N.Y.) in 1969 and Faber & Faber in 1970.

George Steiner's *Language and Silence: Essays 1958–1966* were published by Faber & Faber in 1967 and Athenaeum (N.Y.). William Golding is quoted from the *Guardian*, 20 November 1975; see *Under Siege* pp. 171–2. Alan Young's *Dada and After: Extremist Modernism and English Literature*, Manchester University Press, 1981, is helpful on the Dadaist tradition. R. D. Laing's *The Politics of Experience and the Bird of Paradise* was published by Penguin in 1967 and Pantheon (N.Y.). Colin Greenland's *The Entropy Exhibition: Michael Moorcock and the British 'New Wave' in Science Fiction* was published by Routledge & Kegan Paul in 1983. Peter Stanshill's and David Mairowitz' *BAMN (By Any Means Necessary): Outlaw Manifestos and Ephemera 1965–1970* was published by Penguin in 1971.

The discussion of the theatre owes a great deal to Martin Esslin's *The Theatre of the Absurd*, first published by Anchor

Books (N.Y.) in 1961 and Eyre & Spottiswoode in 1962, and regularly revised. I have used the third edition, published by Pelican in 1980. The Ionesco/Tynan debate is described in Esslin's book. I have used Victor Corte's translation of *The Theatre and its Double*, in Volume 4 of *The Collected Works of Antonin Artaud*, Calder & Boyars, 1974. *The Confessions of a Counterfeit Critic: A London Theatre Notebook 1958–1971*, by Charles Marowitz, was published by Methuen in 1973. *The Encore Reader*, edited by Charles Marowitz, Tom Milne and Owen Hale, was published by Methuen in 1965. Peter Brook is quoted from his lectures, *The Empty Space*, published by MacGibbon & Kee in 1968 and Athenaeum (N.Y.). The description of 'The Public Bath' is from J.C. Trewin's biography *Peter Brook*, published by Macdonald in 1971. I have examined the Lord Chamberlain's copy of the text of *US*, deposited with the Manuscript Division of the British Library. Irving Wardle was writing in *New Society* for 27 October 1967.

The history of little magazines and the poetry revival of the 1960s is described in 'UK Little Magazines: An Introductory Survey' by Geoffrey Soar and R. J. Ellis in *Serials Review* (spring 1982) Volume 8 No.1; 'Little Magazines in the British Isles Today' by Geoffrey Soar and R.J. Ellis in *Book News* for December 1983, and 'The British Poetry Revival 1960–1974', a paper given by Eric Mottram to the Modern British Poetry Conference at the Polytechnic of Central London 31 May – 2 June 1974. John Noyce's *Directory of British Alternative Periodicals* was published by the Harvester Press, Sussex in 1979.

Michael Horovitz is quoted from his anthology *Children of Albion: Poetry of the Underground in Britain*, published by Penguin in 1969. His description of 'Live New Departures' comes from *New Society* 3 June 1965. Malcolm Bradbury's *The Social Context of Modern English Literature* was published by Blackwell in 1971 and Schoken Books (N.Y.)

Julian Mitchell's complaint is in the *London Magazine* for June 1962. *A Group Anthology*, edited by Edward Lucie-Smith and Philip Hobsbaum was published by Oxford University Press in 1963. A. Alvarez's *The New Poetry* was first published by Penguin in 1962, and in a substantially revised edition in 1966. He discusses Sylvia Plath's suicide in *The Savage God*, Weidenfeld & Nicolson, 1971, and Random House (N.Y.). Sylvia Plath's 'Lady Lazarus' is quoted from *Ariel*, Faber & Faber 1965 and Harper & Row (N.Y.).

The 1962 Edinburgh writers' conference was recorded, and the tapes are deposited in the National Sound Archive in London. The conference is described in Michael Barry Goodman's *Contemporary Literary Censorship: The Case History of Burroughs's 'Naked Lunch'*, published by Scarecrow Press, New Jersey in 1981, which is also a useful account of Burroughs's career. His *The Soft Machine* was published by Grove Press (N.Y.) and John Calder, 1961. *Towers Open Fire* and other early film material has been made available as part of a videotape *The Final Academy Documents* by Ikon FCL. Martin Esslin's protest against the 1963 happening was in *Encounter* for December 1963.

Jim Haynes's autobiography *Thanks for Coming* was published by Faber & Faber in 1983 and is an amusing collage-memoir of the period that counter-points Jeff Nuttall's far more serious *Bomb Culture*. Michael Hollingshead's autobiography, *The Man Who Turned on the World*, Blond & Briggs, 1973, describes the spread of LSD.

Wholly Communion, edited by Peter Whitehead, with an introduction by Alexis Lykiard, published by Lorrimer Films Ltd in 1965, gives an account of the Albert Hall reading and reprints some of the poems, including the invocation to Blake. Michael Horovitz is quoted from *The Children of Albion*, Penguin, 1969, Nuttall from *Bomb Culture*, Edward Lucie-Smith from *Encounter* August 1966.

Adrian Henri's *Environments and Happenings*, Thames & Hudson, 1974, is a rapid survey of mixed media art, and Maciunas is quoted from it. Tomas Schmidt is quoted from *Art and Artists*, October 1972, a number which concentrates on Fluxus, and includes 'The Unknown Art Movement' by Victor Musgrave, from which I quote. Gustav Metzger is quoted from *Art and Artists* for August 1966 which concentrates on the auto-destructive art movement, including the work of Yoko Ono. 'Son et Lumière for Bodily Functions' is described in *Studio-International* September 1967. The description of 'Abreakstionspiel' is by Benedict Nightingale in *New Society* 27 July 1967.

Richard Neville is quoted from *Play Power*, Jonathan Cape, 1970, and Random House (N.Y.). Haynes's epitaph for the Arts Lab appeared in *Ark* No. 45 winter 1969. The ICA opening party is described by Michael Kustow in his memoir *Tank*, Jonathan Cape, 1975.

CHAPTER FOUR

Sex, Politics and Society was published by Longmans in 1981. George Melly is quoted from *Revolt into Style*, Allen Lane 1970 and Anchor Books (N.Y.). Philip Bean's *The Social Control of Drugs*, published by Martin Robertson in 1974 is a very useful account of the subject. *IT*'s promotion of LSD appeared in their issue for 28 April 1968.

John Sutherland's *Offensive Literature: Decensorship in Britain 1960–1982*, Junction Books, 1982, contains much useful information and comment. For more on the control of the BBC see my *Irreverence, Scurrility, Profanity, Vilification and Licentious Abuse: Monty Python the Case Against*, published by Methuen and Grove Press (N.Y.) in 1981. Angela Carter's description of the Jagger-Richard trial is reprinted in *Arts in Society*, edited by Paul Barker, Fontana, 1977.

Jeff Nuttall is quoted from *Bomb Culture*. Pamela Hansford Johnson's *On Iniquity* was published by Macmillan in 1967. I quote R.D. Laing on violence first from *The Politics of Experience*, Penguin, 1967, and Pantheon (N.Y.), and then from his speech to the 'Dialectics of Liberation' conference. The major papers at the conference were published in 1968 by Penguin as *The Dialectics of Liberation*, edited by David Cooper, but more of the conference was issued as a set of twenty-three long-playing records by Liberation Records, 20 Fitzroy Square, London W.I, which I was able to listen to at the National Sound Archive. A.M. Fearson was writing in *Freedom* for 25 August 1967. Roger Barnard describes the conference in *New Society*, 3 August 1967. Marcuse's speech is reprinted in *The Dialectics of Liberation*, Penguin, 1968.

Charles Marowitz is quoted from *Confessions of a Counterfeit Critic*, Methuen, 1973. Edward Bond's preface appears in his *Lear*, published by Methuen in 1971. A. Alvarez's 'Extremist Art' appears in his essays *Beyond all this Fiddle*, Allen Lane, 1968. His *The Savage God* was published by Weidenfeld & Nicolson in 1971, and Random House (N.Y.). Yoko Ono is quoted from *The Love You Make*, by Peter Brown and Steven Gaines, Macmillan, 1983.

Henry Luce was writing in *Life*, 4 March 1968; Nick Cohn is quoted from *Pop from the Beginning*, Weidenfeld & Nicolson, 1969, and Stein & Day (N.Y.); Jeff Nuttall's *Bomb Culture* was published by MacGibbon & Kee in 1968, and Delacorte Press (N.Y.).

CHAPTER FIVE

The epigraph comes from *The Hornsey Affair*, by students and staff of Hornsey College of Art, Penguin, 1969. Eric Hobsbawm is quoted from his essay 'Intellectuals and the Class Struggle', reprinted in *Revolutionaries*, Weidenfeld & Nicolson, 1973. *A Sociology of Contemporary Cultural Change* was published by Blackwell in 1981; *Policing the Crisis: Mugging, the State, Law and Order* by Manchester University Press in 1978. David Leigh's *High Time: The Life and Times of Howard Marks*, published by Heinemann in 1984, is an excellent account of the operations of a drug dealer. Stuart Hall and Tony Jefferson edited *Resistance Through Rituals* for Hutchinson in 1976. Guy Debord's *La Societé du Spectacle* was published in Paris by Buchet/Chastel in 1967, and in 'an unauthorized translation' by the Black and Red Press, Detroit, in 1970. Stuart Hall's comments on the theatre of demonstrations come from *Policing the Crisis*; the Hornsey students complaint is from *The Hornsey Affair*. Nigel Young's *An Infantile Disorder? The Crisis and Decline of the New Left* was published by Routledge & Kegan Paul in 1977. *Deviance and Social Control*, edited by P. Rock and M. McKintosh, was published by Tavistock in 1974. Jock Young's *The Drugtakers: The Social Meaning of Drug Use*, was published by MacGibbon & Kee in 1971.

The Anti-University's manifesto is reprinted in *BAMN*, edited by Peter Stansill and David Mairowitz, Penguin, 1971. I then quote *International Times* 5–19 January and 16–19 February 1968, and Roberta Elzey's 'Founding an Anti-University' in *Counter-Culture*, edited by Joseph Berke, published by Peter Owen Ltd and Fire Books, 1969. Charles Widgery's anthology-history *The Left in Britain, 1956–1968*, Penguin, 1976, is an invaluable source of information on alternative politics. Colin Crouch's *The Students' Revolt* was published by the Bodley Head in 1970. The Grosvenor Square demonstrations are described in *Demonstrations and Communication: A Case Study*, by James Halloram,

Notes on Sources

Philip Elliott and Graham Murdock, Penguin, 1970. The Hornsey occupation is described in *The Hornsey Affair*, Penguin, 1969.

Ron Bailey's *The Squatters* was published by Penguin in 1973. The account of the Angry Brigade draws on Gordon Carr's *The Angry Brigade: The Cause and the Case*, Gollancz, 1975. Eric Hobsbawm is quoted from 'Sex and Revolution' in *Revolutionaries*, Weidenfeld & Nicolson, 1973. *Play Power* was published by Cape in 1970 and Random House (N.Y.). The London Street Commune and *Arson News* are quoted from BAMN, Penguin, 1971. Paul Willis's *Profane Culture* was published by Routledge & Kegan Paul in 1978.

Stuart Hall's views on the law and order society appear in *Policing the Crisis*, Manchester University Press, 1978; Bernice Martin is quoted from *A Sociology of Contemporary Cultural Change*, Blackwell, 1981. E.P. Thompson edited *Warwick University Ltd: Industry, Management and the Universities* for Penguin in 1970.

The Arts Council's report *The Obscenity Laws* was published by André Deutsch in 1969. The operation of the Obscene Publications squad are described in John Sutherland's *Offensive Literature*, Junction Books, 1982, which also records the obscenity trials of the Sixties and Seventies. The account of the underground press is gleaned from the papers themselves. The *Oz* case is described in detail in Tony Palmer's *The Trials of Oz*, Blond & Briggs, 1971. Barker and Farren's *Watch Out Kids* was published by Open Gate Books in 1972. Charles Widgery's epitaph for the underground appeared in *Oz* No.41, winter 1973.

Arnold Wesker's *The Friends* was published by Jonathan Cape in 1970. *Goodbye Baby and Amen: A Saraband for the Sixties* was published by Condé Nast and Collins in 1969. Christopher Booker's *the Neophiliacs* was published by Collins in the same year; I quote his comment on the book from his subsequent volume *The Seventies: Portrait of a Decade*, Allen Lane, 1980. Bernard Levin's *The Pendulum Years* was published by Jonathan Cape in 1970. The closing quotation is from R.D. Laing's *Knots*, Tavistock Publications, 1970, and Pantheon, (N.Y.).

CHAPTER SIX

The epigraph is from an essay by Eric Hobsbawm, reprinted in *Revolutionaries*, Weidenfeld & Nicolson, 1973. The Welfare

State's journey is described by Theodore Shank in *Arts in Society*, a periodical published by Wisconsin University Extension, vol.12, No.1, 1975. George Melly is quoted from *Revolt into Style*, Allen Lane, 1970 and Anchor Books (N.Y.). Simon Frith's *The Sociology of Rock* was published by Constable in 1978. Bernice Martin is quoted from *A Sociology of Contemporary Cultural Change*, Blackwell, 1981. Michael Clarke's *The Politics of Pop Festivals* was published by Junction Books in 1982. Mick Farren is quoted from *Watch Out Kids*, Open Gate Books, 1972. Peter York's *Style Wars* was published by Sidgwick & Jackson in 1980.

Catherine Itzin's *Stages in the Revolution: Political Theatre since 1968*, published by Methuen in 1980, is a valuable source for the history of the fringe, as are Peter Ansorge's *Disrupting the Spectacle: Five Years of Experimental and Fringe Theatre in Britain*, Pitman 1975, and John Bull's *New British Political Dramatists*, Macmillan, 1984. Unless otherwise stated, the comments by Howard Brenton, David Hare, David Edgar, Arnold Wesker, John McGrath, and Trevor Griffiths come from *New Theatre Voices of the Seventies*, edited by Simon Trussler, Methuen, 1981. John Arden is quoted from his *To Present the Pretence: Essays on the Theatre and its Public*, Methuen, 1977. The origins of the People Show are described in Jeff Nuttall's *Performance Art Memoirs*, John Calder 1979, and Riverun Press, Dallas. Jenny Harris is quoted from Itzin's *Stages in the Revolution*, Methuen, 1980, as is John Arden on CAST.

The Arts Council published *The Theatre Today in England and Wales* in 1970. John Arden is quoted from *To Present the Pretence*, Methuen, 1977. Jeff Nuttall is quoted from *Performance Art Memoirs*, 1979.

The evolution of the RSC's 'alternative theatre' is traced in Colin Chambers's *Open Spaces: New Theatre and the RSC*, Methuen, 1980. John Arden's criticism of international theatre groups appears in *To Present The Pretence*, Methuen 1977. David Hare is quoted on 'extreme decadence' from John Bull's *New British Political Dramatists*, 1984, as is Howard Brenton on *Lay By*. David Mercer is quoted from Itzin's *Stages in the Revolution* 1980. John Arden's difficulties with the RSC are described in Albert Hunt's *Arden: A Study of his Plays*, Methuen, 1974, Wesker's in his *Distinctions*, Jonathan Cape, 1985. John

McGrath's comments on 1970 and the National Theatre are quoted from *Stages in the Revolution*, as is Trevor Griffiths's first comment on the limitations of the fringe, and his last comment, on television. Howard Brenton's 'theatre is a dirty place' comes from John Bull's *New British Political Dramatists*. Tom Stoppard's *Travesties* was published by Faber & Faber in 1975.

Sex, Politics and Society was published by Longmans in 1981. I have drawn on *The Body Politic: Women's Liberation in Britain*, edited by Micheline Wandor, Stage One Books, 1972, and her *Understudies*, Methuen 1982, together with David Boucher's *The Feminist Challenge: The Movement for Women's Liberation in Britain and the USA*, Macmillan, 1983, for the account of early feminism. Juliet Mitchell is quoted from the *New Left Review* No. 40, Nov/Dec 1966. Sheila Rowbotham is quoted from *The Body Politic*. *The Female Eunuch* was published by MacGibbon & Kee in 1970 and McGraw-Hill (N.Y.).

The self-organization of the fringe is well described in Catherine Itzin's *Stages in the Revolution*, Methuen, 1980. The Artists' Union statement appeared in *Art and Artists*, September 1972. The account of the National Theatre is drawn from John Elsom and Nicholas Tomalin's *History of the National Theatre*, Jonathan Cape, 1978.

CHAPTER SEVEN

The epigraph is from Harold Pinter's *No Man's Land*, published by Methuen in 1975. Robert Hutchison's *The Politics of the Arts Council*, Sinclair Browne, 1982, and Harold Baldry's *The Case for the Arts*, Secker & Warburg, 1981, describe the evolution of the Arts Council. Hugh Jenkins's autobiography, *The Culture Gap*, Marion Boyars, 1979, reveals some of the cut and thrust of cultural politics.

Andrew Brighton was writing in *Studio International*, October 1974, Christopher Finch in the issue for March, 1968. Edward Lucie-Smith's *Art in Britain 1969–70* with Patricia White, was published by Dent in 1970. Lynda Morris was writing in *Studio International*, October 1974; Stuart Brisley in the issue for June 1969. John Latham is quoted from Lucy Lippard's history-anthology, *Six Years: The Dematerialization of the Art Object*

One peculiar and excellent strength of the English creative intellect is its insistence that, in the end, everything has to establish a basis of *some* kind of reasonable utterance, and be defensible (in a way the good-hearted American atmosphere is not) against the bluntest kind of attack. You are encouraged to doubt. You ask questions at readings. It is an admirable asset in a crazy, despairing age.

In the final number of *The Review* in 1972 a young poet, James Fenton, who published his first collection, *Terminal Moraine,* in 1972, foreshadowed a withdrawal from (indeed boredom with) the whole Extremist debate, in this satire of Alvarez.

> He tells you, in the sombrest notes,
> If poets want to get their oats
> The first step is to slit their throats.
>   The way to divide
> The sheep of poetry from the goats
>   Is suicide.

One can only be struck by the bleakness of the world inhabited by Ted Hughes, Alvarez's leading example among English poets. His collections *The Hawk in the Rain* (1957), *Lupercal* (1960), *Wodwo* (1967) and *Crow* (1970) discover in the natural world a modern myth that corresponds to the isolated, violent and disturbed consciousness of contemporary man, a world of cruelty where chaos *is* the most likely explanation, and time offers no hope of amelioration or consolation. 'Pibroch', from *Wodwo* offers this Beckett-like vision.

> Drinking the sea and eating the rock
> A tree struggles to make leaves –
> An old woman fallen from space
> Unprepared for these conditions.
> She hangs on, because her mind's gone completely.
>
> Minute after minute, aeon after aeon,
> Nothing lets up or develops.
> And this is neither a bad variant nor a tryout.

The struggle to create a fresh myth out of the old materials of language and poetic forms can be fruitful. We see the attempt to forge a new view of history in Geoffrey Hill's *Mercian Hymns* (1971), and the conflicts caused by the possession of language

261

from 1966 to 1972, Studio Vista, 1973, and Praeger Publications (N.Y.). Stuart Brisley criticizes Latham in *Studio International*, March 1972.

Peter Fuller is quoted first from *Beyond the Crisis in Art*, Writers and Readers, 1980, and then an article in *Art Monthly*, July, 1977. David Sweet was writing in *Studio International* for October 1969, Lawrence Alloway in July 1969, and Tim Hilton in July 1970. Barry Flanagan is quoted from *Studio International* for October 1969, Richard Long's 1967 sculpture is described in the issue for January, 1969. John Latham is quoted from *Studio International*, December 1966, Barbara Reise in the issue for April 1969. Gilbert and George's dinner is described in the issue for May 1970.

Charles Harrison's comment on Art and Language's 'paradigm shift' was made in *Studio International* for June 1972; Sue Stedman-Jones's criticisms were made in the issue for December 1973. Bruce Maclean is quoted from *Art Monthly*, February 1979. Lucy Lippard's conclusion comes from *Six Years*, Studio Vista and Praeger Publications (N.Y.), 1973. Charles Harrison and Fred Orton's comes from their introduction to *Modernism, Criticism, Realism*, Harper & Row, (N.Y.) 1984.

The Art of the Sixties was published by Phaidon in 1978. Andrew Forge is quoted from *Studio International*, September 1974; 'The Condition of Sculpture' catalogue was published by the Arts Council.

The Reaction Against Experiment in the English Novel was published by Columbia University Press (N.Y.) in 1967. Giles Gordon is quoted from *The Writer's Place*, by Peter Firchow, University of Minnesota Press 1974; *Fiction and the Fiction Industry* was published by the Athlone Press in 1978; Raymond Astbury's *The Writer in the Market Place* was published by Clive Bingley in 1969. Peter Ackroyd's *Notes for a New Culture: An Essay on Modernism* was published by Vision Books, 1976.

The Situation of the Novel was published by Macmillan in 1970. 'The Novelist at the Crossroads' is reprinted in *The Novel Today*, edited by Malcolm Bradbury, Fontana, 1977. Morris Dickstein's *Gates of Eden* was published by Basic Books, (N.Y.) in 1977. *Intellectuals Today* was published by Chatto & Windus in 1968. B.S. Johnson was writing in *Aren't You Rather Young to be*

Writing Your Memoirs?, Hutchinson, 1973. 'Against Dryness' was first published in *Encounter*, January 1961, and is reprinted in *The Novel Today*, edited by Malcolm Bradbury, Fontana, 1977. *A Fairly Honourable Defeat* was published by Chatto & Windus and Viking (N.Y.). Iris Murdoch is then quoted from the *Listener*, 4 April 1968. Bernard Bergonzi is quoted from *The Situation of the Novel*, Macmillan, 1970.

Malcolm Bradbury's 'The Post-War English Novel' is reprinted in his *Possibilities: Essays on the State of the Novel*, Oxford University Press, 1973. William Golding is quoted from the *New Left Review* No. 29 (1965). Angus Wilson's *Hemlock and After* was published by Secker & Warburg, 1952, and Viking (N.Y.). Doris Lessing's *The Golden Notebook* was first published in 1962 by Michael Joseph and Simon and Schuster (N.Y.), who also published the new edition of 1972. John Fowles's 'Notes on an Unfinished Novel' was first published in *Afterwords*, edited by Thomas McCormack, Harper & Row (N.Y.), 1969, and is reprinted in *The Novel Today*, edited by Malcolm Bradbury, Fontana, 1977. B. S. Johnson's *Travelling People* was published by Constable in 1963, who also published his *Albert Angelo* in 1964. Alan Burns is quoted from Charles Sugnet's *The Imagination on Trial*, which he edited with Burns, published by Alison & Busby, 1981.

Malcolm Bradbury is quoted first from his introduction to *The Novel Today*, Fontana, 1977, and then *The Social Context of Modern English Literature*, Blackwell, 1971, and Schoken Books (N.Y.). John Sutherland was writing in *Fiction and the Fiction Industry*, Athlone Press, 1978.

British Poetry since 1945 was published by Penguin in 1970; a revised edition was published by Penguin, and Viking Penguin Inc (N.Y.) in 1985. Jon Silkin's anthology *Poetry of the Committed Individual* was published by Gollancz, 1973. Alan Brownjohn is quoted from his essay in Michael Schmidt and Grevel Lindop's *British Poetry Since 1960*, Carcanet, 1972. Douglas Dunn describes the change in *Poetry Review* in *Encounter*, June 1977. Alan Brownjohn defends reticence in *British Poetry since 1960*. James Fenton satirizes A. Alvarez in his 'Letter to John Fuller', in *The Memory of War*, Salamander Press, 1982. Ted Hughes's

Wodwo was published by Faber & Faber in 1967 and Harper & Row (N.Y.).

Seamus Heaney describes the Belfast Group in an essay reprinted in his collection *Preoccupations: Selected Prose, 1968–1978*, Faber & Faber, 1980, from which I quote. I quote his comment on Berkeley from Blake Morrison's study *Seamus Heaney*, Methuen, 1982, his next comments on English literature are in *Preoccupations*; 'Exposure' concludes *North*, published by Faber & Faber in 1975.

Anthony Thwaite was writing in the *Listener*, 5 April 1973. Grevel Lindop is quoted from his essay in *British Poetry since 1970*, edited by Michael Schmidt and Peter Jones, Carcanet, 1980. Schmidt is quoted from his introduction to *Ten English Poets*, Carcanet, 1976.

Peter Ackroyd's *Notes for a New Culture* was published by Vision Books, 1976; Bradbury's *The Social Context of Modern English Literature* was published by Blackwell, 1971, and Schoken Books (N.Y.). Richard Findlater was writing in the *Observer* colour supplement, 2 September 1975. Bernice Martin is quoted from *A Sociology of Contemporary Cultural Change*, Blackwell, 1981. Christopher Booker is quoted from *The Seventies*, Allen Lane, 1980. Raymond Williams's revised, third edition of *Communications* was published by Penguin in 1975. Margaret Drabble's *The Ice Age* was published by Weidenfeld & Nicolson in 1977; Harold Pinter's *No Man's Land* was published by Methuen in 1975.

CHAPTER EIGHT

The epigraph is from Edward Shils in *Encounter*, April 1955. David Widgery's *The Left in Britain 1956–68* was published by Penguin in 1976. Peter York's 'Recycling the Sixties' is reprinted in his *Style Wars*, Sidgwick & Jackson, 1980. Bernice Martin's *A Sociology of Contemporary Cultural Change* was published by Blackwell in 1981. Raymond Williams's lecture 'The Bloomsbury Fraction' is reprinted in his *Problems in Materialism and Culture*, Verso Editions and New Left Books, 1980.

Michael Frayn describes the Festival of Britain in *The Age of Austerity*, edited by Michael Sissons and Philip French, Hodder & Stoughton, 1963. John Osborne's *Look Back in Anger* was published by Faber & Faber in 1959.

Noel Annan's 'The Intellectual Aristocracy' appears in *Studies in English Social History*, edited by J. H. Plumb, Longmans, 1955. Edward Shils's article was in *Encounter*. April 1955. The quotations from Perry Anderson came from the July/August 1968 issue of *New Left Review*; John Holloway's articles appeared in *The Listener* for 12, 19 and 26 January 1967. Tom Nairn is quoted from his essay 'The English Literary Intelligentsia', reprinted in an anthology from *Bananas*, edited by Emma Tennant, Quartet Books, 1977. Anthony Hartley's *A State of England* was published by Hutchinson in 1963. Malcolm Bradbury was writing in *New Society*, 24 December 1964.

Anthony Sampson's *The Changing Anatomy of Britain* was published by Hodder & Stoughton, in 1982. Dick Hebdige's *Subculture: The Meaning of Style* was published by Methuen in 1979. E.P. Thompson's *The Poverty of Theory* was published by Merlin Press, 1978. The new policy for *Screen* was announced in Volume 12, No.1. Alan Lovell admits the limited interest in semiology in Volume 13, No.2.

Policing the Crisis, by Stuart Hall and others, was published by Manchester University Press in 1978. Alaistair MacIntyre's *Marcuse* was published by Fontana in 1970.

Blake Morrison is quoted from his *The Movement*, Oxford University Press, 1980. Kingsley Amis is quoted from his essays *What Became of Jane Austen?*, Jonathan Cape, 1970, and then *Encounter*, February 1964. *Lucky Jim's Politics* was published by the Conservative Political Centre in 1968. The final quotation from Amis comes from *What Became of Jane Austen?*

The history of the *Critical Quarterly* is drawn from C.B. Cox's account in *From Parnassus: Essays in Honour of Jacques Barzun*, edited by Dora B. Weiner and William R. Keylor, Harper & Row (N.Y.), 1976. *The Black Papers in Education* (1–3) were reprinted by Davis Poynter in 1971. The *Black Paper 1975* was published in that year by Dent. Stuart Hall is quoted from *Policing the Crisis*, Manchester University Press, 1978.

CHAPTER NINE
The epigraph is from Julian Barnes's novel *Flaubert's Parrot*, published by Jonathan Cape in 1984. Julian Maclaren-Ross's *Memoirs of the Forties* was published by Alan Ross in 1965. John Lehmann was writing in *Penguin New Writing* No. 19. *Scrutiny: A*

Retrospect was published by Cambridge University Press in 1963. George Orwell's warning of 1940 appeared in *Inside the Whale*, reprinted in Volume 1 of *The Collected Essays, Journalism and Letters of George Orwell*, edited by Sonia Orwell and Ian Angus, Secker & Warburg, 1968 and Harcourt, Brace, Jovanovitch (N.Y.). Orwell's comment of 1946 comes from 'The Prevention of Literature', in his *Collected Essays*, Volume 4. *The Craft of Letters*, edited by John Lehmann, was published by Cresset Press in 1956. Philip Larkin's 'Going, Going' appears in his *High Windows*, Faber & Faber, 1974.

Bryan Appleyard's *The Culture Club: Crisis in the Arts*, was published by Faber & Faber in 1984. Anthony Sampson's *The Changing Anatomy of Britain* was published by Hodder & Stoughton in 1982. Stuart Hall is quoted from *Resistance through Rituals*, which he edited with Tony Jefferson, Hutchinson, 1976. Luke Rittner is quoted from Harold Baldry's *The Case for the Arts*, Secker & Warburg, 1981. Seamus Heaney is quoted first from 'Feeling into Words', in *Preoccupations*, Faber & Faber, 1980, and then 'Englands of the Mind' in the same volume.

Index

Index

Astor, Michael, 198
Atkinson, Conrad, 242
Atkinson, Terry, 51, 240, 244
auto-destructive art 117–18, 238
Ayres, Gillian, 235

Bacon, Francis, 90, 231
Bailey, David, 73–5, 122, 178; *David Bailey's Box of Pin-ups*, 74–5, 77, 143, 178; *Goodbye Baby and Amen*, 178
Bailey, Ron, 164
Bainbridge, David, 240
Baldwin, Michael, 240
Balocha, Lily, 216–7
Banham, Reyner, 42, 45, 50
Bantock, G.H., 11, 38, 295, 296
Barbican Arts Centre, 57
Barclay, Alan, 237
Bargate, Verity, 200
Barker, Edward (& Farren): *Watch Out Kids*, 175–6
Barker, John, 152, 165–6
Barnard, Roger, 135
Barnes, Julian: *Flaubert's Parrot*, 299
Barr, Alfred, 43
Barth, John, 250
Barthes, Roland, 286
Barton, John, 202
Baverstock, Donald, 29
Bazaar shops, 71
BBC (British Broadcasting Corporation), 130, 171, 227, 277, 278; censorship by, 143; culture diffusionists in, 302; influence of, xiv, 25; Overseas Service of, 26; and pop music, 67, 184; Third Programme of, 280–1; *and see* BBC TV
BBC TV, 10, 12–13, 25–7, 143; and the arts, 25–6, 50; and BBC2, 13, 26–7, 122; and documentaries, 32–3; and drama, 26, 30–3, 34; expansion of, 25–33, 76; news coverage by, 10; and Pilkington Report, 12–13; and satire 27–30, 33; and student revolt, 162; and youth culture, 30, 67
Beardsley, Aubrey, 130, 133
Beat movement, 65, 67, 96, 98, 102, 114, 199
beat music, 51, 63
Beatles, the, 64, 65–7, 68, 184; and drugs, 133, 142–3; and meditation, 177; works mentioned: 'A Day in the Life', 143; *A Hard Day's Night* (film),

69–70; *Revolver*, 142; *Sergeant Pepper*, v, 122–3, 125, 142–3
Beaton, Cecil, 74
Beaulieu Jazz Festivals, 96, 186
Beaux Arts gallery, 232
Beck, Julian, 134, 140, 155
Beckett, Samuel, 86, 88, 90–1, 100, 103, 254; *Eh Joe* 32; *Waiting for Godot*, 86–7; *Watt*, 103
Belfast, 163, 262–3
Belfast Group, 262
Belies, Sinclair, 102
Beloff, Max, 296
Belt and Braces Roadshow, 211
Bennett, Alan, 28
Benveniste, Asa, 96, 155
Bergonzi, Bernard, 295; *The Situation of the Novel*, 249, 250, 252–3
Berio, Luciano, 70
Berke, Joseph, 121, 155
Berkeley, California, 158–9, 262–3
Berkoff, Steven, 204
Berlin, 1, 154–5, 161; Wall, 1
Berman, Ed, 200, 220
Berryman, John, 98–9, 259
Bertrand Russell Peace Foundation, 155
Better Books, 111, 112, 117, 120, 123, 192, 289
Beuys, Josef, 116
Beyond the Fringe (revue) 28, 30, 34
'Beyond Painting and Sculpture' exhibition, 243
Bicât, Tony, 205, 207
Big Table magazine, 101
Bill and Tony (film), 102
Bird, John, 28
Birdsall, Timothy, 4, ill.2
Birmingham, 20, 123; Bull Ring, 56
Birmingham University 17, 285, 292
BIT, information service, 132
Black Dwarf, 162–3, 172, 173
Black Mountain College, 110, 115, 155, 156
Black Papers on Education, 264, 295–6
Black Power, 135, 216
Blackstaff Press: *The Wearing of the Black*, 263
Blake, Peter, 43–5, 49, 50, 54, 178; *Babe Rainbow*, 52; *The First Real Target*, 44; *On The Balcony*, 44; *Sergeant Pepper* sleeve, 142–3; *Self-Portrait with Badges*, 44, 45, 69, ill.1; *Toy Shop*, 44, 52
Blake, William, 113
Blakely, Colin, 202
Blakemore, Michael, 224

329

Index

Index

333

Index

Index

Hurrell, Harold, 240
Huxley, Paul, 54
Hyams, Harry, 55, 56
Hyde Park, free concert in, 186

ICA *see* Institute of Contemporary Arts
'Idea Structure' exhibition, 240
Idiot International, 172, 174
Illustrated magazine, 44
'Image in Progress' exhibition (1962), 54
'In-Stage' theatre group, 90
Independent Group, 42, 44, 45
Independent Television (ITV), 9–10, 12, 13, 25–7
Independent Television Authority (ITA), 35
Independent Theatres Council, 222
India, 100, 154–5, 177
Indica Gallery, 54, 118, 232
Industrial Relations Act (1971), 183
inflation, 21, 56, 79–80, 182–3, 199, 221, 223, 226, 267, 304
Information, Ministry of, 77
Inglis, Brian: *Private Conscience: Public Morality*, 35–6, 275
Ingrams, Richard, 28
Ink magazine, 172–3
inner space, exploration of, xv, 84–6, 102, 177; Beatles and, 143, 177; and drugs, 128–9, 149; and revolution, 137, 168
Institute of Contemporary Arts (ICA), 42, 105–6, 117, 119, 209, 242; and student revolt, 161
Institute for Phenomenological Studies, 134, 155
intelligentsia: British, 59–61, 146, 277, 279–80; European, 281–2, and expansion of higher education, 59–61, 283–4, 294; and revolution, 280–1, 282–5, 287–8; and the Right, 293–4; technical, 60, 153; and TV, 10
Inter-Action Trust, 200–1
International Centre for Theatre Research, 94, 204
International Festival of Poetry (1965), 113–14
International Marxist Group, 157, 162, 173, 217
International Socialism, 212
Internationale Situationniste, 150
International Times (*IT*), 94–5, 107, 119–22, 176; Angry Brigade and, 166; on Anti-University, 155–6; coups at

173; and Dialectics of Liberation conference, 135; and drugs, 128, 131; ideology of, 125; police raids on, 131–2, 174; prosecution of, 172, 174; and violence, 167
Ionesco, Eugene, 86–7, 88–9, 100; *The Bald Prima Donna*, 87; *The Chairs*, 87; *The Lesson*, 86–7; *Rhinoceros*, 87
IRA (Irish Republican Army), 163–4
Iran, Shiraz Festival, 94
Irish TGWU, 209
Irving, Mike, 200
Isle of Wight festivals, 186–7
Itzin, Catherine: *Stages in the Revolution*, 205

Jackson, Glenda, 91–2, 93
Jagger, Mick, 74, 132, ill. 3
Jandl, Ernst, 113, 114
jazz, 21, 58, 62, 108, 186, 191–2; and poetry, 96–7
Jeanetta Cochrane Theatre, 112, 118, 203
Jefferson, Tony, 146
Jeffs, Roger, 51
Jellicoe, Anne: *The Knack*, 70
Jenkins, Hugh, Min. for the Arts, 229
Jennings, Bernard, 51
John, Augustus, 50, 231
John Bull magazine 24
Johns, Jasper, 49, 239
Johnson, B.S., 251, 255–6; *Albert Angelo, Travelling People*, 256; *The Unfortunates*, 255–6
Johnson, Pamela Hansford: *On Iniquity*, 133, 253
Johnson, Paul, 293
Joint Stock theatre group, 205
Jones, Allen, 49, 52, 53, 54
Jones, Brian, 186
Jones, Bryn, 285
Jones, David, 109–10
Journal of the Architectural Association, 108
journalism, 73, 77–8, 302; and music magazines, 188; *and see* magazines, news media, underground press
Joyce, James, 45, 215, 246
Judd, Donald, 239

Kafka, Franz, 87, 205
Kaprow, Alan, 68, 104
Kasmin Gallery, 54, 232
Kasmin, John, 54, 232

337

Index

Index

Index